Shaping Wise Futures

Practice Futures

VOLUME 5

The titles published in this series are listed at *brill.com/pfp*

Shaping Wise Futures

A Shared Responsibility

Edited by

Joy Higgs, Janice Orrell, Diane Tasker and Narelle Patton

BRILL

LEIDEN | BOSTON

All chapters in this book have undergone peer review.

The Library of Congress Cataloging-in-Publication Data is available online at https://catalog.loc.gov

Typeface for the Latin, Greek, and Cyrillic scripts: "Brill". See and download: brill.com/brill-typeface.

ISSN 2665-9263
ISBN 978-90-04-50552-0 (paperback)
ISBN 978-90-04-50553-7 (hardback)
ISBN 978-90-04-50554-4 (e-book)

This book is printed on acid-free paper and produced in a sustainable manner.

Contents

Preface

This journey is about planning our futures.
We need to create practice wisdom through that planning.
Bringing to the challenge, our patterns of knowledge
Guided by our current era, education and cultural preferences.

We can aspire to overcome the wicked problems that befall us.
But we must stand up for the things that inspire us
Like social justice and making
The world better for those who follow us.

As we try to address future needs with judgement and understanding
We build prudence,
Balanced views and social responsibility,
Trying always to see the consequences of our choices.

We attempt to bring moral purpose
And seek to create sustainable futures
Through social, cultural, economic
and environmental means.

We are let down by those who stand in our way,
Those who would do us harm
Our world, our animals, our homes
Strife sent to send us awry.

Can we envision possible, probable and preferable futures
To influence the lives of ordinary people,
The lives of the disadvantaged and the desolate,
The lives of professionals and the creative among us.

There is no single answer.
We have set up this book to be a guide with ways of looking at the task.
Making use of the world as we pass through it
Use the arguments we provide to draw upon your wisdom and insight.

Through our teaching we are motivated
To try a new path

To be better more reliable leaders
To lead our communities more responsibly.

Wisdom is a state of perpetual becoming
Can we build a bridge between planetary and human wellbeing?
Envisaging wise and just living practices for the future.
Let us seek its awakening and use our realisations.

Joy Higgs and Diane Tasker

Acknowledgement

The editors wish to acknowledge the support received by Kim Woodland in checking the references.

Illustrations

Figures

Table

Notes on Contributors

Gulnar Ali

(PhD, MSci Nursing) is Senior Lecturer, Education and Research, at the College of Medicine and Health, Academy of Nursing, University of Exeter, UK. She has engaged in academic leadership and global health research partnerships across the UK, Ireland, USA, India and Pakistan. She also teaches undergraduate/postgraduate courses, doctoral research supervision and education management in universities across the United Kingdom. She is involved in national and international research projects on ontology and existential care aspects of palliative care, trauma, and transformative learning practices. Dr. Ali has developed a reflective framework enabling holistic care; SOPHIE (Self-Exploration through Ontological, Phenomenological, Humanistic, Ideological and Existential Expressions). She is also a Research Consultant, with American Psychiatric Nursing Association (APNA); and a collaborator on a controlled trial of SOPHIE framework, at Purdue University, USA.

Ronald Barnett

(PhD, DLITT (Ed) FRSHE, FHEA, FACSS) is Emeritus Professor at Institute of Education, University of London. He is President of the Philosophy and Theory of Higher Education Society, and Emeritus Professor of Higher Education at University College London. He has produced 35 books and 200 papers on the philosophy and theory of higher education and is the inaugural recipient of the EAIR Award for 'Outstanding Contribution to Higher Education Research, Policy and Practice'. He has also given 150 keynotes in 40 countries.

Tania De Bortoli

(PhD, Speech Pathologist – Retired) lives in the Blue Mountains of New South Wales, Australia, having worked as a speech pathologist for 30 years in community health, in private practice and overseas. She completed her Phd in 2012 through Newcastle University investigating the communication needs of young people with multiple and severe disabilities. She has engaged in academic publication and is currently undertaking independent, community-based research.

Laurence Boulle

(PhD) is Bell Weise Professor of Legal Ethics, Newcastle Law School, Newcastle University, Adjunct Professor, Bond University and ACU, Sydney. Laurence teaches at Newcastle Law School largely in Commercial Dispute Resolution. He has held senior appointments at Australian universities as well as been visiting Professor at Gent University in Belgium, the University of Cape Town and the University of the South Pacific. He has mediated a wide variety of disputes in Australian states and territories, and abroad: within communities and families, relating to native title, workers' compensation, personal injury, intellectual property, in workplaces and organisations. He has written, co-authored or edited over 20 other books on mediation, constitutional law, globalisation, employment law and mediation that have been published in seven countries. His latest book with Rachael Field, is Mediation in Australia (LexisNexis, Sydney, 2018).

Margot Cairnes
(B Educ (Hons)) is a Sydney University graduate and Medal winner, and holds an MBA from UNSW AGSM. Margot started her career managing Darwin Family Centres and oversaw childcare and family support for the Top End of Australia. She also lectured in Urban Sociology and education. After obtaining an MBA she founded The Change Dynamic which became Zaffyre Pty Ltd. Margot has mentored the Boards and senior teams of companies in London and in Australia. She has written 6 books on leadership in times of rapid change and has represented Australia at the World Economic Forum. She is currently writing her 7th book titled *Simple Wisdom for Clever People: Leading Miraculous Lives, Businesses and Communities in Change Times*. She now works extensively in the community, in particular with addicts and those struggling with relationships.

Giovanna Citta
(B Social Work) is a Mental Health Project Coordinator at the Victorian Foundation for Survivors of Torture. Giovanna is a social worker with specialised training and experience in trauma counselling and family therapy. She has worked with individuals/families/groups and communities from CALD and refugee backgrounds for 35 years. She has worked at Foundation House in various roles, and currently is the coordinator of mental health promotion and literacy projects for groups from refugee backgrounds during the covid pandemic. She is committed to working with people from refugee communities using a community development approach.

Philippa Collin
(PhD) is Associate Professor, Political Sociology, at Western Sydney University NSW. She is an Associate Professor in the Institute for Culture and Society at Western Sydney University where she co-directs the Young and Resilient Research Centre. She is an interdisciplinary social scientist who works at the intersections of political sociology, digital media, and health with a focus

on young people. Philippa has championed youth-centred and participatory research, learning from the diverse ways children and young people contribute to knowledge practices and social change. She is the author of *Control Shift: Young People and Digital Society and Young Citizens and Political Participation in a Digital Society: Addressing the Democratic Disconnect.*

Stephen Curran
(PhD) is Consultant & Visiting Professor of Old Age Psychiatry, School of Human and Health Sciences, University of Huddersfield and South West Yorkshire Partnership NHS Foundation Trust, Wakefield, UK. He studied in Leeds and was a Lecturer in Old Age Psychiatry at the University of Leeds. His current post since 1998) is Consultant in Old Age Psychiatry in Wakefield, UK where he manages an in-patient ward for patients with dementia where he was the in-patient consultant for older people. He has been Clinical Lead and Associate Medical Director for Education and Training for the South-West Yorkshire Partnership NHS Foundation Trust since 2017 and an examiner for the Royal College of Psychiatrists. He chaired the Memory Services National Accreditation Advisory Group at the College for 10 years and was appointed visiting Professor of Old Age Psychopharmacology at the University of Huddersfield (2002). His particular interest is old age psychopharmacology and service development.

Agnes Dodds
(PhD) is Honorary Principal Fellow at the Melbourne Medical School, The University of Melbourne Victoria, Australia. She is a Principal Fellow (Hon) in the department of medical education in The University of Melbourne Medical School and an honorary evaluator of programs for Victorian Foundation for the Survivors of Torture. Her research interests and publications are in medical education and she specialises in the application of developmental theory to evaluation and assessment. She currently leads a program of research on the selection and assessment of graduate medical students.

Andrew Dutney
(PhD EdD) is Professor in Theology at Flinders University, and the Adelaide College of Divinity, Australia. He has taught theology and ethics at Flinders University and the Adelaide College of Divinity for more than 30 years. He has been involved in the ethical supervision of research, especially medical research, specialising in the ethics and regulation of Assisted Reproductive Technology, chairing the South Australian Council on Reproductive technology. Andrew has been an influential leader in the field of theological education in Australia where he was the Principal of Uniting College for Leadership and Theology. He is a minister of the Uniting Church in Australia and was its

thirteenth President. Andrew was born on land stolen from the Bidjara nation, in Western Queensland, and lives in Adelaide, on land stolen from the Kaurna nation. Andrew engages with First Nations elders in South Australia working for greater understanding, justice and reconciliation.

Rachael Field
(PhD) is Professor of Law at Bond University, Queensland. She teaches law at Bond University. Her research interest is in dispute resolution which began in her legal practice as a family lawyer. As a volunteer with Women's Legal Service, she became committed to advocating for access to justice for vulnerable women and their children – particularly those in circumstances of domestic and family violence. She has published widely in dispute resolution, women and the law and family law, as well as in higher education including the first-year experience, legal education, and student success and well-being. Her latest book with Lawrence Boulle is *Mediation in Australia* (LexisNexis, 2018).

Anne Fitzgerald
(BSW) is a Social Capitalist. She is a Blue Mountains-based social worker, consulting social researcher and project co-ordinator, specialising in cultural and community engagement, media and communications

David Giles
(PhD) is an Emeritus Professor in Educational Leadership at Flinders University, Associate Professor (University of Adelaide) and Director of Life-Centric Educational Consultancy Ltd. For over 30 years David has contributed to understandings and practices on the relational nature of education and educational leadership. His research interests focus on the relational nature of pedagogy, strengths-based practices, educational leadership, and organizational cultures. He has published both articles and books, the most recent book being *Relational Leadership in Education: A Phenomenon of Inquiry and Practice* (2019, Routledge).

Peter Goodyear
(DPhil, FCIPD) is Member of ALTF and Professor of Education at the University of Sydney, NSW. His research interests include professional education, networked learning and educational design. Peter was awarded a Senior Fellowship of the Australian Learning and Teaching Council in 2008 and an Australian Research Council Laureate Fellowship in 2010. His most recent books include: *The Education Ecology of Universities* (with Rob Ellis, 2019) and *Epistemic Fluency and Professional Education* (with Lina Markauskaite, 2017).

Norman Habel
(ThD) is a Professorial Fellow at Flinders University, Australia. He was awarded a member of the Order of Australia for his contribution to the study of world religions in higher education. He has long been involved in issues of biblical interpretation, eco-justice, and restorative justice for First Nations people. He is a poet and has published numerous academic and children's books. Norman is the editor of *The Earth Bible* series and a founder of the *Season of Creation.* His latest book is *The Wisdom Trinity.*

Anjali Habel-Orrell
(B Behavioural Sci, M Teach (Spec Educ)) is a Teacher of Performing Arts for the South Australian Department for Education with a particular interest in the cognitive benefits that music experiences provide for all students, especially those with learning challenges. She fosters school performances that link to the curriculum, using choirs, bands, Auslan signing, and Tournament of the Minds. Her students have won many competitive school performance awards such as Spirit of Wakakirri, and Best Social Justice Story for the story dance she wrote and choreographed. Anjali is an executive member of the Australian Grihini Advisory Council, supporting non-formal education for Tribal and Dalit girls in Southern India.

Joy Higgs
(PhD) is Emeritus Professor, Professional Practice and Higher Education, at Charles Sturt University NSW. She has worked for over 35 years in higher education and has published extensively producing 42 books and over 360 papers and chapters in the fields of professional reasoning and practice, professional and practice-based education, and practice research. In 2004 Joy received a Member of the Order of Australia award for services to health sciences education in recognition of her contributions to course development, scholarship, research and academic leadership. A key part of Joy's leadership role is mentoring others including supervising 40 Doctoral and Masters students and mentoring local and international colleagues.

Ida Kaplan
(PhD) is Honorary Research Fellow at Victorian Foundation for the Survivors of Torture (VFST). She is a clinical psychologist, research fellow at University of Melbourne, School of Psychological Sciences and has an honorary research appointment at the Victorian Foundation for the Survivors of Torture. She specialises in theorising and developing models of service delivery for trauma survivors, especially in relation to refugee and asylum-seeking experiences. Ida's international publications, lectures and consultancies focus on the intersec-

tion of the human rights, justice and rebuilding of lives of people from refugee background.

Jeanette Lawrence
(PhD) is Honorary Associate Professor at Melbourne School of Psychological Sciences, The University of Melbourne, Victoria, Australia. She is a developmental psychologist and honorary Associate Professor in the University of Melbourne School of Psychological Sciences with an honorary research appointment at the Victorian Foundation for the Survivors of Torture. Her research interests are in personal and social development across the life-course, particularly intergenerational relations and the experiences and well-being of children and young people from refugee backgrounds. She has expertise in developing culturally-appropriate research methods, specializing in the development of computer-assisted interview techniques.

Rosemary Leonard
(PhD) is Professor and Chair in Social Capital and Sustainability at School of Social Sciences at Western Sydney University. She has a background in social psychology and nearly forty years' experience in applied social research. Her particular interest has been the role of social capital as a valuable resource for communities both for community development and building environmental sustainability. Her work has addressed water sensitive urban design, communities affected by coal seam gas development, sustainable intentional communities, and caring at end of life. She also supervises PhD students studying social capital in a variety of contexts including end of life care, climate refugees, and disaster recovery volunteering.

Simon Munro
(B Visual Arts, M Training & Development (Adult Education)) is an Associate Lecturer, Aboriginal Research Academic at the University of Newcastle, NSW. He is a practicing and exhibiting artist. In education and in vocation, Simon has maintained a strong link to his Aboriginal heritage (Anaiwan and Kamilaroi of New South Wales, Australia) paternally. His cultural, educational and community First Nations knowledge brings a strong de-colonising influence to his research and writing. Simon is a primary and adult educator and maintains an honorary role with the University of Newcastle, researching and contributing to equity and access for First Nations students in higher education. His research is in social and cultural justice for Aboriginal and Torres Strait Islanders, language in pedagogy (Yarning), widening higher education participation for Aboriginal and Torres Strait Islanders and art and artefact-based learning.

Lauren Novak
(B Media) is Social Policy Editor, News Corp SA. Her media studies at the University of Adelaide, included an exchange year at University College Maastricht in the Netherlands. She is the Social Policy Editor for News Corp publications *The Advertiser* and *Sunday Mail*, specialising in coverage of domestic violence and child protection and was a State Political Reporter. She has won national and state awards for her work, including an Our Watch Walkley Foundation Fellowship on responsible reporting on violence against women and their children and an International Development Journalism Fellowship in Cambodia. Lauren is a Board Member of the Zahra Foundation Australia, which assists South Australian women and children affected by domestic and family violence, providing pathways toward economic independence.

Janice Orrell
(PhD) is Emeritus Professor, Higher Education and Assessment, College of Education, Psychology and Social Work, Flinders University, Australia. She has a 50-year career in education, including international and higher education including higher degree supervision and research. Her key interest is quality and equity in the delivery of higher education, assessment designed to foster students' self-regulation of their learning; work integrated education (WIE) that is grounded in reciprocal university partnerships with industries and communities and group based research higher degree supervision. She is a lifetime member of both HERDSA and ACEN and a USA CEIA award winner for her contribution to research on cooperative education. She is also a founder of a south Indian Grihini non-formal education school for adolescent Tribal and Dalit girls in remote mountain villages.

Narelle Patton
(PhD, SFHEA) is Associate Professor and Dean (Partnerships and Workplace Learning) at Charles Sturt University, Sydney NSW, Australia. She has extensive experience in professional education, work integrated learning and research that is grounded in a social justice framework and a genuine desire to assist people to reach their full potential. She is committed to achieving optimum work integrated learning outcomes for all stakeholders through harnessing the value of shared wisdom attained by valuing the viewpoints of others. Narelle's key interest is development and widespread implementation of innovative, mutually beneficial work integrated learning activities that meet student and industry/community needs and assist communities to grow and flourish.

Melanie Rogers
(PhD) is a University Teaching Fellow in the fields of Advanced Practice and Spirituality at the University of Huddersfield and is also an Advanced Nurse Practitioner in Primary Care. She is the founder and chair of the Spirituality in Health and Social Care group at the University of Huddersfield; a member of the British Association of the Study of Spirituality scholars' network and in 2009 she was awarded the title of Queens Nurse. She is passionate about integrated holistic care and ensuring patients receive the highest standards of care.

Geoff Scott
(EdD, FACE) is Emeritus Professor of Higher Education & Sustainability at the Western Sydney University, NSW. He has led projects and is widely published in areas ranging from change leadership, sustainability, social entrepreneurship, and professional capability, to what engages students in productive learning, curriculum innovation, assuring achievement standards and quality assurance in higher education. He is currently working with universities and colleges around the world on ways to embed the UN Sustainable Development Goals into the curriculum. He is the recipient of the Australian Higher Education Quality Award and a National Senior Teaching Fellow.

Mardi Stow
(M Social Work) is General Manager of the Community Capacity Building Program, Victorian Foundation for Survivors of Torture, Victoria Australia. She is a social worker who has developed and managed programs for people from refugee backgrounds in Australia for 23 years. As the general manager of community capacity building at the Victorian Foundation for Survivors of Torture, Mardi has responsibilities for leading professional counsellor advocates and community workers to assist people from refugee backgrounds. Her current interests are in assisting community groups to recognise and manage mental health and social relationship issues which have been exacerbated during the covid pandemic.

Diane Tasker
(PhD) was a physiotherapist over 36 years, mostly practising in community settings. She completed a PhD in Community Health in 2013, which examined the complexity of relationships that develop between clients, therapists, families and carers in home-based healthcare. Since then, she has been involved in research and writing about practice wisdom and its place in society.

Skye Tasker

(BA, Hons 1st Sociology) is a PhD Candidate in the Institute for Culture and Society at Western Sydney University where she researches the intersection of data, technology and ethics in adolescent health research. Her research aims to illuminate young peoples' voice, perspectives and everyday experiences in digital society during COVID-19 and her project is affiliated with the Wellbeing, Health and Youth Centre of Research Excellence and the Young and Resilient Research Centre. Skye also works as a youth worker and mentor in her local community. She is passionate about *learning from* and *with* young people about issues which affect youth health and social injustice in society.

John Wattis

(FRCPsych) is a retired Consultant in Psychiatry for Older People. He is still an associate member of academic staff at the University of Huddersfield where he helped found the Spirituality and Compassion Special Interest Group. He has a lifelong interest in relationships in health care and has published on Psychiatry of Old Age, Medical Leadership and Management and, most recently, in the area of the importance of the neglected area of Spiritually Competent Practice in Health Care.

Lilly Xiao

(PhD, FACN) is Professor of Nursing and Aged Care at the College of Nursing and Health Science, Flinders University, Australia. She is an internationally recognised dementia caregiving researcher and is a key contributor to the World Health Organization (WHO) iSupport for Dementia program, which is an online education and skill training program for informal carers of people living with dementia. She is the leader for the Chinese version of iSupport for Dementia project in Australia and Greater China. Professor Xiao is the Fellow of Australian College of Nursing and the Foundation Member of the Australian Hartford Consortium for Gerontological Nursing Excellence.

PART 1

Facing Future Challenges

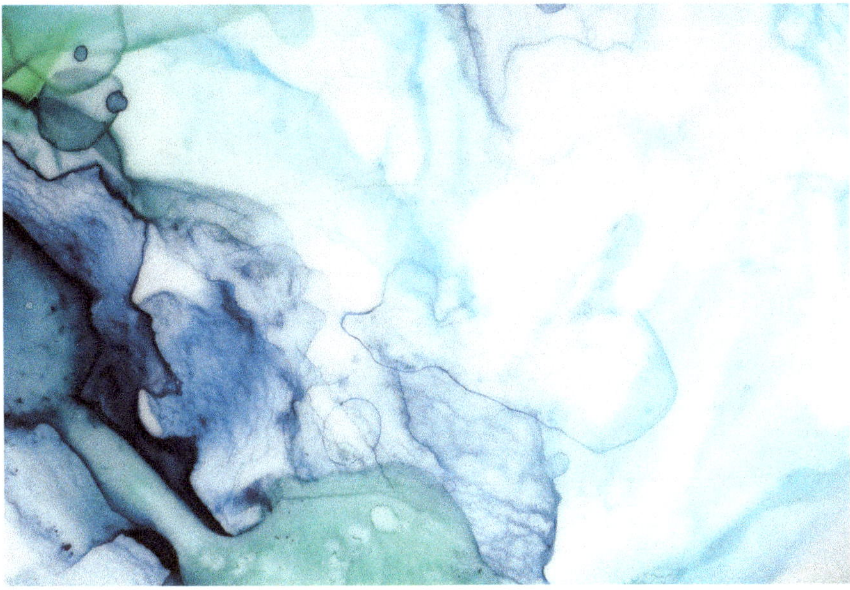

Introduction to Part 1

Joy Higgs

In this part of the book, we address what it means to deal with future challenges. This does not refer to a pre-set future or a future that is focused on one way of thinking by one group of people. Rather it deals with choices people make about their preferred future and the options they have or can have to shape it.

> We live in a world that has many strong assumptions built into it. We assume it's a good idea to examine nature microscopically and to voyage out into space. We believe that human beings develop and nature and society evolves. We trust medicine that is based on research and evidence. We think that it's all right to build roads anywhere and everywhere. We want children to have a standardized education, and we think that prisons are an effective way to deal with crime. We have had a century of remarkable success with these values. Still, I question each of them and ask if we really are better people because of them. (Bourgeault, 2003, p. VII)

> Whatever life's challenges,
> you may face, remember always
> to look to the mountaintop,
> for in so doing you link to greatness.
> Remember this, and let no problem,
> no matter how great it may seem,
> discourage you, nor let anything
> less than the mountaintop
> distract you. This is the one thought
> I want to leave you with.
> (Alfonso Ortiz [b. 1939], in Exley, 1999, n.p.)

> I want to beg you, as much as I can,
> to be patient towards all that is unsolved
> in your heart and to try to love the questions
> themselves like locked rooms and like books
> that are written in a foreign tongue.
> Do not seek the answers, which cannot

 | DOI: 10.1163/9789004505544_001

be given you because you would not be able to live them.
And the point is to live everything.
Live the questions now.
Perhaps you will then gradually,
without noticing it, live along
some distant day into the answer.
(Rainer Maria Rilke, in Exley, 1999, n.p.)

The Critical Decade

The world is on fire, from the Amazon to California, from Australia to the Siberian Arctic. The hour is late, and the moment of consequence, so long delayed, is now upon us. Do we watch the world burn, or do we choose to do what is necessary to achieve a different future? (Figueres & Rivett-Carnac, 2020, p. 1)

Everywhere there are people who, despite finding themselves mired in periods of national darkness or personal marginalisation refuse to give up the thought of a better future or give in to the allurements of deteriorating present. They never lose hope that the values they learned in the best of times or the courage it takes to reclaim their world from the worst of times are worth the commitment of their lives. These people, the best of ourselves, are legion and they are everywhere. … It is the unwavering faith, the open hearts and the piercing courage of people from every level of every society that carries us through every major social breakdown to the emergence again of humanity. In every region, everywhere, they are the unsung but mighty voices of community, high mindedness and deep resolve. They are the prophets of each era who prod the rest of the world into seeing newly what it means to be fully alive, personally, nationally and spiritually. (Chittister, 2019, p. 5)

Doughnut Economics

The twenty-first-century task is clear: to create economies that promote human prosperity in a flourishing web of life so that we can thrive in balance within the Doughnut's safe and just space. It starts with recognising that every economy – local to global – is embedded within society and within the living world. It also means recognising that the household, the commons, the market and the state can all be effective means of provisioning for our many needs and wants, and they tend to work best when they work together. By deepening our understanding of human nature we can create institutions and incentives that reinforce our reciprocity and other-regarding values, rather than undermine them. Once we accept the economy's inherent complexity, we can shape its ever-evolving dynamics through smart stewardship. That opens up the possibility of turning today's divisive and degenerative economies into ones that are distributive and regenerative by design. And it invites us to become agnostic about growth, creating economies that enable us to thrive, whether or not they are growing. (Raworth, 2017, p. 244)

Climate change over the next few decades will mainly act by exacerbating existing health problems. The greatest impacts will occur – indeed, are *occurring* – in populations already burdened by climate-sensitive health problems such as child diarrhoea, nutritional stunting and urban heat extremes. Human-driven warming has increased heat-related death and illness in many locations, while changes in temperature and rainfall have altered the distribution of some waterborne infectious diseases and reduced food yields in some food-insecure populations. The adverse health impacts will widen the existing health gap between regions and between rich and poor. Climate change, unabated, will erode development gains – an issue now of explicit concern to the World Bank and ... the Asian Development Bank.[1] At a worst case, our current trajectory could even: erode the essential foundations of human population health – feed yields, water supplies and the constraints on infectious disease rates, population displacement, conflict and war.[2] (Flannery, 2015, pp. 19–20)

Wisdom can be defined as the "power of judgement rightly and following the soundest course of action, based on knowledge, experience, understanding etc." (Webster's New World College Dictionary, 1997, p. 2533). Such a power would seem to be of vast improvement in a world that at times seems bent on destroying itself. (Sternberg, 2003, p. 147)

Seek Wisdom

The primary purpose of this book is to ground the modern quest for health and sustainability in a clinical philosophy that can be used to tackle the most complex health problems facing people, the human species, and the vast, entangled web of living systems. The philosophical framework for the question is clinical because it has a mission to health systems. Whose dysfunction stands in the way of health and sustainability. … Science is essential for addressing global challenges, but it cannot do so in isolation. A wide range of approaches will be required, including the appropriate use of financial incentives, incorporating not-traditional forms of knowledge, and working with the social sciences and wider disciplines. Science is crucial but it is unlikely to produce all the answers by itself; the science infrastructure works best when it is supported by, and enables, other systems. … In addition to a clinical, wisdom-based orientation towards its task, the quest for health and sustainability will also fare better with a balanced interaction between centralizing and decentralizing forces, as this helps to balance against the asymmetrical advantages that tend to accrue established, centralized sources of power. (Berndtson, 2012, pp. XI–XIV)

Tribal Wisdom

At the dawn of a new millennium
tribal peoples of the world
still echo the voices of their ancestors
as they encourage us
to respect each other …
and the living earth we share.
In their timeless wisdom
lie the seeds of hope,
and the promise of tomorrow…
yet to come.
(Dunn, 1997, n.p.)

And what is it to work with love?
It is to weave a cloth with threads
drawn from your heart
even as if your beloved
were to wear that cloth.
It is to build a house with affection,
even as if your beloved
were to dwell in that house.
It is to sow seeds with tenderness

and to reap the harvest with joy,
even as if your beloved
were to eat the fruit.
It is to charge all the things you fashion
with a breath of your own spirit,
and to know that all of the blessed dead
are standing about you and watching.
(Kahlil Gibran, The Prophet, in Dunn, 1997, n.p.)

Some people – and they are the people we think of as the poorest – live well without doing much of anything. They do not have jobs, they do not work nine to five, they certainly do not work for anyone else. They do not farm; they do not have to take care of animals. They spend their days doing what they do best. Some like making things – they make canoes, to cloth, or pots or carved objects. Some like hunting or fishing. Some people have a talent for staying in touch with another reality; they are priests, shamans, or healers. Some have talent for making other people feel good. People who live very close to earth or the ocean, with very few of what we think of as necessities of life, live well. Sadly, it is not exaggeration to say that as soon as we come and bring them civilization, they plummet into abject poverty and ill health. (Wolff, 2001, p. 81)

The hearth is a simple, quiet, and rustic doorway to spiritual practice, that has its roots as much in utilitarian function as it does in spiritual practices or prayer. This is true of everything in Celtic spirituality if it is practiced authentically. It is not a matter of grandiosity but of simplicity. There is no separation between the Celtic spiritual path and one's daily life. One's life becomes a brightly woven cord of mindfulness that weaves through the ordinarily mundane dimension of living and imbues it with a sacred dimension. In sweeping ashes we discover sacred world. (MacEowen, 2002, p. 194)

Notes

1 McMichael, A. J. (2014). Climate change: Health risks mount while Nero fiddles. *Medical Journal of Australia, 200*(9), 507–508.
2 McMichael, A. J. (2014). Health impacts in Australia in a four degree world. In P. Christoff (Ed.), *Four degrees of global warming: Australia in a hot world* (Routledge).

References

Berndtson, K. (2012). *Seek wisdom: The modern question for health and sustainability.* One Bodymind Press.

Bourgeault, C. (2003). *The wisdom way of knowing: Reclaiming an ancient tradition to awaken the heart.* Jossey-Bass.

Chittister, J. (2019). *The time is now: A call for uncommon courage.* Blue Bridge.

Dunn, P. (1997). *Tribal wisdom.* Axium Publishing.

Exley, H. (1999). *Wisdom for the new millennium.* Exley Publications.

Figueres, C., & Rivett-Carnac, T. (2020). *The future we choose: Surviving the climate crisis.* Manilla Press.

Flannery, T. (2015). *Atmosphere of hope: Searching for solutions to the climate crisis.* The Text Publishing Company.

MacEowen, F. (2002). *The mist-filled path: Celtic wisdom for exiles, wanderers, and seekers.* New World Library.

Raworth, K. (2017). *Doughnut economics: Seven ways to think like a 21st century economist.* Chelsea Green Publishing.

Sternberg, R. J. (2003). *Wisdom, intelligence, and creativity synthesized.* Cambridge University Press.

Wolff, R. (2001). *Original wisdom: Stories of an ancient way of knowing.* Inner Traditions.

Zuckerman, A. (2009). *Wisdom: Peace.* Harry N. Abrams.

CHAPTER 1

Valuing Wise Futures

Joy Higgs

Abstract

Wise futures are aspirations, practices and achievements and through these paths they gain and give value to their users. In essence, they take this powerful and inspiring concept of wisdom and apply it to the setting up of (wise) visions and purposes, the making of (wise) decisions, the arguing of (wise) purposeful intentions and seeking of (wise) goals. It is through the enactment of practice wisdom that we see the true essence of the purpose of this book to create a positive future. The shaping of wise futures takes the path of people seeking wisdom and wise action in their own lives and on behalf of all living things. It may be that wise futures are pursued within the practice (perhaps professional, paradigmatic or artistic practice) that is shaped by knowledges and practices of their deep purpose and practice frameworks.

As we explore our various and changing futures we seek to inform their wise underpinning/substance and to enable wise practice development. It is also to be hoped that we are aiming to make our worlds better places to live in. This pursuit of wise futures includes the support of living futures for cultural and societal communities, for work groups and practice populations (like professions and labour markets), local communities and societies. As well as these practical goals of shaping a multitude of living realities through wisdom perspectives and actions, future realisations of wisdom look at living wisdom itself as an evolution. The shaping of wise futures is a both a means and end. This chapter and the book celebrate valuing wise futures as this outline portrays.

Keywords

value – wisdom – future

1 Reflections and Realisations about a Wiser Future

Two prior books set the foundation for the current book. The first was *Challenging Future Practice Possibilities* (Higgs et al., 2019). In that book we reflected

 | DOI: 10.1163/9789004505544_002

upon possible, probable, and preferable futures in relation to practice and work. Readers are invited to consider how their own engagement in shaping possible futures could support future modes and realities and wisdom of life, practice and work. In the second book "Practice Wisdom" (Higgs, 2019b) the authors argued that practice wisdom is necessary to help people deal with the challenges they face in life, work and society. Readers are invited to consider the place of practice wisdom in pursuing good practice outcomes amidst the turmoil and pressure of life, work and survival today.

I start the opening chapter of the current book with three seemingly simple reflections to commence shaping the argument of the book.

– The first reflection is that any book, conversation or discourse about living futures cannot be driven by concrete rules, absolutes and simplistic definitions. Life is complex. It depends! We need deep knowledge and rich worldviews to pursue life wisdom and live wisely. And, such wisdom needs to be about many things.

Consider, for example, the terms globalisation and nationhood; they represent very different realities from different viewpoints than they did one hundred years ago as terms, lived experiences and expectations. Take the term 'economy' and it is evident that adding the labels 'gig,' EU, 'post pandemic' or 'privileged/disadvantaged' adds significantly different dimensions and actioned interpretations to them. Also the way economists, for instance, explain, interpret and manage economies today involves different interpretive models that are more sophisticated than in simpler times.

– The second reflection is that wisdom can be used as multiple ways of shaping different futures and this interpretation is a richer way of thinking and enacting future paths than seeing the future as something that can be narrowly predicted or defined.

The challenges of realising and imagining possible, probable and preferable futures are large and complicated. What might life, practice and work look like in a range of possible futures and what might our social, natural and physical worlds alongside our lived worlds be like? What would different worldviews prioritise and champion if they differed in substantial ways in relation to such things as artificial intelligence, sustainability, extinction and social justice.

> This seems a straightforward question that simply requires some anticipation of how the world might change and what roles practice might

> play in different future worlds. But asking this seemingly simple question causes us to confront some powerful limitations of human thinking processes. In some ways, it challenges us … authors, … readers, as members of societies that are creating, and preparing for, possible futures – to think in ways that we normally find unthinkable. … We will consider many implications of this (thinking) … including powerful ideas that go largely unchallenged and so leave humanity vulnerable to inevitable surprises, many of which will be undesirable and even potentially catastrophic (Schwartz, 2003). We will touch on some aspects of societal governance that inhibit thinking about *unthinkable* possibilities, (and ways that) … are helping, one another to break free of thinking constraints to make us better prepared for what the future might hold. (Cork & Horsfall, 2019, p. 17)

The idea of "things unthinkable" and "problems unsolvable", or wicked projects are fascinating. They demand of us a quality of attention that we often fail to give to life's greatest challenges. They shake the certainties of our assumptions and "taken-for-granteds", asking us to look anew at why as well as what we believe. Crises also are intense opportunities for wisdom to be realised. It could be argued that regular times can "get away" with using regular rules and actions, crises not only need extra, more powerful and wiser strategies but they hold up to intense scrutiny our regular beliefs and the acceptability of our expected and normally accepted actions.

We cannot appreciate and plan for different futures of places, people and living worlds without acknowledging that they can be different and have to be different to address the emerging and different perspectives and interests of different peoples. Also, we need to acknowledge that multiple influences beyond societal and physical laws will shape not only the choices people make, but also the way they make sense of these choices and their consequences.

- The third reflection is that wisdom is more than an idea or notion. It is a perpetually evolving interpretive space of understanding where wisdom evolves. Wisdom, informed by the situation, contextual challenges and practice knowledge and problem solving, reshapes the emerging future.

Practice wisdom interpretations and models have been the subject of much research, scholarship, debate and critique over different eras. These views and classifications range from the work of Aristotle to ethical practices, from social practice wisdom to sociological imagination and new interpretations. Practice wisdom is interpreted by authors in multiple contexts across professional development, mindful practice, confronting moral issues, embodied practice, practice ecologies, social philosophy, critical reflection, ethico-legal situations, addressing with modern wicked problems in the age of certainty and acknowledging cultural and ethical matters.

What might people across different historical ages, culture and social spaces have otherwise understood as wisdom? Not only would we expect to receive different answers to this question, we would also see the ways that the answers have evolved. We cannot escape the speed and inevitability of such evolution, largely because of the growing interconnectedness of the world and the immediacy of change impacting from global interactions.

2 Wisdom, Practice Wisdom and Wise Practice

Building on the introductory reflections in the primary question, I now turn to the focus phenomena of this book. Within Shaping Wise Futures are multiple legitimate future directions and outcomes that may be constructed, intended, happenstance, optional and perhaps, partially, inevitable, depending on who is driving the changes arising, and whether the changes are collaborative, responsible, environmentally, politically and economically driven.

The second part of this book deals with the nature, experience and interpretation of wisdom. Wisdom (a noun) is like knowledge, a thing, but also like knowing (a verb) cannot occur without action (being wise). In addition, wisdom and being wise has dimensions of behavioural ownership and moral responsibility for actions. Wisdom is linked to ethics and justice, having connotations of goodness and socially acceptable judgements, decisions and actions. It is embedded in humanity, being associated with wellbeing of others. It would be difficult to present a credible case for an argument or decision being wise if it caused harm or injustice. Wisdom is linked to prudence and practicality (involving adult or mature thinking without excluding the possibility of children displaying wisdom or older people have little). We could also add the notion of emotional intelligence and mindfulness, astuteness, serenity and contemplation to wisdom; its realisation and thinking might well be rigorous and hard won, it is unlikely to be chaotically construed, laboriously logical or procedurally argued. Yet, the opposite of argued logic does not set up a barrier to wisdom that limits it from being creative, wordless, beyond overt imagination and from the realm of things invisible, wordless and ephemeral.

> Immeasurables are those typically deep aspects of practice that are impossible or difficult to measure and, at times, to articulate. They are often

> deliberately or inherently hidden and undisclosed, they are often marginalised, they are essentially invisible, unobserved or unspoken, they can be complex and hard to articulate and they are difficult to name. (Higgs, 2014, p. 257)

> The sum of a practitioner's professional knowledge and capacity to use this knowledge in practice is progressively transformed and enhanced, becoming qualitatively different. This increasingly complex phenomenon becomes practice wisdom when it is practised and actuated wisely. This is illustrated in the use of professional judgement, particularly in situations of great complexity and uncertainty where rules and prescribed findings from research are inadequate to deal with wicked problems and lack the essential wisdom of particularity and situatedness. Practice wisdom is finely illustrated in advanced forms of decision-making such as in medical decision-making, which has been portrayed as extending from the novice to expert forms of professional decision-making. … Practice wisdom occurs in spaces beyond the notion of expertise and learned reasoning. Such practice wisdom holds no less responsibility for the quality of practice for the client, but rests on an inherently richer, deeper and more humanly complex realisation of lived reality, creative understanding and human interests. (Higgs, 2019a, p. 4)

2.1 *The Evolution of Wisdom through Practice Experience*

Similar to learning and knowing, wisdom can be derived through practice experience, through theorisation, interpretation (of meanings and patterns) and empirico-analytical thinking. Thus, wisdom can be about life, about practice and about theory including practice and theory perspectives and understandings of wisdom. Wisdom is construed in many different ways ranging from generic wisdom to practice wisdom, and wise practice being inseparable from practical wisdom. In an extensive reflection on various interpretations of wisdom Birren and Fisher (1990) concluded:

> Wisdom brings together experience, cognitive abilities and affect, in order to make good decisions at an individual and societal level. These conceptualisations of wisdom can be placed on a continuum, with wisdom as solely a cognitive ability at one end (Baltes and Smith) and some higher integration of cognition with affect (Kramer) or other subjective forms of knowing (Labouvie-Vief) at the other. Cognitive abilities, action and affect each appear to be a necessary but not sufficient component of wisdom for most authors in this volume. (pp. 325–326)

2.2 *Practice Characteristics*

The nature of practice not only demonstrates its inherent complexity, it also sets wicked challenges for practice wisdom. That is, the practice of an occupation, profession or discipline is a multidimensional and dynamic phenomenon that is:

- Socio-culturally, historically and politically constructed – it is a product of its time, place, peoples and evolving interests
- Shaped by the narrative, discourse and evolution of the discipline/occupation
- Temporally located in eras, generational contexts and prevailing professional, policy and political drivers
- Situational – what practices are useful, optimal and most relevant depends on the circumstances, geography, systems and persons involved
- Ethical (ideally) – since practice is bound up in issues of moral purpose. This can range from contractual obligations to clients and practice communities to professional services with inherent duty of care to clients
- Responsible – as enacted by both the practice community (collectively) and practitioners (personally)
- Consequential – practice in occupational contexts has purposes and consequences if those purposes are not met or if actions taken have negative outcomes
- Embodied – manifested, owned, enacted and realised. Further, Green and Hopwood (2015) emphasise the notion of corporeality, contending that explicit attention to the body "informs and extends our current understandings and conceptualisations of (professional) practice" (p. 4)
- Agential – pertaining to the will and capacity of the practitioner to choose and implement actions and influence
- Owned and interpreted by practice to respect both the norms and standards of the practice community and the personal values and interests of the practitioner
- Governed (regulated, led, managed, monitored) by its practice community/communities
- Current (up-to-date) in the present and future-oriented in its evolution
- Person-centred – people (their interests, characteristics and needs) are the focus and purpose of practice. Without the practice creators, receivers and collaborators practice has no meaning or purpose
- Realised through and embedded in partnerships and collaboration with practice stakeholders including clients, colleagues, employers, practice community leaders and society
- Dynamic, adaptable, flexible and creative – both proactively and in response to changes in circumstances and practice settings

- Encompassing of praxis which refers to "acting for the good", "right conduct" (adopting a neo-Aristotelian view) and as "socially responsible action" (using a post-Marxian view) in the professions. Praxis is inherently reflexive. Praxis is informed by historically generated practice traditions that give substance to praxis, so that praxis is evaluated against historical and evolving standards and expectations that shape and frame the collective practice of professions as well as the conduct of individual practitioners.

2.3 *The Dimensions of Practice Wisdom*

The activities or practices linked to wisdom can be encompassed in the broad label of *Practice* and the activities or *practices* within that field of practice. Practice encompasses doing, knowing, being and becoming (Higgs, 1999) and in practice wisdom they become refined as *dasein, agentia, sapience* and *eudaimonia* (see Figure 1.1).

2.3 *Agentia*

Agentia (Latin), or agency, encompasses a range of ideas including choice, capability, dispositions, self-critique and choice of action and practices. Practitioners (for instance professionals) need to pursue agency in the implementation of their roles and responsibilities and they often act as agents and

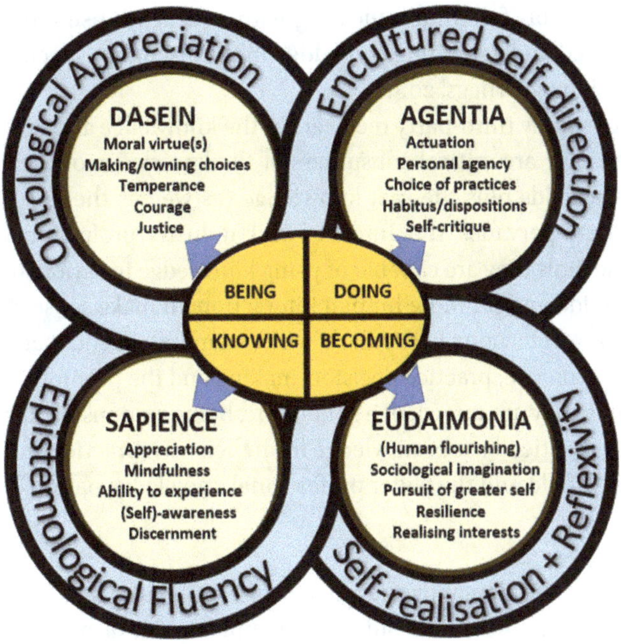

FIGURE 1.1 Practice wisdom: Agentia, sapience, dasein and eudaimonia (Higgs, 2019a, p. 11, reprinted with permission)

advocate for their clients. Their behaviour is informed both by their own self-directed practice decision-making and through the culture of their profession.

2.4 *Sapience*

Knowing extends far beyond having knowledge. Professionals need to be able to derive knowledge from, and use knowledge in, practice. As well as gaining and using knowledge, this includes *appreciating* (with inbuilt critique, valuing and using knowing to generate ideas and judgements), mindfulness (with heightened awareness and attitudes of attentiveness to other and other ideas), self-awareness (self as presence and agent in situations), and being a knowing being with abilities of discernment, metacognition and self-awareness. Such a being is *sapient* (Old French, Latin) meaning having good sense, intelligence, wisdom and the capacity to perceive. Practitioners need to develop not just their practice epistemology and have this capability to inform and expand their practice, their practice knowledge, critical appreciation and development; they also need to develop epistemological fluency.

The idea of fluency, typically applied to language, the spoken word and interactive communication, is particularly useful when thinking about wise practice and practice knowledge including decision-making in practice. Firstly, it refers to having a command of the language, and experienced practitioners need to have this ability. Jargon/technical language of the practice community provides the means and tools for communicating with colleagues using the rich knowledge and shared understanding embedded in the discipline-specific language of the profession (see Higgs, 2019a).

Practitioners are not simply third-party receivers of the knowledge and wisdom of others. Instead they are critical consumers of the knowledge of their own and other relevant fields plus the vast knowledge (as well as the lesser entity, information) that pervades the Internet and industry/professional workspaces. With these tools they are capable of using knowledge in action, to make judgements, to guide and promote human interaction, to make sense of experiences and to inform behaviour, particularly wise and moral practice such as ethical conduct, benevolence, practice decision-making and the promotion of social justice. Further, they are knowledge generators, being responsible for creating and critiquing practice-based knowledge from their own practice and contributing this to their field and the wider professional knowledge base.

2.5 *Dasein*

Being in professional practice demands the pursuit of moral virtues as part of professionalism, expecting the use of ontological appreciation of practice worlds and worldviews to foster understanding, recognition and appreciation of the multiple worldviews of the many participants in professional practice and recognition of the many interests (see Habermas, 1968/1972). Different people, cultures and contexts contribute to the given situation. Practitioners are not just expected to act in line with sound practices of their professions and follow norms and codes of ethical conduct; they are also required to make and enact their own judgements, decisions and practice models and sustain as well as evolve these in the face of uncertain and complex situations, taking responsibility for their choices. Professional practice requires being a person of courage, temperance, virtue and justice. I have chosen the label of *Dasein* for this space: *Dasein* (German: da "there"; sein "being") or presence. Heidegger[1] used the expression *Dasein* to refer to the experience of being that is peculiar to human beings.

2.6 *Eudaimonia*

Neither as self/person or practitioner worthy of the label, does a professional graduate act as a static or non-evolving being. Instead, just as their world of practice and knowledge is growing and changing around them, so too are they developing. People describe this development in many ways. From the general term becoming, there are many other options to be considered. *Eudaimonia* (Greek) is typically translated as human flourishing and living well. In Aristotle's works, *eudaimonia* was used as the term for the highest human good. In practical philosophy the aim is to consider what *eudaimonia* is and how it can be achieved. In pursuit of human flourishing the individual benefits from an under-standing of the human world, a sociological imagination, resilience and creativity. Embedded in human flourishing are the ideas of "*arête*" (virtue and excellence) and *phrónêsis*.

3 Wisdom as a Way of Doing Things: Thinking and Acting Wisely

> Wisdom results from the application of successful intelligence and creativity toward the common good through a balancing of intrapersonal, interpersonal, and extra-personal interests over the short and long terms. Wisdom is not just a way of thinking about things; it's a way of doing things. If people wish to be wise, they have to act wisely not just think wisely. (Sternberg, 2003, p. 188)

Practice wisdom requires the building and critical use of multiple practice knowledges. Aristotle spoke of three forms of knowledge: *epistêmê* (which is today characterised as *epistêmic* or scientific, invariable, context-independent knowledge), *tékhnê* (which is characterised as technical knowledge) and *phrónêsis* (which is characterised as pragmatic, variable, context-dependent and oriented toward action). Knowledge for professional practice requires all three of these.

There is a rich variety of sources for experiential and lived knowledge including knowledge of the lived experience of practitioners, colleagues and clients. Openness to these multiple constructed realities provides a space of diverse and complex understanding of dialectics through ontological appreciation. Wisdom is also manifest in the visible and invisible, explicit and tacit, robust and ephemeral dimensions of practice.

While wisdom may be a dedicated focus of attention in various fields of scholarship and spirituality it is often regarded by 'regular folk' or non-scholars in current generations as a 'soft' and indefinite word far removed from power genre words such as science, political, evidence-based and mathematics. This argument does not reject the value of the knowledges contained and practised in those fields, rather it asks two fundamental questions: upon what epistemologies are these knowledges based and how do these different paradigms give rise to different knowledge truths and discourses? Which epistemological rules govern what counts as truth or epistemologically legitimate in each knowledge paradigm and practice field? Different disciplines, professions, arts and crafts encompass different fields and sub specialities; which can be understood as epistemic cultures and communities of practice as well as fields of work in the labour market. From the perspective of practice wisdom and wise practice, these occupations (the generic term) may appear across this range of jobs and work cultures.

Each occupation and community of practice shares a field of work knowledge skills and activities, often with tacit knowledge. They come together to pursue common interests and activities (e.g. road building, health care, ballet dancing, opera singing, gymnastics, school teaching, research, childcare). By sharing cultural norms, knowledge, quality standards and practices, members of the work community function coherently as members of a group who walk, talk and think (reason) in shared, trained and encultured ways. Over time, paradigms evolve their pursuits and methodologies, and their goals often become more refined and effective in relation to the interests they serve. Paradigms proliferate and new ones emerge as interests change or evolve. For instance, science (including study of the human and the physical worlds) is not static or confined to a single strategy but responds to changing interests.

A key element of learning and working in communities of practice and occupations is recognising and respecting the occupation's worldview (or practice ontology) and how that is linked to the way knowledge is determined and created within that practice world (or practice epistemology) (see Higgs et al., 2004). Being grounded in their own profession's practice, members of the profession typically work across multiple communities of practice with a range of frames of reference (profession-specific, interdisciplinary, organisational and workplace oriented). The use of this knowledge and practice wisdom as part of wise future planning allows for mixed epistemic cultures and recognition that disciplines and practice fields are changing like the economy as mentioned above, and dispute resolution in law where changing practices and socio-legal requirements are changing the way knowledge practices are used.

Increasingly, not all fields follow distinctive epistemic cultures across their disciplines or professions. As an example, consider the health field. Models of health practice largely fit in three categories: the illness or biomedical model, the wellness model and the capability model (in which dis-ability is distinguished from ability). These models are grounded in the empirico-analytical, the interpretive and the critical knowledge paradigms respectively. In some specialties such as biochemistry the epistemic culture is clearly the science-driven empirico-analytical paradigm, in others such as rehabilitation the practice emphasis is on practical knowledge generation and use, while in others such as clinical psychology there is an emphasis on patient or client empowerment and setting aside taken-for-granted practices. Nursing, of interest, is a diverse profession with many sub roles and cultures, demonstrating all three, practice paradigms.

4 Conclusion

The themes proposed in this chapter draw on the shaping of ways of practice wisdom (agentia, sapience, dasein, and eudaimonia) into future practice. It is not enough to create the future, instead we need to create practice wisdom through it.

Note

1 https://plato.stanford.edu/entries/heidegger/#Bib

References

Birren, J. E., & Fisher, L. M. (1990). The elements of wisdom: Overview and integration. In R. J. Sternberg (Ed.), *Wisdom: Its nature, origins and development* (pp. 317–332). Cambridge University Press.

Cork, S., & Horsfall, D. (2019). Thinking the unthinkable: Challenges of imagining and engaging with unimaginable practice futures. In J. Higgs, S. Cork, & D. Horsfall (Eds.), *Challenging future practice possibilities* (pp. 17–28). Brill Sense.

Green, B., & Hopwood, N. (Eds.). (2015). *The body in professional practice, learning and education*. Springer.

Habermas, J. (1968/1972). *Knowledge and human interest* (J. J. Shapiro, Trans.). Heinemann.

Higgs, J. (1999, September). *Doing, knowing, being and becoming in professional practice*. Paper presented at the Master of Teaching Post Internship Conference, The University of Sydney, Australia.

Higgs, J. (2014). Assessing the immeasurables of practice. *Asia-Pacific Journal of Cooperative Education, 15*(3), 253–267.

Higgs, J. (2019a). Appreciating practice wisdom. In J. Higgs (Ed.), *Practice wisdom: Values and interpretations* (pp. 3–14). Brill Sense.

Higgs, J. (Ed.). (2019b). *Practice wisdom: Values and interpretations*. Brill Sense.

Higgs, J., Cork, S., & Horsfall, D. (2019). *Challenging future practice possibilities*. Brill Sense.

Higgs, J., Richardson, B., & Abrandt Dahlgren, M. (Eds.). (2004). *Developing practice knowledge for health professionals*. Butterworth-Heinemann.

Schwartz, P. (2003). *Inevitable surprises: Thinking ahead in a time of turbulence*. Gotham.

Sternberg, R. J. (2003). *Wisdom, intelligence, and creativity synthesized*. Cambridge University Press.

Taylor, R. B. (2010). *Medical wisdom and doctoring: The art of 21st century practice*. Springer.

CHAPTER 2

Building a Wise and Sustainable Future

Moral Purpose and Challenged Assumptions

Geoff Scott

Abstract

The aim of the chapter is to build an argument around the importance of sustainable development and the place of social entrepreneurship in shaping positive local and global futures. It is argued that working collaboratively and wisely at local and global levels to shape a future that takes account of the social, cultural, economic and environmental challenges currently facing the world is now central to building a sustainable future. How the United Nations' Sustainable Development Goals (SDGs) are providing wise leadership, vision and a values-based agenda for action in this arena is outlined.

The focus is on a key message of the book – that shared wisdom, moral purpose, collective and responsible action and effective implementation strategies are needed in combination to wisely shape and enact our global futures. The chapter encourages policy makers, educators, students, business and community members to build on what people are already doing to successfully enact the SDG agenda. It is argued that the work of the UN, as an international agency with the collaboration of more than 190 countries committed to participating in this project, is a strong example of how wise futures can be shaped. The chapter explores not only *what* might be done but *how* to make it happen. It explores what values underpin the SDGs and how they can be put into practice through collective action. The chapter is, therefore, about the big picture of successful change management for a sustainable future. It focuses on what Aristotle called 'practical wisdom' and its key messages are 'good ideas with no ideas on how to implement them are wasted ideas' and 'change doesn't just happen but must be led, and deftly' (Fullan & Scott, 2009). And it highlights how the strategies found to underpin successful change implementation embody the very values that will enable a sustainable future.

Keywords

sustainability – moral action – shared purpose – social entrepreneurship – Sustainable Development Goals

 | DOI: 10.1163/9789004505544_003

1 Introduction

It is argued that, given the events of 2020, it is timely to reflect on exactly what tacit assumptions and values have been driving the 21st century agenda and ask if these are still fit for the purpose of building a desirable and relevant future for people and planet. Doing this requires critical appraisal of accepted beliefs like growth is equally good for everyone, consumption is happiness, ICT is always the answer and global uniformity is great. And it requires us to come to grips with the key challenges now faced in the age of 'acceleration and uncertainty' (Friedman, 2016; Galbraith, 1977). In providing a trigger for such reflection, the COVID-19 pandemic offers an opportunity for a 'reset'. As Rahm Emanuel, chief of staff to former US president Barack Obama, is reported to have said: "You never want a serious crisis to go to waste … And what I mean by that is, it's an opportunity to do things you think you could not do before" (Maley, 2020, n.p.).

Social researcher Hugh Mackay (2020) argues that the crisis has highlighted the importance of values like compassion, caring for others not just oneself, contributing to the greater good, adopting a 'why don't we' not a 'why don't you' approach to life, humility and supporting human dignity, along with the importance of following 'the golden rule', of reciprocal relationships, community support, family, dignity and truthfulness. This contrasts with values like blaming others for personal failure, showing disregard for science, making inflated claims, engaging in vaccine nationalism, pursuing self-interest, withdrawing from forums focused on international cooperation, focusing on winning and remaining in power at all costs, brand boosting, promoting racial intolerance and deception and emphasising divisiveness rather than unity. Giving focus to shaping a wise future leads us to consider exactly what concepts like 'wise' and 'progress' mean in practical terms. This involves understanding that there is a profound difference between change (something simply becoming different) and 'progress' (a value judgement by each individual that what is proposed is relevant, wise, desirable, 'beneficial' and feasible). At the heart of this process of evaluation (making a judgement of worth) are values. Shaping a future which is 'wise' therefore requires those making the judgements about which direction to pursue to be clear on what their values are and to recognise the key role which subjective judgement, emotions and 'moral purpose' play in motivating people to engage with change. In the chapter value-judgement is, therefore, highlighted as the fuel for productive change management and building a wise future.

It is argued that wise futures are shaped by resilient, morally robust and wise individuals and that wise people are developed by an education system which focuses on developing work ready *plus* citizens, using the proven strategies of engaged scholarship and learning (Beaulieu et al., 2018; Scott, 2019a).

Wise, change savvy, adaptable nations are built by wise, change savvy, adaptable individuals. These are people who are able to create, design and deliver desired innovations; and who know how to engage the disengaged with these developments, as they are co-created. As our studies of successful early career graduates in nine professions and work with 3700 Learning and Teaching leaders across the world involved in the international Flip Curriculum Project[1] have shown, work ready *plus* graduates are, sustainability literate, change implementation savvy, inventive (socially not just commercially) and clear on where they stand on the tacit assumptions currently driving the 21st century agenda. As Derek Bok, former president of Harvard University argues, what is now needed are graduates who can:

> … analyze problems successfully; adapt readily to changing conditions and new challenges; collaborate effectively with others in producing creative solutions to novel problems; meet their commitments conscientiously; and interact easily and harmoniously with others from different races, socioeconomic backgrounds and cultures. (Bok, 2020, chapter 9, p. 1)

The chapter highlights the successful ways in which innovatory community groups, organisations and educational institutions are already addressing the challenges we now face using social entrepreneurship projects focused on the SDGs and the key lessons that have been learnt on how to make them work.

2 The UN's Sustainable Development Goals (SDGs)

The Sustainable Development Goals are the blueprint to achieve a better and more sustainable future for all. They address the global challenges we face … The 17 Goals are all interconnected, underpinned by key constructs and in order to leave no one behind, it is important that we achieve them all by 2030.[2]

2.1 *Key Constructs of SDGs*

2.1.1 Change, Progress & Learning

Aiming for learning that is the basis of change that is relevant, wise, desirable, 'beneficial', feasible and observable and an improvement over what went before values as the 'right' thing to do.

2.1.2 Competence

The delivery of specific tasks in relatively predictable circumstances. It enables one to be work ready for today.

2.1.3 Capability

Responsiveness, self-regulation, decisiveness, commitment, creativity, contingent thinking and growth in relatively uncertain times (Scott et al., 2008).

2.1.4 Ethical Principles

The rules of conduct that derive from ethical values […]. Ethics is about putting principles into action and maintaining consistency between what we say we value and what our actions say we value is a matter of integrity" (Josephson, 2002, p. 4).

2.1.5 Moral Purpose

A value that, when articulated, appeals to the innate sense held by some individuals of what is right and what is worthwhile" (Mourkogiann, 2005 p. 1). Michael Fullan (2002) sees it as "… principled behaviour connected to something greater than ourselves, that relates to human and social development" (p. 1), and Kopiyo (2014) as: "… acting with the intention of making a positive difference in the lives of the people it affects" (slide 1).

2.1.6 Wisdom

The ability to make good judgments based on what you have learned from your experience, or the knowledge and understanding that gives you this ability.[3]

Also construed as virtue – the capacity to see what is 'right' without having to be told – as being closely linked to what Aristotle calls *phronēsis*, or practical wisdom (Crisp (2019), residing in where you live and in the nature and impact of what you do to help shape a wise future.

2.1.7 Tacit Knowledge & Assumptions

Tacit knowledge is what people know, but don't necessarily verbalise' (Kopiyo, 2014, point 12).

2.1.8 Tacit Assumptions

"… the hidden beliefs behind what's going on … these shared tacit assumptions influence absolutely everything that happens, but they're not so easy to uncover" (Schein, 2004, cited in Loftus, n.d., p. 1).

2.2 *The Purposes of the SDGs*

The SDGs have been agreed to by 193 of the world's nations. They seek to address the key challenges facing the world over the coming decade and embedded in them is a shared set of values for a better future. They are interconnected and address the four pillars of social, cultural, economic and environmental sustainability. The global challenges that the United Nations Development Programme (2020) identifies the SDGs as addressing are as follows:

1. *No poverty*
   In 2015 more than 735 million people around the world lived on less than US $2 a day.
2. *Zero Hunger*
   In 2017 some 820 million were estimated to be chronically undernourished.
3. *Good health and well-being*
   At present, there is a 31year gap between countries with the shortest and longest life expectancies.
4. *Access to quality education for all*
   Children from the poorest households are up to four times more likely to be out of school than those of the richest households.
5. *Achieving gender inequality*
   At present women earn 77c for every dollar men earn. Only 24% of parliamentarians around the world were women in 2018.
6. *Clean water and sanitation*
   Water scarcity affects 40% of the world's population. In 2015 4.5 billion people lacked safely managed sanitation services.
7. *Affordable, accessible and clean energy*
   One in seven people lacks electricity. Energy contributes 60% of greenhouse gases. 40% of the world's population – some 3 billion people rely on polluting and unhealthy fuels for cooking.
8. *Decent work and sustainable economic growth*
   172 million people were unemployed in 2018.
9. *Sustainable industry, innovation and infrastructure*
   2.3 billion people lack basic sanitation; 2.6 billion do not have access to constant, reliable energy; more than 4 billion don't have access to the internet.
10. *Reduced inequalities*
    "The world's 8 richest people have the same wealth as the poorest 50%" (Goldring, 2017).
11. *Sustainable cities and communities*
    By 2050, two-thirds of all humanity – 6.5 billion people – will be urban.
12. *Responsible consumption and production*
    1.3 billion tonnes of food is wasted every year, while almost 2 billion people go hungry or undernourished. The food sector accounts for around 22% of total greenhouse gas emissions, largely from the conversion of forests into farmland. 6000 kilograms of clothing, mainly 'fast, dispos-

able fashion', is dumped in landfill every 10 minutes. Of the 8.3 billion metric tons of plastic that has been produced, 6.3 billion metric tons has become plastic waste. In 2019 alone, the world generated 53.6 million tonnes of e-waste.

13. *Climate change*
    Greenland lost an average of 286 billion tons of ice per year between 1993 and 2016, while Antarctica lost about 127 billion, tripling in the last decade. Atmospheric carbon dioxide has risen from less than 300 parts per million in 1950 to 420 parts currently and rising. Sea levels are projected to rise 30–122 cm by 2100, threatening many island communities. The annual average economic losses from climate-related disasters are in the hundreds of billions of dollars.
14. *Sustainable life below water*
    Over three billion people depend on marine and coastal biodiversity for their livelihoods. There has been a 26% rise in ocean acidification since the beginning of the industrial revolution. As much as 40% of the ocean is heavily affected by pollution.
15. *Sustainable life on land*
    The value of ecosystems to human livelihoods and well-being is $US125 trillion per year. Forests are home to more than 80% of all terrestrial species of animals, plants and insects. Every year, 13 million hectares of forests are lost. As deforestation increases wild animals get closer to humans and can transmit zoonotic diseases like SARS, Ebola and COVID-19.
16. *Achieving peace, justice and strong institutions*
    By the end of 2017, 68.5 million people had been forcibly displaced as a result of persecution, conflict, violence or human rights violations. Corruption and tax evasion cost developing countries US$1.26 trillion per year. 49 countries lack laws protecting women from domestic violence. Politically there is an increased tendency to focus on fractious division.
17. *Working in partnership to address these goals and challenges*
    The above challenges can only be realized with strong global partnerships and cooperation. The world is more interconnected than ever. Improving access to technology and knowledge is an important way to share ideas and foster innovation.

The Population Division of the United Nations (2019) reports that the world's population is expected to increase by a further 2 billion persons in the next 30 years, from 7.7 billion currently to 9.7 billion in 2050. This has significant implications for almost every one of the SDGs.

2.3 *The UN SDGs – A Global Agenda Driven by a Shared Moral Purpose*

> In these times of unprecedented change and challenge, these goals are a clear framework to review the work we do, how we live our lives and how we individually and collectively can come together to find new ways of working, new opportunities and new ways to solve joint problems … (Hutchinson, 2020, p. 3)

The key values that constitute the moral purpose of the SDG agenda include care and compassion for others; avoiding avarice and over consumption; abiding by the 'golden rule'; pursuing justice, peace and security; fostering intergenerational, interracial and gender equity and opportunities; ensuring peace, security and collaboration for the greater good; inclusive economic and social development; ensuring environmental sustainability; eradication of poverty and hunger; the right to a healthy life; and having equal access to high quality education and life opportunities, job security, and human dignity. As Jan Eliasson (2016), United Nations Deputy Secretary General, has noted:

> (The) fundamental principles that underpin the new goals are interdependence, universality and solidarity. They should be implemented by all segments of all societies, working together. No one must be left behind. People who are hardest to reach should be given priority … This is the underlying moral code of the 2030 Agenda for Sustainable Development. (p. 1)

The values that underpin the SDGs have much in common with the values shared by many of the world's religions (Bouquet, 1969). As the UN Secretary General Annan (2006) emphasised more than a decade ago: "We must stress the basic values that are common to all religions: compassion; solidarity; respect for the human person; the Golden Rule of "do as you would be done by" (para. 16).

Importantly, there is a close overlap between the above values and the key personal and interpersonal capabilities identified in our studies of successful graduates in nine professions and in successful education leaders (Fullan & Scott, 2009; Scott, 2003; Scott et al., 2008, 2012). These distinguishing capabilities include and ability to listen to a wide range of views, work productively and empathetically with diversity, to remain calm under pressure, to tolerate ambiguity, to be true to one's personal values, to take hard but fair and transparent decisions, to engage the disengaged and being authentic and trustworthy.

Enacting the SDGs also has links to what Roger Crisp (2019), Professor of Moral Philosophy at Oxford, identifies as Aristotle's list of virtues which, he says, contains "many of those we still find in our everyday morality: courage, generosity, even temper, moderation, being a good friend (to all), justice, prudence, honesty ... virtues such as patience, tolerance and resilience, ... a life of autonomy and authenticity ... and the virtue of collaborativeness" (Modern Insights, para. 6). Crisp (2019) also makes a distinction between what we do and what we let happen.

> The Sustainable Development Goals (SDGs), ... are integrated – that is, they recognize that action in one area will affect outcomes in others, and that development must balance social, economic and environmental sustainability. (United Nations Development Programme: Programme of Assistance to the Palestinian People, 2021, Section: Sustainable Development Goals, para. 2)

2.4 *COVID-19 Demonstrates How the SDGs Are All Connected*

Pandemics, such. as the COVID-19 pandemic, present 'wicked' sustainability problems and illustrate clearly how the 17 SDGs and the challenges underpinning them need to be addressed in unison. Gopinath, (cited in Whiting, 2020, n.p.). observes that "This is a virus that doesn't respect borders ... so it requires global cooperation to deal with it". (Schuijers, 2020, Section: Public Sector, para. 4) has argued that the diverse responses globally have "demonstrated what can be done differently [forcing] us to alter our behaviour in significant ways, not all of which will necessarily reverse after restrictions are lifted".

For example, dealing effectively with the pandemic has required a concurrent focus on:

- Figuring out how the corona virus and zoonotic transfer work;
- Inventing an effective vaccine and encouraging people to take it;
- An understanding of epidemiology;
- Ensuring clean water;
- Addressing the impact of changed patterns of food production and deforestation;
- Understanding and dealing with cultural difference – e.g. the use of wet markets;
- Fostering new COVID-safe forms of human contact;
- Changing travel regulations; quarantine; and legislation;
- Figuring out how best to balance individual rights with community safety in areas like mandatory mask wearing and bans on public meetings;

- Managing fractious division, disruptive demonstrations and social media-fired misinformation;
- Reducing the impact of poverty and crowed living to slow speed of transmission;
- Fostering renewed international partnerships and cooperation;
- Overcoming the disparity between rich and poor countries in access to health care and avoiding vaccine nationalism;
- Targeting health education on how best to engage the disengaged;
- Rapidly introducing new approaches to teaching and flexible learning, moving away from a purely campus-centric business model (Leonard, 2020), adopting new approaches to international education and managing higher education budget deficits;
- Addressing the digital divide, social media disinformation and new threats to cybersecurity;
- Reducing over-consumption and hoarding;
- Managing the move from instore to online shopping;
- Introducing new patterns of work and adjusting to a changed job market in industries like tourism and hospitality;
- Working together on how to open up borders safely;
- Keeping people in employment as economies move into recession;
- Figuring out how to balance an open, just-in-time approach to free trade with a more locally based just-in-case one.

Many of these COVID-19 triggered issues have raised important moral, ethical and strategic dilemmas and in particular related to the principle of equity, between nations such as vaccine nationalism. Bollyky and Brown (2020) observed that "Vaccine nationalism is not just morally and ethically reprehensible: it is contrary to every country's economic, strategic, and health interests" (n.p.). Kamradt-Scott (2020) noted how the SDGs concerning equity and access are clearly linked to this issue, stating that "rather than being based on equity or need, it [vaccine nationalism] will create global supply problems with those countries that have special deals getting access to the vaccine first (Section: Can We Buy Vaccines in Advance?, para. 5).

The pandemic has also shown up inequity within national populations. Professor Peter Robinson (2020) reports that studies in Europe, the UK and Australia all show that the COVID-19 shutdowns have had a much more significant economic and employment impact on those with low education and in insecure employment than those with higher education. Clearly, this pandemic has hit those living in poverty and crowded conditions hardest. As Vally (2020) reports when discussing the spread of the virus in social housing towers: Physical distancing is almost impossible when you have big families living in two-bedroom units (Section: The Melbourne Tower Blocks, para. 3).

These are important observations and lessons to be learned. Simon Marginson, Director of the Centre for Global Higher Education in Oxford, argues that these emergent challenges of, and responses to, COVID-19 have implications for tertiary education, observed in "there is the need to change the values that govern the way our higher education system functions – and hence the values that students themselves are being taught – so as to put the common good ahead of all other considerations (Margison, 2020, July 25th, Section: A Quasi-market System, para. 9).

In summary, the COVID-19 pandemic has shown us that we can't just assume that what we have been doing in the past is still going to work in the future and that managing such unexpected events requires simultaneous attention to almost every one of the 17 SDGs. And it shows that an effective response requires all involved to reflect critically on the tacit assumptions under which they have been operating.

2.5 *Tacit Assumptions and Shaping the 21st Century Agenda for a Wise, Sustainable Future*

There is an important question to be asked about shaping a wise future. Are the tacit assumptions currently driving the 21st century agenda leading us towards a wise, sustainable future? Individuals, groups and societies are most tested when things go awry or the unexpected happens, it is then that their underpinning values and tacit assumptions about what is most important are revealed. And it is then that people can be triggered to reflect on these taken-for-granted assumptions, habits and ways of behaving and consider changing them.

As just noted, the 2020 COVID-19 pandemic has called into question a wide range of taken-for-granted ways of behaving including those concerning travel, individual rights, social contact, arts and the theatre, secure work and economic growth, quality education, health and well-being, and social interaction and cohesion. As David Suzuki (2020) comments:

> In this moment of crisis, we should be asking what an economy is for … how much is enough and whether we are happier with all this stuff … For me, one of the most dramatic effects of humanity's COVID-19-induced slowdown has been nature's rapid response; clean air over China, fish in the canals of Venice and the sighting of a raptor in my Vancouver backyard … In this disaster lies an opportunity to reflect and change direction in the hope that if we do, nature will be far more generous than we deserve. (paras. 10–15)

When commenting on the difficulties in getting a supply of N95 masks at the outset of the COVID-19 pandemic Rubin (2020) observed that it called into question the assumption that:

> ... the magic of just-in-time-delivery, combined with efficient labour markets and economies of scale ... (will) provide us with whatever we need, in abundance and at the best prices. It shouldn't have taken a bat peeing on a pangolin in Wuhan to teach us this lesson ... that the factories are somewhere else ... the jobs are somewhere else. And, when we need them, the masks are somewhere else too. (pp. 6–7)

The international FLIPCurric project (Scott, 2017) identified the following tacit assumptions under which the 21st century agenda has been operating, many of which have been called into question by the SDGs and the COVID-19 crisis and largely align with the observations just outlined. Prevailing current social assumptions seem to be:
- Growth is good for everyone and is possible forever;
- Consumption is happiness;
- We must live in a plastic world;
- ICT is always the answer;
- Global uniformity is great;
- Inequity is OK;
- Global warming is a problem for future generations not mine;
- Me first.

Frederick Donaldson at Westminster Abbey in March 1925 first put forward in a sermon the so called seven social sins These were: 1. Politics without principles, 2. Wealth without work, 3. Knowledge without character, 4. Business without morality, 5. Science without humanity, 6. Worship without sacrifice, 7, Pleasure without conscience. These social sins were later highlighted by Mahatma Ghandi in his newspaper *Young India* in October 1925 (Crow, 2014; Ravindran, n.d). They have the potential to provide a set of benchmarks against which it is possible to evaluate the tacit assumptions identified above and the values which underpin the SDG agenda).

3 Making It Happen: Effective Ways to Address the SDG Agenda

The SDGs have been signed off by the world's nations but now we have to implement them – a wise future is achieved not just by what is set down in a plan but by what actually changes in practice. In Scott (2019a), I argued that the more we have work ready *plus*, and produce change capable graduates the more we build change capable, resilient, sustainable groups, societies and futures and optimise our capacity to put the SDGs into practice consistently and effectively. Based on this conception, education can be the engine-house of sustainable development and robust social values are its fuel. This is because change is learning and learning is confirmed when we see people behaving differently and demonstrably valuing things differently. Below the key lessons from 20 years' research and experience on taking desired changes like the SDGs and making them happen are summarised (Fullan & Scott, 2009; Scott, 1999; Scott et al., 2008, 2012). First the key lessons on effectively engaging organisations with change and then the lessons on engaging individuals are presented.

3.1 *Engaging Organisations with the SDGs*

1. Never waste a crisis;
2. Develop a 'why bother' case and examples of where the proposed change has worked elsewhere in similar organisations to help build interest in the relevance and feasibility of the change;
3. Seek a senior mentor in the Executive who supports the initiative and who sees it as a way for them to deliver on one of their key accountabilities. For example, in universities, senior executives have become far more interested over the past two years in addressing the SDGs since the introduction of the Times HE SDG Impact Ratings in 2019 (In 2020 my own university – Western Sydney University – was ranked 3rd in the world out of the 766 universities from 85 countries that applied);
4. Undertake a stocktake of what is already happening in your organisation, using the 17 SDGs as a framework and acknowledge what is already underway;
5. Listen, link, leverage and then lead, always in that order. In particular, always listen to 'resisters';
6. Start small and build on your successes. Here the message is to try out a desired innovation under controlled conditions with a small group of interested staff and clients to learn what works best before scale-up, and then use these teams as peer mentors for the next group interested in developing the area;
7. Track participant feedback during early implementation and use this to improve the innovation;
8. Recognise that change is a complex learning and unlearning process for all concerned and that both staff and clients will be continuously considering if what is unfolding is relevant, desirable, clear and, most importantly, feasible for them;

9. 'Moral purpose' engages people far more than ordering change or engaging in public humiliation for inaction or poor outcomes;
10. Promote a 'why don't we' not a 'why don't you' culture; and a culture where there is consensus around the data not around the table;
11. Keep in mind that, for everyone involved, there is a profound difference between 'change' (something becoming different) and 'progress' (a value judgement that this has been 'beneficial');
12. Constantly seek to identify and acknowledged the positive achievements of staff and clients as they occur. Acknowledgement can be highlighted using a team-based institutional award for improved action in the area;
13. Articulate both the business case for the change and also its alignment with the institution's key strategic developments and its mission;
14. Use plain language;
15. Co-design engagement messages using the preferred contact medium(s) of the target group. For example, use social media campaigns to engage young people with key COVID-19 protection strategies (see Bonner et al., 2020);
16. Meet less but meet better in order to give staff room for change;
17. Link up with and learn from those undertaking similar developments elsewhere – network the networks.

In combination, these lessons provide an operational definition of SDG 17.

4 Engaging Individuals with the SDGs

A wide range of strategies are currently being used to engage individuals with the SDGs. They include using citizen educators; networking the many networks already active in this area including the Association of Commonwealth Universities, the International Association of Universities, the Enactus and UN-RCE networks; providing rewards for saving water and energy and minimising waste; co-creating solutions; producing videos on success stories and using popular figures to endorse action; leveraging peer group pressure; using social networking platforms; using targeted analytics and setting up citizen juries like those established by the New Democracy Foundation.[4]

All of the most successful individual engagement strategies recognise that change is learning and that engagement in productive learning, as noted above, requires the individuals concerned to continuously see that what is proposed is relevant, desirable, clear and most importantly feasible. One of the most powerful strategies is to give education a more central role in preparing graduates to address the sustainability agenda through social entrepreneurships projects and community action initiatives focused on the SDGs.

4.1 *The Key Role of Education in Enacting the SDG Agenda*

As all change is learning, education at every level has a central role to play in taking the good ideas embedded in the SDGs and making sure they are actually put into practice. It is schools, colleges and universities that can develop the work ready *plus* graduates and leaders with moral purpose who will be able to take the goals and translate them into practice. As argued in detail in Scott (2019a) this means every educational institution needs not only to develop the key competencies (set skills and knowledge) in its students that enable them to be work ready for today but also the key capabilities (abilities to successfully navigate change and unpredictable moments, adapt, create and implement new directions) that will enable them to be work ready *plus* for an accelerating and uncertain tomorrow.

Work ready *plus* graduates (Scott, 2017) capable of implementing the SDGs are 1. sustainability literate; 2. change implementation savvy in the ways outlined in the previous section; 3. inventive and creative – not just commercially but socially and 4. are clear on where they stand on the tacit assumptions currently underpinning the 21st century agenda; assumptions such as growth is equally good for everyone; consumption is happiness; ICT is always the answer; and global uniformity is great. (See Sections 3.2 and 3.3 in the Getting Started Section of FLIPCurric[5]). Galye DeBruyn (2020), professor of Art and Design at Ferris State University and organiser of the international Wege Prize design competition,[6] observes that, in the current context: "We need wicked problem-solvers ... to respond effectively and inclusively to global system disruptors like pandemics, climate change and social inequity" (pp. 1–2). Many universities and colleges are starting to give much closer attention to what their moral purpose is and consider how it relates to enacting the SDG agenda in their research, engagement, teaching and operations. In doing this many are now giving focus not only to STEM but STEAM (Science, Technology, Engineering, *Arts* and Maths) in recognition of the fact that no scientific or technological breakthrough is value free. As noted earlier, more than 760 HEIs participated in the 2020 Times Higher Education Impact ratings on the SDGs. And more than 170 UN endorsed Regional Centres of Expertise in Education for sustainable development, often led by universities and colleges, are now working around the world with their local communities and international networks on this agenda. In summary, the SDGs provide a morally robust 2020 vision for a shaping a wise and sustainable future and Universities, Colleges and Schools are a key tool for putting them into practice. One way in which HEIs can do this is to give social entrepreneurship projects focused on the SDGs a more central place in their curriculum.

4.2 *Social Entrepreneurship – A Powerful Way to Implement the SDGs*

Over the past five years the use of community-based social entrepreneurship projects focused on the SDGs has grown significantly. How such projects are being developed and implemented aligns with the key lessons of successful change implementation outlined above and highlights the way in which the key values which underpin the goals can be enacted.

4.3 *Defining Social Entrepreneurship*

Social entrepreneurship relates to entrepreneurial action by organisations and individuals that creates significant social value for communities and people. Commercial entrepreneurship is about personal benefit and profit maximisation. Social entrepreneurship is about benefitting others – such enterprises make money but no one takes it out – the profits are dedicated solely to scale up (Yunis, n.d.).

4.4 *Judging That a Social Enterprise Is 'Successful'*

All of the following indicators are being used to judge if a social enterprise project focused on the SDGs is 'successful'. Some (those that focus on demonstrably beneficial impact) are more telling than others of more general nature (e.g. positive press coverage):

- Money is being made out of waste – cradle to cradle design is in place;
- Minimum defaults on micro-finance loans;
- Positive health outcomes;
- 'Gross national happiness' (*Bhutan*);
- Improved social harmony; decreased crime rates;
- Delivery of a well-being budget like New Zealand's in 2019[7];
- More equitable distribution of wealth;
- Increased participation in post-secondary education/employment;
- Positive feedback from participants in each social enterprise;
- Successful scale up and sustainability of the initiative;
- Government and legislative support for scale up;
- Repeat business;
- Positive press coverage;
- Positive rate of return on investment;
- High position on the Times HE SDG Impact Rankings 2019.

4.5 *Characteristics of an Effective Social Entrepreneur*

The most effective social entrepreneurs are work ready *plus*; have a strong, clear moral purpose; are able to listen, link, leverage then lead, always in that order and use a 'why don't we' not a 'why don't you' approach. They are also change implementation savvy, inventive and responsive. Effective social entrepreneurs also possess the key capabilities and dispositions identified in our studies of successful early career graduates, such as the ability to: remain calm when things go awry, tolerate ambiguity, take sensible risks and persevere, work productively with diversity, think laterally, think ahead and adapt, 'read' the unique situation at hand and 'match' a relevant and feasible response, focusing on delivering outcomes endorsed as productive for those intended to benefit. Such social entrepreneurs build, use and sustain productive networks and are business savvy. It can also be argued that these capabilities are the same as those which characterise the culture of organisations and nations which are capable of successfully delivering a wise, sustainable future.

4.6 *Examples of Social Enterprise Projects*

There are hundreds of examples of how giving focus to social entrepreneurship projects can be effective in addressing the good ideas embedded in the SDGs.

They include:

The 'Bringing sustainability to life' initiatives at Western Sydney University including the WSU Riverfarm initiative which was set up as a living laboratory for students and community on social, cultural, economic and environmental sustainability in a rapidly growing peri-urban area (SDG 4, SDG 6, SDG 11, SDG 12, SDG 14, SDG 15, SDG 17).[8]

Professor Athula Ginige and his WSU team are using low cost mobile phones in Sri Lanka to ensure food security, minimise wasteful gluts and optimise productivity (SDGs 8 and 12).[9]

The Spinnifex Project, which is a collaboration between the University of Queensland and local Aboriginal traditional owners, is bringing the world a unique, renewable nanomaterial created out of native spinifex grass (*Triodia pungens*) (SDG 11, SDG 12, SDG 15).[10]

Enactus[11] which engages some 72,000 students on 1730 campuses in 37 countries around the world with collaborative social enterprise projects that address the challenges of sustainable development. The Enactus 2030 Global Goals site[12] gives dozens of examples of which the following are typical:

- In the Right Light project, Enactus students from the University of Southampton provided clean, cheap solar lamps to communities in Africa while increasing income by supporting local entrepreneurs to rent them out and reducing respiratory illnesses (SDG 7, 1, 3 & 8).
- The Enactus team from Kaduna Polytechnic in Nigeria launched an education campaign on the dangers of contaminated water and simple puri-

fication techniques. After one year the livelihoods of over 3,000 people improved and 20 new jobs were created (SDG 6, 2, 4, 11).

- In rural Togo, the Enactus team from the University of Mannheim in Germany, installed solar panels at 10 local health stations, eliminating the need for toxic kerosene lamps while increasing the amount of time the stations can operate. Excess charge loads are sold to power mobile phones. Treatments have doubled from 550 to more than 1,100 (SDG 9, 3 and 7).
- The Enactus team from Gwamile Vocational and Commercial Training Institute in Swaziland started a furniture manufacturing company which is making office chairs by refurbishing discarded steel drums and using waste materials for seat padding. 12 jobs were created (SDG 12, 8 and 13).
- Students from the University of Puerto Rico – Bayamón developed an affordable housing project using plastic bottles as the primary building material (SDG 13, 1, 9 and 12).

In 2020, University of_Birmingham (2020) students initiated an international 'creative hackathon' aimed at inventing technology-based solutions addressing the challenges posed by the COVID-Pandemic (SDG 3 & 11).

The RCE Asia-Pacific Network's Youth Challenge, s upported by the Global RCE network, has engaged over 13,500 youth and 5,000 community members to deliver 39 individual sustainability projects across 9 countries over the last 2 years (SDG 4 and 17).[13]

The Blue Economy project[14] is a world-wide initiative focused on making money out of waste and creating employment and better lives for the poor. Typical Blue Economy projects include:

- In the Pacific Islands, rather than waste the faeces of pigs in a piggery, it is washed into a series of ponds on the side of a hill where algae are grown on the nutrient rich water. Fish feed on the algae, are killed, dried and then fed to the pigs (SDGs 8, 11, 12 and 15).
- To save a failing citrus farm in South Africa not only were orange juice, firewood from plantation offcuts, and mushrooms grown on the leaf litter sold to local game lodges in the adjacent game park, but the left-over orange peels were also used to produce limonene (a valuable, natural detergent oil) and then what was left of the peels was fed to the cattle as an ideal cleansing agent for their first gut (SDGs 8, 10 and 12).
- In Benin maggots are grown on abattoir bones then bled for their valuable natural antibiotic before being fed to fish to produce a local source of protein or to quails whose eggs are sold for a high price in Europe (SDGs 8 & 12).
- The rubbish waste pickers in Delhi make artifacts for tourists using solar 3D printers from filament produced from the plastic they collect in the dumps.

This earns the waste pickers 15 times more than just selling the plastic they collect to recycling depots.[15]

Circular Economy initiatives[16] including the use of cradle to cradle design and circular fashion, are now included in social entrepreneurship courses in a range of colleges and universities (SDG 4 and 12).

Biomimicry[17] provides another source of ideas for SDG-based entrepreneurship projects. Biomimicry inventions are inspired by nature. Examples include:
- Velcro – based on burdock burrs;
- The ridges on humpback fins being used as a model for improving the efficiency of wind turbines by 20%;
- Understanding how fireflies work being used to improve the brightness of LEDs by 55%;
- Creating cement by sequestering carbon in the same way that reefs do;
- Creating permanent colours using how butterflies do it using structural colouration;
- SunTile which uses jackrabbits ears as a model for cooling computer rooms with no energy;
- Use of termite mounds to design the Eastgate Centre in Zimbabwe;
- Eco-friendly sewerage treatment based on the 4 chambers of a cow's stomach (SDGs 6, 9, 11, 12 & 13).

London-based Rob Wilson worked out how to use the 40% of the total bread baked that goes into landfill each year in the UK to make Toast Ale (SDG 12).[18] Morton (2019) reports that researchers have estimated that, if 9 per cent of the world's ocean surfaces were used for seaweed farming, 53 billion tonnes of carbon dioxide would be removed from our atmosphere each year. Kelp has the potential to act as a food source for billions of people. According to the 2040 campaign, "kelp contains more calcium than milk, more iron than spinach and more fibre than brown rice" (SDG 2).

Each year the Social Enterprise World Forum[19] highlights, links and leverages social entrepreneurs from around the world. The British Council's Global Social Enterprise Program supports the development of social enterprise as a means of addressing social and environmental problems in some 30 countries around the world.[20] The Council's report *Social Enterprise in a Global Context* identifies more than 200 HEIs actively engaged with the area (British Council, 2016, p. 10). The British Council's (2020a) Global Social Enterprise Project Report outlines the extensive range of social enterprises and job creation initiatives it currently supports. The UN Entrepreneurs for Social Change and the SDGs project_supports young entrepreneurs "to trigger social transformation in their communities, and thereby contribute to sustainable development in the region"[21] (SDG 4).

The Enterprising Women initiative[22] and the Student Reach Out and Give program[23] undertaken in South Africa by North West University are excellent examples of the many community enterprise programs focused on the SDGs in Africa (SDGs 5, 6,7 8 & 10). The British Council (2020b) has identified many other examples. They include:

- *Afripads* in Uganda manufactures cost effective, reusable sanitary pads. It has so far reached 750,000 girls and women worldwide with its products (SDG 5).
- *Biolite*'s low-cost stove that burns easy to source renewable biomass (twigs, pinecones and wood pellets) as cleanly as gas. This dramatically reduces carbon emissions that result from smoky, open wood fires and requires 50% less fuel than conventional open fires. The HomeStove also generates electricity to power lights and increasingly critically mobile phones (SDG 7).

A key next step is to promote the use of SDG-based social entrepreneurship projects more widely in education and ensure that the students engaged in such projects are given formal course credit for this work. One way to do this is to build trans-disciplinary, social enterprise capstones into the curriculum.

5 Conclusion

This chapter has sought to demonstrate how the UN's SDGs provide a framework for building a morally sound, wise and sustainable future. It has been argued that not only must this agenda for change be owned by those who are to implement it but that a key set of lessons on how to take the good ideas embodied in the SDGs and actually put them into practice needs to be followed. In doing this it has been argued that, as all change is learning, education institutions have a key role to play in developing the ethically considered and work ready *plus* graduates capable of making the agenda happen. It has been also argued that greater focus on developing the key capabilities of collaborative social entrepreneurs is a key path to enacting the goals. The COVID-19 pandemic, in creating a moment of crisis and a fracture point for evaluating old habits, has simultaneously created the opportunity for a 'reset'. This involves stopping to critically appraise the tacit assumptions that, to date, have been driving the 21st century agenda and considering what is necessary to shape a better future for people and planet.

The chapter has sought to provide guidance in this endeavour and has identified some practical ways of addressing the need for change. The stakes are high and it is indeed timely for all of us to consider just how we can both individually and collectively help achieve the equitable and sustainable future embedded in the UN's 2030 goals.

Notes

1 http://flipcurric.edu.au/
2 https://www.un.org/sustainabledevelopment/sustainable-development-goals/
3 https://dictionary.cambridge.org/dictionary/english/wisdom
4 https://www.newdemocracy.com.au/
5 http://flipcurric.edu.au/about-143/about/using-the-guide-and-getting-started
6 http://www.wegeprize.org/
7 https://www.treasury.govt.nz/sites/default/files/2019-05/b19-wellbeing-budget.pdf
8 https://www.westernsydney.edu.au/driving_sustainability/sustainability_education/engagement/community_and_engagement/hawkesbury_riverfarm
9 https://www.researchgate.net/publication/235432607_Building_Social_Life_Networks_through_Mobile_Interfaces-_the_Case_Study_of_Sri_Lanka_Farmers_-_Abstract
10 https://biological-sciences.uq.edu.au/research/hubs/ecology-uq/content/spinifex-project
11 https://enactus.org/who-we-are/our-story/
12 https://enactus.org/globalgoals/
13 https://www.westernsydney.edu.au/rcegws/rcegws/international/sdg_challenge
14 https://www.theblueeconomy.org/innovations.html
15 https://www.youtube.com/watch?v=Ieqqhv_YQOI (SDGs 8 & 12).
16 https://www.ellenmacarthurfoundation.org/circular-economy/concept
17 https://biomimicry.org/what-is-biomimicry/
18 https://www.toastale.com/?_ga=2.220881179.2069057630.1537847534-1379042472.1537847534
19 https://sewfonline.com
20 https://www.britishcouncil.org/society/social-enterprise
21 https://sustainabledevelopment.un.org/partnership/?p=23553
22 https://commerce.nwu.ac.za/bhive/ewp
23 http://www.nwu.ac.za/sites/www.nwu.ac.za/files/files/i-media/I-eish-201702/student-rag.htm

References

Annan, K. (2006). *Stress basic values common to all religions.* United Nations Meetings Coverage and Press Releases. https://www.un.org/press/en/2006/sgsm10733.doc.htm

Beaulieu, M., Breton, M., & Brousselle, A. (2018). Conceptualizing 20 years of engaged scholarship: A scoping review. *PLOS ONE.* https://doi.org/10.1371/journal.pone.0193201

Bok, D. (2020). *Higher expectations:Can colleges teach students what they need to know in the 21st century?* Princeton Press.

Bollyky, T., & Brown, C. (2020, September–October). The tragedy of vaccine nationalism: Only cooperation can end the pandemic. *Foreign Affairs*. https://www.foreignaffairs.com/articles/united-states/2020-07-27/vaccine-nationalism-pandemic

Bonner, C., Nickel, B., & Pickles, K. (2020, August 10). Young men are more likely to believe COVID-19 myths: So how do we actually reach them? *The Conversation*. https://theconversation.com/young-men-are-more-likely-to-believe-covid-19-myths-so-how-do-we-actually-reach-them-143745

Bouquet, A. C. (1969). *Comparative religion*. Penguin.

British Council. (2016): *Social enterprise in a global context; the role of higher education institutions*. https://www.britishcouncil.org/sites/default/files/british_council_social_enterprise_brochure_draft_11_interactive_version_25_05_15.pdf

British Council. (2020a). *Global social enterprise and job creation in Sub-Saharan Africa*. https://www.britishcouncil.org/society/social-enterprise/reports/ssa-jobs-report

British Council. (2020b). *Social enterprises step up to tackle the SDGs*. https://www.britishcouncil.org/society/social-enterprise/news-events/news-social-enterprises-tackle-SDGs

Crisp, R. (2019, September 25). *Virtue in a changing climate: How do we respond morally to global warming?* ABC Religion and Ethics Report. https://www.abc.net.au/religion/roger-crisp-virtue-in-a-changing-climate/11530728

Crow, J. (2014, November 20). Mahatma Gandhi's list of seven social sins. *History, Life, Religion*. http://www.openculture.com/2014/11/mahatma-gandhis-list-of-the-7-social-sins.html

DeBruyn, G (2020, September 5). Why we should empower our students to redesign everything. *University World News*. https://www.universityworldnews.com/post.php?story=20200901155138663

Eliasson, J (2016, January 13). "No-one left behind" is ethical imperative of new development agenda. *UN News*. https://news.un.org/en/story/2016/01/519872-no-one-left-behind-ethical-imperative-new-development-agenda-un-deputy-chief

Friedman, T. L. (2016). *Thank you for being late: An optimist's guide to thriving in the age of accelerations*. Farrar, Straus & Giroux.

Fullan, M. (2002, September). Moral purpose writ large. *School Administrator*. https://michaelfullan.ca/wp-content/uploads/2016/06/13396048660.pdf

Fullan, M., & Scott, G. (2009). *Turnaround leadership for higher education*. Jossey-Bass.

Galbraith, J. K. (1977). *The age of uncertainty*. BBC – Andre Deutsch.

Goldring, M. (2017, January 16). World's eight richest people have same wealth as poorest 50%. *The Guardian*. https://www.theguardian.com/global-development/2017/jan/16/worlds-eight-richest-people-have-same-wealth-as-poorest-50

Hutchinson, B. (2020, July 23). Connect for a better future. *Sydney Ideas Podcast*. The University of Sydney. https://www.sydney.edu.au/content/dam/corporate/documents/engage/events-sponsorships/sydney-ideas/transcript-connectfor-launch-event.pdf

Jaschik, S. (2020, August 19). Higher expectations. *Inside Higher Education.*

Josephson, M. (2002). *Making ethical decisions* (W. Hanson, Ed.). Josephson Institute of Ethics, Los Angeles. https://store.charactercounts.org/wp-content/uploads/sites/10/2015/09/50-0450-E.pdf

Kamradt-Scott, A. (2020, August 17). Creating a COVID-19 vaccine is only the first step: It'll take years to manufacture and distribute. *The Conversation.* https://theconversation.com/creating-a-covid-19-vaccine-is-only-the-first-step-itll-take-years-to-manufacture-and-distribute-144352

Kopiyo, D. (2014). *Fullan's model for change.* https://www.slideshare.net/kopiyosenior/topic-3-moral-purpose-and-change-fullan.

Leonard, W. (2020, September 5). Facing the demise of the campus-centric business model. *University World News.* https://www.universityworldnews.com/post.php?story=20200904145934111

Loftus, E. (n.d.). *Ed Schein: The three levels of organisational culture.* Heart of the Art: The Life of Living Systems. https://www.heartoftheart.org/?p=988

Mackay, H. (2020). *The inner self.* Pan Macmillan.

Maley, J. (2020, May 17). The political art of not wasting a crisis, or getting wasted by it. *The Sydney Morning Herald.* https://www.smh.com.au/politics/federal/the-political-art-of-not-wasting-a-crisis-or-getting-wasted-by-it-20200515-p54tej.html

Marginson, S. (2020, July 25). Pandemic shows need for HE for the global common good. *University World News.* https://www.universityworldnews.com/post.php?story=20200724114218359

Morton, C. (2019, September 9). Groundbreaking seaweed platform creates waves for climate solutions. *MOJO News.* https://www.mojonews.com.au/environment/groundbreaking-seaweed-platform-creates-waves-for-climate-solutions

Mourkogiannis, N. (2005). The realist's guide to moral purpose. *Leadership, 41.* https://www.strategy-business.com/article/05405?gko=bca17

Ravindran, V. (n.d). Seven social sins. *The Urban Engine.* http://theurbanengine.com/blog//seven-social-sins

Robinson, P. (2020, September 17). Who suffers most from Melbourne's extended lockdown? *The Conversation.* https://theconversation.com/who-suffers-most-from-melbournes-extended-lockdown-hint-they-are-not-necessarily-particularly-vocal-145938

Rubin, J. (2020). *The expendables: How the middle class got screwed by globalisation.* Scribe Publications.

Schein, E. H. (2004). *Organizational culture and leadership.* Jossey-Bass.

Schuijers, L. (2020, April 23). *Covid is an opportunity to reset our environmental future.* https://www.thefifthestate.com.au/urbanism/planning/covid-19-is-an-opportunity-to-reset-our-environmental-future/

Scott, G. (1999). *Change matters: Making a difference in education and training.* Angus and Robertson.

Scott, G. (2003). *Learning principals.* New South Wales Department of Education and Training.

Scott, G. (2017). *FLIPCurric.* Australian Government. http://flipcurric.edu.au/

Scott, G. (2019a). Preparing work ready *plus* graduates for an uncertain future. In J. Higgs, G. Crisp, & W. Letts (Eds.), *Education for employability (Vol. 1): The employability agenda* (pp. 107–118). Brill Sense.

Scott, G. (2019b). Social enterprise and sustainable development in the age of acceleration. *Envigogika, 14*(1).

Scott, G., Coates, H., & Anderson, M. (2008). *Learning leaders in times of change.* Australian Government & Australian Council for Educational Research.

Scott, G., Tilbury, D., Sharp, L., & Deane, E. (2012). *Turnaround leadership for sustainability in higher education.* Australian Government.

Suzuki, D. (2020, April 8). How the pandemic may be an opportunity to transform our lives. *Canadian Speakers Spotlight.* https://www.speakers.ca/2020/04/dr-david-suzuki-on-how-the-pandemic-may-be-an-opportunity-to-transform-our-lives/

Tsipursky, G. (2018, February 13). How to talk to students with ill-considered beliefs. *Inside Higher Education.* https://www.insidehighered.com/advice/2018/02/13/advice-professors-talking-about-charged-issues-students-their-classes-opinion

United Nations. (2019). *World population prospects 2019.* Population division, UN Secretariat. https://population.un.org/wpp/

United Nations Development Programme (UNDP). (2020). *Sustainable development goals.* https://www.undp.org/content/undp/en/home/sustainable-development-goals.html

United Nations Development Programme (UNDP): Programme of Assistance to the Palestinian People. (2021). *Sustainable development goals: What are the Sustainable Development Goals?* https://www.ps.undp.org/content/papp/en/home/sustainable-development-goals.html

Vally, H. (2020, July 29). Social housing, aged care and Black Americans: How coronavirus affects already disadvantaged groups. *The Conversation.* https://theconversation.com/social-housing-aged-care-and-black-americans-how-coronavirus-affects-already-disadvantaged-groups-142046

Wallace, C. (2020, September 7). How to win an election? Do the substance as well as the theatre of politics. *The Conversation.* https://theconversation.com/how-to-win-an-election-do-the-substance-as-well-as-the-theatre-of-politics-144795

Whiting, K. (2020, June 3). Gita Gopinath on the economic reset. *World Economic Forum Covid Action Platform.* https://www.weforum.org/agenda/2020/06/covid19-great-reset-gita-gopinath-jennifer-morgan-sharan-burrow-climate/

Yunus, M. (n.d.). *The social business model* [Video]. YouTube. https://www.youtube.com/watch?v=oC3XQ3BTd4o

CHAPTER 3

Linking Science, Spirituality, Ethics and Philosophy in Creating Wise Futures

Narelle Patton

Abstract

As part of this book's exploration of wise practices for better futures, in this chapter I coalesce scientific, spiritual, ethical and philosophical thinking around wisdom and wise practice to better understand how wisdom can be developed and harnessed to achieve desired futures for everyone. Scientific and theoretical knowledge, ethical and spiritual practices and philosophy all provide different ways of thinking and practising that can benefit actions such as sustainability, regeneration, activism and grass roots action. I conceptualise wisdom as a complex, dynamic, and experiential phenomenon that is embedded in the world, embodied in individuals, transformed through actions and grounded in an ethical aim of doing good for and with others. I view wisdom as a capability that encompasses qualities and abilities that can be used to perform actions in unpredictable and challenging situations, and facilitate ongoing development of the individual to perform different actions in the future. Finally, how development of wisdom as a capability for all (not restricted to a select few) can positively contribute to building a more just society with human dignity and wellbeing for all is explored.

Keywords

science – ethics – spirituality – sustainability – activism

1 The Value of Wisdom

In many cultures across the centuries, wisdom has been and continues to be highly valued as a desirable resource representing a perfect integration of knowledge and action, mind and virtue (Baltes & Smith, 2008). Poets and philosophers have long praised wisdom as a key quality promoting individual and group wellbeing (Grossman, 2017). Ancient and modern cultures alike have sought to both better understand and cultivate wisdom. In antiquity,

 | DOI: 10.1163/9789004505544_004

the value of wisdom was considered as being reserved for Divine beings, that was worshipped, but was beyond the reach of mortals (Baltes & Smith, 2008). Aristotle is widely acknowledged as secularising wisdom through his distinguishing between technical knowledge (*techne*) and individuals' disposition towards moral and virtuous action (*phronesis*). Building on Aristotelian beliefs, McKenna (2019), proposed that wise individuals combine intellectual and moral virtues, produce excellence, and in so doing contribute to human and societal flourishing. Today we want citizens to have qualities that extend beyond mere scientific knowledge and that form a disposition toward wisdom and prudence, *phronesis* (Kemmis, 2012). We not only want good citizens but citizens who will do good. This contemporary understanding of Wisdom that was highly valued from ancient times, namely, as a capability to act for societal good, retains its value for 21st century society. It could be argued, that now more than ever, with the rapidly changing contexts of modern society, complete with paradoxical and unresolvable issues created by multiple and diverse stakeholders (Cherry, 2019) emphasise the value of, and need for wisdom.

Science and technology have served enterprise, government and society for many centuries (Cherry, 2019). Scientific investigation and observation have greatly contributed to human flourishing across the centuries, with much of this knowledge taken for granted in many modern societies today. Too extensive to list with any justice, some varied examples of important scientific discoveries include: the wheel, lever, abacus, sanitation, printing press, optical lenses (leading to the creation of the microscope and telescope), internal-combustion engine, electricity, the nature of the earth and the universe, penicillin, analgesics, anaesthetics, space travel, vaccines, DNA sequencing, the Internet, the Pill (launching a social revolution), and semi-conductor electronics (launching the virtual world). There is little doubt that all of these discoveries, and many others, have greatly contributed to human flourishing, emphasising the important contribution of scientific thought as a core and valuable component of wisdom.

Despite the undeniable value of the many and varied knowledges provided by scientific investigation, contemporary widespread use of the Internet and social media have elevated the importance of the contribution of critical reasoning to wisdom and wise practice. Public and academic authority are being increasingly challenged by social media, through contesting of facts and claims of "fake news" (Cherry, 2019). Fake news is false information presented as news or as legitimate information with the intention of misleading. The incidence of fake news has increased with the rise of social media. While it has always been possible to spread fake news, self-publishing and social media mean that false or misleading information can be created and shared incredibly fast, reaching a lot of people before anyone has even stopped to ask if it's true (E-Safety Commissioner, 2021). Famously, the former USA President Donald Trump popularised the term fake news by claiming any reports that were unfavourable to himself were fake news, without any evidence to support his claim. Another example of widespread misinformation occurred as the COVID-19 pandemic dominated the media, both domestically and abroad, and the spread of COVID-19 fake news online itself became viral. In regard to COVID-19 there has been disinformation blaming racial groups, illegal immigrants and even governments for the spread of the virus as well as misinformation including misunderstandings of the disease, wishful thinking about false remedies and fanciful implications drawn on how the spread of the virus will play out (Nyilasy, 2021). In contemporary societal contexts where misinformation abounds, with individuals needing to assess the veracity of information presented on the Internet and via social media, wisdom underpinned by critical reasoning capability is more necessary and valuable than ever.

Wisdom, incorporating knowledge, critical reasoning and moral courage enables individuals to not only discern but enact appropriate strategies to achieve optimum outcomes for all and, in so doing, appropriately break the bonds of unhelpful hegemonic practices in the achievement of desirable futures. French philosopher, Michel Foucault insightfully articulated how social interaction and tradition shapes individuals and their actions. Foucault (1977, 1980) revealed both the pervasive nature and productive capability of power on individual actions. He viewed power within society as circulating rather than functioning within a chain, with individuals circulating within its threads, continually both undergoing and exercising power. Foucault's illumination of the diffuse and entrenched effects of power perpetually operating in all social situations highlights the importance of wisdom including knowledge, skill and moral courage to enable enaction of wise practice.

Moral courage is particularly needed in contemporary society. This is in part because we see so many examples of its lack – in corporate settings and legal proceedings, in politics and sports and entertainment, in personal and social relationships (Kidder, 2006). This lack of moral courage is evident in our political landscape, for example the Australian government's reduction of complex humanitarian crises to two or three-word slogans such as "stop the boats" and "children overboard". This behaviour reduces complex humanitarian issues to simple, and on the surface, acceptable solutions to be presented to the Australian public and indeed the world. We could equally ask how could the Australian public accept immigrant detention practices, demonstrated to be inhumane and condemned globally for so long? These examples highlight the importance of moral courage for contemporary society. Moral courage that means taking action that accords with the core values of honesty, fairness, respect, responsibility and compassion (Kidder, 2006) is needed to achieve human flourishing for all.

The value of wisdom has not decreased over the centuries with wisdom remaining as sought after today as it was in ancient times. Modern day wicked problems produce dilemmas that emerge as we try to engage with them, when trying to do something useful often triggers unwanted and unexpected consequences (Cherry, 2019). Faced with wicked problems, individuals require a wisdom that encompasses qualities and abilities that can be used to undertake ethical action in unpredictable and challenging situations with the ultimate aim of facilitating human flourishing.

2 The Getting of Wisdom: Bestowed, Acquired or Developed

Throughout millennia the gaining of wisdom has been described as a gift from Gods, an immutable essence, difficult to teach and requiring innate potential (Grossman, 2017). Moving beyond viewing wisdom as a gift that is bestowed to worthy recipients, Ancient Greek philosophers linked knowledge, judgement and action to wisdom and began to explore how wisdom could be cultivated (Baltes & Smith, 2008). In contemporary society wisdom is generally believed to be cultivated through a diverse range of positive and negative life experiences. However, life experience on its own is not sufficient to facilitate development of wisdom. Self-reflection has been proposed as one possible way that wisdom can be developed from life experiences (Westrate & Glück, 2017).

Bestowed wisdom can be understood as a gift from God or a spiritual experience. In spiritual texts such as the Epistle of James, people of faith are encouraged to ask God for the gift of wisdom.

> If any of you is without wisdom, let him ask it from the God who gives generously and ungrudgingly to all, and it will be given to him. Yet he must ask in Faith, never doubting, for the doubter is like the surf tossed and driven by the wind. A man of this sort, devious and erratic in all that he does, must not expect to receive anything from the Lord. (The Epistle of James 1: 5–7)

Spiritual texts also contribute to our understanding of wisdom through identification of qualities that accompany wisdom. For example, in the Epistle of St James wisdom is described as innocent, peaceable, sympathetic, impartial and sincere.

> If one of you is wise and understanding, let him show this in practice through a humility filled with good sense. … Wisdom from above is first of all innocent. It is also peaceable, lenient, docile, rich in sympathy and the kindly deed that are its fruits, impartial and sincere. The harvest of justice is sown in peace for those who cultivate peace. (The Epistle of James 3: 13, 17–18)

Khalil Gibran (1883–1930), poet and philosopher, in his best-known work, The Prophet, provides a description of an encounter with Wisdom and in so doing emphasises the value of wisdom. In *An Apparition of Wisdom*, Gibran describes Wisdom as a loving mother who appears to him and provides consolation. Gibran also emphasises wisdom as belonging to the realm of gods in his assertion that a mortal desire to fathom the secrets of the world is folly. In this poem, Wisdom actively discourages mortals from seeking understanding of the world encouraging instead to be like the bee or child and accept everything as it is, as it has been and always will be.

> *An apparition of wisdom*
>
> In the stillness of night, Wisdom appeared to me and stood by my bed. Even as a loving mother, She gazed at me and wiping my tears tenderly, She said: "I heard the cry of your soul and I have come to console it! Open your heart and spread it before me that I might fill it with light! Ask me and I shall show you the way of the truth … You the mortal, you want to see the world with the eyes of a god and fathom the secrets of a world to come with the probing of mortal thought. Such folly! Go you out, go into the wilderness and observe how the bee hovers above the flower and the eagle swoops down on his prey. Enter you into your neighbour's hearth and see you the child blinking at the firelight and the mother busied at her house chores. Be you like the bee and do not waste the days of your spring eying the works of the eagle. Be like the child and rejoice in the warmth of the firelight, and let your mother go about her business. All that you see has been and will always be for your own sake. Wisdom then placed her hand on my feverish forehead and said: "Go forth and never tarry, for forward is the secret of perfection". (pp. 124–125)

In Western philosophical literature, wisdom has long been defined as the experience, knowledge and judgement required for living a good life (Westrate and Glück, 2017). In contemporary accounts of wisdom, acquisition of wisdom for a good life is acknowledged to require time and effort and involves combination of some form of education, practise, apprenticeship, personal experience, and deliberate reflection about life matters (Baltes & Smith, 2008). Individuals' wisdom is also described as socially constructed and maintained and demonstrated through expression of certain attitudes and behaviours during difficult life situations (Grossman, 2017). Three sets of antecedents are thought to be associated with facilitating the development, maintenance, and application of wisdom: general personal factors (e.g. ability, personality), specific expertise related factors (e.g. exposure to life dilemmas and significant life events, motivation and mentorship) and context (e.g. age, cohort, historical period, culture) (Baltes & Smith, 2008). It is widely assumed that in the course of development, all individuals have access to and acquire part of this socially shared knowledge system and approximate different levels of expertise (Baltes & Smith, 2008).

Wisdom has been a highly valued commodity across the centuries and continues to be highly valued by contemporary societies. Wisdom once understood as a gift from gods to the select few, is now understood as a human capability that can be developed through life experience and reflection on that experience.

3 Wisdom Underpinned by Knowledge and Sound Reflective and Critical Reasoning

Knowledge of truth gained by repeated observation, testing traditions of scientific, philosophical and spiritual realms alongside sound reflective and critical reasoning capacities underpins wisdom in contemporary societies. Our concept of factual knowledge, similar to Aristotle's theoretical wisdom, involves deep understanding of human nature, lifelong development, alongside social norms and their implications, (Baltes & Smith, 2008). In our digitally connected world, where content knowledge is accessible to all, contested, and continually displaced by new content, practical wisdom, involving knowing how and when to apply one's knowledge is needed in the construction and implementation of plans to achieve desired future outcomes.

The rise of entire civilisations such as the Aztec, Roman and Chinese empires was founded on their superior knowledge, positing knowledge as a universal, anthropological characteristic of the human race (Stehr, 2001). It has taken centuries of painstaking observation, measurement, calculation and deduction to establish knowledge that most of us now take for granted, for example the earth is round not flat (Ingold, 2011). The privileged status of scientific and technical knowledge in modern society is derived not from the fact that scientific discoveries are generally considered to be credible, objective, in conformity with reality, or even indisputable, but from the fact that this form of knowledge, does not usually live up to the reputation of infallibility it possesses: it is often disputed, and despite its social standing scientific knowledge is almost always questionable (Stehr, 2001). In contemporary society knowledge is not only growing at an exponential rate but is also contested, increasing its fluid nature. Knowledge changes according to the way it is valued by society, where humanities give way to science; small-scale forms of knowledge production give way to large-scale forms; knowledge for its own sake gives way to applied knowledge and problem-solving in situ; and propositional knowledge is supplemented by experiential knowing (Barnett, 1997). Societal anxieties and concerns that arise as a consequence of new scientific knowledge and new technologies highlight the inadequacy of knowledge development on its own to positively contribute to achievement of desired futures and human flourishing. For example, scientific advances including embryonic stem cells, genetically modified foods, biotechnology weapons, genetic engineering, and reproductive cloning highlight societal concerns around consequences of unfettered expansion of scientific knowledge (Grundmann & Stehr, 2003).

The embedded nature of contemporary knowledge creation by individuals in specific circumstances places a spotlight on reflective and critical thinking as knowledge generation capabilities. The idea that knowledge is developed through reflection is not new. John Dewey (1916) identified reflection as underpinning knowledge development in education at the beginning of the 20th century. Building upon Dewey's work, Schön (1983, 1987) introduced a new epistemology of learning for professions, moving the focus from technical rationality to reflection on experiences as underpinning development of professional knowledge. Barnett (1997) and Brookfield (1995) expanded Schön's reflective practice through incorporation of social and critical dimensions in their descriptions of knowledge as socially constructed and sustained and argue that critical thinking incorporating social processes is central to the development of professional knowledge. Barnett (1977) described critical thought as intentional, purposeful, nuanced and sensitive to its context, with an unbounded quality that allows transfer of skills across contexts. Further, the development of professional knowledge in practice requires critical use of concepts and ideas embedded in well-established practice traditions (Patton & Simpson, 2016) to achieve optimal outcomes for their clients, often in uncertain and complex contexts (Patton & Higgs, 2018).

The ubiquitous, contested and consequently fluid nature of knowledge in contemporary society underscores the centrality of reflective and critical thinking capacity to individuals' ability to discern wise actions. Only through reflective and critical reasoning are individuals able to adapt codified knowledge to achieve best outcomes for others in particular circumstances, and thereby positively contribute to human flourishing.

4 Wisdom as a Complex and Dynamic Phenomenon

Wisdom is a complex, dynamic and experiential phenomenon that is embedded in the world, embodied and transformed through individual performances and grounded in an ethical aim of doing good for others. Wisdom as an expertise is not an intelligence in the usual sense, but a substantially more complex system of knowledge, procedural strategies, and intuition (Baltes & Smith, 2008). Wisdom arises from the deep self and enables meaningful and ethical possibilities. A capability for wisdom includes more than knowledge and technical skills, crucially, built on reflective and critical thinking capacity and a well-developed ethics and values system, wisdom enables an ability to discern and facilitate ways forward that benefit other individuals and society more generally.

The need for a dynamic wisdom is emphasised by the escalating rate of change evident throughout contemporary society. Many forms of modern life are united by their fragility, temporary nature, vulnerability and inclination to constant change (Bauman, 2012). As an example, contemporary work life is undergoing rapid, profound and ubiquitous change, influenced by both technological development and the global economy (Lehtinen, 2008). In this environment there is growing certainty that change is the only permanence, and uncertainty the only certainty (Bauman, 2012). Societal practices continually evolve as they respond to changing contexts and are transformed by individual performances. These practices have been described by Schatzki (2002) as a temporally evolving open-ended set of doings and sayings, emphasising the dynamic nature of societal practices as well as individual contribution to the evolution of those practices.

Wisdom, as a dynamic and responsive phenomenon, is further challenged by contemporary society's broad continuum of ethics and values. There are many versions of a good life, which means that there are also many ways to achieve excellence within the constraints of socially accepted values and ethics (Baltes & Smith, 2008). This variety of ways to achieve a good life emphasises the importance of a strongly developed, ethical and moral compass to guide discernment of wise actions. For example, introduction of the contraceptive and morning after pills and legalisation of abortion in Australia have brought legal, religious, political and cultural value systems into conflict requiring individuals to discern wise ways forward in specific circumstances.

Wisdom qualities are evolving and responsive to historical and cultural change (Baltes & Smith, 2008). Novel societal and personal dilemmas emerge over time, and the ways and means to deal with recurring dilemmas are revisited and updated with prudence (Baltes & Smith, 2008). A salient example of changing ways to deal with emergence of societal dilemmas over time is comparison of the Bubonic plague in the 14th century with the 21st century COVID-19 pandemic. In the 14th century the Bubonic plague was thought to be transmitted by miasmas (disease carrying vapours) that emanated from corpses, purulent material or the breath of infected people; punishment from God; or astrological and natural phenomena. The only remedies involved inhalation of aromatic vapours from flowers and herbs or begging forgiveness from God (Firth, 2012). People died with such rapidity that proper burial/cremation did not occur (Firth, 2012). There was great economic and social upheaval, crops could not be harvested, travelling and trade was curtailed, and food and manufactured goods became short (Firth, 2012). Ultimately, the instigation of public health controls isolating victims from healthy people (quarantine) and preventing ships with disease from entering ports curtailed the spread of the plague (Firth, 2012). While in the 21st century we have a better understanding of the cause (virus) and transmission (air and on surfaces) of COVID-19 as well as more effective treatments, parallels with the experience of the Bubonic plague in the 14th century are startling. During the height of the COVID-19 pandemic people died with such rapidity that mass burials/cremations occurred, there has been and continues to be great economic burden and social upheaval, travelling has been curtailed and social isolation and quarantine remain a first line strategy to prevent spread of the virus. Interestingly, while scientific and medical advances have significantly improved how we treat disease, the current COVID-19 pandemic has also highlighted how societal expectation, and proliferation of social media including access to information (public health messages and rules) and misinformation (fake news) have significantly influenced the way we are able to respond to challenges from pandemics, including our ability to critically evaluate and appropriately act on information.

Wisdom, understood broadly as a dynamic and complex phenomenon, demands more than a combination of propositional knowledge, practice knowledge, personal knowledge and technical skills. Wisdom requires individual abilities (e.g. knowledge and critical thinking capacity), personal qualities (e.g. integrity, empathy and ethical courage), judgement and potential to act ethically in uncertain, unfamiliar and dynamic environments.

5 Wisdom Requires Action

Wisdom and action are irrevocably entwined. Praxis, considered as practical reasoning about what is wise, right and proper to do in a particular situation, also encompasses subsequent actions (Kemmis, 2012). Critical thinking seeks to analyse and produce alternative actions, with the expression of a critical thought being a definitive interaction in the world (Brookfield, 1995; Barnett, 1997). While people may have exemplary values and develop great skill at moral reasoning and ethical decision-making, such mental activity counts for little if their decision sits unimplemented on the shelf (Kidder, 2006). Wise people are able to challenge and change current practices and possess the courage to change both themselves and the world for the better.

Praxis, oriented and informed by practice traditions, is grounded, embodied, embedded, and morally committed action (Kemmis & Smith, 2008). Praxis recognises that a person who acts in response to the practicalities of a given situation, does the best they can on the day, the best they can do under the circumstances to achieve optimum outcomes for others (Kemmis, 2012). Through experiencing consequences of their actions, individuals become wiser about making action choices when they encounter future uncertain practical situations (Kemmis, 2012). The practice knowledge and wisdom developed in this manner are pragmatic, variable, context dependent, and oriented towards action (Kinsella & Pitman, 2012). In this way, praxis is transformative for the individual, the practice tradition and the people with whom the individual works.

This embedded, embodied and action-oriented understanding of wisdom underscores the importance of understanding contextual and individual influences including individual dispositions (such as moral and ethical courage and integrity) on development of wise actions. Wise action requires development of a broad range of capabilities, qualities and skills. Enacting wise practice requires ethical courage, underpinned by sound decision-making capabilities including the ability to select relevant and credible actions for the situation at hand. It also requires confidence in the appropriateness of those decisions, and the courage to undertake selected and deliberate actions for the good of others, even in the face of pressure to conform to hegemonic practices (Patton, 2014). Courage is required as these actions may carry with them risks of humiliation, ridicule, and contempt, not to mention unemployment and loss of social standing (Kidder, 2006). Importantly, this courage is frequently seen in the deeds of ordinary individuals building piece by piece a more ethical world (Kidder, 2006).

Observable indicators of wisdom in action include such verbal behaviours as exceptionally good judgement; good advice; insightful commentary about uncertain matters of life and nonverbal behaviours associated with good conduct, emotion regulation, and empathy in interpersonal and group contexts (Baltes & Smith, 2008). Unfortunately, observable indicators of a lack of wisdom in action are also evident in contemporary society. Our lack of success in combating climate change provides a pertinent example. The robustness and consensus in the scientific community about human-caused climate change has in recent years not only increased in strength, but recent studies point to far more dramatic and longer lasting consequences of global warming than previously thought (Stehr, 2013). In such a circumstance, how is it possible, many scientists ask, that such evidence does not provoke political action in societies around the world? The still dominant approach to climate policy shows little evidence of success (Stehr, 2013). A 2021 Australia Talks survey with 60,000 respondents provided a clear indication that Australians believe the Government needs to do more to tackle climate change (81% of respondents believed the Australian Government is not doing enough to tackle climate change). However, 46% of respondents believe that climate change action should not come at the expense of Australian jobs. These Australians know more needs to be done to address climate change, but are reluctant to make lifestyle and/or economic sacrifices to address climate change. In short, there is a lack of ethical courage to undertake required but difficult action.

Wise action is underpinned by knowledge, skills and personal qualities. To make positive change in the world individuals require relevant critical thinking and decision-making capacities alongside ethical courage to enact decisions that will positively contribute to human and environmental flourishing.

6 Wisdom: A Social Capability for All

Wisdom for positive change and enablement of desired futures requires broad capability including knowledge, technical skills, cognitive ability and individual qualities. In particular, ethical or moral courage is needed to enact wise actions. Further, to achieve desired futures for all, wisdom must be considered as a capability for all, not a select few. Indian philosopher, Amartya Sen's description of capability as a positive form of freedom (2005) provides a way of thinking about wisdom to inform how everyone can be given opportunity to meaningfully contribute to achievement of desired outcomes for all.

Amartya Sen draws attention to the influence of both intrinsic individual dimensions and extrinsic environmental dimensions on capability in an effort to address social inequities (2005). What people can positively achieve is influenced by economic opportunities, political liberties, social powers, and the enabling conditions of good health, basic education and the encouragement and cultivation of initiatives (Sen 1999). This acknowledgement of individual and environmental factors on capability development allows us to view capability as a positive form of freedom; the substantive freedom to achieve various and valued outcomes. Viewing capability in terms of freedom enables us to discern whether individuals are able to do the things they value doing and whether they possess the means or instruments or permissions to pursue what they might like to do (Sen, 2005). This focus on capabilities as freedoms, rather than outcomes, draws attention to the often neglected influence of human diversity, complex social relations, the sense of reciprocity between people. Central to this notion of human diversity and reciprocity in human relations is the appreciation that people can reflect reasonably on what they value for themselves and others, and on what people are ultimately able to do or be (Walker & Unterhalter, 2007).

In a search for deeper understanding of the capabilities that underpin wisdom, the understanding of capability as a freedom draws attention to an important, but previously neglected, influence of context and an individual's ability to influence the development of wisdom. This understanding of capabilities, which implies democratic participation, access to opportunities and real scope for action, provides a tangible basis to the concept of freedom (Lambert, Vero, & Zimmermann, 2012). Lambert el al contend that the capability approach places people at the heart of action through focus on individuals' freedom to accomplish; that is, their power to achieve meaningful outcomes. These authors also highlight a significant contribution of environment to capability development, they contend that individual, social and environmental factors must be taken into account when understanding capability development. Importantly, Lambert et al recommend a shift of emphasis from a narrow appetite to learn, to a broader, more upstream idea of capability for aspiring to learn, which incorporates various factors both internal and external to the individual. This capability for aspiring to learn is future oriented; it requires resources for participating and acting as well as contesting and challenging when change is required and is essentially both an individual and a social matter.

The American Philosopher Martha Nussbaum also contributed to the development of a broad approach to understanding capability linked to contributing to the common good. Nussbaum (2006) identified three capacities that are essential to the cultivation of democratic citizenship; capacity for critical examination of oneself and one's tradition, capacity for global citizenship and capacity for narrative imagination. At the heart of all three capacities is freedom: the freedom to engage critically with tradition; the freedom to imagine citizenship in both national and world terms and the freedom to reach out in the imagination, allowing another person's experience into oneself (Nussbaum, 2006). Thus, attention has been drawn to a significant contribution of individual capacity for critical examination, societal relationships and empathy (through imagination obtaining an insight into the experience of another) to capability development.

At the core of development of wisdom for all is a call to people with power to take responsibility to bring about changes that would enhance human development in the world. Wisdom development can positively contribute to building a more just society with human dignity (Nussbaum, 2006) and well-being for all (Sen, 1999). Viewing wisdom in terms of freedom allows us to discern whether individuals are able to do the things they value and whether they possess the means, instruments or permissions to pursue what they might like and in so doing develop wisdom. This freedom can also extend to freedom to relate to the realms of nature, the living environment and the spiritual world of First Nations Australians.

7 Conclusion

Across the centuries, wisdom has been described in terms of something given to a deserving recipient, highly prized, and as excellence in mind and virtue. In this chapter, wisdom has been conceptualised as a valued, complex, dynamic and experiential phenomenon that is embedded in the world, embodied in individuals, transformed through actions and grounded in an ethical aim of doing good for, and with, others. This understanding of wisdom highlights an important contribution of individual abilities and qualities including ethical judgement, integrity, empathy, and courage to enable ethical actions in uncertain and dynamic environments. To make positive change in the world individuals require critical thinking and decision-making capabilities. Along with these cognitive capabilities they require the ethical courage to enact decisions that contribute to human and environmental flourishing. Finally, wisdom cannot be restricted to a select few, all individuals require the freedom to accomplish that is to make a meaningful difference in the world.

References

Australian Government E-Safety Commissioner. (n.d.). *Fake news*. Retrieved June 20, 2021, from https://www.esafety.gov.au/young-people/fake-news

Baltes, P. B., & Smith, J. (2008). The fascination of wisdom: Its nature, ontology and function. *Perspectives of Psychological Science, 3*(1), 116–124.

Barnett, R. (1997). *Higher education: A critical business.* The Society for Research into Higher Education & Open University Press.

Bauman, Z. (2012). *Liquid modernity.* Polity Press.

Brookfield, S. (1995). *Becoming a critically reflective teacher.* Jossey-Bass.

Cherry, N. L. (2019). Contested practice. Being "wise" in an age of uncertainty. In J. Higgs (Ed.), *Practice wisdom. Values and interpretations* (pp. 29–38). Brill Sense.

Dewey, J. (1916). *Democracy and education. An introduction to the philosophy of education.* McMillan.

El-Desouky, A. A. (2010). *Kahlil Gibran: An illustrated anthology.* Octopus Publishing Group.

Foucault, M. (1977). *Discipline and punish: The birth of the prison* (A. Sheridan, Trans.). Penguin.

Foucault, M. (1980). *Power/knowledge: Selected interviews and other writings 1972–1977* (C. Gordon, L. Marshall, J. Mepham, & K. Soper, Trans.). Pantheon.

Grossmann, I. (2017). Wisdom in context. *Perspectives Psychological Science, 12*(2), 233–257.

Grundman, R., & Stehr, N. (2003). Social control and knowledge in democratic societies. *Science and Public Policy, 30*(3), 183–188.

Higgs, J., & Gates, A. (2013). Realising exemplary practice-based education. In J. Higgs, D. Sheehan, J. Baldry-Currens, W. Letts, & G. Jenson (Eds.), *Realising exemplary practice-based education* (Vol. 7, pp. 277–297). Sense.

Ingold, T. (2011). *Being alive: Essays on movement, knowledge and description.* Routledge.

Kemmis, S. (2012). Phronesis, experience and the primacy of practice. In E. A. Kinsella & A. Pitman (Eds.), *Phronesis as professional knowledge: Practical wisdom in the professions* (pp. 147–167). Sense.

Kemmis, S., & Smith, T. J. (2008). Conclusions and challenges enabling praxis. In S. Kemmis & T. J. Smith (Eds.), *Enabling praxis: Challenges for education* (pp. 263–286). Sense.

Kidder, M. (2006). *Moral courage.* Harper Collins Publishers.

Kinsella, E. A., & Pitman, A. (2012). Engaging phronesis in professional practice and education. In E. A. Kinsella & A. Pitman (Eds.), *Phronesis as professional knowledge: Practical wisdom in the professions* (pp. 1–12). Sense.

Lambert, M., Vero, J., & Zimmerman, B. (2012). Vocational training and professional development: A capability perspective. *International Journal of Training and Development, 16*(3), 164–182.

Lehtinen, E. (2008). Discussion. Bridging the individual and social in workplace learning and motivation. *International Journal of Educational Research, 47*, 261–263.

McKenna, B. (2019). Social Practice Wisdom. In J. Higgs (Ed.), *Practice Wisdom. Values and interpretations* (pp. 29–38). Brill Sense.

Nussbaum, M. (2006). Education and democratic citizenship: Capabilities and quality education. *Journal of Human Development, 7*(3), 385–395.

Nyilasy, G. (2021). *Fake news in the age of Covid-19*. https://fbe.unimelb.edu.au/newsroom/fake-news-in-the-age-of-covid-19

Patton, N. (2014). *Clinical learning spaces. Crucibles for the development of professional practice capabilities* [Unpublished PhD dissertation]. Charles Sturt University, Albury, Australia.

Patton, N. (2016). A praxis perspective: Musings on the works of Kemmis and Wilkinson. In J. Higgs & F. Trede (Eds), *Professional practice marginalia* (pp. 37–46). Sense.

Patton, N., & Higgs, J. (2018). Professional practice. In N. Patton, J. Higgs, & M. Smith (Eds.), *Developing practice capability: Transforming workplace learning* (pp. 3–14). Brill Sense.

Patton, N., & Simpson, M. D. (2016). Co-writing discourse through practice and theory. In J. Higgs & F. Trede (Eds), *Professional practice marginalia* (pp. 11–16). Sense.

Schatzki, T. R. (2002). *The site of the social.* The Pennsylvania State University Press.

Schön, D. (1983). *The reflective practitioner. How professionals think in action.* Ashgate.

Schön, D. (1987). *Educating the reflective practitioner.* Jossey Bass.

Sen, A. (1999). *Development as freedom.* Alfred A Knopf.

Sen, A. (2005). Human rights and capabilities. *Journal of Human Development, 6*(2), 151–166.

Stehr, N. (2001). A world made of knowledge. *Society, 39*(1), 9–92.

Stehr, N. (2013). An inconvenient democracy: Knowledge and climate change. *Society, 50*(1), 55–60.

Walker, M., & Unterhalter, E. (2007). The capability approach: Its potential for work in education. In M. Walker & E. Unterhalter (Eds.), *Amartya Sen's capability approach and social justice in education* (pp. 1–18). Palgrave McMillan.

Weststrate, N. M., & Glück, J. (2017). Hard-earned wisdom: Exploratory processing of difficult life experience is positively associated with wisdom. *Developmental Psychology, 53*(4), 800–814.

CHAPTER 4

Social Movements within the Australian Context for Wiser Futures

Anne Fitzgerald and Diane Tasker

Abstract

The twenty-first century has ushered in existential challenges for life on earth. This chapter explores some of the social movements preceding and responding to these challenges. As the urgency for change increases, we reflect upon the reasons for the successes and failures of relevant long-term campaigns within the Australian context: First Nations rights and environmental conservation. We ask what wisdom can be gleaned from reflections on past and continuing social movements to assist humanity's rise to the challenges of the twenty-first century?

Keywords

existential challenges – social movements – environment – First Nations – shape-shifting

> We can make mountains as we run as long as we climb towards that as one meaning. We can shape the sea as we sail and the only way we can fail is to not learn from the journey and the only way to triumph is to share what we know to be true.
>
> GORMAN (2021)

∵

1 The Authors' Position

We, the authors of this chapter are white Australians. We have been fortunate to experience good health, education, and productive working lives, and exist

 | DOI: 10.1163/9789004505544_005

within a privileged culture that has encouraged us as individuals, and particularly as women, to achieve our goals. We do not take this for granted, for we could equally have been born in a different time and place, which did not provide these opportunities. We acknowledge that our perspectives reflect this privilege and work to challenge our unconscious biases.

Our education and careers, as social worker, journalist, therapist, mothers and active local community members, contributes to our thinking for this chapter. We consider the questions we raise at a time when we are keenly attuned to the urgent call for humans to achieve a more sustainable future for all species, and for the planet. We do not pretend to have specialist knowledge regarding social movement development, relying upon our participation in ongoing collective actions aimed at restoring planetary health and achieving better social justice, and upon our engagement with activists and with writings on the related themes.

2 Introduction: Life at the Crossroads

The twenty-first century has ushered in existential challenges for life on earth. Developments in science, technology and production over the past three hundred and sixty years have had an inevitable and unsustainable impact on Earth's environment and ecosystems.

From this vantage point, we observe an exponentially increasing human population, continuing unsustainable levels of consumption (Shah, 2001), and unmitigated lethal impacts of industrialisation through the production of toxic waste and emissions. Increasingly 'unprecedented' natural disasters are now more openly attributed to climate change (United Nations, 2020). We are witnessing new levels of concentration of globalised wealth and power with increasing inequality between peoples. Problems of climate related displacement and food insecurity are being experienced by more nations, especially in the Asian Pacific region (Salem, 2020). Increasingly precarious geopolitical situations are demanding global responses and cooperation on a scale that tests the capacity of our species to achieve.

Governments worldwide are to varying degrees rising to the challenge to arrest and address environmental harm and its causes and consequences: some are achieving significant reductions in polluting emissions and managing the necessary shifts from old to cleaner industries and economies. However, others, including China, the USA and Australia, are dangerously slow to transition, despite the urgency and the scale of the current threat posed to life on Earth. The calls of small island nations experiencing immediate climate devastation are overshadowed as the international community deals with the secondary and tertiary impacts of the changing world; disasters, war, refugees and pandemics. A taste of things to come hangs in the air. New futures with better outcomes will require, to varying degrees, reshaped politics, industries, and economies and governments that are fit for purpose. It is not yet clear whether or how these changes will come about. In Australia the political will is still significantly invested in redundant industries and wedge politics.

We are poised at the crossroads between a past that is outgrown, and a choice of futures; poised at a time when the term 'tipping point' has moved from an ominous prospect to a cliché. Citizen responses rush to fill the void left by leadership. As political cultures struggle to come to terms with the need for adaptability and agility, citizens, through their involvement in social movements, are emerging as blocs of unwieldy players in the emerging political field.

3 Social Movements for Change

Citizens and the social movements they build have been the driving force behind responses to significant shifts in human history, striving to bring about change or to prevent change. The rise of citizens' social movements at this time of challenge prompts reflection. According to conventional western wisdom, for a social movement to become successful and sustainable, it is necessary for it to be framed in such a way that prospective new members become interested and feel they can commit to ongoing involvement (Little & McGivern, 2014).

Social movements for change provide a necessary disruption in the working of healthy democracies. In authoritarian settings, social movements face greater challenges, as the epic but ill-fated 2019/2020 Hong Kong democracy protests demonstrated. However the template for the most successful form of activism, *non-violent civil disobedience* was founded in Mahatma Ghandi's campaign for Indian independence from the British Empire. Persistence, timeliness and sheer numbers of people, along with a disciplined approach to civil disobedience, enabled Gandhi and the people surrounding him to achieve their aims, albeit at the considerable sacrifice of many. Many social movements have succeeded using non-violent direct action including the Tasmanian Franklin River blockade. More recently it is the chosen model of the international Extinction Rebellion movement.

Recent, significant social movements have formed to pressure for change to the status quo (e.g. *Occupy Wall Street*, the *Arab Spring*, *Extinction Rebellion*) and to prevent a change to the status quo (e.g, Anti-uranium mining, Anti-dam building). Concurrently we are witnessing the growth of movements promoting the rights of the disenfranchised (for example, Aboriginal rights, deaths in custody, 'change the date' of 'Australia Day'; refugee rights movements; and the *#Metoo* and other women's rights movements). This trend is being met by a concurrent rise in conservative movements attempting to deny such rights (for example, the *Incel* movement, and *MAGA*-associated white supremacy movements).

In the age of social media, and at a time when the climate emergency is undeniable, the plethora and prominence of movements is arguably unprecedented. Powerful movements have persisted, in shifting forms, for centuries, achieving incremental victories and enduring multiple frustrations. Many movements, which have been exemplary in their execution, have not been successful, as exhausted environmentalists (e.g. *Save the Tarkine* forest campaign in Tasmania).[1]

Movements succeed when the context allows. There are few movements with such enduring and creative effort as that of Australian Aboriginal activists over time. Where conventional activism has failed to achieve justice, activists have undertaken extraordinary and desperate campaigns to draw international attention to their plight:

- In 1928 activist Anthony Martin Fernando picketed Australia House in London dressed in a costume of toy skeletons – "this is all Australia has left of my people"[2],
- The 1969 Aboriginal delegation to the New York office of the UN Secretary-General[3],
- In 1988 Burnum Burnum planted the Aboriginal flag on an English beach to claim Britain for the Aboriginal people (Farnsworth, 1997) and
- As recently as 2019 12-year-old Dujuan Hoosan addressed the UN Human Rights Council: "I want my school to be run by Aboriginal people. I want adults to stop cruelling 10-year-old kids in jail. I want my future to be out on land with strong culture and language".[4]

Despite this, and demonstrating the contextual limitations of activism, the movement has had minimal impact on Aboriginal claims for sovereignty and justice to date. Exemplary non-violent direct action has and can be ignored without political and public will to accept and act upon inconvenient truths.

Even following successful campaigns, activists reeling from the shock of hard-won victories rarely leave the activism arena for long, as it is unusual to achieve immediately the deep systemic impact that their proponents seek. For example, as successful international marriage equality and gay rights movements have demonstrated, there can persist a myriad of ongoing challenges to universal acceptance, and ongoing efforts to revoke or water down the changes achieved. Similarly, the land rights gains, hard won in the High Court by Eddie Mabo for the Meriam people, and by the Wik people of Cape York, were quickly eroded by the Howard government.[5]

As the climate emergency deepens, and as the lived experience of people renders irrefutable, the evidence that change is upon us, citizens look to their leaders. When clear and reasonable leadership is wanting, citizens, through social movements, are forcing their way into the vacuum to participate in the contest of ideas for new futures. Prominent among these social movements in Anglo European countries are those which challenge white cultural dominance, and contest the environmental impacts of economic determinism in the creation of new futures; as well as the obverse, right-wing extremist and anti-science movements. From *QAnon* to *Black Lives Matter*, *#Metoo* and *Extinction Rebellion*, citizen movements are becoming significant forces for disruption, and potentially for revolution, as citizens use their numbers as consumers and voters, to challenge or preserve old power.

4 Evolution of Social Movements in Australia

Within the Australian context, contemporary activism bears a resemblance to that occurring across its modern history. The Australasian League was formed in 1851 from a social movement formed to end convict transportation to the colonies.[6] The way in which the movement grew throughout the 1840s reflects many of the ways that contemporary activists work to win hearts and minds. Newspaper campaigns, rallies, inter-colonial conferences, lobbying the government (in England), and the development of a flag under which to unite were all strategies that are familiar to the modern activist. It is interesting to note that the banner of this radical movement, the *Australasian League Flag*, royal blue with the stars of the Southern Cross and the Union Jack in the top right corner would become the national flag in 1901.

4.1 *Social Media to Organise Activism*

In the last 30 years the rise of digital technology has influenced the shape and prevalence of social movements, culminating in the advent of digital activism and the capacity to respond globally to global as well as local issues. Activists can protest online and their impact can be amplifies. For example, as the *Black Lives Matter* movement rose quickly to global prominence global in 2020, it in turn benefitted the local movement against Aboriginal deaths in custody as the global context of this largely overlooked campaign helped break through prejudice.

In many countries citizens have unmediated access to social media and its boundless streams of information, misinformation and disinformation. It is almost impossible to be apathetic to unprecedented concentrations of globalised wealth and power, and the impact of this on people and planet, when people are subjected to a daily diet of outrage memes. Digital content demand brings to our devices a stream of world news, which graphically portrays the impacts of, and emotional human responses to, worrying world events. The climate crisis becomes more relatable when it becomes stories about seaside homes being washed away, fires and floods, food security, population stability and conflict. The impact of a strong narrative becomes immediate through digital media, stimulating ongoing dialogue and building depth of feeling and motivation.

Social media seems inadvertently custom-built to aid activism. In the hands of an alarmed and agitated population, it provides a direct line to pervasive and unmediated digital platforms (as long as their owners, their algorithms, communications companies and governments allow). In this new world, the battle for influence is not waged to the inevitable advantage of the wealthy and powerful. Increasingly, digital activists are growing their capacity to share information, to satirise and to organise, and at times their creative and opportunistic activism is shaking traditional institutions to their foundations. Creative campaigning is increasingly evident:

– Traditional environmental movements like *Friends of the Earth* have pivoted to combine forces with the international *BankTrack* network to build investor climate activism through *Market Forces*.[7] The *Market Forces* ethical superannuation campaign is a good example of their digital campaigning,
– The *Australasian Centre for Corporate Responsibility* (ACCR)[8] uses high level shareholder activism to target corporate Australia (companies, industry associations, and investors), on their performance in managing climate, labour, human rights and governance issues and
– Small investors using the Reddit social media platform collectively undermined the modus operandi of hedge funds by raising and holding the value of targeted stock (Woods, 2021).

In the current digital activism landscape, targeted institutions are confronted by a new agile activism, which has both swelled the engagement of concerned citizens and enabled the internationalisation of their campaigns. However, the capacity of social media to empower movements in this way does not discern; it is available to movements that avail themselves of it, including those founded upon misinformation.

4.2 *'Rabbit Warrens' and 'Echo Chambers'*

The algorithm rules in this digital battleground.The effect (beyond the bulging bottom line of platform owners) is an unregulated social experiment with far-reaching impacts. Major platforms' content-feeds are designed to maximise view-time and profit by delivering 'more of the same' to viewers, creating what is known as a 'rabbit warren' effect. It is this effect that draws potential activists together, creating an 'echo chamber' of information and strengthening the sense of community and identity for users.

Within the 'rabbit warren', it is difficult to discern the veracity of what is shared. Disinformation and misinformation can be re-shared and 'corroborated' within the trusted online community of interest. The warrens create fertile grounds for misguided and mischievous players, including domestic and foreign political players, to influence masses for their own personal or political ends. The ability for warrens to create clusters of like-minded and action-ready movements, which can be activated by high profile social media celebrities, has contributed to some of the most remarkable mass mobilisations witnessed, such as Greta Thunberg's *School Climate Strike*, the 2019/2020 *Black Lives Matter* protests, and the insurrection on Capitol Hill, USA in January 2021. It is hard to imagine any of these movements growing to have such massive, immediate impact before the arrival of social media. However, this does not directly translate to their effectiveness in achieving lasting change. The 'arrival' of such movements as major forces and players in the field presents huge challenges for activists and governments alike as the battleground for hearts and minds becomes crowded.

5 'Shape-Shifting' Social Movements in Response to Change

In this next section of the chapter, we take two of the pre-eminent social movements operating within the Australian context and examine how their presence and development through our history have evolved and how they may connect with each other. Movements for environmental protection and the movements for First Nations/'Black Lives' justice are experiencing unprecedented engagement. Both of these social movements are 'shape-shifting' in response to macro changes within society. Over time activists in both movements have sustained the 'fire in the belly', which triggered their movements' origin, and both are simultaneously gathering momentum as their truths resonate with more and more people. These particular social movements are exploiting the reach afforded by social media, as well as employing more traditional strategies including non-violent direct action.

5.1 *First Nations Justice/Black Lives Matter in Australia*

The oldest of the social movements in the Australian continent's recent history has as much to teach modern Australians as campaigners, or as those who have looked away or were oblivious. Modern Australia has grown alongside persistent campaigns for justice waged by the continent's First Nations peoples and their supporters. What began as the *Black Wars* following invasion, morphed through centuries of campaigns for land rights, human rights and constitutional recognition, to the current persistent demands for justice and recognition, recently amplified through the lens of the international *Black Lives Matter* movement. Mainstream attention to 'suddenly' popular movements like *Back Lives Matter* and *Extinction Rebellion* naturally evokes raised eyebrows amongst First Nation activists who have a centuries-old tradition of rebellion against the continuing consequences of invasion that caused the near extinction of the peoples of many First Nations, and the decimation of others.

In Australia, at the time of colonial invasion and since the *Black Wars*, passionate non-violent protest has persisted in many forms throughout the continent and has received shamefully poor response in view of the injustices perpetrated on First Nations peoples. Public discourse in Australia has largely failed to acknowledge that the *Black Wars* ever began or ended. The dispossessed First Nations peoples' desperate campaigns for justice, which began in the 18th century and persisted throughout the nineteenth and twentieth centuries to the present day, have most often been met with a combination of cultural blindness and shrewd political dismissal from 'white Australia'.

The persistent protests by Aboriginal activists reveal their desperation and creativity in trying to draw attention of Australian people and of the world to their calls for justice: for return of lands, for an end to slave-like conditions, for an end to the removal of their children, and for sovereignty over their un-ceded lands. In addition to the international protests outlined above, local activism has been met with attention, but muted action, on the part of government representatives of white Australia. Examples include major protests on significant anniversaries of European occupation:

- In 1938, on the sesqui-centenary of European occupation, the *Aboriginal Progressive Association* declared a Day of Mourning and held an Aboriginal conference in Town Hall, Sydney.
- On the bicentenary in 1988, 40,000 protestors joined the inaugural '*Survival Day*', protest march across the Sydney Harbour Bridge.[9]
- Twelve years later, for *Corroboree 2000*, Sydney, Melbourne and Brisbane marches organised by Reconciliation Australia saw over 600,000 Australians march in support for fundamental reckoning (Trask, 2020).

- Additional powerful activism was undertaken in the 1960s and 1970s, including the *Freedom Ride* of 1965 when Charles Perkins and fellow University of Sydney students undertook a 15 day bus tour to shine a light on the poor state of Aboriginal health, education and housing and on discrimination against Aboriginal people in country NSW.[10]
- First Nations activists' frustrating eleven-year campaign leading to the 1967 referendum was marked by ingenious disruptive strategies, such as the tabling of petitions every parliamentary sitting day for 15 months (total 100,000 signatures) rather than all at once. The successful 'yes' referendum saw inclusion of Aboriginal people in the census and enabled the Commonwealth to make laws affecting Aboriginal people (Thomas, 2017).
- A permanent *Aboriginal Tent Embassy* was erected in 1972 on un-ceded land within the Australian Parliament House precinct in Canberra in response to the government's rejection of land rights.[11]

Aboriginal workers engaged in protest and strike action in order to carve out their rights to equality and freedom from subjugation. On 1 May 1945 the three-year Pilbara pastoral strike, known as the *Black Eureka* commenced. This milestone protest in the fight against their dispossession by pastoralists and the slave like conditions of Aboriginal workers was the first of many which engaged organisations in support of the cause, and created a turning point in Aboriginal recognition and justice. It is revealing that withdrawal of labour appears to have been such an effective way through which Aboriginal people have gained rights.[12] Other significant gains have been achieved through court action for land rights in the Mabo and Wik cases.

Before and since these successful actions successive governments have failed to substantially address the impact of colonisation and honour the legitimate claims of First Nations people. This is despite centuries of justified protest, and the extent of public support for Aboriginal justice that has been evident since the 1960s. Exemplary social action alone has failed to substantially compel governments to prioritise the rights and needs of Aboriginal people.

In Australia the power of social movements was dealt a body blow in the era of the Howard government (1996–2007). The failure of the *Corroboree 2000* bicentennial marches to dent the government's inaction on Aboriginal justice was magnified when in response, the Prime Minister John Howard refused to say sorry for past wrongs, asserting that current generations are not responsible for the deeds of the past.[13] Three years after the *Corroboree 2000* yet another massive crowd of half a million people gathered in Hyde Park in Sydney to protest the invasion of Iraq. Again the government of the day failed to heed the action. The combination of these two events sent a clear message to activists: demonstrations were now symbolic and would probably not bring about change. Subsequent *Invasion Day* marches have been well-attended and powerful symbols that the protest will not go away.

In 2020, across the Pacific, the death of George Floyd, a black man, at the hands of police in the USA was captured on video and shared on a day when the social media algorithm was favourable to such material becoming viral. The outrage of Australians when they saw the disturbing footage mirrored that expressed worldwide but it became more complicated when similar footage of David Dungay, an Aboriginal man in custody, also began to circulate across Facebook and Twitter. Outraged Australians had ignored the plight of black people within our own country, whose appalling fate within our justice system had been the subject of a Royal Commission and numerous other enquiries; none of which had helped save David. Tens of thousands of Australians responded by attending *Black Lives Matter* protests in capital cities, despite the Covid 19 pandemic and police warnings (Henriques-Gomes & Visontay, 2020). This led to yet another inquiry, but a palpable shift in activism persists; from demanding justice to also promoting First Nations Voice in parliament and Aboriginal parliamentary candidacy.

Symbolism is not in short supply in Australia. However, the process of making the necessary change to the complex, existential and legal crises at the heart of the nation and the racism embedded in its institutions, strikes at the heart of the Australian experiment. This requires that government members act as though the problem was important, and have the ticker' to tinker with the very foundations of Australia's development as a country. Movements are building that may usher in such new politics, and the timing may well finally be better as sadly and ironically, *Country* is suffering and European ways are failing. Finally, Aboriginal knowledge and cultural practice are attracting serious and urgent attention from the 'settlers' as the devastating impacts of successive government policies on this fragile land become inescapable. While First Nations voices have for too long been silenced, now they are more often sought. Rising numbers of committed environmental activists, scientists, farmers and everyday non-Indigenous Australians are belatedly discussing the connection between the needs of the environment and Traditional Owners.

5.2 *Australian Environmentalism*

Despite persistent and at times successful campaigns for environmental conservation in Australia the plight of our environment is dire. Australia's fragile ecosystems are enduring catastrophic damage from the effects of global warming, mining, deforestation and farming, and from the lack of traditional land management practices that shaped the Australian landscape and its ecosystems.

Here and elsewhere environmental movements have frequently overlooked the critical connection between environmental wellbeing and First Nations justice. Since European occupation of this continent, Traditional Owners have struggled to exercise their cultural obligation to care for *Country* in the face of dispossession and repression of culture. Alongside and often oblivious to this struggle have grown a plethora of non-Indigenous-led movements calling for protection and 'conservation' of the natural environment on this continent. These movements range from localised to larger scale national and international movements.

In the nineteenth and twentieth centuries the destructive impact of forestry, mining, farming and development became the subject of campaigns by 'bushwalking' clubs and conservation organisations, that fought hard and with some success to create legislated 'reserves' of country. These reserves were usually protected on the basis of human-less ecosystems, a concept that overlooked the millennia of Aboriginal land management of Australia and the relationships within *ngurra*, a concept alien to the occupying people.

> The Dharug and Gundungurra concept of *ngurra* takes in everything within the physical, cultural and spiritual landscape – landforms, waterways, air, trees, rocks, plants, animals, food, medicine, minerals, stories and special places and includes cultural practice, kinship, knowledge, songs, stories and art, as well as spiritual beings and people past, present and future. (Blue Mountains City Council Acknowledgement of Country)

The legal basis for occupation of these lands occurred on the false assumption of *terra nullius,* that is, a land belonging to no one. Evidence of traditional land management practices that were witnessed and recorded by colonists and subsequently have largely been devalued from the time of invasion. Even after intensive scrutiny as reserves of land gained protection through the UNESCO World Heritage listing of places like the Blue Mountains and South West Tasmania World Heritage National Parks, the extent of human agency in the pre-colonial management is underappreciated. The devastating and continuing impact of denying Traditional Custodians agency in land management, and freedom to care for *Country* over time has increased the vulnerability of ecosystems.

Compounding this problem, many traditional Nations struggle to retain the knowledge needed to care for *Country*, which is gained and maintained via a dynamic process of engagement within the natural world, as well as by the human transmission of knowledge over millennia. At this stage traditional knowledge is critically endangered in many parts of the continent, along with the species that this knowledge traditionally cared for and protected. This growing tragedy coincides, unsurprisingly, with the natural destruction of environment in now disaster-prone landscapes.

Environmentalism that promoted the protection of 'untouched wilderness' inadvertently fostered a colonial, romantic notion of conservation, The effect of governments responding to the 'white fella' interpretation of 'conservation' and 'environment' was to compartmentalise the natural world in a way that allowed continuation of its destruction, whilst creating museums or laboratories of selected reserves. This failed to address the reality that to deeply and sustainably care for the environment requires more than just conserving pieces of it. The health of the environment on this continent depends upon the ongoing and interconnected engagement with, not just land, but *ngurra.* It requires active cultural engagement with *Country* everywhere.

5.3 *Developing a Deeper Australian Environmentalism*

Communities in many nations have become exasperated with inaction in the face of a need to urgently adapt to the changing world. Here and elsewhere they are using movements to flex their collective muscles: disrupting stock markets, undermining the influence of media moguls and engaging in shareholder activism and consumer boycotts. In Australia activists are also pivoting, having grown frustrated by governments disregarding mass protests of over half a million people, or that dismiss historic opportunities out of hand such as Prime Minister Malcolm Turnbull's dismissal of the *Uluru Statement from the Heart.*[14] Increasingly there is public concern that major political parties are responding to the demands of donors rather than to the needs of the nation.

Environmental campaigners in Australia have embraced the international *Extinction Rebellion* movement, which was developed in England and coincided with the publicised pleas to the world of a child, Greta Thunberg, to stop continuing as though there is no existential crisis looming. Not everyone, including *Extinction Rebellion*'s rebels, has overlooked the irony of Australians embracing an extinction rebellion movement imported from England, whilst failing to make effective the 230 year old, customised extinction rebellion being waged on our continent.

Imported movements are not without merit. However, failure to reflect upon our unique Australian context has undervalued the unique history of struggle and First Nations activism on this continent. The ecological crises in Australia demand our most effective response to our unique intercultural and historical dilemmas. Australia must restore to Traditional Owners their cultural authority to lead if we are to find a way to live sustainably and respectfully on this land. While the dominant culture and government continues to promote dispossession and cultural genocide this can only rarely occur. Urgent opportunities for respectful and practical engagement must be made and seized upon, in order to commence overdue transformation in the culture and institutions of Australia. This requires preparedness to accept necessary but deep changes to the status quo within Australian culture and politics.

Natural disasters and social media campaigns have swelled the numbers of people making the shift from environmental concern to activism. Increasingly, from the very young to the very old, people are joining movements. A deeper shift in understanding is occurring in Australia, thanks in part to the timely publication of works explaining the relationships within the natural world and the integral role of Aboriginal land management in the creation of pre-colonial Australian landscapes, and the macro Australian environment. Mainstream and social media attention is amplifying the impact of the works of writers like Bill Gammage (2012) (*The Biggest Estate on Earth: How Aborigines Made Australia*), Bruce Pascoe (2018) (*Dark Emu: Aboriginal Australia and the Birth of Agriculture*) and Victor Steffensen (2020) (*Fire Country*), particularly as they apply to the possibility of addressing the problem of increasing natural disasters.

6 Lessons in a Time of Necessary Outcomes

The prominence and acceptance of both the environmental movement and First Nations/Black Lives justice movements on the international scene has grown over the past decade. Formerly treated as fringe movements, both environmental activist Greta Thunberg and the *Black Lives Matter* movement have recently received nominations for the Nobel Peace Prize. In Australia there is some history of crossover of activism between these two social movements (Mason, 2017) but it is growing and becoming more mainstream. At a government level minimal effort has been made to do more than polemically denounce Australia's historically genocidal policies and actions, and much effort is made to effectively ignore the sovereignty of Aboriginal Australia. Atrocities, by action and omission, continue. However, there is evidence that more Australians are now understanding the nexus between First Nations justice and environmental wellbeing. The voices of First Nations peoples are being heard with a sense of urgency that has not existed before the climate emergency. Growing numbers of environmental activists are supporting Aboriginal activism, both at protest sites on *Country* and in the cities (Gregoire, 2020). Shareholder activism is being used to sanction cultural vandalism, as in the case of the 2020 destruction of the Juukan Gorge by Rio Tinto (Lannin & Puppazoni, 2021).

Aboriginal leaders have developed both expertise and extraordinary tolerance in cross-cultural relations and creating opportunities for respectful, constructive engagement with non-Indigenous people. Respectful cross-cultural participation of non-Indigenous activists 'on the ground' in support of local direct actions requires cultural competence that can be lacking in well-meaning protestors who 'don't know what we don't know'. It is asking a lot to expect that after 230 years of continuous struggle to defend *Country*, front-line Aboriginal activists will divert limited energy to educate well-meaning non-Indigenous Australians who are often beginning their cultural learning journey.

Our national challenge is to rapidly transform from an unquestioning culture that craves achievement and avoids retrospection, to a mature nation that knows its truth. Australia is a new nation with a continuing history of atrocity and denial that has been built upon stolen lands of the oldest surviving cultures on earth. How we come to terms with this as individuals and as a nation, and how we move to a better place is a process that requires urgent and deep contemplation and action. For Australia's oldest movement, incremental change will not achieve its mission: the full restitution and wellbeing for people and *Country*. The mission of climate activists begins with a reduction in carbon dioxide emissions but their ultimate goal is not unlike that of the First Australians: the wellbeing of the planet and its life forms. Both require little short of revolution, and both are pragmatically interdependent.

In Australia there is evidence that fundamental change is beginning:

- In March 2021 the Victorian government announced a landmark *Truth and Justice Royal Commission* as part of Aboriginal Treaty talks (Dunstan, 2021);
- Following reaction to the Liberal National Party government's rejection of the *Uluru Statement From the Heart*, the Australian government has established a Senior Advisory Group to work on a co-design process for an *Indigenous Voice To Government*;
- Throughout Australia the *Voices 4 Community-minded Independents* movement has grown exponentially from the original *Voices for Indi* and Warringah electorate movements which unseated conservative party representatives. These integrity and community values-based movements have grown in response to the failure of parties to respond adequately to the climate emergency.

6.1 *Adapting Our Political Scene for a Wiser Future*

Emerging independence movements may well absorb the energies of members of social movements as they move beyond protest to adaptation, refreshing parliaments and rendering them fit for a future that demands our best responses to urgent challenges. Governments will need to be increasingly agile to respond to the challenges of the twenty-first century, and back the capacity of their citizens to take local initiatives that mitigate the problems of life on a heating planet.

Social movements are becoming repositories of hope for citizens who can no longer hide from the challenges we face. Despite the efforts of successive conservative Australian governments to ignore the protests, they will continue because symbolism matters. Serious citizens will undertake civil disobedience because disruption reminds the community that business as usual has ended.

7 Conclusion: Does the Koala Care?

The ways that community concerns give rise to social movements has evolved over decades, refining and reforming social concerns to reflect societal change, social perceptions and acceptance of concerns by ordinary people.

Wisdom has been developed by activists, who have maintained sustained efforts; fuelled by concern for *Country* and its life forms, and particularly for future generations. Such wisdom is hard won because it is born of the pain and grief that comes from acceptance of overwhelming problems. It comes out of denial, sits with complexity and uncertainty and despite the mess, sustains our effort and that of those around us to continue fighting for what we need and love for our future.

Whilst many have lauded the work of environmental activists, the same people have mostly ignored the simultaneous, existential rebellions being waged by First Nations people around the world. We are becoming more conscious of our 'white gaze'. There is a risk of despondency when we acknowledge the damage that this 'white gaze' has wreaked. Although there will be despondency in acknowledgment of past mistakes, new awareness comes with hope. Business as usual has ended. New futures require a 'new gaze" upon our concerns and 'a new worldview'.

In the end the question for the path forward is as simple as

Does the koala care?

Notes

1 https://www.sbs.com.au/nitv/explainer/australia-day-invasion-day-survival-day-whats-name

2 https://www.austlit.edu.au/austlit/page/A146776

3 https://www.preceden.com/timelines/485674-civil-rights-movement---australia---usa

4 https://www.sbs.com.au/news/timeline-indigenous-rights-movement

5 https://antar.org.au/sites/default/files/120807_native_title_fact_sheet.pdf
6 https://www.aph.gov.au/About_Parliament/Senate/Powers_practice_n_procedures/~/~/link.aspx?_id=010D9F7D451E4425AAA8A681CE3A5DC7&_z=z
7 https://www.marketforces.org.au/
8 https://www.accr.org.au/about/#:~:text=The%20Australasian%20Centre%20for%20Corporate%20Responsibility%20%28ACCR%29%20is,managing%20climate%2C%20labour%2C%20human%20rights%20and%20governance%20issues
9 https://www.sbs.com.au/nitv/explainer/australia-day-invasion-day-survival-day-whats-name
10 https://www.nma.gov.au/explore/features/indigenous-rights/civil-rights/freedom-ride
11 https://www.nma.gov.au/defining-moments/resources/aboriginal-tent-embassy
12 https://www.ymac.org.au/remembering-the-1946-pilbara-strike/ AND https://www.nma.gov.au/defining-moments/resources/wave-hill-walk-off
13 https://www.abc.net.au/am/stories/s47078.htm
14 https://ulurustatement.org/

References

Dunstan, J. (2021, March 8). Victoria announces landmark truth and justice royal commission as part of Aboriginal treaty talks. *ABC News*. https://www.msn.com/en-au/news/australia/victoria-announces-landmark-truth-and-justice-royal-commission-as-part-of-aboriginal-treaty-talks/ar-BB1enwoK

Farnsworth, C. H. (1997, August 20). Burnum Burnum, 61, Fighter for Australia's Aborigines. *The New York Times*. https://www.nytimes.com/1997/08/20/world/burnum-burnum-61-fighter-for-australia-s-aborigines.html

Gammage, W. (2012). *The biggest estate on earth: How Aborigines made Australia*. Allen & Unwin.

Gorman, A. (2021). Making mountains as we run. *Harvard Magazine*. https://www.harvardmagazine.com/bacow29-poet-18#

Gregoire, P. (2020, October 16). Get the hell out of bed with Santos, Gladys, warns Extinction Rebellion. *Sydney Criminal Lawyers*. https://www.sydneycriminallawyers.com.au/blog/get-the-hell-out-of-bed-with-santos-gladys-warns-extinction-rebellion/

Henriques-Gomes, L., & Visontay, E. (2020, June 7). Australian Black Lives Matter protests: Tens of thousands demand end to Indigenous deaths in custody. *The Guardian*. https://www.theguardian.com/australia-news/2020/jun/06/australian-black-lives-matter-protests-tens-of-thousands-demand-end-to-indigenous-deaths-in-custody

Lannin, S., & Puppazoni, R. (2021). Rio Tinto hit by huge protest vote on executive pay over Juukan destruction. *ABC News*. https://www.abc.net.au/news/2021-05-07/rio-tinto-investor-revolt-over-juukan-caves-destruction/100122824

Little, W., & McGivern, R. (2014). Chapter 21: Social movements and social change. In *Introduction to sociology* (1st Canadian ed.). Creative Commons. https://opentextbc.ca/introductiontosociology/chapter/chapter21-social-movements-and-social-change/

Mason, A. (2017, January 25). A history of student engagement in Aboriginal rights. *Honi Soit.* https://honisoit.com/2017/01/a-history-of-student-engagement-in-aboriginal-rights/

Pascoe, B. (2018). *Dark emu: Aboriginal Australia and the birth of agriculture.* Magabala Books.

Salem, S. (2020, February 18). Climate change and food security in the Pacific. *E-International Relations.* https://www.e-ir.info/pdf/81898

Shah, A. (2001, September 26). Effects of over-consumption and increasing populations. *Global Issues.* https://www.globalissues.org/article/216/effects-of-over-consumption-and-increasing-populations

Steffensen, V. (2020). *Fire country.* Hardy Grant Travel.

Thomas, M. (2017). *The 1967 referendum.* Parliament of Australia. https://www.aph.gov.au/About_Parliament/Parliamentary_Departments/Parliamentary_Library/FlagPost/2017/May/The_1967_Referendum

Trask, S. (2020, May 25). It's 20 years this week since the Reconciliation Walk across Sydney's Harbour Bridge. *SBSNews.* https://www.sbs.com.au/news/it-s-20-years-this-week-since-the-reconciliation-walk-across-sydney-s-harbour-bridge

United Nations. (2020). *UN75, 2020 and beyond: Bridging the divide.* https://www.un.org/sites/un2.un.org/files/un75_inequality.pdf

Woods, M. (2021, January 28). Why GameStop stock soared as part of a Reddit Forum's quest to take down hedge funds. *Huffpost.* https://www.huffingtonpost.ca/entry/gamestop-stock-market-reddit-explained_ca_6012f58fc5b6aa4bad322010

CHAPTER 5

Practice Dimensions and Drivers Shaping Wise Futures

Joy Higgs

Abstract

Practical wisdom can be interpreted as "the right way to do the right thing", or perhaps, avoiding the definite article and its certainty; right *ways* of doing right *things*. In this chapter a model for shaping wise futures is presented. It explores wise practice dimensions and drivers that are shaping wise practice futures.

Keywords

practice dimensions – shaping wise practice

> We do not inherit the earth from our ancestors, *we borrow it* from our children.
>
> NATIVE AMERICAN PROVERB

1 A Model for Shaping Wise Futures

This chapter presents a model for shaping wise futures. The key features of this model are:
- key spaces of attention
- key drivers of future directions
- key goals of these potential directions
- key challenges of future shaping strategies
- key opportunities and barriers to shaping wise futures (see Figure 5.1)

 | DOI: 10.1163/9789004505544_006

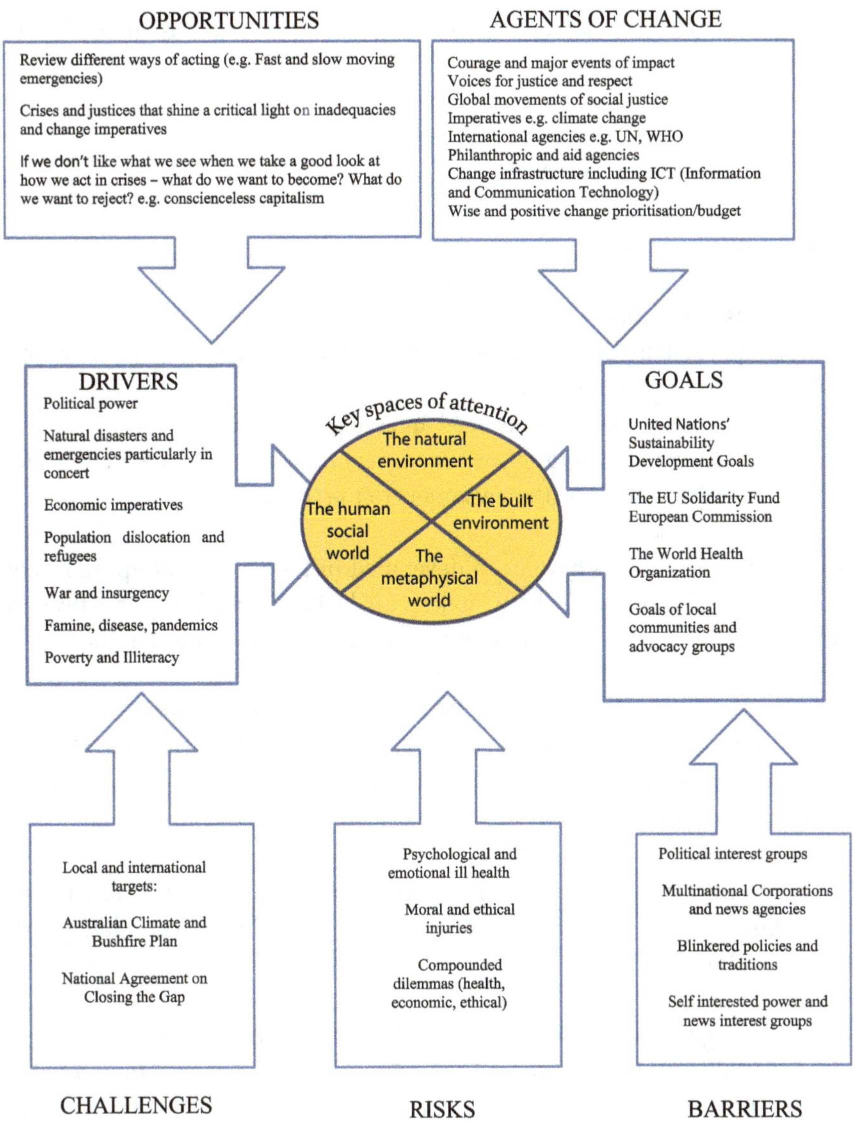

FIGURE 5.1 Key spaces of attention in the natural world, the human social world, the built environment, the metaphysical world

Wisdom including practice wisdom of doing, knowing, being and becoming provides the bedrock for the planning of this model, its dimensions and strategies. It draws on the words of sages and clever, wise people. It is like standing on their shoulders, to gain the capacity to see further into the future. We can see and feel through their hearts and place humanity and the desire for better places at the centre of this model. Through this we can envisage the intent of such wise futures and ensure that a critical gaze and collaborative intent is ever present.

2 Different Starting Points

In planning wise futures, where do we start:
- at basic and universal needs of humans and other species?
- at extensively debated decision frameworks such as a Bill of Rights?
- at very particular points that address the expectations of specific communities, groups or occupations?
- at crisis points of tremendous need and enlightenment?
- at learned points, where experienced people like wise leaders can share their practice wisdom with newcomers to the field?

Numerous wise models have been developed in the past to set up frames of reference for shaping pathways to make wise decisions and frame wise futures. Where we start depends on what is our goal and what do we stand for. Consider the following for models or foundations, for instance.

Maslow's Hierarchy of Needs. "a theory of human motivation (the reasons why people do particular things), developed in 1954 by Abraham Maslow, which says that people will only satisfy some needs after more basic needs have been satisfied". From basic to highest level these needs are: physiological, safety, love and belonging, esteem, and self-actualisation.[1]

The World Health Organization (WHO) definition of health is often used to categorise types of health care needs: "Health is a state of complete physical, mental and social well-being and not merely the absence of disease or infirmity".[2]

Human rights are rights inherent to all human beings, regardless of race, sex, nationality, ethnicity, language, religion, or any other status. Human rights include the right to life and liberty, freedom from slavery and torture, freedom of opinion and expression, the right to work and education, and many more. Everyone is entitled to these rights, without discrimination. The foundations of this body of law are the Charter of the United Nations and the Universal Declaration of Human Rights, adopted by the General Assembly in 1945 and 1948, respectively.[3]

Members of professions are held to a higher level of responsibility for the service they provide to their clients (including school children, patients, legal clients etc.). The following are six essential expectations of such workers: humanity, professionalism (including ethical conduct), professional decision-making, self-critique and reflexivity, effective communication and profession-relevant technical capabilities. By setting these expectations we create a list of targets for higher education of professionals, for the self and professional regulation of their conduct, for the expectation of the ongoing delivery and advancement of the standard of their practice. This list could be diversified to formulate a list for other groups' action and learning, (politicians for instance).

Frameworks for ethical decision-making are used in situations where ethical considerations of life, quality of life standards of business and service of care are required. In such cases key principles, recognitions and actions, are vital to form the platform for that decision-making including:

- Recognition that difficult decisions need to be made through crises and should be sustained by credible ethical principles that define the group, profession, organisation etc.
- Such decisions need to be consistently and transparently made, based on these defining principles, during the process and review of the ensuing decision-making.
- Recognition that during ethical crises we run the risk of moral injury and subsequent post-traumatic stress and ensuring that part of the decision-making is how to deal with these risks.
- Recognition that the survival of the group or organisation after the crisis is validated by the ethics, values and principles of the group.
- Understanding that people face loss of certainty and usual capability to deal with the dilemmas of their work. In the absence of such certainty the essential element is that people act in good faith.
- Ethical decision-making requires acts of discretion and justification of the choices based on the purpose, values and the principles that sustain these decisions.
- Finally, there is the aim to emerge from the crisis into a position and future that is also supported by the organisation's purpose, values and principles (possibly those arising through the crisis changes) (Longstaff, 2020).

We see through these expectations and aspirations, examples of how people may go about planning for positive futures and what they might plan for. It is interesting that when we sit down to say what matters in the targets we are seeking to attain in our "planning of wise futures", we are at the same time developing other lists, for example, what matters most to us as a culture of people, what areas of development in life and the world we live in we want to give priority to, what factors influence us and what we allow and want to influence us, what we know about future directions of priorities, influences and rewards, how much we want to be the people driving our futures or just the ones who let others take the brunt and blame for where we end up and what is our responsibility?

This is a good time to ask very clearly – why is this book about *wise* futures? In the first industrial revolution the word progress was paramount. Wise was not necessarily required or considered. Progress despite, for instance, destruction of forests, progressive extinction of species etc was what mattered most. Wise questions were not so prevalent about equity, diversity and equality of access to the things like education, which could further promote personal and collective gain in comparison to helping the rich get richer. Two core aspects of Paolo Freire's (1972, 1995) principal work on critical pedagogy, *Pedagogy of the Oppressed*,[4] raised awareness of these important questions in critical pedagogy:

- How might education build a voice for the oppressed and provide a 'pedagogy of hope'? Freire was concerned with 'conscientization' or 'developing consciousness that has the power to transform reality' (Taylor, 1993, p. 52).
- How can education be linked to lived experience of the participants expand learners' literacies?

In these discussion points the implications that future decision-making can be short or long term, urgent or more gestational, our problem as well as "someone else's". And, there are times when people feel disempowered, "what's the point" or engaged, "we all have a part to play". Bigger challenges pose bigger questions like responsibilities for future generations.

Future planning prompts reflection on processes as well as goals for change e.g. involvement of first nations people, youth and the elderly (and their agents) in decision-making. How, what, why and who, all need review as does meta-level planning, that is, planning about planning. This book poses the question what is wise planning? This is the challenge we pose to our readers. It is of course, linked to, "according to whom?" and how will we ascertain if the planning has been wise when we look at its outcomes. Of particular relevance to this point is that we need to hear different voices and perspectives seeking wise solutions and we need to see opportunities for people with different interests being able to shape futures in collaboration.

3 Key Goals of Future Planning

Part of wisdom in future planning is having a focus and frame of reference that is credible, defensible and sustainable. For instance, Arup Australasia Chair, Peter Chamley advocated through CEDA (The Committee for Economic Development of Australia) that industry has an obligation to ensure infrastructure spending after COVID-19 is informed by the United Nations Sustainable Development Goals. He argued that since January 2020, public sentiment about the nation's top issues has swung from climate change action to healthcare, to the economy and then to job security and now back to healthcare as COVID-19 cases spike again in Melbourne. Will this cycling of on-going crises be the new rhythm of life, our business as usual for the foreseeable future? Such a 'Focus. Refocus. Refocus again' syndrome will inevitably wear us down. To cope with these times, we need some form of stabiliser, a framework for the future that will guide decision-making through the turbulence. We should remember that we already have this with the United Nations Sustainable Development Goals (UN SDGs), which are simultaneously far-reaching, sensible and enduring.[5] The SDGs exist as the result of extensive international collaboration seeking to establish focussed, high priority goals for international development, thus providing wisdom in shaping goals and strategies for sustainable development. Why waste such amazing collaborative effort in the development of wise plans of action or wise collaboration in implementation and learning from the attention of funded jurisdictions and well-meaning agencies in these powerful goals.

4 Key Spaces of Attention

From time to time we enter a space of significant re-evaluation. 2020 will be remembered as one such time and space with the Covid-19 pandemic. When Winston Churchill was working to form the United Nations after WWII, he famously said, "Never let a good crisis go to waste". Recently a discussion group reflected on the current 2020 pandemic and asked the following questions to deal with today's crisis:

- What are today's primary survival questions?
- What long-term changes would we like to take with us out of this crisis? People listed: a much better labour market, a very much better climate control strategy, a program for closing the gap in relation to First Nations people's health, wellbeing and education, radical improvement in social housing, better emergency (particularly bushfires and wildlife impact) management, wider reflection on and attention to unemployment support; there was a sense of a return to goodwill and affirmation of others alongside a sense of discarding the selfish disregard of the interests of others that pervades more "normal" times.
- What do we want our society and culture to be like? Are we satisfied with these perceptions by others of our society's priorities and practices of support for others?
- Who's going to pay the cost for future recovery?

At the very least the spaces of our attention in shaping wise futures should include the human social world and the natural environment (encompassing all living and non living natural things), systems, resources and the built environment incorporating infrastructure, transportation, communication and information systems.

> We're a part of the environment. We are one aspect of the environment. We're not separate from it or better than it. … We've got to stop being so prideful about the fact that we're doing something that the world needs. It's not a matter of pride, It's a matter of dire necessity, internally and externally. (Alan Arkin, as cited in Zukerman, 2003, p. 18)

Internationally climate change priorities are a key driver of future planning. Recently a key national planning initiative in Australia, for instance, built on recent bushfire disasters (Mullins et al., 2020). The major conclusion was "Without action on climate change, any response to the bushfire crisis will be ineffective" (p. 1). The report writers reminded readers: "While unprecedented, this tragedy was not unforeseen. For decades climate scientists have warned of an increase in climate-related disasters, including longer and more dangerous bushfire seasons" (p. 4). The top priority recommendation from this widespread consultation across multiple jurisdictions and communities was:

> Tackling the climate crisis 1. The Federal Government must address the root cause of the climate crisis and worsening bushfires through a national commitment to net zero emissions, strengthening of Australia's 2030 emissions reduction targets, and the managed phase-out of all fossil fuels. (p. 5)

5 Climate Change Activists – Quotes[6]

> Many individuals are doing what they can. But real success can only come if there is a change in our societies and in our economics and in our politics. (David Attenborough)

> Climate change is a huge challenge, but it can be brought in line if governments, businesses and individuals work together. (Sir Richard Branson, Founder of Virgin Group)

> We really need to kick the carbon habit and stop making our energy from burning things. Climate change is also really important. You can wreck one rainforest then move, drain one area of resources and move onto

another, but climate change is global. (Sir David Attenborough, Natural World Broadcaster)

Twenty-five years ago people could be excused for not knowing much, or doing much about climate change. Today we have no excuse. (Desmond Tutu, Former Archbishop of Cape Town)

We are the first generation to feel the effect of climate change and the last generation who can do something about it. (Barack Obama, Former US President)

Climate change knows no borders. It will not stop before the Pacific Islands and the whole of the international community here has to shoulder a responsibility to bring about sustainable development. (Angela Merkel, Chancellor of Germany)

The world is reaching the tipping point beyond which climate change may become irreversible. If this happens, we risk denying present and future generations the right to a healthy and sustainable planet – the whole of humanity stands to lose. (Kofi Annan, Former Secretary-General of the United Nations)

Climate change is the single greatest threat to a sustainable future but, at the same time, addressing the climate challenge presents a golden opportunity to promote prosperity, security and a brighter future for all. (Ban Ki-Moon, Secretary General of the UN)

The time for seeking global solutions is running out. We can find suitable solutions only if we act together and in agreement. (Pope Francis, 266th Catholic Pope)

Climate change is real. It is happening right now, it is the most urgent threat facing our entire species and we need to work collectively together and stop procrastinating. (Leonardo Di Caprio, Actor & Environmentalist)

Adults keep saying we owe it to the young people, to give them hope, but I don't want your hope. I don't want you to be hopeful. I want you to panic. I want you to feel the fear I feel every day. I want you to act. I want you to act as you would in a crisis. I want you to act as if the house is on fire, because it is. (Greta Thunberg, 16-year-old Swedish Activist)

> Animal extinction rebellion activities often run in parallel to climate change initiatives. Dr Jane Goodall, Scientist and Activist argues: '*What you do makes a difference, and you have to decide what kind of difference you want to make*'.

The human social world with its many goals, strategies and systems could be the focus of many explorations and subdivisions of wise future planning including nations, communities, global markets, international laws, human rights demands and widespread human conflicts and crises. Social practice issues are manifest in the chapters of Part 3 of this book and key reflective chapters in Part 4 considering the place of wisdom in futures the of young and old, the leaders, politicians and opinion shapers. The current Covid-19 times are of particular significance in considering what directions could be considered to be wise and might result in wise foci and strategies and outcomes.

In 2020 the Australia Together[7] alliance launched The National Community Recovery Summit to help build a roadmap for national-level reforms and local leadership to leave a positive legacy from the trauma of the Covid pandemic. Interestingly this group demonstrates a strong emphasis on recognising positive population attitudes and support in crises, recognising the need for applying these positive attitudes to addressing enduring challenges and valuing local community leadership. Group discussions have led to planning activities around key initiatives and need areas including:
- Jobs, skills and enterprises
- Engaging local communities
- Early childhood development
- Social and community housing.

Parallel initiatives are addressing homelessness, the need for a living wage and calls for significant expansion of social housing. Some of the activities are addressing direct pandemic health demands, like social distancing and isolation, the need for street dwellers to be housed while other initiatives focus on the economic sequelae of homelessness and unemployment. None of these changes seem to be mentioned or constructed or *demanded*, without clearly holding up a stark and critical mirror of social housing deficiencies and associated lack of human supportiveness. A key report arising from this social housing scrutiny and championship is the Social Housing Acceleration and Renovation Program (SHARP).[8] The report concluded:

> At this difficult time the Government's emergency measures to support businesses and workers will bring much-needed relief to many

> Australians. Equally, it's imperative that we plan now for a government-driven stimulus program to kickstart our country's post-crisis recovery. This will be vital in getting people back into jobs fast, and also in enhancing building company confidence to retain workers. (p. 1)

This SHARP program would have four overlapping 'waves' ensuring that the programs would be immediate, and its outcomes, of high quality:

WAVE 1	WAVE 2	WAVE 3	WAVE 4
social housing maintenance and upgrading	acquisition of sites and properties requiring renovation completion which are suitable for social housing	social ready projects	longer term new development projects

Looking back at such major points of reflection help to put today's events and issues in perspective. In 1995 two significant events were concurrently occupying the minds and interests of two major groups:

- a thousand participants from around the world met at the Banquet Hall of the University of Copenhagen to debate the great social issues of the closing years of the millennium.
- Nearby 120 heads of state and governments met to deliberate upon and adopt a set of commitments and planned actions for global social development – a Social Charter for the Twenty-First Century.

Building on this time of debate and reflection, UNRISD, the United Nations Research Institute for Social Development, invited social analysts and distinguished writers to reflect on fundamental processes that were driving momentous social change at the time.

In commenting upon the UNRISD event Johan Galtung emphasised the apparent patterns of social disintegration. He left us with this quote (Galtung (1995): "One day the present First world may ask the present Third world for advice about social development. If that happens, the world would have taken a major step forward" (p. 157).

6 Identifying Key Drivers of Future Directions

How do we come to grips with drivers of future directions? This section explores pathways that people, industries, businesses, nations or individuals might take. In recording these insights my challenge to readers is to reflect on what can be learned from the pathways, how they might by used by the group or individual in question and how might wisdom be interpreted if used in this context of planning wise futures? How do values and roles in the world influence how the agency shapes their own future priorities and strategies and those of their clients and constituencies?

- The World Future Council is an independent body formally founded in Hamburg, Germany on 10 May 2007. Formed to speak on behalf of policy solutions that serve the interests of future generations, it includes members active in governmental bodies, civil society, business, science and the arts.[9]
- Futurists are people whose specialty or interest is futurology or the attempt to systematically explore predictions and possibilities about the future and how they can emerge from the present, whether that of human society in particular or of life on Earth in general.[10]
- The United Nations Sustainable Development Agenda. With just under ten years left to achieve the Sustainable Development Goals, world leaders at the SDG Summit in September 2019 called for a Decade of Action and delivery for sustainable development, and pledged to mobilise financing, enhance national implementation and strengthen institutions to achieve the Goals by the target date of 2030, leaving no one behind.[11]
- The goals of the European Union are[12]:
  - Promote peace, its values and the well-being of its citizens.
  - Offer freedom, security and justice without internal borders.
- PricewaterhouseCoopers[13] is a multinational professional services network of firms headquartered in London, United Kingdom, operating as partnerships under the PwC brand. PwC ranks as the second-largest professional services network in the world and is considered one of the Big Four accounting firms, along with Deloitte, EY and KPMG. Roles of central offices include: managing the global brand, and developing policies and initiatives, to creating a common and coordinated approach in areas such as risk, quality, and strategy. Dispersed components provide client services.
- WHO values[14]: WHO, as the directing and coordinating authority on international health within the United Nations system, adheres to the UN values of integrity, professionalism and respect for diversity. The values of the WHO workforce furthermore reflect the principles of human rights, universality and equity established in WHO's Constitution as well as the ethical standards of the Organization. These values are inspired by the WHO vision of a world in which all peoples attain the highest possible level of health, and its mission to promote health, keep the world safe and serve the vulnerable,

with measurable impact for people at country level. WHO is individually and collectively committed to put these values into practice.

7 Key Challenges of Future Shaping Strategies

The section above focuses on planning at a global scale and outlines influential factors on that planning. In this next section the shift is towards planning of a particular group by that group or organisation. It is taken from a business organisation but could be adapted (e.g. remove reference to profit and loss, replace employees with collaborators). The issue is to develop and implement a planning framework that is tailor-made to the current need. It could relate to planning the individual's future career or the organisation's direction.

1. *Succession*
   How does the organisation plan and prepare for leadership succession? What training and development is required?
2. *Life Balance*
   How does this relate to the workers in question? How does the company deal with this issue for the company as a whole?
3. *Clients*
   Who are the clients and what are their interests? What are the implications of this for planning, systems development and evolution of the company?
4. *Generation Y*
   Much has been written about Generation Y and their different work and life values to "Baby Boomers" and even Generation X. Understanding your workers and their values plus the contributions they can make to the company is important to their development and meeting their incentive needs.
5. *Competition*
   How does the business compare to competitors in the market? What is the value of such competition in planning and presence in the marketplace?
6. *Business Processes*
   What processes, values and systems comprise and epitomise the company? How do leadership and system management operate together?
7. *Cost Structure*
   Cost structure of the business – planning, cost-benefit and sustainability provide important considerations in organisation planning.

8. *New Technology*
   How is technology involved in the business and the effectiveness of workers? How might future changes in technology influence the production, communication, marketing and operations aspects of the business – including worker capabilities and endurance?
9. *Value Drivers*
   How are the company's values manifest in the business purpose and operations? How do they influence the ways the company deals with workers?
10. *Service Delivery*
   How is service delivery currently implemented? Does this provide insights and imperatives for future plans for service delivery?

8 Conclusion

In modern times we tend to think of "wisdom" as the opposite of "practical". Wisdom is about abstract, ethereal matters like "the way" or "the good" or "the truth" or "the path". We tend to think that wisdom is something for sages, gurus, rabbis, and scholars.

> Aristotle's teacher, Plato shared this view that wisdom was theoretical and abstract, and the gift of only a few. But Aristotle disagreed. He thought that our fundamental social practices constantly demanded choices – like when to be loyal … and that making the right choices demanded wisdom. … The wisdom to answer such questions and to act rightly was considered distinctly practical, not theoretical. It depended on our ability to perceive the situation, to have the appropriate feelings or desires about it, to deliberate about what was appropriate in these circumstances and to act. (Schwartz & Sharpe, 2010)

In this wisdom, futures and planning as ideas and practices have been pulled apart and related again as dimensions of future planning. The model in this chapter places these features in relationship and together offers a framework for planning wise futures.

Notes

1 https://dictionary.cambridge.org/dictionary/english/maslow-s-hierarchy-of-needs?q=Maslow%27s+hierarchy+of+needs

2 The bibliographic citation for this definition is: Preamble to the Constitution of WHO as adopted by the International Health Conference, New York, 19 June–22 July 1946; signed on 22 July 1946 by the representatives of 61 States (Official Records of WHO, no. 2, p. 100) and entered into force on 7 April 1948.
3 https://www.un.org/en/charter-united-nations/ https://www.un.org/en/universal-declaration-human-rights/
4 https://infed.org/mobi/paulo-freire-dialogue-praxis-and-education/
5 https://www.ceda.com.au/Digital-hub/Blogs/CEDA-Blog/July-2020/A-sustainable-legacy-for-our-post-COVID-infrastructure-spend
6 https://www.curious.earth/blog/climate-change-quotes#:~:text=%22We%20don't%20have%20time,It's%20life%20or%20death.%22&text=%E2%80%9CBy%20polluting%20the%20oceans%2C%20not,there%20is%20no%20planet%20B.%22
7 https://australiatogether.org/
8 https://www.communityhousing.com.au/wp-content/uploads/2020/05/SHARP-Program.pdf?utm_source=Council+to+Homeless+Persons+E-news+list&utm_campaign=58aa91876a-EMAIL_CAMPAIGN_2018_06_25_05_11_COPY_01&utm_medium=email&utm_term=0_47e37fdcf8-58aa91876a-422982093&mc_cid=58aa91876a&mc_eid=6e3b93c793
9 https://www.worldfuturecouncil.org/
10 https://en.wikipedia.org/wiki/Futurist
11 https://www.un.org/sustainabledevelopment/development-agenda/#:~:text=At%20the%20core%20of%20the,and%20address%20the%20climate%20emergency
12 https://www.google.com/search?q=european+union+goals&rlz=1C1JZAP_enAU793AU793&oq=european+union+goals&aqs=chrome..69i57j0l7.6977j1j4&sourceid=chrome&ie=UTF-8
13 https://en.wikipedia.org/wiki/PricewaterhouseCoopers
14 https://www.who.int/about/who-we-are/our-values

References

Freire, P. (1972). *Pedagogy of the oppressed* Penguin.

Freire, P. (1995). *Pedagogy of hope: Reliving pedagogy of the oppressed.* Continuum.

Galtung, J. (1995). On the social costs of modernization: Social disintegration, anatomie'/anomie and social development, *Altenativas. Cuadenos de Trabajo Social, 8.*

Longstaff, S. (2020). *Ethical decision making during a crisis.* CEDA Webinar.

Mullins, G., Bradshaw, S., & Pearce, A. (2020). *Australian Bushfire and Climate Plan: Final report of the National Bushfire and Climate Summit 2020.* Emergency Leaders for Climate Action & the Climate Council of Australia.

Schwartz, B., & Sharpe, K. (2010). *Practical wisdom: The right way to do the right thing.* Riverhead Books.

Taylor, P. (1993). *The texts of Paulo Freire.* Open University Press.

Zukerman, A. (2009). *Wisdom, peace.* PQ Blackwell in association with Abrams.

PART 2

Exploring Practice Pathways

Introduction to Part 2

Joy Higgs

In this part of the book, we explore ideas of wisdom and seek practice pathways to shed light on what we can learn from wisdom and how it can light future possibilities.

> There is a deep and pristinely clear 'something' in each of us, regardless of the outer circumstances of our lives, that has the capacity to recognize Wisdom when we meet it, and it is the nature of wisdom teaching to call this 'something' forth. But until the spark of recognition actually goes off in us, Wisdom remains invisible. (Bourgeault, 2003, p. 14)

> … one of the greatest gifts one generation can give to another is the wisdom it has gained from experience. (Zuckerman, 2009, p. 3)

> Knowing others is intelligence;
> Knowing yourself is true wisdom.
> Mastering others is strength,
> Mastering yourself is true power.
> (Lao Tzu, 6th century BCE, in Benedict, 2010, p. 39)

> Understanding involves negotiation and agreeing to differ knowingly. (Davey, 2006, p. 10)

> To the mind that is still, the whole universe surrenders.
> To know, yet to think that one does not know is best;
> Not to know, yet to think that one knows will lead to difficulty.
> Original nature can intuit all happenings.
> In original nature is the essence of goodness.
> Be natural in your actions and you will always be pure and still.
> (Lao Tzu, 6th century BCE, in Benedict, 2010, p. 38)

> It is not truth that makes man great, but man that makes truth great. (Confucius, in Benedict, 2010, p. 23)

> Notice that I capitalise the word *Wisdom*, for I am not referring simply to a generic of subjective quality of being but to a far more precise lineage of

 | DOI: 10.1163/9789004505544_007

spiritual knowledge. Wisdom is an ancient tradition, not limited to one particular religious expression but at the headwaters of the great sacred paths. (Bourgeault, 2003, p. 4)

Wisdom means keeping a sense
of the fallibility of all our views
and opinions, and of the uncertainty
and instability of the things
we most count on.
(Gerald Brenan, in Exley, 1999, n.p.)

The summary definition of *wisdom* is as follows: Capacity of judging rightly in matters relating to life and conduct; soundness of judgement of the choice of means and ends; sometimes, less strictly, sound sense especially in practical affairs; opposed to folly. (OED, 1933, pp. 191–192)

The term *practical wisdom* sounds like an oxymoron to modern ears. We tend to think of 'wisdom' as the opposite to 'practical'. Wisdom is about abstract, ethereal matters like 'the way' or 'the good' or 'the path'. And we tend to think it is something for sages, gurus, rabbis, or scholars … It was the particular and concrete issue in what to do in a *particular* circumstance; … It depended on our ability to perceive the situation, to have the *appropriate* feelings or desire about it, to *deliberate* about what was appropriate in the circumstances, and to act. (Schwartz & Sharpe, 2010, p. 5)

The wise one embraces oneness
and becomes a model for the world.
Not self-centred, she is enlightened.
Not self-righteous, she is a shining example.
Not self-glorifying, she accomplishes
glorious things.
Not boastful, she groups large inside.
She alone does not compete.
And so the world can never overcome her.
The wise one is always there to help others
so that no-one is forsaken
She is always there to see things
so that nothing is lost.
This is called being clothed in light.
(Lao Tzu, in Dunn, 1997, n.p.)

Ideas of Wisdom	
Robinson	*Three historical definitions* *Greek*: an intellectual, moral, practical life; a life lived in conformity with truth, beauty. *Christian*: a life lived in pursuit of divine, absolute truth. *Contemporary*: a scientific understanding of laws governing matter in motion.
Csikszentmihalyi and Rathunde	An evolutionary hermeneutical approach to the study of wisdom suggests that wisdom is a *holistical cognitive process*, a virtue of compelling guide for action, and a good, desirable state of being.
Labouvie-Vief	A smooth and balanced dialogue between two sets of attributes; outer, objective, logical forms of processing (*logos*) and inner, subjective, organismic forms (*mythos*).
Baltes and Smith	Wisdom is *expertise* in the domain of *fundamental life pragmatics*, such as, life planning or life review. It requires a rich factual knowledge about life matters, rich procedural contexts and values or priorities, and knowledge about the unpredictability of life.
Chandler and Holliday	Contemporary philosophy of science limits conceptualization of wisdom to a technologic type of knowing. A more accurate description of wisdom may need *well-defined, multidimensional, prototypically organized contemporary descriptors*. It involves recovering age-old types of knowledge that have been forgotten.
Sternberg	Wisdom is a *metacognitive style* plus sagacity, knowing that one does not know everything, seeking the truth to the extent that it is knowable.
Orwoll and Perlmutter	A personologic study of wisdom suggests that wisdom is a multidimensional balance of *integration of cognition* with *affect*, affiliation and social concerns. An advanced development of personality together with cognitive skills is the essence of wisdom.
Meacham	Wisdom is an *awareness of the fallibility of knowing* and is a striving for a balance between knowing and doubting. Age is explicitly not a component of wisdom; in fact, one may lose it with age. Age is associated with change in wisdom, from simple to profound manifestation.

(*cont.*)

Ideas of Wisdom	
Kitchener and Brenner	Wisdom is an intellectual ability to be aware of the limitations of knowing and how it impacts solving ill-defined problems and making judgements, characteristics of *reflective judgement.*
Arlin	Wisdom is closely associated with *problem-finding ability,* a fundamental cognitive process of reflection and judgement.
Pascual-Leone	Wisdom is a *mode of symbolic processing* by a highly developed will. It is a dialectical integration of aspects of the personality, including affect, will, cognition, and the life experiences.
Kramer	Wisdom is the organismic intration of relativistic and dialectical modes of thinking, affect, and reflection; *a perspective of reality* developed with interrelationships.
Birren and Fisher	Wisdom is the integration of the *affective, conative and cognitive aspect* of human abilities in response to life's tasks and projects. Wisdom is a balance between the opposing valences of intense emotions and detachment, active and inaction, and knowledge and doubts. It tends to increase with experience and therefore age but is not exclusively found in old age.

References

Benedict, G. (Ed.). (2010). *Sacred wisdom, Chinese wisdom: The way of perfect harmony.* Watkins Publishing.

Bourgeault, C. (2003). *The wisdom way of knowing: Reclaiming an ancient tradition to awaken the heart.* Jossey-Bass.

Davey, N. (2006). *Unquiet understanding: Gadamer's philosophical hermeneutics.* State University of New York Press.

Dunn, P. (1997). *Tribal wisdom.* Axium Publishing.

Exley, H. (1999). *Wisdom for the new millennium.* Exley Publications.

Schwartz, B., & Sharpe, K. (2010). *Practical wisdom: The right way to do the right thing.* Riverhead Books.

Sternberg, R. J. (1990). *Wisdom: Its nature, origins, and development.* Cambridge University Press.

Zuckerman, A. (2009). *Wisdom: Peace.* Harry N. Abrams.

CHAPTER 6

Restoring the Balance

Wisdom and the Spirit of the Age

John Wattis, Melanie Rogers, Stephen Curran and Gulnar Ali

Abstract

Facing multiple challenges, from coronavirus to climate degradation, we need to re-examine where we are now and ask how individuals, organisations and society can move forward to a better future. Attention to issues, such as 'spirit' and 'spirituality', is a vital part of this movement. Based on a model developed to encourage relational aspects of health care practice, we argue that the complexity of contemporary issues requires a holistic approach incorporating three different angles: organisational culture, personal development and specific spiritual competencies. We explore how our culture is out of balance and suggest ways to build a better future.

Keywords

spirit – spirituality – wisdom – restoring balance

1 Shaping the Future

During the Covid-19 pandemic one of the authors saw a child's painting in the window of a house in England. The picture of a rainbow and the earth was accompanied by praise for UK National Health Service workers, telling them 'you are out of this world'. Faced by the pandemic, inequality, racism, climate change and numerous other issues, our thinking needs to be 'out of this world'. We need to challenge the dominant unbalanced worldview of our time, which is pushing the world towards disaster. We need to shape the future and repair the great post-enlightenment 'divorce' between 'objective' reductionist science and the subjective richness of lived experience (Wattis et al., 2019). In healthcare, we have found the terms 'spiritual' and 'spiritually competent practice' (Wattis et al., 2017) helpful in seeking to restore the balance between technical excellence and compassionate kindness. Spirituality is not esoteric but

 | DOI: 10.1163/9789004505544_008

extremely practical in helping movement from the predominant worldview to something more balanced.

2 What Do We Mean by Spirituality?

2.1 *Brief History of the Word Spirituality*

The word 'spirituality' first came into the English language from 17th century French denoting direct knowledge of the divine or supernatural (McGrath, 2011). It derives from the Latin spiritus which serves as the root for words such as inspire (used both literally and metaphorically) conspire and respiration. The meaning of spirituality has gradually migrated so that it (and the related words spirit and spiritual) are used both inside and outside of religious understanding. While it is a 'slippery' concept (Swinton & Pattison, 2010) and hard to define, the issues of meaning, purpose, hope, values, and connectedness with other people (and perhaps 'the transcendent') are at the core of spirituality.

2.2 *Metaphorical and Experiential Senses of Spirit*

When we talk about the 'spirit of the age' (German *zeitgeist*) or the 'spirit of an organisation' or a 'spirit of co-operation' we are using the word metaphorically. We are not speaking of something physical that we can measure but of something that nonetheless has a reality that, through the metaphor, can be grasped (and even 'assessed') by human reason. When we talk about our own 'spiritual experience' or the 'spirit' of a person, some would say that we are still using language metaphorically. Others would argue that we are speaking of an experience or reality that cannot be limited to metaphor but is a description of 'lived experience'. People will argue about how our experience relates to (ontological) reality depending upon their theory of knowledge (epistemology). For present purposes we will embrace a philosophical position of limited realism (King & Brooks, 2017). This combines a realist ontology with a constructivist epistemology. This holds that intangible phenomena such as culture, social forces and mental phenomena are as real as measurable physical phenomena. It also acknowledges that we cannot remove subjectivity from our understanding of that reality.

3 Spirituality and Philosophy in Healthcare and Life

Writing about the spiritual dimension in health care Swinton (2012) made the helpful distinction (based on neo-Kantian philosophy) between *nomothetic* and *idiographic* knowledge. Nomothetic (rule-based) knowledge is the kind that is studied by (empirical) science and is falsifiable, replicable and generalisable. It is usually advanced by testing hypotheses. Idiographic knowledge, on the other hand is based on experiential knowledge. No less valid and 'real' than nomothetic knowledge, it cannot be proved or disproved in the same way. Spiritual experience falls into this idiographic domain. Religion, one way in which people experience and express their spirituality, often involves practices such as attendance at services or daily prayer. These practices can be counted and are sometimes used as a surrogate for spirituality in research using quantitative techniques (Koenig et al., 2012). Qualitative methods can be used to study idiographic knowledge directly. Qualitative study may lead to the formulation of ideas that can be operationalised in a way that allows them to be reliably scored (and 'measured') by trained raters. Carl Rogers' (2003) client-centred therapy, with its principles of empathy, congruence and unconditional positive regard, has been verified by hypothesis-testing as well as qualitative research over the years (Kirschenbaum & Jourdan, 2005). There have been attempts to score spirituality through measures such as the spiritual wellbeing scale (Paloutzian et al., 2012). However, this measure involves indirect scoring rather than direct measurement and relies on two subscales (existential and religious) potentially confounding existentialism, religion and spirituality. For a fuller discussion see Wattis et al. (2017, pp. 6–7).

Another helpful distinction from philosophy comes from Martin Buber whose work *Ich und Du*, published in German in 1923, has been translated into English as *I and Thou* (Kaufmann, 1970/1996; Smith, 1937/2010). Buber distinguished I-It experiences, corresponding to nomothetic knowledge, from I-Thou relationships, which fall in the idiographic domain. He asserted that I-Thou relationships not only happen human to human but also between humans and other creatures and things, as when an artist looks at a landscape. This corresponds to Swinton's idea of how a human being can appreciate (relate to) a waterfall as a beautiful and inspiring whole (idiographic knowledge). The I-It approach would be to collect and analyse the water as H2O a (nomothetic knowledge). Buber asserted that we can also treat other people as depersonalised 'its' and this has increased as reductive science (and some strands of neoliberal thinking) have failed to recognise the importance of I-Thou relating. Carl Rogers had a public dialogue with Martin Buber (Anderson & Cissna, 1997). Tom Kitwood (1997), the originator of the concept of person-centred care for people with dementia, also acknowledged his debt to Buber's thinking. Kitwood (1997) summarised Buber's distinction between I-Thou and I-It nicely:

> Relating in the I-It mode implies coolness, detachment, instrumentality. It is a way of maintaining a safe distance, of avoiding risks; there is no danger of vulnerabilities being exposed. The I-Thou mode, on the other

> hand, implies going out towards the other; self-disclosure, spontaneity – a journey into uncharted territory. (p. 10)

Buber's work provides a link between transcendental, ethical and socio-psychological concepts of personhood.

One consequence of the 'Enlightenment' was a divorce between biomedical science, with its reductionist approach and the inter-personal aspects of clinical care. Though the biomedical approach has led to amazing progress in technical care, psychological, relational and social phenomena have sometimes fallen casualty to a focus on reductionist methods. This led Engel (1977, 1980, 1992) to propose an alternative *biopsychosocial model*. This is a systemic approach, allowing for the interaction between body, mind and the social dimension. It emphasises the importance of relationship (Borrell-Carrió et al., 2004) and potentially includes the spiritual aspects of care (Sulmasy, 2002). Person-centred and holistic care models also include spirituality as part of care. They all embrace *I-Thou* as well as *I-It* approaches.

4 The Concept of Spiritually Competent Practice and Living

We developed the concept of spiritually competent practice to deal with issues around the variety of definitions for spirituality in the clinical literature and the problem of differentiating spirituality from religion. We believe it is also a useful framework for understanding how to live better in other contexts. Spiritually competent practice was made explicit in the PhD of one of our former colleagues at the University of Huddersfield (Jones, 2016) in relationship to Occupational Therapy. Her work involved direct observation of occupational therapists in practice followed by discussion to establish how they enacted spirituality in practice. We widened her description of spiritually competent practice to include other disciplines in health care. We currently describe it as follows:

> Spiritually Competent Practice involves compassionate engagement with the whole person as a unique human being in ways which will help them find and sustain their sense of meaning and purpose, where appropriate connecting with a community where they experience a sense of wellbeing, addressing suffering and developing strategies to improve their quality of life. This includes the practitioner accepting a person's beliefs and values, whether they are religious in foundation or not, and practising with cultural competency. (Modified from Wattis et al., 2017, p. 3)

Spiritually competent practice requires three elements to be present in some degree:

- Spiritual Competencies (which can be taught)
- Personal Qualities of compassionate motivation and engagement (which can be developed) and
- Opportunity (provided by political/organisational practices).

We believe that (with some modification) these elements can be applied more widely to life, society and the wisdom of positive change. For this purpose, the specific elements are described more broadly and considered in the reverse order.

4.1 *Political and Organisational Culture* (*Opportunity*)

A culture that values wisdom as more than mere knowledge is important. Wisdom is more than a thinking tool, though it uses both convergent and divergent thinking. Before coming to a decision or judgement wisdom broadens the options and considers the issue(s) under consideration in their social, political and economic context (Wattis et al., 2019). Wisdom is compassionate and relates to others in a whole person (*I-Thou*) way, seeking balanced solutions to problems. Wisdom puts due emphasis on those things which cannot be measured but can be valued and evaluated qualitatively, like kindness, trust and compassion. Wisdom uses metrics in balance with other considerations, not allowing itself to be governed only by what can be measured. Wisdom in healthcare management gives doctors, nurses and other clinicians, time to attend to the need of patients for compassionate, person-centred, human interactions as well as for routine tasks. During the coronavirus epidemic, intensive care staff maintained human connection between patients and their relatives even when visiting was not allowed. Wisdom in the governance and management of life more generally gives room for interpersonal connections and does not just focus on metrics. Later, we will consider the current state of society and how a wisdom that includes spirituality might improve the organisation of society and the workplace, leading to a better future.

4.2 *Personal Qualities for Compassionate Engagement*

Most people enter the helping professions with a strong sense of vocation, compassion and commitment. An over-emphasis on the technical aspects of training and 'professional distance' can educate the compassion out of people. Good healthcare education values personal qualities like compassion and the ability to be 'present' with people. We suggest that the same principles can be applied to develop people for a more balanced, wiser future.

4.2.1 Ontological Development for Compassionate Engagement

Using multiple case-study methodology Ali (2017) investigated the teaching of spirituality in three English University Schools of Nursing. She found a lack of systematic approach and a hunger for learning and development in this area. She proposed a framework based on self-determination, ontological development, personal reflection and humanistic concern for others. Ontological approaches emphasise and facilitate authenticity and self-determination, presence, curiosity and commitment to care (compassionate engagement) (Ali & Snowden, 2019; Benner et al., 2010; Hartrick-Doane & Varcoe, 2015; Kang, 2003). Integrating transformative learning practices, facilitating reflexivity, coaching and mentorship in health care education, can promote ontological development (Ali & Snowden, 2019). Just as embracing authenticity and recognising self-care needs enables personal transformation in health care professionals (Newman, 1999) it also can enable personal transformation for others. The reflective model, developed through Ali's (2017) study, SOPHIE (Self-exploration through Ontological, Phenomenological, and Humanistic, Ideological, and Existential expressions) can be applied in other contexts and is briefly summarised here.

The diagram (Figure 6.1) is a symbolic expression of an intuitively expanding self. As a drop in the ocean produces waves, so the person addresses basic issues, radiating from exploration of self, a sense of being and encounter with

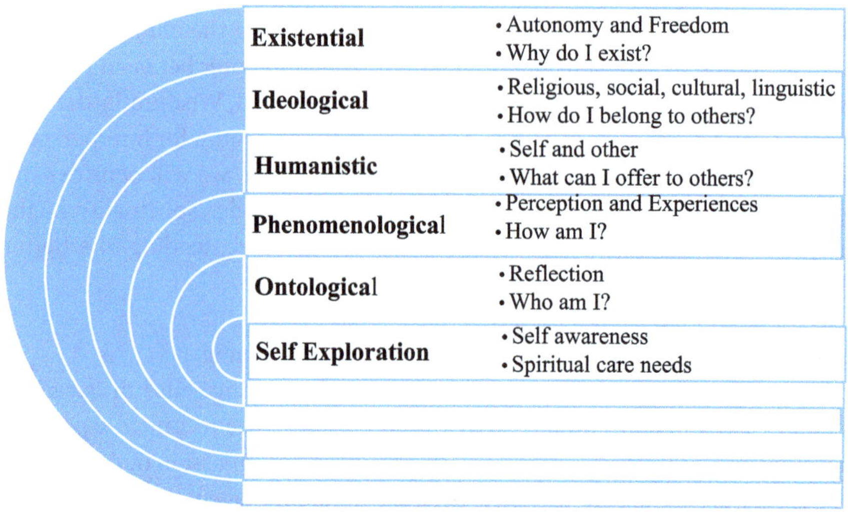

FIGURE 6.1 SOPHIE – A framework for approaching spiritual care needs (Ali & Snowden, 2019, p. 112, reprinted with permission)

the outside world to an understanding of the importance of relationships and finding personal meaning in life (Ali, 2017). This model provides a series of questions that can be applied in all areas of life.
- WHO am I?
- HOW am I in the world?
- WHAT can I offer others?
- HOW do I relate to others?
- WHY do I exist/WHAT is the meaning of my life?

Considering these questions, through self-reflection and creative learning, can help develop an authenticity and capacity for compassionate engagement (Ali & Snowden, 2019).

4.2.2 Personal Qualities of Availability and Vulnerability

The Availability and Vulnerability in healthcare framework was derived from the 'rule' of the (Celtic Christian) Northumbria community (Northumbria Community, 2020). The two key principles of availability and vulnerability were found to be useful in Rogers' own work as an Advanced Nurse Practitioner. Using hermeneutic phenomenology, she studied other Advanced Nurse Practitioners' approaches to spirituality (Rogers, 2016). This involved interviews with practitioners, exploring their own experiences of spirituality in practice. Participants were then given details of the Northumbria Community's rule. A second interview, conducted around eighteen months later, intentionally explored the utility of ideas of availability and vulnerability in understanding the practitioner's experiences. A secularised version of the concepts of Availability and Vulnerability was found to be useful in operationalising spiritual care in Advanced Nursing Practice. Below we have expressed these principles for more general application.

4.2.3 Availability to Self, Others and the Community

Availability to self, calls for self-acceptance and reflection on the spiritual dimension of the meaning and purpose in one's own life. Availability to others involves being fully 'present' (*I-Thou*) with people we meet, offering time, acceptance and understanding. Availability to community involves being open to the needs of the wider society and taking action, within our sphere of influence, to help meet those needs.

4.2.4 Vulnerability to Self, Others and the Community

Vulnerability to self means being willing to accept that being genuinely available to people exposes our vulnerability. This includes acknowledging we can never 'know it all' and allows a more authentic relationship to develop. It involves embracing accountability, engaging in reflection alone and with others, accepting constructive criticism, sharing uncertainty in an open, honest and transparent way, and acknowledging mistakes and limitations. Vulnerability to the community means willingness to stand up for people in need, questioning authority on their behalf (Rogers, 2016; Rogers & Wattis, 2020).

Availability is the easier of the two concepts to understand and embrace. Offering time, care and presence (*I-Thou*) to those in need is a natural human response. Vulnerability is an inevitable part of Buber's *I-Thou* relating. Social Scientist and researcher Brené Brown has written and spoken extensively about vulnerability. In 2011 she gave a TED talk (Brown, 2011) on vulnerability, which went viral. Her message has resonated globally with many people disillusioned with individualism. Brown (2010) suggested that many people feel spiritually or emotionally empty. She challenged people to "be seen" authentically, accepting the risk and uncertainty associated with this. She recognised that vulnerability is the birthplace of joy, love and gratitude and being vulnerable enables true connection, which is important to wellbeing. Vulnerability is seen not as weak, but as courageous. Human to human connection is present when we are willing to be available to ourselves and others and when we engage with others with all our vulnerabilities.

The concepts of availability and vulnerability echo the theological virtue of love found in the Hebrew Bible חֶסֶד (*chesed*), *and New Testament* Greek ἀγάπη (*agápē*, Latin caritas) which suggest that love and caring compassion be offered to all. Within the concept of caritas, used in nursing literature, being present is paramount (Lindström et al., 2014). Alvsvåg (2014) suggested that caritas be offered with discernment which is moral, practical and professional. This discernment necessitates emotional involvement, an aspect of vulnerability (Martinsen, 2006). Templeton (1999) emphasised that concepts analogous to *agápē* can be found in Judaism, Islam, Hinduism, Buddhism, Taoism, Confucianism and Native American spirituality. The Values in Action organisation, which adopts a broadly humanistic position, also has a cluster of character strengths (Values in Action Institute on Character [VIA], 2020) called:

> *Strengths of HUMANITY:* centred around relationships to others which cover the same area of steadfast loving kindness as *chesed* and *agápē*,
> 1. The capacity to love and receive love
> 2. Kindness
> 3. Social intelligence.

This suggests there is universality about the importance of these ideas.

4.2.5 Spiritual Competencies

Spiritual competencies tend to have elements that are specific to different occupations and contexts. Based on general spiritual competencies in healthcare (Wattis et al., 2017), we suggest that the three broad areas below can be used in summarising spiritual competencies in all areas of life:

- Managing and organising to enable and enhance consideration of spiritual issues.
- Spiritual self-awareness
- Communication and actions concerning spiritual matters

Managing for Consideration of Spiritual Issues

In positions with managerial responsibility, do we strive to create an environment in which personal and spiritual issues are taken seriously or do we just focus on the financial bottom line? Do we think about the meaning and purpose of what we are doing, or do we let the bottom line and performance indicators become a rod with which to beat others (and ourselves), leading to a bullying culture? At the level of our peers, are we open to these issues? If we are brave enough, do we try to improve the workplace and social environments from the 'bottom up'?

Spiritual Self-Awareness

Spiritual self-awareness develops from reflecting, perhaps using Ali and Snowden's (2019) questions above, on what gives our own lives meaning, purpose and hope; where our own values come from; and how we connect with others (and perhaps 'the transcendent' or 'God'). Reflective practice is an important part of clinical professional and other disciplines; but reflection is also important more generally in self-understanding and in developing relationships and interests in the family and the wider world. The practice of Mindfulness, borrowed from Buddhist practice supports this as do meditation and contemplation and other religious and secular practices

Communication about and Acting on Spiritual Matters

This concerns how our spiritual self-awareness influences our communication with and behaviour towards other people in all aspects of our life. Are we open to other people's concerns about the core issues of spirituality? Do we listen sensitively and empathetically to people who express those concerns? Are we genuine in our responses and compassionate in our actions? Do we relate to them as fellow human beings (*I-Thou*) regardless of race, gender, etc. or do we 'other' them and treat them like (*I-It*) objects?

5 Developing a Wiser Future – Where Are We Now?

5.1 *Worldviews*

The concept of worldview is close to what is expressed by *zeitgeist* or 'the spirit of the age'. Worldviews relate to the presuppositions, often unconscious, which form the substrate of a given culture or society and they relate to matters of ultimate concern. Worldviews have four characteristics. Firstly, they have a series of assumptions about how the world *is*, expressed through narrative stories. Secondly, they answer basic questions about human existence such as who are we, where are we, what is wrong and what is the way to move forward? Thirdly, the stories are expressed symbolically through events and artefacts. Finally, the worldview, its associated narratives, questions and symbols lead to a way of being and behaving in the world (Wright, 1992). The radical theologian Walter Wink (2000) suggested that there are only a handful of religious/spiritual worldviews. Two are of most interest to us here: the 'materialist' worldview, which admits of no reality that cannot be reduced to purely material terms and an 'integral' worldview, which sees everything as having an outer material aspect and an inner spiritual aspect. There are two variants of the integral worldview, one in which the spiritual and material are intimately linked with nothing beyond them, and one in which they sit within a transcendent reality (Wattis et al., 2017) identified by some as divine. In the West today, secular materialism and neoliberalism are dominant.

5.2 *Neoliberalism*

In the West, five hundred years ago, the dominant worldview was based on the Christian religion with its questions about morality, forgiveness, and life after death, and its symbols including cathedrals, churches and feast days based on the Christian calendar. The neoliberal worldview's narrative can be summed up (perhaps rather pejoratively) by questions about how to get money and persuade other people to buy what we want to sell (products or labour). Its symbols include the January sales, 'Black Friday', regular reports on the FTSE100 and Dow Jones index, celebrity culture, shopping malls and massive buildings in the financial centres of London, New York and elsewhere. Its way of being is through market competition resulting in success or failure for individuals and organisations. This involves commercial advertising and political 'spin' to encourage consumption and compliance.

The term neoliberalism was first used at a conference in Paris in 1938 (Monbiot, 2016). The presupposition of neoliberalism is that competition and the 'market' lead to the optimum outcomes for humanity, by rewarding efficiency and punishing inefficiency, delivering benefits that, it is claimed, could never be delivered by state level planning and regulation. Neoliberalism was founded on ideas of individual consumers exercising choice through buying and selling. It believed that the market should be free, as far as possible, from 'unnecessary' constraints. Theories of natural selection in evolution were extended to a social level. It gathered strength from the development in the 1930s and 1940s of national income accounting in the form of GDP (Gross Domestic Product) and GDP *per capita* (Coclanis, 2019).

Neoliberal thinking developed through the mid-period of the 20th century but did not gain political ascendancy till the late 1970s with Margaret Thatcher in the UK followed by Ronald Reagan in the USA. It has indeed delivered prosperity to some people in some countries; but there is a downside. Its antipathy to regulation by the state has led to exploitation of workers and the environment. Another unintended consequence of this worldview has been the growth in financial inequality so that currently the world's eight wealthiest people own the same wealth as the 3.6 billion making up the poorest half of humanity (Hardoon, 2017). Although neoliberals talk of wealth being 'created' by the wealthy and 'trickling down' to benefit those less well off, others think that those at the top of the wealth 'pyramid' extract wealth from those lower down. Even more importantly, the exploitation of our planet and consequent global warming are near the point of irreversible damage to the future of humanity. Campaigner and wildlife expert, Sir David Attenborough (Selby, 2020) warned world leaders that we are facing our 'last chance' of averting catastrophe.

5.3 *How Did We Get Here? The Making of the Modern World*

Of the many influences that have shaped the modern world, five stand out as especially influential:

- The imperial age and persistent related racism
- The gradual and incomplete establishment of democracy based on market fundamentalism rather than religious values.
- The Enlightenment and the divorce of reductionist science from other branches of reason
- Industrialisation and the dehumanisation of production
- Globalisation and the power of multinational corporations

Beginning in the 16th and 17th centuries and lasting into the 19th and mid twentieth century, the age of colonisation and imperialism is largely over, though some would argue that economic imperialism still exists with big international corporations exerting more power than governments. Modern democracy began to develop with the overthrow of European monarchies in 17th and 18th century but is still far from perfect with 'first past the post' systems, dependence on high financial stakes and susceptibility to media manipulation. The 'Enlightenment', also beginning in the 17th century, questioned traditional authority and advocated rational thinking as the way forward for humanity. Before this, natural philosophy, the precursor of modern science, was part of the wider discipline of philosophy; but the humanities, ethics and other aspects of philosophy became 'divorced' from the approach of reductionist science. However, ethics (moral principles that govern conduct and behaviour) remained an important factor for the healthcare and other professions.

The 'Industrial Revolution' followed, in the eighteenth century, and led to a dehumanisation of the methods of production, remarked upon by proto-socialist John Ruskin in his 1862 collection of essays *Unto this Last* (Ruskin, 1985). Frederick Taylor in 1911 (cited in Muller, 2018) coined the term 'scientific management'. This aimed to improve industrial efficiency by careful study and standardisation of workforce behaviour, typified by work study methods and the production lines introduced on a large scale by Henry Ford at the beginning of the 20th Century.

Political developments, such as neoliberalism, also relied on what can be counted (especially money). Muller (2018) discussed how, through *principal-agent* theory, these have led to a suspicion that those employed in institutions cannot be trusted and need their activity to be monitored, using *performance indicators*, with financial incentives for achieving or exceeding 'targets'. *Performance indicators* were introduced into many fields such as education and healthcare in the late 20th century often with disbenefits that outweighed the benefits (Muller, 2018). The use of *external* motivation is symptomatic of a loss of trust in the workforce's *intrinsic* motivation to do a good job. This is often accompanied by a tendency to treat the workforce as objects rather than as fellow human beings (*I-It* rather than *I-Thou*). The mid-20th century Toyota Production System – management by means rather than targets – attempted to put this right. It emphasised continuous improvement and *respect for all the people in the workforce,* maximising their ability to contribute to outcome rather than 'driving' them to predetermined targets (Johnson & Brom, 2008).

5.4 *Whatever Happened to Morality and Ethics?*

Adam Smith (1999), in his *The Wealth of Nations* first published in 1776, argued for the division of labour and the 'invisible hand' of the market but also warned that there could be negative as well as positive consequences. His earlier work *The Theory of Moral Sentiments* first published in 1759 (Smith, 2010) argued that conscience developed from social relationships through a process of mutual sympathy. Writing over two centuries later, a prominent neoliberal economist,

Roy Griffiths, adviser to Prime Minister Margaret Thatcher, challenged both secular socialism and capitalism and emphasised the importance of mediating structures, such as "the family, the school, the workplace, the village, the neighbourhood, the trade union, the professional organisation, the church" (Griffiths, 1982, p. 11) in mediating between the private life of the individual and the state *and in transmitting values*. His solution was specifically Christian and capitalist; but his contention that the market and Marxist socialism could not *of themselves* produce a moral or ethical framework to produce a just society was sound. Like many right-wing thinkers, he seems to have been unaware of the Christian ethical socialism behind much of the British Labour movement. Others have looked more specifically at the environmental damage done by our present way of living and argued that religions which believe in a creator God can provide a moral imperative to treat 'creation' better (Shah-Kazemi, 2011; Rohr, 2019). A well-argued secular philosophical analysis (Goff, 2019) of the phenomenon of consciousness develops the theory of pan-psychism. Goff argues that this means that we need not live exclusively in the human realm but, recognising our oneness with nature, we can find a place in the universe and create a better world, providing a (debatably) non-religious framework for the same conclusion.

5.5 *Coronavirus and Change*

Mair (2020) argues that the dominant idea of the current neoliberal system is that exchange value is equivalent to use value and markets are the way to match productive capacity and use value. He argues that the coronavirus epidemic has demonstrated the flaws in this system, for example by highlighting that it undervalues many of the most critical societal services such as health and social care. These are labour intensive and cannot easily increase productivity through mechanisation and information technology. At the same time many of these critical jobs are not highly valued in monetary terms by society as compared, for example, to jobs in advertising and the financial sector. The coronavirus epidemic has highlighted the immediate importance of members of society who provide health, social and other essential services. It has forced governments to respond to the crisis in a way that highlights this issue. For example, Spain has nationalised private hospitals and the UK and other countries have provided income support for workers. Government has also assumed at least temporary control over other essential activities. So, are we right to assume that the 'neoliberal consensus' of forty or fifty years has been challenged by this emergency? It has certainly highlighted areas where balance is lacking and a change in the 'spirit of the age' is needed to address this.

5.6 *Areas Where Balance Is Lacking in Our Current Society*

The tremendous success of analytic, reductive scientific understanding has led to a relative under-emphasis on the more holistic approach that wisdom requires. Nomothetic (rule-following) knowledge has been elevated over idiographic (experiential) knowledge. Non-material aspects of life including hope, meaning, purpose and values, together with the human sense of interconnectedness with others (and possibly the transcendent), have been crowded out by an obsession with what is measurable. Lack of attention to values has led to attitudes in which social and economic justice and compassion have been relegated to a secondary status. Changes in production methods in industry have led, in some cases, to workers being seen as mere instruments who need to be 'driven', like cattle rather than people who, themselves, have something to contribute to improving the quality of products. The Toyota production system, mentioned earlier, has restored some human value to the workers. In clinical work, front line workers have had to work hard to maintain the importance of person-to-person contact as part of the healing process. The Virginia Mason system (Kenney, 2010) has recognised the value of frontline clinicians and patients themselves in designing and improving services.

Neoliberalism has become the dominant political force, occupying the place that religion had previously filled in some cultures. Its emphasis on metrics like GDP and the commercial 'bottom line' has sometimes led to moral and other failures. As neoliberalism has grown, so also has exploitation of workers through 'zero-hours contracts', pseudo-self-employment and the so-called 'gig economy'. Exploitation of the planet has led to a point where climate breakdown is imminent. Exploitation of the world financial system arguably led to the global financial collapse of 2008.

6 Restoring the Balance – Spiritually Competent Living

Whether we argue from a religious or a secular viewpoint, the 'spirit' of the current age needs to change. We need to value each other through *I-Thou* relating and to value the world of which we are a part. The climate emergency urgently demands action, which politicians have so far failed to deliver. Looked at from a political and organisational point of view, at a national and international level, we need to embrace issues like social justice, climate justice and economic justice. We need to educate people of all ages to value the non-reducible aspects of human experience and to develop values that can be used to mitigate political excesses. In the past these values would have come from traditional religions and for many people they still do; but in a multicultural society we need shared values that embrace as many people in society as possible. To look at this in more detail we will use the following three categories described earlier.

6.1 *Political and Organisational*

Mair (2020), a research fellow in ecological economics, has proposed four possible (political) futures. On one axis he places what we value. "Do we use our resources to maximise exchanges and money or do we use them to maximise life?" (n.p.). His use of 'life' in this context perhaps echoes Ruskin's conclusion in 1862 that "There is no wealth but life" (Ruskin, 1985, p. 222). On the other axis Mair placed centralised versus decentralised styles of governance. This resulted in four possible combinations. The first he dubbed state capitalism, the current dominant global response, prioritising exchange value and centralised governance. The second was barbarism with a decentralised response prioritising exchange value but not extending protection of life to those locked out of markets by illness or loss of paid work. The third resulted from measures, which put protection of life, for its own sake, before the protection of exchange value, and embodied centralised governance. This he called state socialism and the final, combining protection of life with decentralisation, he called mutual aid. He discussed all these possibilities and their possible consequences in more detail and this brief summary does not do justice to all his caveats.

An even more fundamental issue (regardless of the particularities of politics) is developing a society based more upon treating all people as valued individuals and urgently recognising our oneness with and dependence upon nature. This would be consonant with spiritual values as expressed in Buber's vital distinction between *I-Thou* and *I-It* and with secular and religious understanding of our oneness with nature/creation. Principles such as respect for all stakeholders in society and methods for enabling this at a political level could be developed following the lead of the Toyota Production System in manufacturing and the Virginia Mason Institute's practices in health care.

6.2 *Personal Qualities That Can Be Developed*

This is not just a 'tick-box' exercise. Plato listed four 'cardinal' virtues or character strengths; *Wisdom, Courage, Temperance* and *Justice.* Christian, Islamic and other religious thinking also makes *love* central. Humanistic thinking agrees about the need for 'virtues', typified by the Values in Action list of twenty-four character strengths, derived from a study of a wide range of cultures and philosophical and religious thinking (VIA, 2020). These have been clustered into groups largely corresponding to Plato's *Wisdom, Courage, Temperance* and *Justice.* Two further clusters have been identified: *Humanity,* representing love, kindness and social intelligence and *Transcendence,* representing appreciation of excellence and beauty, gratitude, hope, humour and spirituality. We argue that whilst all the character strengths are important, it is those focused around loving kindness and compassion in our (*I-Thou*) relationship to others and to the world we live in that are foundational. We develop them through connecting to others, creative activities and reflection, using frameworks like those discussed above.

6.3 *Spiritual Competencies*

Managing to enable and enhance consideration of spiritual issues has largely been dealt with in the section on political and organisational governance and culture above. Creating an organisational culture in which *I-Thou* relating and mutual respect flourish, improves the quality of life for all. This is also true of family and other relationships outside of work. This is the most rewarding aspect of attention to spirituality. Creating an organisational culture, which respects our oneness with nature and the need to act urgently to preserve the environment that supports us is equally important.

Spiritual self-awareness depends on maintaining the habit of reflection. Socrates is quoted as saying the "the unexamined life is not worth living". Perhaps this competency aspect of spirituality is about regularly setting aside time for examination of our own lives, reflecting on where we find meaning, purpose and hope, where our own values come from and how we connect with others and the world around us (perhaps including 'the transcendent' or God).

Communication about and acting on spiritual matters also needs to be practised. Too often these are squeezed out of modern discourse by time pressures, data collection and the concerns of a consumer society. We need to educate people to be much more comfortable talking about the things that really matter and give our lives meaning. We also need to de-emphasise the tendency to manage from the top down by imposing targets rather than by encouraging and trusting people's intrinsic motivation to do well.

7 Conclusion

In this chapter we have argued that spirituality, properly understood, is distinct from religion (though, for many of us, the two overlap). Spirituality can be understood as relating to subjective aspects of life, expressed through hope, meaning, purpose and values. The current materialistic neoliberal 'spirit of the age' could lead to disaster by treating people and the planet as objects to be exploited. We have asserted the need to find a new worldview, based in *I-Thou* relating and the importance of recognising that our humanity is part of nature, to rescue us from this disaster. Put bluntly the choice is between competitive consumerism and compassionate co-operation that respects the planet we live on. This requires us to de-emphasise materialism and develop a wiser more spiritually reflective way of dealing with the world and each other. Then we may all live to see a better future.

References

Ali, G. (2017). *Multiple case studies exploring integration of spirituality in undergraduate nursing education in England* [Unpublished doctoral dissertation]. University of Huddersfield. http://eprints.hud.ac.uk/id/eprint/34129/

Ali, G., & Snowden, M. (2019). SOPHIE (Self-Exploration through Ontological, Phenomenological, Humanistic, Ideological and Existential Expressions): A mentoring framework. In M. Snowden & J. Halsall (Eds.), *Mentorship, leadership, and research: International perspectives on social policy, administration, and practice* (pp. 107–116). Springer AG.

Alvsvåg, H. (2014). Philosophy of caring. In M. R. Alligood (Ed.), *Nursing theorists and their work* (8th ed., pp. 38–42). Elsevier.

Anderson, R., & Cissna, K. N. (1997). *The Martin Buber-Carl Rogers dialogue: A new transcript with commentary*. State University of New York Press.

Benner, P., Sutphen, M., Leonard, V., & Day, L. (2010). *Educating nurses: A call for radical transformation*. Jossey-Bass/Carnegie Foundation for the Advancement of Teaching.

Borrell-Carrió, F., Suchman, A. L., & Epstein, R. M. (2004). The biopsychosocial model 25 years later: Principles, practice, and scientific inquiry. *Annals of Family Medicine, 2*(6), 576–582.

Brown, B. (2010). *The gifts of imperfection*. Hazelden.

Brown, B. (2011, January 4). *The power of vulnerability* [Video]. YouTube. https://www.youtube.com/watch?v=iCvmsMzlF7o

Coclanis, P. A. (2019, June 10). Why we urgently need a real alternative to GDP as an economic measure. *NewStatesman*. https://www.newstatesman.com/politics/economy/2019/06/why-we-urgently-need-real-alternative-gdp-economic-measure

Engel, G. L. (1977). The need for a new medical model: A challenge for biomedicine. *Science, 196*(4286), 129–136.

Engel, G. L. (1980). The clinical application of the biopsychosocial model. *American Journal of Psychiatry, 137*(5), 535–544.

Engel, G. L. (1992). How much longer must medicine's science be bound by a seventeenth century worldview? *Psychotherapy and Psychosomatics, 57*(1–2), 3–16.

Goff, P. (2019). *Galileo's error: Foundations for a new science of consciousness*. Rider.

Griffiths, B. (1982). *Morality and the marketplace*. Hodder and Stoughton.

Hardoon, D. (2017). *An economy for the 99%*. Oxfam International. https://www.oxfam.org/en/research/economy-99

Hartrick-Doane, G., & Varcoe, C. (2015). *How to nurse: Relational inquiry with individuals and families in shifting contexts*. Lippincott Williams and Wilkins.

Johnson, H. T., & Brom, A. (2008). *Profit beyond measure*. Nicholas Brealey.

Jones, J. E. (2016). *A qualitative study exploring how occupational therapists embed spirituality into their practice* [Unpublished doctoral dissertation]. University of Huddersfield. http://eprints.hud.ac.uk/id/eprint/27857/

Kang, C. (2003). A psycho spiritual integration frame of reference for occupational therapy. Part 1: Conceptual foundations. *Australian Journal of Occupational Therapy, 50*(2), 92–103.

Kaufmann, W. (1996). *I and thou* (M. Buber, Trans.). Simon and Schuster (Touchstone edition). (Original work published 1970)

Kenney, C. (2010). *Transforming health care: Virginia Mason Medical Center's pursuit of the perfect patient experience*. CRC Press.

King, N., & Brooks, J. M. (2017). *Template analysis*. Sage.

Kirschenbaum, H., & Jourdan, A. (2005). The current status of Carl Rogers and the person-centered approach. *Psychotherapy: Theory, Research, Practice, Training, 42*(1), 37–51.

Kitwood, T. (1997). *Dementia reconsidered: The person comes first*. Open University Press.

Koenig, H., King, D., & Carson, V. (2012). *Handbook of religion and health*. Oxford University Press.

Lindström, U., Lindholm Nyström, L., & Zetterlund, J. (2014). Theory of caritative caring. In M. R. Alligood (Ed.), *Nursing theorists and their work* (8 ed., pp. 171–201). Elsevier.

Mair, P. (2020, March 30). What will the world be like after coronavirus? Four possible futures. *The Conversation*. https://theconversation.com/what-will-the-world-be-like-after-coronavirus-four-possible-futures-134085

Martinsen, K. (2006). *Care and vulnerability*. Akribe.

McGrath, A. E. (2011). *Christian theology: An introduction* (5th ed., pp. 108–109). Wiley-Blackwell.

Monbiot, G. (2016, April 15). Neoliberalism: The ideology at the root of all our problems. *The Guardian*. https://www.theguardian.com/books/2016/apr/15/neoliberalism-ideology-problem-george-monbiot

Muller, J. Z. (2018). *The tyranny of metrics*. Princeton University Press.

Newman, M. A. (1999). *Health as expanding consciousness* (2nd ed.). National League for Nursing Press.

Northumbria Community. (2020). *Our rule of life*. https://www.northumbriacommunity.org/who-we-are/our-rule-of-life/

Paloutzian, R. F., Bufford, R. K., & Wildman, A. J. (2012). Spiritual well-being scale: Mental and physical health relationships. In M. C. Cobb, C. M. Puchalski, & B. Rumbold (Eds.), *Oxford textbook of spirituality in healthcare* (pp. 353–358). Oxford University Press.

Rogers, C. (2003). *Client-centred therapy: Its current practice, application and theory.* Constable and Robinson.

Rogers, M. (2016). *Spiritual dimensions of advanced nurse practitioner consultations in primary care through the lens of availability and vulnerability: A hermeneutic enquiry* [Unpublished doctoral dissertation]. University of Huddersfield.

Rogers, M., & Wattis, J. (2020). Understanding the role of spirituality in providing person-centred care. *Nursing Standard, 35*(9), 25–30.

Rohr, R. (2019). *The universal Christ.* SPCK.

Ruskin, J. (1985). *Unto this last and other writings.* Penguin Classics.

Selby, J. (2020, April 19). Sir David Attenborough warns world leaders they have a 'last chance' to save the planet and stop climate change. *i News.* https://inews.co.uk/news/sir-david-attenborough-warns-world-leaders-save-planet-stop-climate-change-419886

Shah-Kazemi, R. (2011). Seeing God everywhere: Quranic perspectives on the sanctity of virgin nature. *Sacred Web: A Journal of Tradition and Modernity, 27,* 5–38.

Smith, A. (1999). *The wealth of nations.* Penguin Classics.

Smith, A. (2010). *The theory of moral sentiments.* Penguin Classics.

Smith, R. G. (2010). *I and thou* (M. Buber, Trans.). Bloomsbury Revelations. (Original work published 1937)

Sulmasy, D. P. (2002). A biopsychosocial-spiritual model for the care of patients at the end of life. *The Gerontologist, 42*(Suppl. 3), 24–33.

Swinton, J. (2012). Healthcare spirituality: A question of knowledge. In M. Cobb, C. Puchalski, & B. Rumbold (Eds.), *Oxford textbook of spirituality in healthcare* (pp. 99–104). Oxford University Press.

Swinton, J., & Pattison, S. (2010). Moving beyond clarity: Towards a thin, vague and useful understanding of spirituality in nursing practice. *Nursing Philosophy, 11*(4), 226–237.

Templeton, J. (1999). *Agape love: A tradition found in eight world religions.* Templeton Foundation Press.

Values in Action Institute on Character [VIA]. (2020). *Character strengths.* https://www.viacharacter.org/character-strengths

Wattis, J., Curran, S., & Rogers, M. (2017). *Spiritually competent practice in health care.* CRC Press.

Wattis, J., Rogers, M., Ali, G., & Curran, S. (2019). Bringing spirituality and wisdom into practice. In J. Higgs (Ed.), *Practice wisdom: Values and interpretations* (pp. 155–170). Brill Sense.

Wink, W. (2000). *The powers that be*. Bantam Doubleday Dell.
Wright, N. T. (1992). *The New Testament and the people of God*. SPCK.

CHAPTER 7

Wisdom and Spirituality

Norman Habel

Abstract

As part of the book's exploration of wisdom and spirituality this chapter explores the conceptions and approaches adopted by the Wise (people) of the Ancient Near East who were the scientists of their time. In doing so it draws knowledge from their ways of thinking, discerning and enquiring to consider what might be wise practice for the modern world. Finally, it establishes alignment between Ancient Near Eastern wisdom and what may be considered wisdom and spirituality in the contemporary world.

Key words

the Wise – the Wisdom School – wisdom – spirituality

1 The Way of the Wise

This chapter investigates the dimensions of wisdom that were identified by the Wise (people) in the Wisdom School of the ancient Near East, with particular focus on the spirituality dimension. The ancient Near East, in the context of this chapter, includes Israel, Egypt, Babylon and nearby countries. The chapter begins by introducing the Wisdom School of these ancient Near Eastern lands and identifies the technical terms employed by the Wisdom scientists of this school in their research practice and critical analysis. The Wisdom School represents a community with a distinctive way of thinking and living.

At the outset, it needs to be recognised that the wise of the Wisdom School were equivalent to the scientists of the ancient world. As scientists, their goal was to discern Wisdom by direct observation and critical discernment, not by receiving a revelation from a divine being or by simply accepting the traditions of the past. As we shall discover, these scientists discerned dimensions of Wisdom that we would also identity as spiritual. The ancient Wisdom scientist discerned Wisdom in the realms of wonder, mystery and the primordial, embedded throughout the many phenomena of the cosmos.

 | DOI: 10.1163/9789004505544_009

The primary source of the analysis in this investigation is the Wisdom Literature of the Hebrew Bible, but more specifically three classic texts, namely:

- The Wisdom Magna Carta, a text describing the discernmentt of Wisdom in nature inserted as a Wisdom School text (Job 28) by the Wisdom narrator of the Book of Job.
- The Testimony of Wisdom, a text in which Wisdom, a primordial female presence, testifies to the essential role she played in the design and creation of the cosmos (Proverbs 8:22–31).
- The Challenge of the Wisdom Mentor, a text in which Job and the Wisdom student are challenged to answer a plethora of questions about how Wisdom functions in the eco-system of the cosmos (Job 38–39).

While two of these texts are found in the Book of Job, it needs to be recognised at the outset, that the sufferings of Job are not pivotal for this analysis. Rather, the Book of Job is the work of a brilliant Wisdom narrator who uses the story of Job as the background for constructing a bold superstructure in which Wisdom is the pivotal reality being analysed.

2 The Wisdom School

The Wisdom School refers to the thinking, techniques and traditions of a major body of citizens, known as 'the wise'. The wise were a discrete part of their community, distinct from the priests, prophets, royalty and other leading figures in society. There is evidence to suggest that in Egypt and Israel there were actual 'schools' of wise in locations like the royal court where they explored questions about how to pursue research, live wisely and give counsel to the leaders in society (Whybray, 1965).

In the analysis pursued in this investigation, I use the term 'Wisdom School' in its wider sense: referring to a Wisdom cosmology and modus operandi rather than to a specific school of royal scribes. The Wisdom School refers to an orientation that involves learning via critical observation and rational analysis, rather than revelation from a deity or messages from religious leaders. This school of thought included close observation of both the natural world and human behaviour. Wisdom thinking was akin to what today we would call 'scientific analysis': the wise were the 'scientists' of old, and the subject of their analysis was understood as both a spiritual mystery and a natural reality.

Von Rad (1972) argues that the wise were searching for the rule/laws/structures that govern and guide creation. Their research was indeed a search for the rational, the inbuilt laws in the various realms of creation. In the worldview of the wise, however, the rational was embedded in a universe of mystery and wonder, a cosmos saturated by the spiritual. The question that naturally arises, given our contemporary perspective on the sciences, is whether the understanding and observation of nature by the ancient wise scientists also incorporated what we would today call a 'spiritual dimension'.

3 The 'Scientific' Modus Operandi of the Wise

To appreciate the modus operandi of the wise in ancient Israel, especially their way of interpreting nature, I suggest we begin with the key technical terms used to describe the process of research and analysis in the Wisdom School.

a. 'observe' (*ra'a*)
Like good scientists, the wise are expected to 'discern' through 'observation' and critical analysis. The task is to 'observe' closely and discern the 'way': the determining innate characteristic of that phenomenon. The Wisdom to be learned does not necessarily come first and foremost from tradition or the teacher, but by direct observation and examination of the subject.

b. 'discern' (*bin*)
The verb 'discern' and the noun 'discernment' refer to the process of rational and critical analysis to ascertain the true essence of a subject or distinguish between the truth and falsity of a given reality. The aim of this act of discernment is to determine the 'way' (*derek*) and/or the 'place' (*maqom*) of a particular phenomenon of nature or society.

c. 'acquire' (*qana*)
To 'acquire' Wisdom is the mission and task of every student of Wisdom. In the traditional Wisdom community, acquiring empirical Wisdom was the primary goal. The wise, over the centuries, observed the behaviour of humans, nature and society, observations that led to an accumulation of acquired Wisdom known as proverbs. Acquiring Wisdom was also achieved by observing and analysing nature where Wisdom may be discerned as an innate force.

d. 'place' (*maqom*)
In the ordering of phenomena on Earth, in the thinking of the Wisdom School, everything has its 'place'. In The Wisdom Magna Carta (Job 28), the 'place' of things is made explicit. The rocks of Earth, for example, are the 'place' of sapphires. It is central to the role of a student of the Wisdom School to determine the locus or 'place' of a given phenomenon in the world of nature. The ultimate question posed by the Wisdom School is 'Where can Wisdom be found? Where is its 'place' in the cosmos?

e. 'way' (*derek*)
Just as the term 'place' has Wisdom significance, so too does the key term *derek* (way), which is usually translated as 'way'. In Wisdom contexts we hear about the 'way' of the eagle in the sky and the 'way' of a snake on a rock (Proverbs 30:18). Every living creature has its 'way' according to the school of Wisdom – a 'way' that is equivalent to a Wisdom compass embedded in a phenomenon of nature (Habel, 2014).

4 Four Dimensions of Wisdom

Wisdom promoted in the Wisdom School can be divided into four primary dimensions, each of which are examined in detail.

a. *Innate Wisdom*: a discrete lifeforce in all living creatures that determines their driving characteristics and a deep force programmed into the cosmos that governs the realms and laws of nature.
b. *Acquired Wisdom*: a life-giving knowledge acquired by scientific observation and critical analysis of tradition.
c. *Cosmic Wisdom*: a pervasive spiritual power and presence in the primordial and current eco-system of the cosmos.
d *Experienced Wisdom:* the deep mystery that manifests itself in the many phenomena of the universe arousing both Wisdom consciousness and spiritual awareness.

Each of these dimensions of Wisdom may prove to be relevant for those of us pursuing research into evolution, ecology, education and spirituality, if we move beyond simply accepting these Wisdom insights as relics of an ancient culture.

4.1 *Innate Wisdom*

There are two types of innate Wisdom, the first relating to Wisdom in living creatures, the second to Wisdom in realms of nature. These two definitions and the definitions that follow are refinements of definitions in *Discerning Wisdom in God's Creation* (Habel, 2015).

> Innate Wisdom is the lifeforce in all living creatures of the natural world, a compass that guides their driving characteristics and the distinctive roles of their existence. (p. 21)

In the Wisdom School, a person interested in becoming wise was expected to 'observe' nature and understand its 'ways' closely. Following this practice, the individual may not only learn lessons about life, but also about the phenomenon being observed, its 'way' or inner Wisdom. The *derek* or 'way' of a phenomenon is the innate Wisdom programmed into its very being so that it remains true to its essential nature.

4.1.1 The 'Way' of the Ant

The student of the Wisdom School is encouraged by wise mentors to watch the ant as an example and 'observe' its distinctive code of behaviour – the innate Wisdom found in ants – and so gain some personal Wisdom:

> Go to the ant, you lazybones!
> 'Observe' its 'way' and be wise!
> Without having any chief
> or officer or ruler,
> it prepares its food in summer,
> and gathers its sustenance in harvest. (Proverbs 6:6–8)

The Wisdom in an ant colony is, according to these ancient scientists, an inner capacity to function as a corporate body without any hierarchy, a mystery that modern scientists still find fascinating. Another dimension of ant Wisdom, according to these ancient scientists, is its instinctual/intellectual capacity to gather food in summer and store it for the winter when conditions for finding food are difficult. The Wisdom embedded in the ant enables it to anticipate a wise future and plan ahead, a Wisdom based on the evolution of its 'way'.

Celia Deane-Drummond (2006), in her discussion of natural wisdom in evolutionary biology, returns to the example of the ant and asks whether modern scientists are now better informed than ancient Wisdom scientists to distinguish the Wisdom innate in ants. Biological diversity still challenges scientists to explore the mystery of evolution involved in the process of creating the unique character of each living being. The Wisdom School would argue that each species has its own unique 'way', its innate Wisdom. From each species we can learn new dimensions of the Wisdom embedded in all life forms, dimensions that may help facilitate a wise future for them and for us.

The contemporary observer may examine the ant in its current form, a form, which exhibits how its current 'way' or innate Wisdom has evolved. Millions of years ago these creatures existed in an earlier form, each with its innate Wisdom, its drive to evolve and to be a discrete species. The innate Wisdom of the ant, therefore, may reflect a long history of the innate drive to become the precise living being it is now. In terms of the Wisdom School, innate Wisdom in living creatures can be considered tantamount to the innate drive of evolution in such beings.

While Wisdom scientists in books like Proverbs, explore a range of mysteries both in society and in nature, one Wisdom scientist claims he lacks the capacity to understand all the mysteries that surround him (Proverbs 30:1–3). There are four wonders, four 'ways' in nature, he declares, that are too wonderful to comprehend fully:

> The 'way' of an eagle in the sky,
> the 'way' of a snake on a rock,
> the 'way' of a ship on the high seas,
> the 'way' of a man with a girl. (Proverbs 30:18–19)

This innate Wisdom is frequently represented as a mystery (cf. Proverbs 30:18–31). The challenge before us, in the light of our appreciation of innate Wisdom is, whether, when we are exploring the realms of botany, biology or human nature, we should be aware that there is a deep dimension, a Wisdom compass in each living being under examination that is unique, spiritual and awesome, a dimension to be considered as we plan for the future. Innate Wisdom relating to the realms of nature is a driving force programmed into the cosmos, a force that governs each of the diverse realms of creation and controls the laws of nature.

4.1.2 The Wisdom Magna-Carta

We now move from the innate world of living creatures to the innate laws and forces at work in the inanimate realms of nature. The Wisdom dimension for this tradition is preserved especially in what has been designated The Wisdom Magna Carta (Job 28), a discrete chapter inserted by the Wisdom narrator into the Book of Job to alert the reader that the focus of the book is not really on the person of Job but the nature and function of Wisdom, especially Wisdom in nature.

The Wisdom Magna Carta is an imaginative portrait of where and how a model ancient Wisdom scientist discerned Wisdom innate in the driving forces and realms of nature. This portrait is the creative work of a narrator from the Wisdom School. To highlight the spiritual significance of this discernment, the narrator depicts this ideal Wisdom Scientist as God.

4.1.3 The 'Place' of Wisdom

The ultimate question posed in this Magna Carta is: Where can Wisdom be found? Or, in other words, what is the 'place' of Wisdom in the ecosystem of the cosmos? The Wisdom School concept of 'place' (*maqom*), the locus or habitat of a phenomenon in the ecosystem network of the universe is crucial for an understanding of this tradition. In the design of creation there is an appointed 'place' for each realm, creature or component of nature.

In The Wisdom Magna Carta, the Wisdom School narrator, takes the question of the essential 'place' of everything in the universe and asks the question: 'Where is the 'place' of Wisdom herself?' The answer to that question might seem to be obvious: the source or the original 'place' of Wisdom is within God. In the course of this poem, however, the Wisdom narrator leads us on a search that ends in another location—the world of nature! The opening verse of this Magna Carta immediately focuses on the question of the 'place' of various phenomena in creation, entities such as silver and gold:

> Truly, there is a source for silver and a 'place' for the gold they refine. (Job 28:1)

As indicated above, everything has its appointed 'place' in the order of creation, and more specifically on Earth. Gold has its 'place' in Earth (Job 28:1); precious gems have their 'place' in stones (Job 28:6); rocks too have a 'place' on Earth (Job 14:18); Earth has its 'place' in the cosmos (Job 9:6); and each mortal has a 'place' on Earth (Job 7:10). By establishing that precious commodities have a specific 'place' in the design of the universe, the Wisdom narrator prepares the way for posing the ultimate question about the 'place' of Wisdom, the most precious find of all (Job 28:12).

The Wisdom sought in this Magna Carta is of far greater value than any other precious commodity. A knowledge of Wisdom innate in nature can only be acquired by the skills of close observation and critical analysis as demonstrated by the Wisdom Scientist of The Wisdom Magna Carta.

4.1.4 Discerning the 'Way' of Wisdom

In the final verses of The Wisdom Magna Carta, the Wisdom narrator imagines God to be the one who first undertook a successful search for Wisdom. This imagined divine Sage-cum-Scientist is depicted as searching far and wide across Earth to find Wisdom. Unlike other deities of the ancient world, who claimed to possess great Wisdom, the God portrayed by the narrator of the Wisdom School searches for Wisdom. In the ancient Near East, the God *Ea* was known as "the wisest of the gods who knew every sort of thing" (Kalugila, 1980, p. 30). The wisdom of *Marduk* was considered a mystery never understood by humans. While the sun god *Shamash* was not only wise and mighty, "he was his own counsellor" (ibid., p. 30).

The 'place' where the divine Sage of The Wisdom Magna Carta begins to search for Wisdom is not a distant realm among the gods or the council of heaven. The 'way' of Wisdom that the Wisdom 'scientist', discerns is not in the 'mind' of God or a personal divine capacity. Rather, it is like this:

> God 'discerned' [*bin*] her 'way' [*derek*],
> and came to know her 'place' [*maqom*],
> for God looked to the ends of Earth
> and 'observed' [*ra'a*] everything under heaven. (Job 28:23–24)

The model scientist is here portrayed as searching the ends of Earth, including every realm 'under heaven'. The model Wisdom scientist 'observes' and scrutinises the entire landscape of the planet. The 'place' of Wisdom is on and in Earth!

4.1.5 Findings of Innate Wisdom Research

When we finally reach the climax of The Wisdom Magna Carta, where God, the imagined Wisdom scientist, is portrayed by the Wisdom narrator as discovering Wisdom in nature. This discovery of Wisdom, however, is not depicted as a recent event. It is specifically linked to the origin of the meteorological realms in the cosmos. These specific domains, it would seem, are representative of all the realms of nature.

> When God fixed the weight of the wind
> and meted out the waters by measure,
> when God made a rule [*choq*] for the rain
> and a way [*derek*] for the thunderstorm,
> then God observed [*ra'a*] her and appraised her,
> established her and probed her. (Job 28:25–27)

A crucial focus of the search for Wisdom portrayed in The Wisdom Magna Carta, is not the specific realms of nature themselves, but on an innate feature of these realms where Wisdom is to be found. The use of the technical terms 'way' (*derek*) and 'rule/law' (*choq*) identify the innate character of these phenomena – whether they be the wind, the waters, the storms or the rain.

The model Wisdom Scientist in this text does not merely 'observe' a given phenomenon, he 'discerns' its 'way' (*derek*), its inner code, its innate character. By discerning the 'ways' of these phenomena of nature, the Wisdom Scientist discovers innate Wisdom. Wisdom, then, is not separate from these phenomena of nature, but a driving force, an innate dimension of nature. By employing the research methods identified in The Wisdom Magna Carta, the Scientist of the Wisdom School may also discover Wisdom as a 'network of forces in' nature.

The Wisdom findings discovered by the Wisdom Scientist in The Magna Carta focus on Wisdom as a force innate in the laws of nature. Accordingly, the ancient Wisdom Scientist is a model for students of the ancient Wisdom School. This model, however, may be relevant for those doing research in the world of nature today. The laws of nature are not to be taken for granted, but may be investigated and discerned as mysterious innate forces. A Wisdom search, then, may be interpreted as both scientific and spiritual, a search for the innate that has a spiritual precedent in the primordial, in the origins of creation.

4.2 *Acquired Wisdom*

Acquired Wisdom is life-giving knowledge acquired from the observation of nature, the insights of wise mentors or the probing of tradition and imbibed to become a valuable means of creating a vibrant community and a sustainable planet.

4.2.1 The Council to Acquire

The famous normative injunction of the Wisdom School is for students to 'acquire wisdom'.

> The beginning of Wisdom is this: acquire Wisdom.
> and whatever else you acquire, acquire insight.
> Prize her highly, and she will exalt you;
> she will honour you if you embrace her. (Proverbs 4:7–8)

Humans are enjoined to acquire Wisdom by heeding the instruction of their mentor (Proverbs 3:1, 4:1) and by following the Wisdom tradition of the Wisdom School (Proverbs 1:1–6). Wisdom may also be acquired by observing the 'way' or innate Wisdom of living creatures such as ants (Proverbs 6:6), or even the 'way' of Wisdom in the cosmos. Today, the very term 'acquire' might well carry with it the association of a collection of items 'acquired'. In educational contexts, that may include the accumulation of intellectual information or data that would be valuable assets in life. In Proverbs, however, it becomes apparent that Wisdom is far more than an accumulation of intellectual assets and valuable traditions. To acquire Wisdom is the ultimate goal of life that can be compared to receiving the gift of life itself (Proverbs 3:18).

To acquire Wisdom means to locate Wisdom, imbibe Wisdom and make her, and all she embraces, an integral part one's being. The Wisdom acquired activates the innate Wisdom already present in humans from birth. This acquired Wisdom is not a gift to be kept on the shelf, but a driving force for humans to employ for building community, healing lives and establishing peace. Acquiring Wisdom enhances Wisdom consciousness and potential spiritual awareness.

An appreciation of acquired Wisdom is relevant for a contemporary society that may often pursue education or personal development primarily for economic success or popularity. The goal of the Wisdom School was to develop a Wisdom consciousness, an awareness of the presence of Wisdom that can be acquired and to employ the natural processes of learning from the environment to locate life-giving knowledge that will create a healthy community and a vibrant planet.

4.2.2 The Testimony of Wisdom

Perhaps the most striking tradition relating to acquiring Wisdom is found in the famous Testimony of Wisdom where Wisdom, as a primordial female, relates her own story (Proverbs 8:22–31). In spite of some well-known translations such as the Revised Standard Version of the Bible, the original Hebrew of the text, where Wisdom makes her famous speech, reads,

> The Lord acquired [*qana*] me first,
> his way [*derek*] before his works.
> From of old, from antiquity I was established,
> from the first, from the beginnings of Earth. (Proverbs 8:22–23)

The Creator is portrayed here as 'acquiring' Wisdom prior to the creation of the world. Wisdom introduces herself as the 'way' that this Creator acquires before any of the works of creation. Wisdom is the primordial 'way', the primal blueprint for the creation of the universe.

Wisdom testifies that she is primordial. She is not just knowledge accumulated over time, but an eternal reality that precedes and activates all forms of constructive knowledge that humans may acquire. To acquire knowledge is to link one's thinking and planning to the very 'way' employed in the creation of the universe, the spiritual beginnings of the cosmos and community.

The primordial remains a mystery that many cultures have long sought to understand, whether in terms of a specific divine presence or as an inherent primal impulse. In the Wisdom School, Wisdom represents a great mystery present in the primordial prior to creation. The question is whether, following the lead of the Wisdom School, we may be able to discern that impulse alive in creation today as we follow the modus operandi of the Wisdom School. It is significant to recognise that the Creator Spirit is portrayed as a model for the wise of the world to follow. Our goal is to acquire Wisdom as did the imagined Creator and then employ that Wisdom in a creative process to construct a cosmos, an integrated community alive with the forces, designs and wonders that enable one to be true to the 'way' that each human possesses, like the 'way' acquired by the Creator Spirit.

Whether or not one believes in a primal Creator or a primordial evolutionary process, Wisdom, in the ancient Wisdom School of thought, is a primordial spiritual energy that persists in our cosmos and community today. Acquiring Wisdom today involves observing how and when we can discern Wisdom 'truths' about our cosmos that will sustain our community and our planet, a truth especially relevant in the context of our climate change crisis.

4.3 *Cosmic Wisdom*

Cosmic Wisdom is a primordial spiritual power and presence in the primal design and current eco-system of the cosmos. Cosmic Wisdom is the underlying principle that governs the plot, orientation and spirituality of the classic Wisdom text we have identified as *The Challenge of the Wisdom Mentor* (Job 38–39). We have already encountered features of this primordial principle in our analysis of the Innate Wisdom explored by the divine Wisdom Scientist in *The Wisdom Magna Carta* and acquired by the divine Wisdom Scientist according to the *Wisdom Testimony*.

4.3.1 The Wisdom Mentor

The background to *The Challenge of the Wisdom Mentor* is the story of Job, who, though a man of integrity and justice, experiences great disasters and debilitating trauma, apparently at the hand of a cruel God. Job is portrayed as accusing God of cruel injustice. In *The Challenge*, however, the divine Wisdom Mentor takes Job and the Wisdom student on a journey through the cosmos posing a series of challenges designed to illuminate the listener about the mystery and role of Wisdom in the eco-system of the cosmos. The voice of the Wisdom mentor emanates from a mighty whirlwind (Job 38:1).

The voice of the Wisdom mentor confronts us and Job with the 'design' (*'etsa*) of the master-plan of the cosmos. Reference to the 'design' of the cosmos in his opening words of *The Challenge*, the mentor indicates that we are being confronted with the big picture and, in particular, how the many dimensions of the cosmos combine under the influence of Wisdom to form the coherent ecosystem of the universe. Inherent in this picture are the beginnings of a cosmic ecology already active in the ancient Wisdom School. The 'design' of the cosmos is tantamount to the 'Wisdom Blueprint' already identified in our discussion of *The Testimony of Wisdom*.

4.3.2 Our Journey with the Wisdom Mentor

In the course of our journey through the cosmos with the Wisdom Mentor, we are confronted with three realms: the primordial, the natural world and the world of the wild. Each of these domains are interrelated parts of the cosmos with Wisdom being a common integrating factor that we and Job can experience in person during the three main stages of the cosmic journey, The Primordial, The Realms of Nature and The World of the Wild.

Stage One – The Primordial

In Stage One of the journey, we are taken back to the primordial, the origins of the cosmos. The Wisdom Mentor begins by asking Job whether he has the 'discernment', the research skills of a Wisdom scientist from the Wisdom School, to go back in time and witness the origins of Earth, Sea and other realms of the cosmos. The origin of Earth is depicted as a cosmic moment of celebration; it is not a fragment from a Big Bang but a magnificent construction to be celebrated across the cosmos.

> Who set its [Earth's] cornerstone
> when the morning stars sang together
> and all the sons of God shouted for joy? (Proverbs 38:6–7)

The Wisdom narrator is leading us to the realisation, that the origins of key components of the cosmos are not meaningless moments in the past—they are events celebrated in the beginning and deserve our praise in the present. Today, the Wisdom narrator would probably be asked to join us in celebrating the moment before the birth of the Big Bang as we connect with contemporary scientific perceptions of that primal impulse of the cosmos. The metaphor used to describe the creation of Earth in this legend is that of a mighty edifice with a grand cornerstone that can be seen across the skies.

The origin of Sea is portrayed poetically as a birth from a cosmic womb with the baby being swaddled in dense clouds. This image might be overlooked as a colourful metaphor, but the crucial feature is control of the potential force of the mighty ocean in a primal plan for the cosmos:

> I prescribed my 'limit' for him,
> by fixing bars and doors, and saying:
> thus far you may come and no further!
> Here your proud waves break. (Job 38:10–11)

The laws of nature that contain the oceans and beyond are here understood to be part of the primal Wisdom blueprint of the planet. We, under the guidance of the Wisdom Mentor, are led to understand the mystery of cosmic Wisdom, the source of the primal design that orders creation.

With Job, we are also asked to explore light and darkness, the Deep and the vast expanses of Earth (Job 38:12–19), forces beyond the control the world of humans. The laws of nature, reflected in the movement of light and darkness, control the potentials of the wicked as well as the patterns of life on Earth. The Wisdom narrator presents the laws of nature—rather than an intervening God—as a factor in the fate of humans, demonstrating that cosmic ecology and primordial ethics are interrelated.

Especially significant is the question of whether Job has 'discerned' the expanses of Earth. Ancient Wisdom School scientists discern dimensions of Wisdom by close investigation and observation, not by faith or tradition. Along with Job, we are challenged to employ our Wisdom skills to gain a Wisdom consciousness of the vast extent of Earth in the original design of the cosmos, a challenge that contemporary researchers may also consider.

Stage Two – The Realms of Nature

Stage Two on the journey includes the realms of nature – including lightning, thunder, rain and cloud cover (Job 38:22–38). The Wisdom of the thunderstorm is also linked to the wilderness where no humans live. Some humans may presume that rain is sent for their benefit, as a blessing for their fields and gardens. On this journey, however, we gain a Wisdom consciousness that the ecosystem of the weather provides blessings for all the realms of the landscape (Job 38:26–28). There are features of the weather system, however, that remain a mystery. What is the ultimate source of rain or ice or hoarfrost (Job 38:28–30)? They are active components of the ecosystem that represented a genuine challenge for the ancient wise scientist.

Perhaps the most famous test at this stage in the cosmic journey is the explicit challenge: Who put Wisdom in the clouds (Job 38:36)? This challenge makes it abundantly clear that the driving force in the various domains of nature is Wisdom, and, in the cosmic context of this whole chapter, this force is cosmic Wisdom, the blueprint for the cosmos (Job 38:2).

One of the most contemporary issues on this journey is the challenge to discern the laws of space, a mystery that still confronts a cosmic ecologist. The challenge remains relevant today:

> Do you know the laws of the sky?
> Can you establish their order on Earth? (Job 38:33)

However, the pivotal question relates to the 'laws' (*chuqoth*) of the skies (Job 38:33). The focus is clearly on innate Wisdom as a realm for scientific investigation, not on some deity who controls the heavens or manipulates the stars. Today, we might identify the cosmic laws in the skies with contemporary understandings of gravity and astral forces. Just as Wisdom is found by the Wisdom Scientist in the 'laws' of nature associated with the weather (Job 28:25–26), we are here challenged to discern the same cosmic Wisdom functioning in the laws of space.

These laws are understood to establish an ordered world on Earth, a genuine mystery of ancient ecology or astrophysics. This question relates to the very core of ecology as a science. How do the laws of one domain interrelate with those of another domain? How do the laws of space interact and affect the modus operandi of planet Earth? How do the laws of the cosmos relate to each other to facilitate the operation of the universe and the place of Earth in that universe? How does Wisdom function in the design of the cosmos?

Stage Three – The World of the Wild

Stage Three of the journey is into the world of the wild to explore the ecosystem of life on Earth, the life of creatures in the wild and how they are related to human beings. These creatures include the lion, the ibex, the wild ass, the wild ox, the horse, the hawk and the eagle. In relation to the latter creatures, for example, the Wisdom mentor asks:

> Is it by your Discernment [*bina*] that the hawk soars, spreading its wings to the South? Does the eagle mount at your command and build his nest on high? (Job 39:26–27)

The challenge is not only to recognise that hawks and eagles possess the innate Wisdom needed to soar in the sky and find abodes for their nests on mountain ridges, but also that they are not dependent on humans to live successfully in these domains. The 'place' of the eagle is to fly freely in the sky and nest safely on the mountain, not in some location where humans can control them or dominate them. The same is true of the wild ass and the wild ox.

This text highlights again the relevance of discerning the innate Wisdom in any creature or domain of nature that a Wisdom student or scientist may wish to examine. The task is to discover the innate Wisdom that enables the subject to be true to its essential character and to relate to the cosmic environment in a positive way that is consistent with its innate Wisdom.

Following these three stages in our journey through the cosmos, from the primordial to the present, from the origins of Earth to the laws of space, from Wisdom in the clouds to discernment in the eagle, we may activate our Wisdom consciousness, a spiritual awareness of the presence of cosmic Wisdom throughout this world and the universe, an awareness we will explore further in the following analysis of Experienced Wisdom.

4.4 *Experienced Wisdom*

Wisdom is a profound mystery that manifests itself in the many natural phenomena of the universe, a mystery that may arouse, in the wise, a sense of sheer wonder, Wisdom consciousness and deep spiritual awareness.

4.4.1 Experiencing the Mystery of Wisdom

Having explored the several dimensions of Wisdom, we are now faced with the question of how we might respond to this profound spiritual mystery. How do we experience Wisdom in creation?

We might respond in a mechanical way and collect the reams of knowledge that, we, like ancient scientists, might collate and categorise. Findings from the observation of animals and plants, or the domains of nature and the realms of space, have the potential to create an encyclopedia about the natural world and its many mysteries. The challenge we face here is to discern levels of response to the mysteries of Wisdom in nature that are personal, deep and spiritual. Consistent with the Wisdom School cosmology, we can identify at least three discrete experiential approaches that are recognised by Wisdom School scholars. I believe these three approaches can be classified as:

- Sheer wonder
- Wisdom consciousness
- Spiritual awareness

4.4.2 Experiencing Wisdom as Wonder

One way of responding to an experience of innate Wisdom as a spiritual mystery is a sense of awe – whether as quiet amazement or exploding wonder. To be in the presence of such a pervading mystery may cause us to be mesmerised in amazement. Alternatively, the challenge of such a mystery may move us to delve even deeper into a phenomenon filled with mystery and seek spiritual meaning or ultimate causes.

Scientists may be struck with wonder as they contemplate the origins of the universe. The very design of the cosmos evokes sheer amazement amongst nuclear physicists. They are likewise astounded by the very existence of atoms when it might be expected that all matter and corresponding antimatter would cancel each other out and leave but a glow of cosmic radiation (Deane-Drummond, 2006).

4.4.3 Experiencing Wisdom Consciousness

Another experiential response may be designated 'Wisdom Consciousness': an acute sense of the presence, power and significance of Wisdom in all domains of our environment; a mindset that recognises Wisdom as an innate force driving nature and, ultimately, the cosmos.

Psychologists may identify a range of ways in which consciousness emerges from an individual's inner self or brilliant brain. Wisdom consciousness, as retrieved from the thinking of the Wisdom School involves an innate awareness of an external presence. My internal innate Wisdom compass becomes aware of an external innate Wisdom presence in my surroundings. My innate Wisdom is conscious of innate Wisdom around me.

If I walk through my garden, a rainforest or a wild wilderness, I am surrounded by numerous forms of life: everything from ants to amoeba, from giant eucalypts to wallabies. Beneath my feet are life-forms in the soil and the sand. Above my head there are life-forms in the atmosphere and beyond. If I am Wisdom-aware, I become conscious of Wisdom embedded as a spiritual presence within each of these life-forms, even though I cannot actually see it. If I now look out to sea and discern the horizon or view the expanses of a mountain range and the laws that sustain order on our planet I may discern the innate Wisdom that governs their function in the cosmos. Your Wisdom consciousness may also be aroused if you scan the skies.

Scanning the Skies

Stand under the sky late at night.
Gaze deep into space and back into time,
observing distant stars, local planets and the blanks beyond.
Before you is the entire cosmos
a vast universe of matter and anti-matter,
a world of lights coming from explosions,
many of which occurred billions of years ago.

Before you is Wisdom, the blueprint of creation,
the design of the cosmos
that reaches back to the very beginning of creation,
before any Big Bang or soft whisper.

And you are connected to that beginning,
a tiny piece of matter in that cosmic design.
Let your mind reach back to read the primal blueprint,
to discern cosmic Wisdom before your very eyes,
the spiritual core of the cosmos.

4.4.4 Experiencing the Spiritual

Profound as these experiences may be, we may ask whether they could lead to a spiritual awareness or a spiritual experience. A priori, we need to recognise that 'spiritual awareness' or 'spiritual experience' in the Wisdom tradition may differ from that in the world of prophets, preachers or religious leaders.

The experience of sheer wonder or Wisdom consciousness may be tantamount to spiritual awareness for some of the would-be-wise observing nature or exploring the cosmos. I suggest, however, that the response of Job to his Wisdom consciousness experience may offer a deeper appreciation of spiritual awareness. The ultimate challenge from our Wisdom mentor is to comprehend how all those domains where Wisdom was a driving force contributed to the 'design' of the cosmos. The Wisdom consciousness we may acquire is indeed a form of 'cosmic consciousness'. But this new awareness may also be a 'spiritual experience'.

Job's response to his tour of the cosmos is revealing (Job 42:1–6). He recognised that the Wisdom mentor was challenging him to understand the *'etsa*: the 'primordial design', the blueprint for the cosmos. Job admits that he had not been true to his Wisdom tradition, that he had not used his 'discernment' to interpret the cosmos or what is happening in his physical world. Previously, he had focused on the question: Where can justice be found? Now he is faced with the question: Where can Wisdom be found? He declares:

> I heard of you with my ears, but now my eyes 'see' you. (Job 42:5)

What does Job mean when he claims to have 'seen' God? Surely such a cry is an admission that he has now had a spiritual experience of some kind. What kind of experience? The context is the ancient Wisdom School; the meaning of this pivotal cry is relevant to our understanding of his response and the nature of his spiritual experience.

A significant feature of this response is the use of the term *ra'a* (see/observe). As we noted earlier, this verb is a technical term in the Wisdom School. A key step of the wise scientist of old was to 'see' or 'observe' a particular phenomenon closely so as to 'discern' its very nature. Now Job, the newly initiated Wisdom scientist, claims to have 'seen/observed God'. How? Where? Or, in the language of the Wisdom School: 'Where can God be found/seen?' Can one claim to have seen God as an 'observable phenomenon' or a celestial being present of the universe? Since the initial assertion of the Wisdom mentor was that someone, namely Job, has been obscuring the cosmic design (Job 38:2), Job has been led by his divine Wisdom mentor to journey across the cosmos—from primordial realms to the world of wild animals. With Job, we have been challenged to discern the presence of cosmic Wisdom encoded in all the laws and realms of the universe.

What has been seen/discerned is Cosmic Wisdom not a discrete celestial being! Cosmic Wisdom, as we have come to recognise, is a force and a presence in nature with its many dimensions. In line with Wisdom School thinking, it would seem that by 'seeing' or 'experiencing' Wisdom as a cosmic force in nature, we, along with Job, have experienced the spiritual, not as a dominant celestial being but as a permeating presence and power called Wisdom.

The spiritual, in ecological terms, is that deep dimension of the cosmos that is interrelated with all the other dimensions of the cosmos and discernible through the many. The would-be wise who dare to journey through the many realms of the cosmos have the innate capacity and environmental opportunity to have a spiritual experience with Wisdom as their cosmic compass.

5 Conclusion

If we now reflect on wise practice is the light of our preceding analysis of the dimensions of Wisdom reflected in the thinking and practice of the wise in the Wisdom School of the ancient Near East, a number of relevant insights deserve consideration in our contemporary, and for our future, society.

5.1 *Wise Practice Involves Developing Wisdom Awareness*

Appropriate education is important for cultivating Wisdom awareness. So often we have limited education to gaining and measuring knowledge acquisition and developing practical skills. If we recognise that from infancy a child possesses innate wisdom, the goal of early education is to stimulate an awareness of the innate Wisdom compass guiding thinking and actions. As children grow the task is to assist them in appreciating that their innate self is their true self, an amazing gift they are privileged to express throughout their lives.

In school, the role of the teacher, as a Wisdom mentor, is to further cultivate individual children's innate Wisdom and to help them strengthen that Wisdom by acquiring Wisdom through observation, research and experience. To do this children need guidance in developing their capacity to notice, to discern, to enquire and to engage with their life-world (Jackson, 2010). Wise practice also involves creating an awareness that each person has an innate Wisdom that is the core of their character, the essence of their identity. Education involves developing a respect for other people and their distinct character, working with them to establish a community, celebrating differences, but maintaining peace.

5.2 *Wise Practice Involves Developing Wisdom Discernment*

Research is pivotal for developing Wisdom discernment. From the earliest age the Wisdom student should be challenged to explore all the realms of nature in order to discern the character, function and location of innate Wisdom in those natural realms.

This research is designed to make the researcher aware that every component of the environment is more than mere matter or lifeless energy. Every component of the cosmos, from the clouds in the sky to the crabs in the ocean, from the oxygen in the atmosphere to the penguins in the Antarctic, possesses an active element, which in the past was called Wisdom. That element still exists even if scientists chose to give it another name, such as DNA.

Wise practice involves exploring not only the existence of the innate Wisdom in all phenomena of nature, but also involves exploring how the Wisdom of these phenomena are interrelated. Wise practice demands that we enquire into and sustain the innate Wisdom of these phenomena. Importantly, we must discern how we have intervened in order to understand fully how our actions have impacted on nature, for example, to become a cause for destructive climate change and other forms of collateral damage in nature. To be wise, we must also appreciate the wisdom of those who have studied the Wisdom in nature, in other words our modern scientists, to discern how we might change our practices to shape a positive and less destructive future.

5.3 *Wise Practice Involves Recognising Wisdom Experience*

Experiencing the spiritual in nature is also a potential impulse for Wise practice. The spiritual is not a reality necessarily associated with a divine being. The spiritual may be experienced when a person is confronted with sheer wonder, a reality that evokes awe and amazement. The spiritual may also be experienced when a mystery of nature overwhelms us with a response that may lead to works of art, imaginative exploration or inspiration in song. The spiritual may happen when Wisdom surfaces and confronts us with surprise. Perhaps the most powerful spiritual experience is 'cosmic consciousness', an awareness of Wisdom as the cosmic compass that guides, governs and celebrates the cosmos, of which and in which each of us is a living being.

For a person to be wise in practice, whether it be in education, engineering, science or archaeology, a Wisdom experience provides a deep motivation to connect with Wisdom in whatever field one is working, exploring, researching or relating to in an artistic way.

References

Deane-Drummond, C. (2006). *Wisdom and wonder: Conversations in science, spirituality and theology.* Templeton Foundation Press.

Habel, N. (2014). *Finding wisdom in nature: An ecological reading of the Book of Job.* Sheffield Phoenix Press.

Habel, N. (2015). *Discerning the wisdom in God's creation.* Morning Star Publishing.

Hall, S. S. (2010). Wisdom: From philosophy to neuroscience. In J. Fieser & B. Dowden (Eds.), *Internet encyclopaedia of philosophy.* University of Queensland Press.

Jackson, N. (2010, June 10–11). *Developing creativity through life-wide education: Proposition for a more complete education* [Keynote presentation]. 8th annual Galway Symposium on higher education, Galway, Ireland.

Kalugila, L. (1980). *The wise king: Studies in royal wisdom as divine revelation in the old testament and its environment.* AMS Press.

Von Rad, G. (1972). *Wisdom in Israel.* Abingdon.

Whybray, R. N. (1965). *Wisdom in proverbs.* SCM Press.

CHAPTER 8

Professional Practice and Knowledgeable Action in Turbulent Times

Rediscovering Métis

Peter Goodyear

Abstract

There are many ways of describing and categorising the forms of knowledge bound up in professional practice. Some approaches use the language and constructs of empirical psychology to focus on how knowledge may be represented in the mind, and how it may be learned and applied. Other approaches draw inspiration from philosophy, preferring its accounts of how knowledge ought to be. Or sociology, and its careful descriptions of how knowledge is created by real people in complex institutions. All of these perspectives have merits and it is likely that real progress is to be made by finding and forming more of their connections. In this chapter, I tap into some relatively recent writing about a very old epistemic tradition, briefly revisiting Aristotle's depiction of *epistêmê, téchnê* and *phrónêsis,* before adding and arguing for a fourth conception of knowledgeable action: *métis.* On some accounts, *métis* is everywhere in ancient Greek culture, yet the species of "cunning intelligence" it names is neither very visible, nor widely applauded. My aim is to remedy this ignorance, assist in the rediscovery and rehabilitation of *métis* and show how it may be just what we need when looking for wiser ways of surviving – and even flourishing – in turbulent times.

Keywords

ways of knowing – practical wisdom – *métis* – *phrónêsis* – action and change

1 Introduction

It is in the nature of turbulent times that doubts arise about the kinds of capabilities that will be of most value in navigating and shaping uncertain futures. In universities, for example, we periodically check the relevance of our courses and their alignment with workplace and community needs. Gaining a sharper

 | DOI: 10.1163/9789004505544_010

understanding of valued capabilities can prove useful as a way of improving course, curriculum and assessment design. More careful attention to the nature of workplace skills and knowledge has informed the development of richer ideas about the attributes that make university graduates more employable. Among other things, such work has added a list of important "soft skills" to complement graduates' mastery of specialist technical knowledge. The intellectual coherence and robustness of research and practical development work in this broad area is quite variable. For example, the difficulty of translating ideas between workplace vernaculars and psychologically-plausible accounts of knowing and learning is exacerbated by the lack of relevant expertise among many of those who shape university curricula. This makes it all the more important to strengthen our shared understanding of the capabilities education should be seeking to foster. Moreover, we need to look well beyond the narrow desiderata for employability and workplace productivity. Educating new professionals so that they can play knowledgeable roles, with other citizens, actively engaging in responses to major social and environmental challenges, is also vitally important. Working with others to find ethical transitions to more sustainable ways of living depends upon a wider and deeper set of capabilities (Higgs et al., 2019; Manzini, 2015; Markauskaite & Goodyear, 2017).

In this chapter, I explain and provide an argument for the Greek concept of *métis*. Some well-established accounts of knowledge and ways of knowing have traced routes back to Ancient Greek philosophy to find and repurpose three key terms: *epistêmê, téchnê* and *phrónêsis*.

Epistêmê involves abstract generalisations and can be positioned as the core of scientific ways of knowing. *Téchnê* refers to technical know-how: knowing how to get things done. *Phrónêsis* is practical wisdom, derived from social practice and imbued with moral purpose. All three can play a part in understanding wisdom and wise living practices – the topic(s) at the heart of this book. The rediscovery of a fourth term – *métis* – can be credited to two French scholars of Greek literature, culture and myth: Marcel Detienne and Jean-Pierre Vernant. *Métis* can be translated narrowly as a form of "wily intelligence", archetypally displayed in hunting and fishing. It is strongly associated with Odysseus/ Ulysses and the skills of the seafarer that are needed and tested in turbulent waters: *métis* allows the sailor to outwit a malevolent storm and avoid disaster. Detienne and Vernant (1974, 1991) make a bolder claim: that *métis* is foundational. It is needed to engage with *epistêmê, téchnê* and *phrónêsis*.

The idea of *métis* has been explored more recently by de Certeau (1988), Baumard (1999) and Mentz (2015). It has not been picked up widely in writing about education: exceptions being Lynch and Greaves (2016) and Markauskaite and Goodyear (2017), who mention it in passing. McKenna (2019) finds a place for *métis* in thinking about the many contradictions encountered in organisational life.

The chapter proceeds as follows. I start by providing a short working definition of *métis* and then, with the help of selected authors, elaborate on the core ideas – ideas that might be generative in thinking about education for professional practice and the shaping of wise futures. I locate *métis* in relation to some existing terms used widely in the literature on ways of knowing: particularly *epistêmê, téchnê* and *phrónêsis*. I then turn to the main text on *métis*: Michel Detienne and Jean-Pierre Vernant's *Les Ruses de l'Intelligence: La Métis des Grecs* (1974). This wide-ranging exploration of early Greek literature and culture appeared in English translation in the 1980s, though most of the writing in English about *métis* has been by Francophone authors. Detienne and Vernant explore, explain and elaborate on *métis* by examining the wider semantic field which it inhabits. My summary is aimed at demonstrating the particular relevance of *métis* for thinking about themes of professional work and wise living in a changing world.

After that, I draw on more recent work by three authors who have used *métis* in writing about: management, organisations and tacit knowledge (Baumard, 1994, 1999); tactics in the practices of everyday life (de Certeau, 1988) and workplace studies and ergonomics (Wisner, 1995a, 1995b). The fourth author appearing in this section is Steve Mentz (2015), who combines an examination of *métis* with an analysis of contemporary ecological challenges to argue, among other things, for a much more dynamic conception of the circumstances within which knowledgeable action is needed.

Finally, I explore some implications for professional knowledge and action. My sense is that there are many areas ripe for exploration, but I have focussed on what may be two aspects of a common challenge: (i) the framing (or "building") of complex problems faced by professionals and their clients and (ii) marshalling the resources needed to fight for more sustainable ways of living and working.

In its title and content, the chapter dwells on the motif of "turbulent times", which I take from Mentz (2015) and from Pitman and Kinsella (2019). Pitman and Kinsella have provided us with a thoroughgoing account of *phrónêsis* in professional practice (see especially Kinsella & Pitman, 2012). In their 2019 chapter, Pitman and Kinsella use the term "turbulent times" to refer quite broadly to contemporary contexts for professional work in which neoliberal economics and managerialist regimes of accountability have been eroding professional autonomy and making it harder to exercise professional responsibility in the service of clients' best interests. This moral foundation is, they argue, a distinguishing feature of *phrónêsis*. As will become clear, in this chapter, drawing particularly on the imagery and arguments of Mentz, I use "turbulent times" with a greater sense of drama, uncertainty, volatility and threat. On this view, we need to supplement *phrónêsis* with *métis,* to equip ourselves, our colleagues, and those who rely upon us, against various forms of shipwreck.

2 Rediscovering *Métis*

Métis is often glossed as a form of intelligence that is "wily", "cunning" or "crafty". It relies on the use of tricks to outwit a stronger or more capable opponent. On this reading, it is not a *heroic* virtue. Indeed, it would be disparaged by those who claim to love a "fair fight" on a "level playing field" and who denounce subterfuge. The redemption of *métis* is quite straightforward, once one recognises this "fair play" framing of competition as a rhetorical device used by those who are accustomed to bringing superior resources to what is billed as a "fair fight" and/or by those who have no skin in the game. (The 18th Century generals of European armies, who took such pride in the formalised manoeuvres of their regiments, rarely came under fire themselves.) There are, of course, occasions when joint subscription to a clear set of rules is important. But there are also many situations in which people are struggling to find a way forward in much less well-defined circumstances, where they are not matched evenly against well-behaved forces. Mentz (2015) makes the point most sharply by using the example of sailors' skills in moments of threatened shipwreck – *métis* as "skilled, tool-driven work … in which human actors modify and engage with a threatening and dynamic environment" (p. 77). The threats may not be so intense or overpowering in everyday workplaces, but the need to act smartly isn't hard to find. For example, McKenna (2019) sees a role for *métis* when managers in complex organisations are trying to reconcile competing, distorting pressures: such as the need to protect workers' well-being in times of rampant cost-reduction.

> Wise managers are not remote people perpetually engaged in contemplation. Rather, they must display the capacity of *métis*, a cunning intelligence based on knowledge of power and administrative practices that can be used to produce desirable outcomes. (McKenna, 2019, p. 138)

There is something here (in *métis*) that is not salient, and may not be present, in Aristotle's more familiar ideas about forms of knowledge and ways of knowing: *epistêmê, téchnê* and *phrónêsis* (Hager & Beckett, 2019; Higgs, 2019; Kinsella & Pitman, 2012).

Epistêmê is often used to connote: abstract generalisation; universal (context-independent) knowledge that is worth preserving and teaching; objective, scientific knowledge, mainly expressed in laws and principles, explicit rather than tacit.

Téchnê refers to specific capabilities; the "know how" needed to accomplish a specific (well-defined) task. It is context-specific, pragmatic and involves a practical rationality.

Phrónêsis is the closest of the three to the core concerns of this book – a combination of prudence and wisdom; personal forms of social and practical wisdom, developed through lived experience, often intuitive and hard to articulate; above all, operating within a strong moral framework.

On a first pass, we might say that what *métis* adds is the ability to orchestrate these other ways of knowing, to outplay superior forces.

3 Detienne and Vernant's Exploration of *Métis*

Detienne and Vernant (1974, 1991) are quick to point out that in Greek scholarship, *métis* is conspicuous by its absence, appearing just below the surface, missing from accounts of what Greek intelligence has to say about itself. Its traces are everywhere, but it is rarely singled out, named and analysed. They look for it, and find expressions of it, across a very wide range of literature, myth, and story, as well as in philosophical and technical accounts of military arts, medicine, politics and craft. On their view, it can be seen as a type of intelligence and thought, as a way of knowing:

> ... a complex but very coherent body of mental attributes and intellectual behaviour which combine flair, wisdom, forethought, subtlety of mind, deception, resourcefulness, vigilance, opportunism (Detienne & Vernant, 1991, p. 3)

> ... a whole gamut of operations in which the intelligence attempts to make contact with an object by confronting it in the guise of a rival ... combining connivance and opposition. (Ibid., p. 6)

And they go on to explain why this is useful: that it appears in

> ... situations which are transient, shifting, disconcerting and ambiguous, situations which do not lend themselves to precise measurement, exact calculation or rigorous logic. (Ibid., pp. 3–4)

The word itself derives from the Greek goddess Metis – daughter of Ocean, mother of Athena, first wife of Zeus – who, jealous of her gifts, swallowed her. *Métis* sits in a wider semantic field, and its associated meanings and resonances have been traced across a thousand years, from Homer ("the figure of Odysseus, the human embodiment of *métis*" (ibid., p. 47) to Oppian.

> In every confrontation or competitive situation – whether the adversary be a man, an animal or a natural force – success can be won by two means, either thanks to a superiority in 'power' in the particular sphere in which the contest is taking place, with the stronger gaining the victory; or by the use of methods of a different order whose effect is, precisely, to reverse the natural outcome of the encounter and to allow victory to fall to the party whose defeat had appeared inevitable. (Ibid., p. 13)

The outcome may be seen in one of two contrasting ways: disdainfully, as the consequence of cheating, or with (sneaking?) admiration for "thinking outside the box". But the success of *métis* depends upon more than creative thinking. It works across past, present and future.

> During the struggle, the man of *métis* – compared with his opponent – displays at the same time a greater grip of the present where nothing escapes him, more awareness of the future, several aspects of which he has already manipulated, and richer experience accumulated from the past ... [a] state of vigilant premeditation, of continuous concentration on activity that is already in progress. (Ibid., p. 14)

Detienne and Vernant also observe that the semantic field within which *métis* can be found also includes visual images – colourings, sheens, signs of shifting movement – such that *métis* becomes particularly associated with "turbulent movement" and "incessant change" (ibid., p. 19). And while it is associated more strongly with age and experience than with youth, this dynamism distinguishes it from "armchair wisdom" and disengaged contemplation.

> Why does *métis* appear thus, as multiple (*pantóië*), many-coloured (*poikilē*) shifting (*aiolē*)? Because its field of application is the world of movement, of multiplicity and of ambiguity. It bears on fluid situations which are constantly changing and which at every moment combine contrary features and forces that are opposed to each other. In order to seize upon the fleeting *kairós* [opportune moment], *métis* had to make itself even swifter ... In order to dominate a changing situation, full of

> contrasts, it must become even more supple, even more shifting, more polymorphic than the flow of time: it must adapt itself constantly to events as they succeed each other and be pliable enough to accommodate the unexpected so as to implement the plan in mind more successfully. It is thus that the helmsman pits his cunning against the wind so as to bring the ship safely to harbour despite it. (Ibid., p. 20)

In exploring the many contexts in which *métis* can be found, and valued, Detienne and Vernant do not restrict themselves to tales of gods and heroes. They find *métis* at work, and of value, among hunters and fishers – whose qualities include "agility, suppleness, swiftness, mobility ... [and] dissimulation, the art of seeing without being seen" (ibid., p. 30), vigilance and "a keen eye" (p. 31) – as well as among the animals hunted, including the fish:

> It is the *métis* of the fish which obliges the fisherman to deploy an intelligence full of finesse. (Ibid., p. 33)

> ... a being of *métis* slips through its adversary's fingers like running water. It is so subtle as to be polymorphic; like a trap, it is the opposite of what it seems to be. (Ibid., p. 44)

In sum, we can understand *métis* as embodied intelligence in action: fit for uncertain times, ambiguous spaces and unequal competitions. In thinking about professional work, we can see *métis*, more narrowly, as a resource for resolving or side-stepping the tensions and contradictions that arise in organisations that are being shaped by complex, competitive forces (McKenna, 2019). We can also see it more broadly as an inspiration for tackling much larger social, political and environmental challenges.

4 Elaborations of *Métis* in More Recent Literature

Before looking more closely at *métis* in professional practice, I need to supplement the insights of Detienne and Vernant with some more recent scholarship.

4.1 *Baumard: Métis and Ways of Knowing in Organisational Life*

The most extensive application of the concept of *métis* to thinking about organisational life and professional knowledge is to be found in the work of Philippe Baumard (1994, 1999). It is in Baumard's writing that we find *métis* contrasted with, and finding a place alongside, *epistêmê*, *téchnê* and *phrónêsis*.

Baumard's broader aim is to explore the place of tacit knowledge in organisations, and *métis* stands out as an important, neglected kind of knowledge, or way of knowing: "conjectural knowledge" that is particularly suited to dealing with ambiguous and puzzling situations, while committed to action and its consequences. Following Detienne and Vernant, Baumard (1999) sees *métis* as "relegated to the shadows" by philosophers, after the 5th century A.D.

> In the name of a metaphysics based on Being and immutability, the conjectural and oblique knowledge of the clever and the prudent was rejected as non-knowledge. (p. 65)

Baumard outlines a process of learning, through which a flair for working with ambiguity is developed, and within which people

> … penetrate the rules, and infiltrate the hard knowledge that disconcerts them and prevents them from achieving their goals … they use 'conjectural and oblique knowledge' … [to] skilfully implement their plans to outwit these very rules, now having at their disposal knowledge that is 'polymorphous and rich'. (Ibid., pp. 66–67)

Baumard (1999) also talks about individuals making transitions between different modes of knowing, especially in encounters with the new, with changing and unfamiliar situations. When the world becomes "unsettled and disconcerting, and no longer open to measurement" (p. 101), the habitual application of *epistêmê* and *téchnê* no longer works. Instead, success depends upon a way of knowing (*métis*), which is derived from social practice (*phronesis*) and which supplies the ruses and the cunning that people need to extract themselves from difficult situations.

4.2 *De Certeau: Métis and the Practices of Everyday Life*

Michel de Certeau (1988) also draws upon Detienne and Vernant (1974) in applying ideas about the intelligence of practice to what he describes as the practices of everyday life.

> Many everyday practices (talking, reading, moving about, shopping, cooking etc) are tactical in character. And so are, more generally, many 'ways of operating': victories of the 'weak' over the 'strong' (whether the strength be that of powerful people or the violence of things or of an imposed order, etc), clever tricks, knowing how to get away with things, 'hunter's cunning', maneuvers, polymorphic simulations, joyful

> discoveries, poetic as well as warlike. The Greeks called these 'ways of operating' *métis*. But they go much further back, to the immemorial intelligence displayed in the tricks and imitations of plants and fishes. From the depths of the ocean to the streets of modern megalopolises, there is a continuity and permanence in these tactics. (de Certeau, 1988, pp. XIX–XX)

De Certeau (1988) offers three ideas to distinguish *métis*, each of which can be expressed as a relation: to the situation, to disguise and to "paradoxical invisibility" (p. 82). Firstly, *métis* is a temporal practice: it is timely, recognises and acts on opportunity, involves a capacity to draw on accumulated knowledge and experience to intervene at just the right moment (*kairos*). Secondly, it masks itself: it subverts, it tricks, works around and/or disrupts conventional arrangements and ways of doing things. Finally, it "disappears into its own action" (p. 82); in succeeding, it leaves no obvious trace.

For de Certeau (1988), *métis* is also characterised by economy: obtaining maximum effects from the minimum of force: "the multiplication of effects through the rarefaction of means" (p. 82). And it depends upon a certain kind of knowledge for its success – knowledge characterised by "the duration of its acquisition and its composition as an unending summation of particular fragments" (p. 82) – the experience of age against the thoughtlessness of youth.

4.3 *Wisner: Tasks and Activities in the Workplace*

In a pair of papers in the mid 1990s, Alain Wisner drew together some recent ideas from cognitive psychology, anthropology, education and the learning sciences to make a case for more thoroughgoing studies of how workers actually tackled the tasks given to them, and, in particular, how they "built" (rather than simply solved) problems arising in the course of their work. In this, he was especially influenced by Lucy Suchman's workplace studies at Xerox, including her distinction between plans and situated actions (Suchman, 1987). In contrast to prevailing accounts of problem-solving in research on human cognition and artificial intelligence, Suchman argued that human action cannot be reduced to the execution of plans; plans might more accurately be seen as resources for talking about action. Wisner made a related distinction:

> The plans are the instructions, the task and the work prescribed and the situated action is the real work. (Wisner, 1995a, p. 1549)
>
> An essential concept is clearly shown here: the difference between the prescribed work (the task) and the real work (the activity) linked to the concrete difficulties of the situation, to their perception by the operator,

> to the strategies (s)he adopts to satisfy the demands of the work and, in particular, to the hazards. (Wisner, 1995b, p. 597)

In accounting for these creative aspects of work *activity*, Wisner drew on old ideas, newly rediscovered: the "intelligence of practice" – the "crafty intelligence" distinguished as *métis* by Detienne and Vernant (1974, 1991).

Wisner's distinction between (a) the official, sanctioned, prescribed, formalised, "manager's" view of the task and (b) the actual activities engaged in by workers in order to do the job, the real work has been generative in a number of areas of social, ergonomic and educational research. For example, mapped onto students' reconfigurations of tasks set for them by their teachers, it plays a central explanatory role in Activity-Centred Analysis and Design (Goodyear et al., 2021).

The fourth and final source of commentary on *métis* that I want to bring into this discussion takes us back to historical and literary research.

4.4 *Mentz: Métis, Shipwreck and Ecological Catastrophe*

Steve Mentz's book *Shipwreck Modernity* (Mentz, 2015) takes the idea of *métis* from Homer's *Odyssey* and applies it to thinking about seafaring. Within tales and experiences of seafaring, danger is never far away, and Mentz makes effective use of the spectres of shipwreck to comment more broadly on past and contemporary catastrophes and especially on crises in human affairs associated with ecological change. His book covers a great deal of ground and water but for this chapter I will focus on three of his key contributions. Firstly, there is the idea of *métis* as an invaluable resource when facing catastrophe, with shipwreck as the emblematic case, but with relevance to other forms of impending or actual dramatic change. Secondly, and associated with such perils, there is an important consideration that may be overlooked by modern minds: that forces of nature, fate, or the actions of gods, may be understood as malevolent. Applying *métis* to avoid shipwreck may involve defying the gods or trying to outwit savage nature. Thirdly, Mentz (2015) sees in the sailors' craft a cunning intelligence that we might call "socio-technical". "The ocean's essential term is *métis*: skilled, tool-driven work" (p. 77).

In describing this *instrumented* character of sailors' work, Mentz calls on Latour's (2005) actor-network-theory.

> It is important to recall that *métis* combines the technological with the social. A Latourian perspective suggests the fundamental continuity among the contributions of disparate actors that include social networks, human laborers, and inanimate tools. Maritime labour provides an exemplary case of collaboration between human and nonhuman actants. In

> forming this sort of network, the important thing is to have reliable collaborators, human and not. (Mentz, 2015, p. 80)

While the capacity to form, sustain and work with(in) such networks is important for the efficient conduct of routine activity on board ship, as elsewhere, it takes additional forms of resourcefulness when things are going badly wrong. *Métis* gives a name to those qualities of seamanship that are needed to act in a timely fashion, in uncertain, complicated, dynamic circumstances. Stripped to its heart, *métis* is what a sailor shows when dealing with shipwreck.

> The interaction between human hands and precise tools assumed paramount importance during crises at sea. To rebuild a fracturing anthropotechnological assemblage (i.e. a ship and her crew) during a storm required a special combination of skill, tools, social organization, and the ability to manage all these things under chaotic conditions. (Ibid., p. 81)

In histories of shipwreck, the sea, waves, the wind and rocks may each be seen as terrible: as agents of disaster, as actively malevolent. Fatalistic sailors may see impending shipwreck and death as the will of the gods. "Against this theological anger, seaman-like *métis* keeps the ship afloat, enabling sailors to bear witness of God's displeasure" (ibid., p. 124).

Mentz makes a further, profound, point. *Métis* may help a sailor bring the ship to safety, but it is also needed when shipwreck is unavoidable: to make the best of dreadful circumstances. He urges us to make sense of our current predicaments – climate change, pollution of the oceans, rising sea levels, mass migrations of climate refugees, through realising that we are already living in a shipwreck, and that, by implication, *métis* is what we need right now.

> The world in which humans live is not a stable space into which we can project our desires, literary culture imagines ways to endure disorder, not correct it. The essential counterweight to oceanic catastrophe is narrative. Stories, with their structural imperative to bring together unlike things, represent the intellectual infrastructure through which disorderly environments become provisionally legible. By telling stories, literary writers, like other humans, construct ways to make sense of our encounters with disruptive and changing spaces such as the ocean. For our age of ecological crisis, the ancient story of shipwreck tells topical tales. (Ibid., p. 172)

> It turns out that it is not so bad living inside shipwreck. It becomes easier if you stop hoping that there is solid ground somewhere. ... Humans have

> been floundering about inside disorder for a long time. We have gotten good at inventing ways to reimagine disorder as order. (Ibid., p. 163)

Rather than craving order – which causes us to be "pole-axed with dread" and "melancholy with nostalgia for things we believe we have now but are about to lose forever" (ibid., p. 164) – we should get used to being wet. "The ecological future is for swimmers, not sailors" (p. 181).

In the last main section of the chapter, I try to use some of these connotations of *métis* to sketch their implications for knowledgeable action in professional practice. What follows may be two faces of the same fundamental dilemma.

5 Exploring the Scope and Potential of *Métis* in Reconsidering Professional Practice

5.1 *Professional Problems: Design, Wicked Problems and Social Innovation*

Markauskaite and Goodyear (2017) offer a simple categorisation of the kinds of problems that emerge in professional practice by introducing two dimensions along which problems vary: structure and stability. Problems vary in terms of the degree to which they are "ill-structured" or "well-structured" and the degree to which they remain stable during the activities involved in finding a solution. "Well-structured" problems appear much more frequently in educational programs of preparation for professions than they do in the messiness of professional practice. Well-structured problems are used a good deal in formal education – including at school and university – to help students learn to *apply* what they know (Jonassen, 2011). Typically, well-structured problems are presented with all the information needed to solve the problem, they are solvable through the application of a small number of well-defined operations, and there is agreement on a correct solution. When students encounter well-structured problems, they usually know that their main challenge is to spot what kind of problem this is, so that they can then apply a well-defined set of transformations to the problem to arrive at a solution. However, ill-structured problems are much more common in professional practice. They often involve one or more of the following:

> conflicting goals, multiple solution methods, unanticipated problems, multiple forms of problem representation, one or more unknown problem elements, multiple solutions, uncertainty about knowledge applicable to the problem and a need for personal judgements or reliance on personal beliefs. (Markauskaite & Goodyear, 2017, p. 556)

In such circumstances, knowing what kind of problem one is facing, and working out what kinds of knowledge may be needed, can be very difficult. Neither *epistêmê* nor *téchnê* will suffice.

Problems can be said to be stable (or "tame") if a consensus can be reached in advance, by all the parties involved, about what the problem is and about how the parties would know that the problem has been solved. Problems are better characterised as unstable (or "wild" or "wicked") if the nature of both problem and solution remain dynamic: where some kind of collective action and inquiry process needs to be agreed upon, to "build" the problem and find a good way forward (Goodyear & Markauskaite, 2019; Nelson & Stolterman, 2014; Rittel & Webber, 1973; Wisner, 1995b).

Many recent accounts of the capabilities citizens will require if they are to play active roles in social innovation – working together to create more sustainable ways of living – emphasise the skills and dispositions needed to participate in complex, collaborative, inquiry-rich design (Costanza-Chock, 2020; Cottam, 2019; Manzini, 2015; Yelavich & Adams, 2014). The distribution of skills in such work can vary, with professionals and other experts taking greater or lesser roles (Goodyear, 2019). Drawing upon the idea of *métis*, we can now take this a little further, building in some provision for the forms of dynamism that flow from conflict and environmental change. In short, many social innovations generate opposition from powerful interest groups jealous of their privileges. Few processes of social innovation unfold against the static background of an unchanging world. Identifying the workings of privilege, and improvising ways of resisting its powers, can only take us so far. Beyond that, successful innovation involves strategising and needs all the talents associated with *métis* if entrenched powers are to be out-witted. Similarly, as Mentz (2015) argued, we no longer have the luxury of time, or a static world: stories imbued with *métis* provide equipment for thinking in the midst of ecological catastrophe.

5.2 *Knowledgeable Professional Action in Times of Crisis*

Contemporary academic commentary on professional life often resorts to the language of crisis. Professions for which we have some affinity are painted as if their souls are at risk. So while it is tempting to make blunt use of Mentz's arguments about shipwreck, catastrophe and *métis* to characterise current predicaments, I suggest we too are under an obligation to find some credible resources for hope. The rise and rule of neoliberal economic and political thought, over the past 40 years or so, accounts for some of what has happened in the "softer" professions: the attacks on autonomy; growth of managerialism; the imposition of accountability measures and performance metrics; the underfunding, undermining and privatisation of public services; the over-use of internal markets; outsourcing; the decoupling and commodification of services, and so on.

So successful has this ideological movement been, and so thoroughgoing has been the "normalisation" of its assumptions and workings, that politicians and pundits can say "there is no alternative".

But the climate crisis and the COVID-19 pandemic say otherwise: biology eats ideology for breakfast. It is quickly becoming clear to increasing numbers of people that concerted action is needed to deal with the interleaved global problems of climate change, poverty, inequality, forced migration, social exclusion and discrimination (Ghosh, 2017; Krznaric, 2020; Latour, 2017; Raworth, 2017). This realisation is being expressed through (some) traditional political parties and trades unions, but also through new forms of social movement and through myriad examples of local social innovation (see e.g. Castells, 2015; Cottam, 2019; Gerbaudo, 2017). Ezio Manzini (2015) cautions that social innovations leading to more sustainable ways of living are at an early stage, and yet what we can readily perceive may under-represent what is actually happening.

> All these ideas, the activities they refer to, and the relationships they generate seem to me beautiful islands of applied cultural and socioeconomic wisdom. They are islands in the sea of unsustainable ways of being and doing that is, unfortunately, still the mainstream throughout the world. The good news is that the number of these islands is growing and generating a wide archipelago. An archipelago that could be seen as the emerging dry land of a rising continent: the already visible expression of a new civilization. (p. 26)

What does this mean for our conceptions of professional practice and its ways of knowing? For one thing, it promotes ways of framing the world, and the problems arising in professional work, that refuse to accept rigid notions of what is possible. But this is arguing for something that is much more than a critical reflex. Seeing the world, in Mentz's terms, as Blue, not just Green, watery as well as sedimented, means learning to thrive in fluid, turbulent, sometimes alarming, situations – where judicious application of *métis* can beat overwhelming odds and seize opportunities to save or make what we truly value. Using a different metaphor, this involves an ontological trick: refusing to see rigidities, and acting with others to make the most of uncertain times.

To be clear, none of this absolves professionals from acting in line with the best of what is known about recurrent problems of practice – *epistêmê* and *téchnê* remain as relevant as ever. Nor does it mean we should extinguish *phrónêsis*: that "beacon of light, hope, and belief" in a morally-directed professional practice that puts the long-term needs of clients and society first (Kinsella & Pitman,

2012, p. 166). Rather, *métis* can help animate *epistêmê, téchnê* and *phrónêsis* with the tactical prowess needed to take on the powerful, and win.

6 Concluding Comments

In this chapter, I have suggested that the ancient Greek conception of *métis* may turn out to be an essential complement to *epistêmê, téchnê* and *phrónêsis* when considering wise professional practice in times of great change and uncertainty. In particular, some of the ideas associated with *métis* may help us think more adventurously about the nature and limits of "acting for the common good". I also suggest that *métis* has a role to play in expanding our sense of "wise futures" and how to make them.

Acknowledgement

I acknowledge funding from the Australian Research Council through grant DP200100376 (Developing interdisciplinary expertise in universities).

References

Baumard, P. (1994). *Oblique knowledge: The clandestine work of organizations*. Cahier de recherche DMSP, n°228. Université de Paris-Dauphine.

Baumard, P. (1999). *Tacit knowledge in organizations*. Sage.

Castells, M. (2015). *Networks of outrage and hope: Social movements in the Internet age* (2nd ed.). Polity Press.

Costanza-Chock, S. (2020). *Design justice: Community-led practices to build the worlds we need*. MIT Press.

Cottam, H. (2019). *Radical help: How we can remake the relationships between us and revolutionise the welfare state*. Little Brown.

De Certeau, M. (1988). *The practice of everyday life*. University of California Press.

Detienne, M., & Vernant, J.-P. (1974). *Les Ruses de l'Intelligence: La Métis des Grecs*. Flammarion.

Detienne, M., & Vernant, J.-P. (1991). *Cunning intelligence in Greek culture and society* (J. Lloyd, Trans.). University of Chicago Press.

Gerbaudo, P. (2017). *The mask and the flag: Populism, citizenism and global protest*. Hurst Publishers.

Ghosh, A. (2017). *The great derangement: Climate change and the unthinkable*. The University of Chicago Press.

Goodyear, P. (2019). Networked professional learning, design research and social innovation. In A. Littlejohn, J. Jaldemark, E. Vrieling, & F. Nijland (Eds.), *Networked professional learning: Emerging and equitable discourses for professional development* (pp. 239–256). Springer.

Goodyear, P., Carvalho, L., & Yeoman, P. (2021). Activity-Centred Analysis and Design (ACAD): Core purposes, distinctive qualities and current developments. *Educational Technology Research and Development*. https://doi.org/10.1007/s11423-020-09926-7

Goodyear, P., & Markauskaite, L. (2019). The impact on work and practice of wicked problems and unpredictable futures. In J. Higgs, S. Cork, & D. Horsfall (Eds.), *Challenging future practice possibilities* (pp. 41–52). Brill Sense.

Hager, P., & Beckett, D. (2019). *The emergence of complexity: Rethinking education as a social science*. Springer.

Higgs, J. (2019). Appreciating practice wisdom. In J. Higgs (Ed.), *Practice wisdom: Values and interpretations* (pp. 3–14). Brill Sense.

Higgs, J., Crisp, G., & Letts, W. (Eds.). (2019). *Education for employability (Volume 1): The employability agenda*. Brill Sense.

Jonassen, D. (2011). *Learning to solve problems: A handbook for designing problem-solving learning environments*. Routledge.

Kinsella, E. A., & Pitman, A. (Eds.). (2012). *Phronesis as professional knowledge: Practical wisdom in the professions*. Sense.

Krznaric, R. (2020). *The good ancestor: How to think long term in a short-term world*. WH Allen.

Latour, B. (2005). *Reassembling the social: An introduction to actor-network-theory*. Oxford University Press.

Latour, B. (2017). *Facing Gaia: Eight lectures on the new climatic regime*. Polity Press.

Lynch, J., & Greaves, K. (2016). Michel de Certeau: Research writing as an everyday practice. In J. Lynch, J. Rowlands, T. Gale, & A. Skourdoumbis (Eds.), *Practice theory and education: Diffractive readings in professional practice* (pp. 55–70). Taylor & Francis.

Manzini, E. (2015). *Design, when everybody designs: An introduction to design for social innovation*. MIT Press.

Markauskaite, L., & Goodyear, P. (2017). *Epistemic fluency and professional education: Innovation, knowledgeable action and actionable knowledge*. Springer.

McKenna, B. (2019). Developing wise organisations. In J. Higgs (Ed.), *Practice wisdom: Values and interpretations* (pp. 127–140). Brill Sense.

Mentz, S. (2015). *Shipwreck modernity: Ecologies of globalization, 1550–1719*. University of Minnesota Press.

Nelson, H., & Stolterman, E. (2014). *The design way: Intentional change in an unpredictable world* (2nd ed.). MIT Press.

Pitman, A., & Kinsella, E. A. (2019). A place for *phrónêsis* in professional practice: A reflection of turbulent times. In J. Higgs (Ed.), *Practice wisdom: Values and interpretations* (pp. 57–68). Brill Sense.

Raworth, K. (2017). *Doughnut economics: Seven ways to think like a 21st century economist*. Penguin Random House.

Rittel, H., & Webber, M. (1973). Dilemmas in a general theory of planning. *Policy Sciences, 4*(2), 155–169.

Suchman, L. (1987). *Plans and situated actions: The problem of human-machine communication*. Cambridge University Press.

Wisner, A. (1995a). Situated cognition and action: Implications for ergonomic work analysis and anthropotechnology. *Ergonomics, 38*(8), 1542–1557.

Wisner, A. (1995b). Understanding problem building: Ergonomic work analysis. *Ergonomics, 38*(3), 595–605.

Yelavich, S., & Adams, B. (2014). *Design as future-making*. Bloomsbury Academic.

PART 3

Examining Options

∵

Introduction to Part 3

Joy Higgs

In this part of the book, we explore different ways of using wisdom to illuminate wise practice in many different avenues.

> It's awfully sad that with our clever brains, capable of taking us to the moon and developing all those sophisticated ways of communicating around the planet that we seem to have lost wisdom; and that's the wisdom of the Indigenous people who would make a major decision based on how that decision would affect people seven generations ahead. We're making decisions based on the bottom line. How will this affect me now? ... So although we think we're caring about our children and grandchildren, we're actually stealing their future. (Jane Goodall, in Zuckerman, 2009, p. 105)

> Peace is the greatest weapon for development that any people can have. (Nelson Mandela, in Zuckerman, 2009, p. 114)

> If the experience of South Africa means anything to the world at large, we hope that it is in having demonstrated that where people of goodwill get together and transcend their differences for the common good, peaceful and just solutions can be found even for those problems which seem intractable. (Nelson Mandela, in Zuckerman, 2009, p. 117)

> We're a part of the environment. We are one aspect of the environment. We're not separate from it or better than it. ... We've got to stop being so prideful about the fact that we're doing something that the world needs. It's not a matter of pride, it's a matter of dire necessity, internally and externally. (Alan Arkin, in Zuckerman, 2009, p. 18)

> First of all it is important to know that each one of us can make a contribution. Too frequently we think we have to do spectacular things, and yet if we remembered that the sea is actually made up of drops of water, and each drop counts – each one of use can do our little bit where we are and it is those little bits that can come together and can almost overwhelm the world. And so it's important to try to be senders of peace. Each one of us can be an ounce of peace. (Desmond Tutu, in Zuckerman, 2009, p. 12)

 | DOI: 10.1163/9789004505544_011

We have to move away from this idea that only 'me' can do it, because that's not true. (Chinua Achebe, in Zuckerman, 2009, p. 87)

A new life begins for us with every second. Let us go forward joyously to meet it. We must press on, whether we will or no, and we shall walk better with our eyes before us than with them ever cast behind. (Jerome K. Jerome, in Exley, 1999, n.p.)

The most I can do for my friend
is simply to be his friend.
I have no wealth to bestow on him.
If he knows that I am happy in loving him,
he will want no other reward.
(Henry David Thoreau, in Exley, 1999, n.p.)

I compared notes
with one of my friends
who expects everything
of the universe,
and is disappointed when anything
is less than the best,
and I found that I begin
at the other extreme,
expecting nothing,
and am always
full of thanks
for moderate goods.
(Ralph Waldo Emerson, in Exley, 1999, n.p.)

The wisdom of the world cannot simply be defined as only past or present because one leads to the other – the past has created the present. More than that, we need an understanding of the past in order to find our way through the limitations of the past to the best of the age that is dawning. (Chittister, 2014, as cited in Dreyer, 2014, n.p.)

'Wisdom' in common speech is prudence, showing careful thought about consequences. It is shown in balanced judgement, in being skilled or well informed. We ask, 'Is that wise?' meaning 'Is it sensible?'. Wise choices are made after due consideration, weighing the best advice we can get, and thinking about possible consequences. The dictionary definition is 'the quality that develops within a specified society or period'. To be wise is 'having or showing experience, knowledge and good judgement'. It is being aware, and knowing how to act. (Wakeman, 2013, pp. 129–130)

...the wise professional, whether working as a nurse or a teacher, is constantly making judgements that take into account perceptions of the actual or potential feelings of those with whom they work. (Bondi, 2011, p. 132)

In sum, the components of intelligence are at the base of successful intelligence, creativity, and wisdom. They are applied in intelligence, broadly defined, to experience in order to adapt to, shape and select environments. When the components are involved in fairly abstract but familiar kinds of tasks, they are used analytically. When they are involved in relatively novel adaptations to, shaping of, and selection of environments, they are used practically. ... Creative intelligence is a part of, but not the entirety of, human creativity. Creativity also involves aspects of knowledge, styles of thinking, personality, and motivation, as well as these psychological components in interaction with the environment. An individual with the intellectual skills for creativity but without the other personal attributes is unlikely to do creative work. ... Wisdom results from the application of successful intelligence and creativity toward the common good through a balancing of intrapersonal, interpersonal, and extrapersonal interests over the short and long terms. Wisdom is not a way of thinking about things; it is a way of doing things. If people wish to be wise, they have to act wisely, not just think wisely. We all can do this. Whether we do is our choice. (Sternberg, 2003, p. 188)

We leave behind the memory of the way we treated strangers, how we loved the individuals closest to us, how we cared for those who loved us, how we spoke to them in hard times, how we gave ourselves away to satisfy their needs. (Chittister, 2008, n.p.)

References

Bondi, L. (2011). On the gender of professional wisdom. In L. Bondi, D. Carr, C. Clarke, & C. Clegg (Eds.), *Towards professional wisdom: Practical deliberation in the people professions* (pp. 125–139). Ashgate.

Chittister, J. (2008). *The gift of years: Growing old gracefully*. BlueBridge.

Chittister, J. (2014). Foreword. In E. Dreyer (Ed.), *Accidental theologians: Four women who shaped Christianity*. Franciscan Media.

Dreyer, E. (2014). *Accidental theologians: Four women who shaped Christianity*. Franciscan Media.

Exley, H. (1999). *Wisdom for the new millennium*. Exley Publications.

Sternberg, R. J. (2003). *Wisdom, intelligence, and creativity synthesized*. Cambridge University Press.

Wakeman, B. E. (2013). *Knowing through poetic reflection*. Pen Press.

Zuckerman, A. (2009). *Wisdom: Peace*. Harry N. Abrams.

CHAPTER 9

Living Practices

Moving from the Past towards a Wiser Future

Tania De Bortoli and Diane Tasker

Abstract

Wisdom creates a process, which allows the individual and collective mind to use learned principles, life rules and past experience to inform and generate a better future. In this chapter, we discuss the need for imagining and realising a wiser future. How can we value what has been learned from the past and use this to imagine a future, which incorporates wise and just ways for citizens to engage within their local communities and wider society. Our way of living is at stake because of climate change and widening social inequality. We must develop wiser ideas and ways of thinking as well as the means for putting these into practice.

Keywords

collaboration – participation – proactivity – change and complexity

•••

> A wise citizenry is one that takes an active, informed role in looking at its past in order to reason about its future. It cannot properly reason unless it articulates its values, asks if its behaviour is congruent with those values, and calculates the costs of its behaviours, changing them if necessary. In other words, a wise citizenry is one that comes to know itself, warts and all.
>
> MAUER (2015, para. 4)

∴

 | DOI: 10.1163/9789004505544_012

1 Introduction

Individually and as a society, we need to be fully aware of the direction society is taking and make informed choices at the appropriate times in order to reach a situation where humans, animals and the environment are properly cared for and about. Ultimately this is about our survival and that of other species. We need to be wise and far-sighted in our endeavours and we argue that this requires a multi-faceted form of wisdom, including both the historical wisdom of elders and myriad expressions of new information, data and knowledge of this fast-developing age (The University of Queensland [UQ], 2020). Wise living practices will need to develop in many different spaces within society, ranging from families in their homes to CEOs running big organisations and governments endeavouring to support our society. Whilst big changes need a top down approach to achieve any degree of success (UQ, 2020), we argue that society also needs the finer detail of change emerging from a base of individual and community-based wisdom, based on community level approaches and the wise living and resilience of each one of us.

In Part 3 of this book, authors were encouraged to explore the notion of wise living practices and to provide examples. This introductory chapter to the third part of the book highlights two viewpoints. The first is about valuing what has been learned from the past and using this to imagine different futures for society. The second is about envisaging living practices that are wise and just ways for citizens to engage within their local communities and wider society. We then turn our attention to what might be broadly involved in developing and implementing wise living practices to inform and shape the way we could live. This involves not just ideas and ways of thinking (ideologies) but also how such ideas might be put into practice in a relevant and meaningful way for people in their particular situations and in response to changes over time. For us as authors, wise living practices means making conscious decisions about what we can do in order to make our world a better and safer place in the future. There is nothing value-free about the stance we take in this chapter. We wish to consciously include socially collective and environmentally responsible stewardship strategies for a wise future.

Research consistently shows that beyond a certain level of personal income or wealth, emotional wellbeing does not necessarily increase (Kahneman & Deaton, 2010). In fact, the opposite may occur. A better world is one with a broader focus on an equality of happiness and fulfilment for all people. It should be acknowledged that in the past, economists thought that economic growth overall would improve happiness. Instead we have witnessed a widening of social inequality even though there has been a significant reduction in extreme poverty in the world (Nieuwkoop, 2018).

Most people would say that a better world includes clean air, a healthy natural environment and care for the world's flora and fauna. Unfortunately, the fracturing of the complex relationships between humans and the world we live in has led to climate change of tragic dimensions as our planet's boundaries for the use of resources are breached. Kate Raworth's (2017) Doughnut Model for Sustainability clearly explains the problem of balancing the areas of climate change, with regards to biodiversity loss, land conversion and nitrogen and phosphorus loading which have breached the limits that our planet can cope with. In addition, many foundations of social functioning, including access to food, water, electricity, peace and social justice, political voice, health, housing and gender equity are not being achieved or sustained globally. The results of such imbalances are leading us to tipping points in our planetary and societal functioning, beyond which, we will not be able to return. Raworth (2017) argues that we must live within our planet's limits. Wise living practices are needed to enable society to better operate and allow the long-term continuation of society. Such important living practices may be seen in fragments of past ways of living. How can we value what has been learned and envisage and enact living practices that are wise and just. What are the consequences of not learning from the past and not developing wise practices?

2 Valuing and Learning from the Past

> When I want to understand what is happening today or try to decide what will happen tomorrow, I look back. (Khayyam)[1]

Most countries have used the measure of Gross Domestic Product (GDP) as an indicator of economic progress but use of such a lens on human wellbeing may not be as useful as was once thought. Indeed, its originator warned society of its limitations. "The welfare of a nation can scarcely be inferred from a measurement of national income" (Kuznets, 1934, as cited in Kohler & Chaves, 2003, p. 336). We need to see the welfare of people being integrated within society in terms beyond just money.

Although many millions of people have been lifted out of poverty in recent decades, ratios of inequality continue to increase (United Nations General Assembly, 2020). Increases in prosperity have been coupled with an increase in inequality due to human population, concentrations of wealth to a small percentage of people in society and the resultant pressures on governance. Simplistic and homogenised societal infrastructures can result in othering and polarisation of ideas. A clear illustration of this can be seen in the example of punishment and imprisonment within society. Across the world, differing pictures of imprisonment range from the positive pictures of,

- emptying prisons in the Netherlands (Taylor, 2016) and
- truly rehabilitative prison centres in Finland (Bischell, 2015)
- imprisonment of young adults with disability and mental health problems in Australia, where such people are six times more likely to be imprisoned than the rest of the community. (Australian Human Rights Commission [AHRC], 2019, Section Four) and
- imprisonment of people with mental illness in the USA (Roth, 2018).

GDP often includes activities, which are clearly not in the best interests of society, such as the inclusion of prison services (especially if they are privatised) in measures of national prosperity. When we blame the most damaged people amongst us, it becomes obvious that our systems are failing and a rethinking of basic policy is gravely needed. We need to be more discerning, to identify useful and wise practices to take forward, while discarding those that are less useful or no longer serve us.

2.1 *Building a Bridge between Economic Progress and Planetary and Human Wellbeing*

Economic progress continues to outweigh the importance of planetary and human wellbeing in major discourse and popular culture. Unfortunately, the dominance of the 'for profit' paradigm in our society has resulted in an increasing percentage of the society being impacted by corporatisation and casualisation of the work force. People can then be regarded in a utilitarian way as instrumental sources of labour. This practice can deny those people any possibility of reaching their chosen potential, to flourish, or to explore what they are capable of being and doing. As long as the 'for profit' paradigm dominates our discourse, it makes it very difficult to properly envisage and put into place wiser living practices.

By moving away from a narrow focus on economic growth other measures of human wellbeing, such as happiness and trust can be embraced. The United Nations is "committed to developing broader measures of progress to complement gross domestic product" (United Nations General Assembly, 2015, p.15). An interesting example may be seen in the Himalayan country of Bhutan, which initiated a Gross National Happiness Index (GNHI) in 1972, in which national development has become sustainable and holistic, concentrating on non-economic aspects of wellbeing (Oxford Poverty and Human Development Initiative [OPHI], 2020).

The GNHI includes nine domains (OPHI, 2020, Section 2):
- Psychological wellbeing
- Health
- Education
- Time use
- Cultural diversity and resilience
- Good governance
- Community vitality
- Ecological diversity and resilience
- Living standards

More recently, New Zealand has adopted the GNHI as a lens on policy-making and spending for five main government priorities (Ellsmore, 2019):
- improving mental health,
- reducing child poverty,
- addressing the inequalities faced by Indigenous Maori and Pacific Islander people,
- thriving in a digital age and
- transitioning to a low-emission, sustainable economy

3 Envisaging Wise and Just Living Practices for the Future

> Change happens not by trying to make yourself change but by becoming conscious of what is not working. (Gawain, 2015, p. 152)

Shakti Gawain (2015) argued that realisation of a chosen future needs to start with the process of creative visualisation; knowing the reality of the present and asking how do we see our world in the future. How do we work with the present and future challenges to create a future in which we can flourish rather than just exist? What could the future be like and how can it shape the way we, as its people interact with it and each other?

Baughman McLeod (2020) asked questions of future thinkers about how our world could be in 50 years, asking a broad range of questions, which give indication of the breadth, complexity and difficulty of society's efforts to plan ahead. Through this Imagineering, we can see possible ways forward.

> Who will run the world?
> Which country will have the most powerful economy?

What kind of companies might be most important?
What could cause the biggest conflicts?
How will people earn a living?
How will we communicate with each other?
How will we entertain one other?
What will we eat?
How will we die?
What will we wear?
How will we find love?
What kind of stories will we tell?
How will we get information?
What forms of transportation will we use?
What will cities be like?
What will our borders be like?
Will we have ventured to other planets?
What will our most valuable resource be?
What will be the biggest change to our natural world ?
Will our world be more equal or less equal?
What technology will bring about the biggest change in society?

3.1 *Multi-Faceted Lenses on Decision-Making: Altering Mindsets*

> We cannot solve our problems with the same thinking we used when we created them. (Albert Einstein)[2]

Society is grounded in its history. However, given the nature of the complex and existential challenges we face, there is a need to depart from purely historical approaches to more contemporary problem solving. When societal structures are rigid, effective responses to challenging situations may not be realised. Challenging situations are often complex and therefore require a diversity of approaches if we are to respond adequately to them. Some deeply entrenched social problems (often called "wicked problems") have been approached in radically different ways to those previously imagined.

Following the dismantling of Apartheid in South Africa, (for instance) the new government, led by the African National Congress, established a Truth and Reconciliation Commission. This process was designed to support the building of new, racially tolerant and peaceful societal structures. By moving away from oppression and bloodshed, healing was seen to be possible through knowing the truth and forgiving the past. At the time of its introduction, many people had difficulty seeing how such an approach would work because it was so new. Retrospectively, the wisdom of this approach and that of its leader, Nelson Mandela, has been more fully appreciated.

One option is to take seriously the complexity and contradictions of realities we face and then find ways of navigating through new concepts and discourses. Creativity is crucial (Ang, 2011). The shaping of a sustainable future is likely to require complex and innovative decisions being made in multiple spaces (UQ, 2020). This necessitates changing our thinking or adjusting our mind sets, for example by shifting from linear/mechanistic thinking, consistent with the drive for efficiency, to systems or complexity thinking that more accurately reflects our interconnectedness with the natural world. Systems or complexity thinking includes multiple components of systems that not only operate at and across multiple layers, but are also interconnected and interact in non-linear ways, for example, individual, community and societal considerations.

3.2 *Individuals and the Collective*

> Each of us is ensnared within numerous all-encompassing spider webs, which on the one hand restrict our movements, but at the same time transmit our tiniest jiggle to faraway destinations. (Harari, 2018, p. XI)

When dialogue occurs about whether wise living practices should be implemented at the level of individuals, communities or society, use of a complexity lens helps us to understand that all layers of involvement are important. Individuals are nested within ever more complex systems, which they influence and are influenced by. For meaningful and on-going change to occur, interventions need to happen at every different layer of society, from individual to the planet. Change emerges from interactions between different layers of a system over time and the overall effect may be greater than the sum of its parts. Change cannot necessarily be imposed, controlled or simplistically determined at the outset. For example, not all wise practices come from academics or government but can emerge "on the ground", which suggests a need to build capacity and resilience within communities (Holmgren, 2017).

Change outcomes can be unpredictable. The Butterfly Effect Theory suggests that changing one component in a complex system, such as individual practices, can influence the entire system (Lorenz, 2000). However, because of the complexity of interactions involved, it is not possible to know exactly how changes will manifest on a broader scale (Lorenz, 2000).

Paradox may also be embedded within complex systems. Paradox involves contradictory but inter-related processes that exist simultaneously within systems and persist over time. The tension of opposites interacting over time can have "emergent, surprising and often uncontrollable effects" (Cunha & Putnam, 2019, p. 98). A paradox of the emergent properties of complex systems can be seen in the compounding effects of the climate change crisis with its inter-related tipping points. A part of such complexity is the discourses that can influence individuals and communities.

4 Communicating and Building Useful Discourse

> In a world deluged by irrelevant information, clarity is power. In theory, anybody can join the debate about the future of humanity but it is so hard to maintain a clear vision. (Harari, 2018, p. IX)

People are finding it difficult to discern and make sense of the many discourses currently occurring in society, for example, globalism and nationalism. In a world which has valued and developed specialisation through the industrial age, fragmentation of information and silos of expertise and thought add to the difficulty of managing the integration of information for better understanding of complex contexts – the bigger picture.

4.1 *Barriers to the Development of Wise Living Practices*

Excluded or disadvantaged discourses include the discourses of refugees and Indigenous people, where inter-generational trauma perpetuates, making it difficult for those communities to flourish. The effects of such trauma present potential obstacles towards envisaging or realising an enriched future because trauma impacts greatly on cognitive functioning and the ability to imagine, problem-solve and plan.

While the discourses of marginalised people include experiences of systemic inequality, human rights abuses, natural disasters, terrorism, displacement, and other complex humanitarian emergencies, they may also include experiences of resilience, community building and living sustainably. These excluded discourses may therefore include important areas of concern, as well as knowledge and experience that we need to discuss and develop in our efforts to create wiser futures for our society. For example, we may need to consider what the *Black Live Matters* movement has to offer broader society. Lack of awareness of these discourses can cause other parts of society to misunderstand the needs and potential contributions of other people. While these discourses are being excluded, other discourses are being binge-promoted in ways that serve the interests of a few; those with access to wealth and power.

Charismatic leaders, corporations and governments often push certain agendas without accurately informing the public or having regard to the views of the majority of people. In this information environment, abuses of power can begin to intensify. In addition, polarised political agendas develop rifts between different sections of the community, undermining possibilities of cooperation that could benefit the community. Wise practices could mean being more discerning about the development and circulation of discourses.

Breakdown of trust can result from the imposition of profit-driven and neoliberal political agendas. In addition, the dominant neoliberal and patriarchal systems perpetuate the underrepresentation or lack of acknowledgement of the everyday acts of political engagement, citizenship and leadership that are occurring both on and offline. Social and digital media can enable a greater volume of reporting about issues of concern, for example, climate change, biodiversity loss, natural disasters, violence, and the recurrent waves of pandemic. Such widely differing messages can result in people feeling disillusioned about being able to make any difference to the wicked problems and important societal issues we face. Being overloaded with information, regardless of its credibility can also contribute to people 'shutting down' to public discourse or opportunities to make a difference.

Language and dialogue are important. We need to reflect on how our society is portrayed. Then we can change the predominant discourse and its narratives so that they can better contribute towards developing wise living practices. For example, a more positive discourse could promote the view that it is acceptable for people to receive help and support if they need it. Furthermore, that it is better for individuals and society as a whole, if people are not left in poverty with all its resultant complications; human misery and despondence, crime, lack of good health and limited economic contributions to society.

Dialogue needs to be consistent with living practices that enact the concept of valuing people as well as the planet. We need to enrich our public language with words that embrace complexity, promoting the idea that rather than fear and disaster we can achieve wiser futures with flair and style. Society could begin by moving away from reactivity and use of words such as 'restriction' and 'austerity'. Wiser futures do not have to be impoverished.

4.2 *Platforms for Connection, Reflection, Exploration and Communication*

Techniques and strategies need to be put in place for the development and communication of discourses to promote wise living practices. We need platforms and tools for reflecting, exploring and communicating what is important and really matters to the community. While different online platform capabilities currently restrict debate and dialogue, there are other mechanisms that can promote alternative discourse as well as collective action. Strategies and techniques could include mindfulness practices, opportunities for public dialogue, asking questions, the use of metaphor and narrative for clearer messaging, and actions such as those currently being used by *Black Lives Matter* and School Strike 4 Climate. Rather than promotion of certain agendas by the few, the development of wise living practices will necessarily involve participation of the majority of people.

Mindfulness allows us to make time to reflect on current happenings and issues and to discuss these with other people. Time for reflection can be brought into the schema of people's days, for example, meditation and yoga for school children. Many people are exploring meditation as a way to promote peaceful and compassionate behaviour. By slowing down and "stepping aside" for relatively short periods each day, people can become able to achieve a state of calm and clarity of thought that enables them to build quiet happiness and an appreciation of peace and beauty in times of difficulty. This background state of being promotes more critical thinking and a sense of the interconnectedness of people and the world around them.

As a society, we need to enable people to imagine and explore other mindsets and ways of being and living and provide sufficient opportunity for those ideas to be developed. Such envisaging does not happen automatically. In order to start to imagine what are wise living practices, we need time for personal reflection, community dialogue and conscious decision-making through consensus. There is a place for mindfulness at both the personal and the collective level.

Cultures of kindness and reflective conversation can be created to provide opportunities for active listening and growing connections in the community and across cultures. When such communication is also lifted to the level of the body politic, further action and sometimes legislation and funding can also be brought to bear on difficult issues such as dealing with the incarceration of young Indigenous people. Public inquiries are an important example of a platform that provides such opportunities. At the time of writing this chapter, Australia has seen a Royal Commission into Institutional Responses to Child Abuse. Other similar inquiries are underway into Aged Care Facilities, the Disability Sector and Bushfire and Climate Change. It is significant that the global pandemic has set the focus on major issues with Elder Care. These processes of inquiry necessarily include the collective reflections mentioned above. Questioning how current institutions and practices are really serving us may help to decide whether they are really what we want into the future.

In order to gain clarity within complex contexts, we need to ask "what if" questions, for example, 'what if we did it another way?' Such speculative thinking can stimulate wiser thinking and open up paradigms for critical investigation. Businesses use risk management strategies to manage legal and economic risk and to look at ethical decision-making that can arise from the performance of their entities. The same techniques could be employed for the overall good of society and the planet into the future.

The outcomes of community reflection and dialogue and the asking of 'what if' questions could address the need for more accessible and timely processes for people to receive help and support when this is needed, for example, during and after bushfires. Positive cultural change can be achieved by embedding accepted practices such as checking in with people and listening. Another example, a positive practice might be the enabling of men to contact a support person when they are feeling violent towards those around them. It is possible for people who may share an interest or goal to come together from different backgrounds and roles in life, to develop their ideas before putting them into action. When the use of positive discourse, metaphor and narrative is fully translated into actions, practices and behaviour, we will begin to see change at different levels within our society.

5 Implementing Wise Living Practices

Our discussion in this chapter so far has highlighted the need for processes and activities most likely to assist us towards wiser living practices. We argue that a proactive approach is better than a reactive response. Many events may be predicted but are not prepared for adequately, for example, pandemics and climate emergencies. There are processes and activities currently underway that could also be refined to better address wicked societal problems. These may be springboards that have the benefit of giving us a starting thinking point.

What might be the possible characteristics of springboard activities within society? We have listed some suggested characteristics in Figure 9.1. The list is not intended to be exhaustive.

5.1 *International Organisations Providing Springboard Activities for Wiser Futures*

International organisations are providing springboards for wise action by the gathering of broad consensus on different global issues. A prominent example is the United Nations, which convenes the United Nations Framework Convention on Climate Change (2020). This is the main international and intergovernmental process for formulating integrated global responses to climate change.

Characteristics of springboard activities towards future wise living

- Consistency within the context of an overarching crisis of climate change
- Generation and incorporation of the best of our scientific knowledge and thinking into governmental and global policy
- Planning for the essential interest of people and the natural environment (the planet) for the benefit of the majority of people
- Promotion of participatory democracy and a countering of accumulation of wealth and power
- Enrichment of the holistic well-being of people, animals and environment rather than the lowest common denominators of existence
- Inclusivity and opportunity for the voice of individuals and community groups to be heard and their concerns acted upon.
- Cross-cultural respect of different ways of knowing and learning
- Community-based collaboration between different levels of government
- Encouragement of participation by engaging people in different ways
- Decentralisation of essential services to better respond to disasters, for example, community gardens and food co-ops
- Establishment of value of place and the particular characteristics of place for the people who live there to better balance the needs of progress, history and community concern
- Allowance for monitoring of impact and evaluation of possible negative consequences
- Focus on communicating and educating people for civic participation
- Encouragement of creativity and innovation to encourage people to make their life in a fashion that really suits them
- Inclusion of plans for implementation

FIGURE 9.1 Characteristics of springboard activities towards future wise living

It relies on up-to-date scientific information from the Intergovernmental Panel on Climate Change (IPCC) for the development of policies and actions (United Nations Framework Convention on Climate Change, 2020). This forum influences discourse about climate change and informs collaborative action on the part of national governments to respond to climate change and foster sustainable development, which will "require unprecedented transitions in all aspects of society" (IPCC, 2019, p. VI).

The United Nations has also adopted the 2030 Agenda for Sustainable Development (UN General Assembly, 2015). This document sets out seventeen goals aimed at building a better future for all people through ending poverty, saving the planet and creating conditions for sustainable, inclusive and equal societies. It contains a transformational vision where a better world for all is envisaged. The document also defines means of implementation through an integrated approach requiring collective endeavour and reflecting "deep interconnections" (United Nations Department of Economic and Social Affairs, 2020, p. 2). It calls for "solidarity" and cooperation between international institutions, all levels of government, the private sector and business, non-government organisations and community groups, Indigenous people, the scientific and academic community and civil society (United Nations General Assembly, 2015).

Another example is the World Health Organization's documents: The International Classification of Functioning, Disability and Health (ICF) and The International Classification of Functioning, Disability and Health – Children and Youth version (ICF-CY). These documents provide a framework for the consistent communication of research findings internationally, and development of national policies and design of health care systems. The role of these documents as springboards is around changing social discourse about disability. The documents define the role of social and environmental factors in the construction of disability and see participation and inclusion of people living with disability as a chief outcome of societal practices. The documents set a framework for taking a long-term view of the wellbeing of people living with disability (World Health Organization [WHO], 2001, 2007).

5.2 *Ground Level Social Movements Providing Springboard Activities for a Wiser Future*

Other philosophical and cultural movements with potential to be springboards for wise living practices include such ground level social movements as Permaculture, Voluntary simplicity, Meditation, the Wellbeing movement and Regenerative culture. These perspectives all offer clear and practical guidelines for how people can lead sustainable and healthy lives, and engage with community-based initiatives to build resilience in the face of what David Holmgren calls 'energy descent', that is, a future with declining energy use and natural resource availability (Holmgren, 2017). Permaculture, for example, gives people thinking and practical tools for responding positively to social inequity, resource depletion and environmental degradation by making changes in one's own life towards a sustainable future (Holmgren, 2017). While these social movements are mainly intended to be relevant at the individual or household level, it is still important to consider what can be taken from them, in order for their effects to have wider societal impact.

5.3 *Collaboration between Different Levels of Government and the Community*

In an increasingly complex society, benefits for all are most likely to be achieved through activities based on collaboration. At our local level in the Blue Mountains, there are recent examples of collaboration between government and the community that could be considered springboards towards wise living practice. Across the Blue Mountains, there have been widespread and varied community responses to the 2019–20 bushfires. Our state, New South Wales has established the position of a Commissioner for Resilience and local areas, for example, our local Blue Mountains City Council have established Bushfire Recovery Committees. The purpose of these organisations is to collaborate with all interested and relevant community organisations, researchers and individuals to promote the holistic wellbeing of residents in the aftermath of devastating bushfires. The local Council has also established a community advisory group to support the recovery of wildlife in a similar way. While these initiatives have responded to current emergencies, they also provide frameworks for local residents to participate in the development of practices that can build future community resilience and better care for people and the environment. Even prior to the bushfire emergency situation, the Blue Mountains City Council had implemented a lengthy process of engaging local residents in the development of a Local Planning Statement. This Statement is in essence, a position determined by the people about the extent of development permissible in their city, as well as a vision of quality of life in a zero carbon emissions future. We are commenting here on our local area particularly but there are obviously many other examples around the world of such collaboration.

In a similar fashion, in the time of the COVID-19 pandemic, there have been practices implemented with cooperation between government, businesses and community organisations, for example, working from home and the equivalent of a universal basic income (income assistance). Advocates of such practices have not been able to implement them previously but now in a pandemic situation, they have become acceptable and therefore possible, enriching peoples' lives in many ways; emotionally, intellectually, creatively and socially. These examples suggest that we need to and can do more than just react to situations. We need to enact change not only in response to current emergencies but with a view to how we want our future to be shaped. So, we face the questions and challenges associated with making sustained change a reality; that is implementing change.

5.4 *Change and Implementation*

For the types of existential challenge we are facing, change will need to occur in multiple spaces and at multiple administrative levels, from the individual to global. It is also required at an accelerated rate, given the urgency of our situation. Research findings from the healthcare sector where implementation of important science discourse originates, suggest that the influence on professional practices of factors such as legislation, policies, social discourse and individuals' skills and knowledge may be mediated by other contextual factors. It seems that contextual factors at multiple levels may also interact to influence the implementation of practices. These factors range from characteristics of individuals, to organisational structures and cultures, collaboration between agencies, and community participation – a very complicated picture. Hence, supports may be required at as many levels as possible, and across as many factors as possible, in the direction of desired practices in order to increase the likelihood of effective implementation (Fixsen et al., 2009).

Change and implementation are not the same thing. Implementation is the process of practices being enacted, and includes the mechanisms that enable the realisation of that enactment. Change may ensue when practices are sufficiently embedded for benefits and other positive outcomes to be manifested and experienced. It does not seem possible in most situations to move straight from envisaging practices to positive change. Implementation needs to be planned with supports provided over time. These will include communication and education. We need to acknowledge these issues around implementation, including that implementation takes time, particularly where influencing attitudes and perspectives, organisational culture and social discourse is required. If we do not acknowledge that implementation is a complex issue, change will not occur in a resilient or ongoing way.

6 Anchoring Reality: Conclusions and Beginnings

Many people continue to grapple with how to cultivate wise living practices in the face of the overwhelming enormity of the challenges we face. Practices such as mindfulness and voluntary simplicity support individuals to make conscious decisions about the focus of their time and attention. What do you choose to think about and where do you focus your attention? Such focused thinking has considerable potential when embedded within a broader context of decision-making and actions. Given the enormity of the challenges we face and the complexity of their solutions, collective and political action is crucial for achieving the required scale of wise living practices.

It is clear that large-scale actions will also be required to support wise living practices for society. This can be seen in examples such as the UN Agenda for 2030 Sustainable Development Goals mentioned above and implementation of the Paris Agreement (United Nations General Assembly, 2015). However, decentralised societal structures may be much more supportive of localised wise living practices, given the global challenges that we face. Harari (2018) for example, has also suggested that there may be a need to pull back from globalisation because villages have a human size/human scale that give people a context within which to make their sense of reality by investigating and seeing what is happening in their surroundings. This is where the potential of Permaculture, Regenerative culture and other practices may be realised to create broader benefits. This is a part of the collective and distributed social action mentioned above. Such structures afford more opportunities for individuals to participate in collective wise living practices, such as the collaborative initiatives between local government and community organisations mentioned above, and this requires people to consciously make wise choices as they move forward in life. As a society and as individuals and families, we may feel more comfortable with 'baby steps' but now is also the time to have the courage to rise to the challenge of our world and take more 'adult steps' into the future.

We know that it is possible for people to make significant changes in their lives, and that this can happen on a large scale, as witnessed in times of pandemic. The paradox of COVID-19 can be seen in the co-existence of some concerning practices and others that could be envisaged as wise living practices. While there has been loss of work and social isolation for many people, there has also been a pre-empting of a universal basic income or social wage. In addition, working from home has allowed people to live a more local life in their neighbourhood with attendant social and environmental benefits. There are also large-scale opportunities for individuals, community organisations, businesses and government agencies to participate in collective reflection and dialogue about future practices. This can be seen in the previously mentioned Royal Commissions of Inquiry and indeed other formal governmental inquiries that can be viewed as vehicles to raise awareness and shift social mores. Large volumes of people are already taking the opportunity; becoming involved and getting their voices heard. This can help society take larger steps forward even if it may just mean that what is acceptable to talk about, changes.

Wise living practices will be shaped in no small way by the power and energy of the coming new generation. The push to be heard and to influence wise living practices for a better future for all can be clearly seen in the *Black Lives Matter* movement and the School Strike 4 Climate movement driven by young people. The voices of our young people are urging us to shape a better future. As the quote used by Mauer at the beginning of this chapter says, each one of us is called upon to:

- Be active and participate
- Be informed about our past

- Articulate our values
- Ask if our behaviour is congruent with those values
- Calculate the costs of our behaviours, and
- Change those behaviours if necessary. (Mauer, 2015, para. 4)

Our planet and our societies need everyone to connect with each other and participate together towards wiser living practices.

Notes

1 https://www.brainyquote.com/quotes/omar_khayyam_391496
2 https://www.brainyquote.com/quotes/albert_einstein_121993

References

Ang, I. (2011). Navigating complexity: From cultural critique to cultural intelligence. *Continuum, 25*(6), 779–794. https://doi.org/10.1080/10304312.2011.617873

Australian Human Rights Commission [ARHRC]. (2015). *Face the facts: Disability rights.* https://humanrights.gov.au/our-work/education/face-facts-disability-rights

Bauman McLeod, K. (2019). *We asked some of the boldest thinkers what the world will be like in 50 years: Here's what their answers tell us about the future.* Adrienne Arsht-Rockefeller Foundation Resilience Center. https://www.onebillionresilient.org/post/we-asked-some-of-the-boldest-thinkers-what-the-world-will-be-like-in-50-years-heres-what-their-answers-tell-us-about-the-future

Bichell, R. E. (2015, April 15). In Finland's 'open prisons', inmates have the keys. *The World.* https://www.pri.org/stories/2015-04-15/finlands-open-prisons-inmates-have-keys

Cunha, M. P., & Putnam, L. L. (2019). Paradox theory and the paradox of success. *Strategic Organisation, 17*(1), 95–106.

Ellsmoor, J. (2019, July 11). New Zealand ditches GDP for happiness and wellbeing. *Forbes.* https://www.forbes.com/sites/jamesellsmoor/2019/07/11/new-zealand-ditches-gdp-for-happiness-and-wellbeing/#51711db11942

Fixsen, D. L., Blasé, K. A., Naoom, S. F., & Wallace, F. (2009). Core implementation components. *Research on Social Work Practice, 19*(5), 531–540.

Gawain, S. (2015). *The Shakti Gawain essentials featuring creating visualization, living in the light developing intuition.* FranklinCovey Co. https://play.google.com/books/reader?id=dcLCCQAAQBAJ&pg=GBS.PT149.w.4.0.80

Harari, Y. N. (2018). *21 questions for the 21st century.* Spiegel & Grau.

Holmgren, D. (2017). *Permaculture: Principles and pathways beyond sustainability* (Rev. ed.). Melliodora.

Intergovernmental Panel on Climate Change (IPPC). (2019). *Global warming of 1.5 degrees Celsius.* https://www.ipcc.ch/site/assets/uploads/sites/2/2019/06/SR15_Full_Report_High_Res.pdf

Kahneman, D., & Deaton, A. (2010). High income improves evaluation of life but not emotional well-being. *Proceedings of the National Academy of Sciences, 107*(38), 16489–16493.

Kohler, G., & José Chaves, E. (2003). *Globalization: Critical perspectives.* Nova Science.

Lorenz, E. (2000). The butterfly effect. In R. Abraham & Y. Ueda (Eds.), *The chaos avant-garde: Memories of the early days of chaos theory* (Series A, Vol. 39, pp. 91–94). World Scientific.

Mauer, B. J. (2015, September 2). How do you make a society wise? *Huffpost.* https://www.huffpost.com/entry/how-do-you-make-a-society_b_8078718?guccounter=1&guce_referrer=aHR0cHM6Ly91ay5zZWFyY2gueWFob28uY29tLw&guce_referrer_sig=AQAAABb2GQQH-iWxHkkhT3P2_zgd9iBy9hZPTRSDf3SFdU7CAJ1IzLlV1p6bINhqQx_gHRWbriXZhMIvpS5tPMWJab7nreXOt1I2zmuAB47cQcj1yrIhrSzISYWr-uFf_odZHNIZu6FFWtz96pb5aX7_sI433vxqtono1o7dAkhjMJA2

Nieuwkoop, M. (2018, October 22). Ending hunger to end poverty, ending poverty to end hunger. *World Bank Blogs.* https://blogs.worldbank.org/developmenttalk/ending-hunger-end-poverty-ending-poverty-end-hunger

Oxford Poverty and Human Development Initiative (OPHI). (2020). *Bhutan's Gross National Happiness Index.* https://ophi.org.uk/policy/national-policy/gross-national-happiness-index/

Raworth, K. (2017). *Doughnut economics: Seven ways to think like a 21st-century economist.* Random House Business Books.

Roth, A. (2018, March 31). A 'hellish world': The mental health crisis overwhelming America's prisons. *The Guardian.* https://www.theguardian.com/society/2018/mar/31/mental-health-care-crisis-overwhelming-prison-jail

Taylor, A. (2016, July 8). The Netherlands has a strange problem: Empty prisons. *Washington Post.* https://www.washingtonpost.com/news/worldviews/wp/2016/07/08/the-netherlands-have-a-strange-problem-empty-prisons/

The University of Queensland. (2020). *UQ changemakers: A new global economy – are we entering a new industrial revolution?* [Panel discussion]. https://alumni.uq.edu.au/changemakers-events

United Nations Department of Economic and Social Affairs. (2020). *World social report 2020: Inequality in a rapidly changing world.* United Nations. https://www.un.org/development/desa/dspd/wp-content/uploads/sites/22/2020/01/World-Social-Report-2020-FullReport.pdf

United Nations Framework Convention on Climate Change. (2020). *Science in the negotiations.* https://unfccc.int/topics/science/the-big-picture/science-in-the-negotiations

United Nations General Assembly. (2015). Transforming our world: The 2030 agenda for sustainable development. *Resolution 70/1*, p. 15. https://sustainabledevelopment.un.org/content/documents/21252030%20Agenda%20for%20Sustainable%20Development%20web.pdf

World Health Organization [WHO]. (2001). *International classification of functioning, disability and health.* World Health Organization Press. apps.who.int/iris/bitstream/10665/42407/1/9241545429.pdf

World Health Organization [WHO]. (2007). *International classification of functioning, disability and health – Children and youth version.* World Health Organization Press. apps.who.int/iris/bitstream/handle/10665/43737/

CHAPTER 10

Future Oriented Practice Spaces

Creating Socially and Environmentally Responsible Workplaces

Margot Cairnes and Rosemary Leonard

Abstract

Workplaces as we have known them are fertile sources of experience from which a person might develop wisdom. However, three interconnected social changes; the increased use of AI technology, high levels of unemployment or insecure work, and addiction to screens, exacerbated by the COVID 19 pandemic, restrict the opportunity for personal growth. Kegan's framework for adult brain development can guide experiences for dealing with change including education; collective activities, spiritual practices, addressing mental health and screen addiction. Wisdom demands that we accept change and look for ways of using our innate human capacity to become masters at working with it.

Keywords

wisdom – workplace – brain development – working with change

> The Cambridge English dictionary defines wisdom as 'The ability to use your knowledge and experience to make good decisions and judgments'.[1]

1 Introduction

Workplaces as we know them are a great source of experiences from which a person might develop wisdom. They often offer opportunities to work with a range of people (e.g. customers, clients, co-workers, managers) in diverse ways;

 | DOI: 10.1163/9789004505544_013

they can be sites of continuous learning of both content and skills; the need to deal with the expectations of other people, especially those with some control over your work situation; managing one's own power over others; obtaining feedback on one's performance; obtaining work-life balance; putting oneself forward for new work or new positions; and dealing with negative experiences such as being cheated, bullied, or harassed. Drawing on the adult development literature, which addresses expected changes through the lifespan, for example, employment, marriage, parenthood, retirement) there is evidence that people can grow from life experiences but not all do so. For example, Erikson and Erikson (1998) found that at each life stage there was a choice point for developing as an adult: Intimacy versus isolation; generativity versus stagnation; integration versus despair. Moving through the stages to achieve wisdom is not necessarily easy and can involve a good deal of self-awareness and re-examination sometimes accompanied by a period of depression. Self-development is not something that can be forced onto people. Each person will choose to learn or resist the lessons embedded in workplace experiences. Each person will perhaps learn something different from the same experience. All a workplace can do is provide a supportive environment where people can have varied experiences and room for self-reflection, learning, and emotional growth. Kegan et al. (2014) reviewed two companies that have created such cultures leading to happier healthier staff and improved business performance.

For 30 years, first author Margot Cairnes, worked as a change agent at the level of boards and senior teams of large global companies. Her work involved helping leaders go up the levels of adult development, build healthy relationships that involved self-disclosure, truth telling and robust discussion, then bringing these skills and attributes to formulating and implementing billion-dollar strategic changes. The evidence of her eyes, ears and research showed that when companies were prepared to create environments where healthy and induced growth, were anchored in the reality of the business strategy, everything worked better. People were happier; grateful to be seen and heard as real people, not having to invest so much energy in hiding their real selves and playing time-consuming and dysfunctional political games. Honest conversations allowed for real issues to be raised, examined and solved. This increased trust between all parties and built healthy relationships, which allowed for decisions to be made and quickly enacted. All of this led to increased business success (Cairnes, 1998).

The key areas of resistance encountered were from those who were more interested in controlling their staff than achieving results. Those wanting to achieve and learn were happy to face the real problems and work them through honestly and constructively. Those wanting to maintain the status quo were happy for 'training" or "counselling" or superficial "team building" as long as it was kept separate from the business of the business.

Within western societies, personal growth is generally seen as an individual responsibility. Indeed, in a society dominated by an ideology of liberal individualism (Rubens, 2014) almost all life activities are seen in terms of individual choice. Promoting personal growth is rarely seen as a collective or institutional responsibility of the workplace. Reuben refers to 'job-ocracy', describing the way in which liberal individualism has evolved to define people by the single dimension of their work in which creativity and imagination are rarely encouraged. However, just as companies are required to invest in workers' financial futures through superannuation (pension) schemes, they could be required to invest in their workers' personal growth. Those workplaces that do provide support to workers often employ external agencies to provide individual counselling to help them with individual personal problems rather than fostering resilience for their workplace community.

However, such strategies assume that there is a workplace where workers gather with some type of shared identity, but this is often no longer the case. This chapter argues that as the world of work has changed significantly due to technological innovation and more lately COVID 19 restrictions, the very nature of wisdom at work needs to change too. Wisdom now requires the ability to use your knowledge and experience to make good decisions in an uncertain and rapidly changing environment where there are few certainties and many unknowns. Knowledge then becomes a state of being familiar with change.

2 Is Change Real?

COVID 19 hit the world early in 2020, wiping out around 255 million full time equivalent jobs (International Labour Organization [ILO], 2021). The impact of job loss has been uneven across different parts of the workforce with young workers, women, the self-employed and low and medium skilled workers being hardest hit. The ILO (2021) predicts that while there will be some economic bounce back, post vaccination, the job loss figure is still likely to be 130 million.

As societies around the world have gone into lockdown there has been an increase in the number of people shopping and entertaining themselves online. Computer games and social media encourage addiction to our screens (an addiction being something that we do to excess and can't give up even to improve the quality of our health and lives (Schaef & Fassel, 1988). In the documentary *The Social Dilemma* (Orlowski, 2020), ex high-level staffers from Facebook, Google and Pinterest, along with a range of commentators, reveal the tactics used to monetarise social media, which effectively encourage addiction to social media. As 45% of humans, that is, 3.5 billion people use social media this is important. 90.5% of millennials, 77.5% of GenX and 48.2% of boomers who are active users for an average of three hours a day. This is seen to be increasing anxiety, depression and alienation particularly in the young. *Social Dilemma* reveals that from 2009–2015, girls aged 15–19 had a 62% increase in admission to hospital for self-harm (for girls 10–14 that was a 189% increase) and a 70% increase in suicide (for girls aged 10–14 the increase was 151%). This was correlated with unrealistic beauty standards and rising levels of anxiety and insecurity.

The world of work is increasingly becoming the world of screens. The requirements for social distancing have meant that more and more people are home-based workers and every day new apps appear to service their needs. Many people work at home on computer screens and communicate via apps such as Zoom, Skype and Facetime. An in-house, worldwide study by Nitro Analytics (2020) claims that productivity has increased since people have been working from home. Without the impost of long commutes and with the cancellation of many distractions and increased flexibility, many home-based workers are working longer, more productive hours.

In all we now spend many more hours attached to screens because of our thirst for social media, the rising importance of AI and now distance working and the need for social distancing. Many of us have become extensions of our phones, tablets and desktops.

The phenomenon of people either not working or working from home has hastened the advancement of AI (artificial intelligence) and the gig economy. A number of international leaders have spoken out about the increases in the pace of development of many AI and bio-tech technologies. For example, Jonathan Medved, founder of OurCrowd and one of Israel's leading high-tech venture capitalists recently told a World Economic Forum[2] audience that COVID has led to huge advances. He quoted the CEO of Microsoft as saying that in the first two months of COVID, AI was advanced an equivalent of two years in progress. Google Futurist, Ray Kurzweil (2017), tells us that within the next 10 years, computers will be smarter than most humans. For example, a $100,000 computer may then be better than the average human mind. Everything will be cheaper because we will have nanotechnology-based manufacturing and electronic implants will change the way we live and think. Kurzweil sees these things as improvements. Bill Gates (2019) and Elon Musk (Clifford, 2017) however are less positive about the impact of AI on society. Not only does Elon Musk tell us that robots will do everything better than us and therefore take over the economy, but they may also take over the world and cause WWIII. Less dramatically, Israeli historian, Harari (2017), author of *Homo Sapiens, Homo*

Deus and *21 Lessons for the 21st Century*, tells us that as AI takes over, we will move towards a situation where we have technologically modified and thus upgraded superhumans who control the algorithms and the rest of us who will be economically "irrelevant".

Many people losing their jobs through COVID may never return to the workforce. We are seeing a clearing of the economic decks facilitated by the mass introduction and advancement of AI assisted technologies. Just ten companies – including Microsoft, Alphabet (Google's parent company), Apple and Facebook between them have over US$720 billion in cash reserves (ValueWalk, 2017). If these US tech giants were collectively a country, they would be the 5th richest in the world. The US Government has cash reserves of $140 billion which is overshadowed by the $3464 billion cash reserves of China ("List of countries by foreign-exchange reserves," 2021).

Both Chinese and US tech giants control huge amounts of "big data" and the algorithms that command how AI operates. The ethical and operational future of the world rests in a very few hands. These hands are faced with a huge vacuum created by the demise of thousands of companies and the clearing of the job market by the COVID 19 pandemic. A handful of very rich companies have the funds to finance our technological future and AI is ready and waiting (Krantz, 2020). In a private conversation, a banking executive, who wishes to remain anonymous, reported that his employer had the AI capability to completely replace their call centres. "AI doesn't get sick, it works 24/7, takes no holidays and no smokos" (n.p.). More than that, it is programmed to read and respond to the emotional rhythm of the caller. AI never makes the same mistake twice and forgets nothing. The bank's only problem, he remarked, was the huge political fallout that would follow if they sacked their 150 humans currently in the call centre and replaced them with AI. Well now there are no longer 150 humans in the call centre, or the factories or so many other industries. There is no longer a myriad of individual companies run by humans who know and care for their employees.

In contrast to the power of the tech giants, many individuals are facing a future without huge (if any) cash reserves, worried about how they are going to pay the rent, feed themselves and their families and adapt to an uncertain and chaotic world. There are people isolated in their homes scared about a pandemic that is changing the world forever.

Even before the advent of COVID we had seen massive restructuring of the global workforce. With globalisation came the need to be globally competitive. This led world-wide companies to seek out cheaper sources of labour. Simultaneously, we saw jobs shifted offshore and a rapid increase in less secure forms of employment. Currently, Australia has 3.3million people working on contract or in casual or gig jobs or as labour hire (Actuaries Institute, 2020). When COVID 19 arrived, a third of the Australian workforce was without paid sick or holiday leave entitlements. It is very hard to be wise when you cannot pay the rent or feed your children. While those in secure employment were entitled to Job Keeper, the second-tier workforce of casuals, contractors, gig workers and those on labour hire, were not (Forsyth, 2020).

Inequality is growing – both within countries and between countries. In USA the top CEOs earn around 350 times as much as the average worker. Overall, the richest 10% of adults in world own 85% of global household wealth, while the bottom 50% collectively own barely 1%. The average person in the top 10% owns nearly 3,000 times the wealth of the average person in the bottom 10%. (Davies et al., 2006) Those with secure well-paid work, the beneficiaries of Job Keeper, paid sick leave, holiday leave and parental leave weathered COVID more easily than those who were laid off (or had their hours reduced) due to COVID and had no paid entitlements (from employers or the Government) on which to fall back.

Inequality is not wise. Pickett and Wilkinson (2009) argue that almost everything "from life expectancy to depression levels, violence to illiteracy is affected not by how wealthy a society is but by how equal it is." Societies with large gaps between the rich and the poor are bad for everyone including the well off. This was painfully illustrated with the US response to the COVID pandemic. While the poor were most severely affected the whole country paid a huge cost in terms of illness, personal restriction and economic shut down. If we want to live in a healthy society, we need to provide good health services for everyone. If we want to live in a wise society, we need to make education that builds skills, critical thinking and wisdom into the whole population. To increase wisdom for a whole population we need a strong understanding of how our brains work and the possibility for change. That brings us into the world of neuroscience.

3 Wisdom and the Brain

Neuroscientists (e.g. Norman Doige, 2010) tell us that our brains exhibit plasticity, that is, our brains can change their physical structure as a result of learning. When we learn a skill or a language, for example, we strengthen some neuropathways more than others, thus altering the brain in real and measurable ways. Ironically, our brains don't particularly like change. One way of looking at the brain is as a triune[3] (MacLean, 1990). In this model, the first of the three parts of our brain to develop was the reptilian brain, which interprets the world in terms of survival. When we feel emotionally or physically threatened, we immediately switch into our reptilian brain, which views the world through a filter of fear. The reptilian brain only has three possible responses to fear: freeze, fight or flight. The next part of the triune brain to develop was the mammalian brain otherwise known as the limbic system, paleo-mammalian complex or the midbrain. This part of the brain is unique to mammals and was developed to process emotion and relationships so that we were able to live in social groups. The final part of the brain to develop was the neo cortex. The neo-cortex is part of the cerebral cortex. It is involved in higher functions such as sensory perception, generation of motor commands, spatial reasoning, conscious thought and, in humans, language.

3.1 *Reacting from a Reptilian Brain*

Messages come to our brain somatically, through sensations and feelings perhaps stirred by unconscious memories or feelings and from the world around us; through our senses such as sight, hearing and tactile input. In the first instance, these messages are sent to the thalamus. The *thalamus* is a mostly grey matter structure of the diencephalon that has many essential roles in human physiology. The *thalamus* is composed of different nuclei each of which serve a unique role, ranging from relaying sensory and motor signals to regulation of consciousness and alertness. The thalamus decides in a nanosecond beyond our conscious awareness, if the messages received are Safe, Familiar or Authentic. If they are not processed as Safe, Familiar and Authentic, messages are sent to the reptilian brain. We unconsciously go into freeze, fight and flight.

In times of very rapid change very few received messages will feel Safe, Familiar or Authentic. Everything is changing and we do not know how to act. In times of uncertainty very few of us feel safe so, we go into the fear response: freeze, fight or flight. In times of rapid change and uncertainty, most of us are in reptilian brain most of the time. With the increasing speed and complexity of change we see an upsurge in what is usually labelled "mental ill health": aggression, anxiety, depression, self-harming and a plethora of diagnosable maladies; more awfully, we see a growing incidence of suicide.

3.2 *Wise Brain*

When the limbic system and the neo-cortex work together it is called limbic resonance or *wise brain*. It is the wise brain that allows us to function strategically in times of rapid change. When we come from our *wise brain,* we can see reality as it is, feel and balance our emotions appropriately and work

Nokia story

For most of the early 21st century Nokia dominated the world mobile phone market. In 2007, Google announced the launch of their Android Operating system. Olli Pekka Kallasvuo, CEO of Nokia at the time, realised that Google's forthcoming smartphone would outmatch Nokia's Symbian software platform. He knew they had around 2 years to update their technology. They failed.

Huy and Vuori (2015) claim that strategy is 5% thinking and 95% execution, and that strategy execution is 5% technical and 95% people related. They posit that Nokia lost its winning place in the world mobile phone market because the Nokia people went into fear, which led to bullying and inertia. While Nokia had highly intelligent people, sufficient time and all the necessary resources to maintain their market position, they didn't because fear led to freeze, fight and flight responses, which disabled the whole company.

FIGURE 10.1 Nokia story

our relationships and actions to achieve positive outcomes. In times of rapid change those who are in their wise brains can realistically assess changes in the environment, think through an appropriate response and work successfully with key stakeholders to co-create and innovate, successful ways forward. If the thalamus processes messages as Safe, Familiar and Authentic, they go up into the wise brain where we can consciously decide the best course of action, feel our feelings, choose our behaviours and work our relationships to achieve the best outcome. There are a few complications here but at least if messages go up to the *wise brain* we are in with a chance of developing wisdom (Maclean, 1990). Wisdom in such a world is to find ways to use the plasticity of the brain to help us thrive, to master and use the energy of change. This will require huge shifts in our society, our economy and our work, education and health systems.

3.3 *Obstacles to Developing Our Wise Brain*

There are strong forces thrusting us away from wisdom. One such force is the relatively easy availability of "cheap thrills". Greenfield (2000) argues from a neuroscience perspective that the most basic form of consciousness is intense emotion, not cool reason. People seem driven to seek a loss of identity or letting go as a respite from the more complex brainwork of maintaining meaning and memory. They find it through orgasm, dancing, drug-induced euphoria, or a cold dip on a hot day. Through such things we recover a childlike state of pure feeling. The job of these cheap thrills, according to Greenfield, is to build a transient neural network, which registers sensation intensely. However, they prevent us from engaging larger networks, which would bring in the slowly grown personality laid down inside an adult brain. We regard thrills as cheap because we sense that they have to be kept in check in deference to the mind's larger concerns.

A ubiquitous force against wisdom is our growing addiction to screens. In describing *The Addictive Organization*, Schaef and Fassel (1988) describe a long list of negative impacts of any addiction which include dishonesty, ethical deterioration, fear, self-centeredness, and a crisis orientation and show how they are evident in organisations as well for individuals. Greenfield (2014) believes that our addiction to social media and computer games means we are constantly in a state of reaction rather than building our capacity to grow as creative beings, constructing our own world views and realities. Thus, we deaden our innate capacity to be human.

If Harari (2017) and Kurzweil (2017) are right, we will increasingly be connected to screens through having chips and nano computers inserted in our own beings. Greenfield (2014) postulates that this will simply make us more pliable, controllable and subservient to the powers of those with the algorithms and the money, who control the machines. She argues that our over reliance of screens and our constant seeking for cheap thrills, infantilises us and undermines our capacity to grow our wisdom and advance to adult stages of consciousness. It is our adult stages of consciousness, which allow us to weather change, develop full rich independent lives, and flourish as creative beings. She cannot understand why people want to be more like machines and opt to have chips implanted in their being (Greenfield, 2014). She feels that it makes more sense to use the skills and advantages of machines while developing that which was innately ours, that is, our human consciousness. Thus, it is our humanness that is our competitive advantage over machines. It is the development of this very human consciousness that equates to wisdom in a rapidly changing world.

4 Development of Human Consciousness

One useful way of looking at the development of human consciousness is through Kegan's (2013) levels of adult brain development. He outlines stages of adult mind development; the Imperial Mind, the Socialised Mind, the Self-authoring Mind; and the Self-transforming Mind.

Other writers have developed similar categorisations. For example, Graves' (1966) Spiral Dynamics Model which maps the evolution in thinking of social groups describes an Orange Meme which is equivalent to Kegan's (2013) socialised mind, a Green Meme similar to the Self-authored mind and a Yellow meme similar to the Self-transforming mind. He also presents them as a hierarchy: Orange, lowest then Green, and Yellow highest, but adds that from Green to Yellow is a quantum leap in development and perspective. Another related framework is Bakan's (Bakan, 1966) model of agency and communion where agency is about asserting oneself in the world and communion is about social connections. As argued by Wiggins (1991) and Leonard (1997) agency and communion are two independent constructs so a person can be high in one and low in the other or high in both or low in both. However, agency and communion are not placed within a hierarchy as both are necessary for healthy functioning. Kegan's and Graves' typologies add a third dimension that of personal development which reflects ideas from Eastern traditions whereby people can reach a higher level of thinking and action through mental practices such as meditation and self-reflection.

We have chosen to focus on Kegan's typology and examine each category in terms of people's likely response to rapid change.

4.1 *The Imperial Mind*

The imperial mind is highly egocentric, although many at this level have stunted adult lives (many ending up in prison) it does not necessarily limit success. Kegan (2013) estimates they make up 6% of the adult population. One can be the head of a company, amass a great fortune, or lead a country at this level – usually at the expense of many others (Gillespie, 2017). Those operating from Imperial mind view others as a means to getting their personal needs met. They care about how people see them only if those perceptions have concrete consequences for them. Dominated by greed or fear of personal pain or loss, those at the level of Imperial mind will follow rules and laws only if they fear the consequences of being caught.

The Imperial mind is consistent with agency without communion. Bakan (1966) describes the negative consequences of excessive agency but it is not so much the amount of agency that is the problem but rather the lack of communion. Large expressions of agency in the service of other or society generally are not a problem but if there is a failure of empathy then that agency becomes toxic. There has been a worrying trend for a decline in empathy. For example, Cameron et al.'s (2019) study of 14,000 American college students found they exhibited approximately 40% less empathy than their peers in 1980.

Such people are well adapted for rapid changes because they are not restricted by their previous relationships or commitments. They simply look for the short-term advantage in any situation. Indeed, the rapid changes mean that their history is easily hidden and working via the internet can give them anonymity (Gillespie, 2017). They represent a threat to anyone affected by their bullying, aggression, manipulation, or direct violence. Identifying and managing such people will become even more difficult in the new dispersed and fragmented work environments.

4.2 *The Socalised Mind*

At this stage of development, the individual gains their sense of identity from outside of themselves. Kegan (2013) estimates they make up 58% of adult population. So, status, wealth, appearance, and other socially sanctioned assets are very important to the socialised mind. The most important things for the socialised mind are the ideas, norms and beliefs of the people and system to which they identify (this could be the family, the wider culture or a hippie or bikie gang); whereas the Imperial mind avoids cheating for fear of punishment. The socialised mind avoids cheating because they feel guilty for upsetting others and because cheating transverses the values of right and wrong of their primary group (we would call this group think or peer group pressure). Consequently, those at the Socialised level are continually looking for external validation because this is what gives them their sense of self. At the level of the Socialised Mind, we are who our significant others (directly or indirectly) tell us we are. This can result in socialised thinkers being overly responsible for the feelings and actions of those around them, which is often referred to as co-dependency.

Although someone with a Socialised Mind might have extensive knowledge about a subject gained through experience or study, at this level of development, self-identity is based on group sanctioned "knowledge". When the pace of change was slower, leaders liked to have a highly socialised workforce because such a work force was easier to control. Managers like control. The socialised mind is consistent with communion with little agency. Much has been written about the difficulties for women from excessive communion (Wiggins, 1991), however, strong social relationships and shared identity are almost always positives. It is most likely a limited sense of agency that is the difficulty for the socialised mind (Leonard, 1997).

From a Socialised Mind perspective: safe means "I understand how you feel and what you want so that I can give it to you in return for group acceptance"; familiar means "nothing changes" and authentic means "don't you change, that way I can continue to read what I have to do to win and keep my existing role in the wider group". In times of rapid change these mindsets can be paralysing. When the environment changes rapidly, we need to use our knowledge and experience to make good decisions and judgments in an unknown and uncertain world. Those with a Socialised mind can quickly feel out of their depth because the things they know might rapidly be becoming redundant. As group-sanctioned knowledge becomes outmoded, the socialised person has nowhere to turn for direction and there is a high risk they will react with their reptilian brain. When the only options are flight, freeze or fight the Socialised Mind is likely to freeze and risk falling into what is called mental ill health.

4.3 *The Self-Authoring Mind*

Those with a Self-Authored mind understand that they are a person with thoughts, feelings and beliefs that are independent from the standards and expectations of their environment. They can distinguish the opinions of others from their own and can thus formulate their own set of judgments (Kegan, 2013). A sense of who "I am" develops, with a personal sense of values and purpose. Those with a self-authoring mind can question the expectations and values of others. They can take a stand, set limits, and solve problems with independent mind frames. The self-authoring mind can explore other's thoughts and feelings and create a personal sense of authority or voice. This means they can take responsibility for their own inner states and emotions. Self-authoring minds can generate a personal understanding of the world and are not unduly shaped by the context in which they find themselves. The self-authored mind draws on both agency and communion. Kegan estimates 35% of the adult population have a Self-authoring Mind.

Wisdom from the level of self-authorship is often highly personalised. For example, an "Anti-masker" or "Anti-vaxxer" might well be coming from self-authoring mind. They have written their own story. A socialised anti-vaxxer might simply be fitting into a social group but self-authored minds will have reached their position through their own value sets and internet research.

Applying Graves' (1966) Spiral Dynamics model, Wilber (2000) suggests that this is the level of most Cultural Creatives. They are socially conscious, multi-cultural, and believe that truths are relative. This thinking, according to Wilber dominates in the social sciences and academia. Wilber argues cultural creatives are an "odd mixture of remarkably creative intelligence coupled with a dose of narcissism". This sentiment is echoed by Jungian Analyst, James Hillman in "We've had 100 years of psychotherapy and the world is getting worse". He claims that many at the level of the self-authoring mind have become so fascinated with their own values, views, and perspectives that they have grown increasingly narcissistic. Such narcissism risks reducing self-authoring minds to the level of Imperial minds. In the first author's experience working with community and business groups is that the narcissism and self-righteous certainty that can come with the self-authored mind can easily blind people to reality, impair their capacity to change quickly and therefore undermine their ability to make wise choices.

For those at Self Authoring mind Safe, Familiar and Authentic means "I can find a place that is compatible with my internally generated seat of judgment and personal authority and where my personal limits and boundaries are respected". Familiar means "I have found my tribe, a place where I fit in and feel accepted for being myself" and authentic means "I can fathom who you are and from where you are coming emotionally and philosophically".

Although in times of slow change, this holds the self-authored mind in fairly good stead, in times of paradigm shift (total systems change – which is what is currently happening) even the self-authored mind struggles because all the boundaries can change apparently simultaneously. For example, COVID 19 turned many people's world upside down. Many lost their jobs and therefore their incomes, could no longer have face-to-face contact with their peers, social groups and even loved ones. Many had to move to a new house at the same time. In times of rapid change there is no certainty that what we thought of as normal will remerge. Under conditions of change and therefore stress it is not uncommon for primary relationships to break down or for loved ones to become mentally unstable, physically ill or even die. This is a huge amount of change for anyone to accept and tolerate. COVID showed us that system change can be rapid, not pervasive and become the new normal. Those with a self-authoring mind can o accommodate change over time. The problem with very fast, discontinuous, systemic change is that there are so many changes, so quickly, that we don't get time to recover from one before the next one hits. Under such conditions, old hurts and wounds are likely to emerge at the very time when you have insufficient resources to deal appropriately with them. This weakens us when we have a whole range of present day here and now challenges to face simultaneously.

Faced with such conditions even the self-authored mind feels unsafe (I no longer know who I am in this rapidly changing reality), nothing seems familiar (not even myself), and authenticity can seem to disappear in the mass of uncertainty and the plethora of unknowns and unknown unknowns.

4.4 *The Self-Transforming Mind (1% of the Adult Population)*

At this level, one's sense of self is not tied to particular identities or roles, but constantly created through exploration of ourselves internally or in relation to others and the world around us. This allows us to evolve as the world around us and as our relationships grow and change. Our very being and identity are in a constant state of evolution and flux (Kegan, 2013).

Those with a self-transforming mind can both self-author and work with the authority in others and themselves. Thus, they are no longer a prisoner to their own identity. Life becomes a rich and evolving tapestry full of possibilities into which they can expand and reinvent their identities. They can hold multiple thoughts and ideologies and can thus embrace paradox, and many different (even conflicting) perspectives, simultaneously.

In times of rapid and complex change, such as the present moment, the acquiring of a self-transforming mind assists in building wisdom. It is only a mind attuned to the world as it changes that has 'the ability to use…. knowledge and experience to make good decisions and judgments' when reality is changing very fast, and in many ways simultaneously. As Megginson (1963) said:

> it is not the most intellectual of the species that survives; it is not the strongest that survives; but the species that survives is the one that is able best to adapt and adjust to the changing environment in which it finds itself. (p. 4)

The self-transforming mind is best suited to thriving in times of chaos and rapid systemic change. For those with a self-transforming mind, change is normal. They have been seeking it inside themselves and their worldview, possibly for a lifetime. They are comfortable in times of confusion, paradox and easily tolerate opposing forces and worldviews. For the self-transforming mind, chaotic change is simply life on life's terms. They are comfortable and familiar with change and so they can ride out the crises and losses, seeing them as opportunities to further develop their humanity, their creativity and the fullness of their inner and outer lives

5 What Are the Implications for Wisdom at Work?

Workplaces as we know them now might become rare. Many people will work from home either for just one employer or for several. Even if they go into a particular place to work, they may not belong in the way staff do currently. As work becomes increasingly casualised it will become less reliable and harder to find as there are more people unemployed. The current conservative government is developing legislation to hasten this trend. So, we need to re-examine both work and place as separate entities. Do we need to divest from work as our site of identity formation? Some will invest in communities of practice through professional or trade organisations. Can we invest in local geographical community through the process of re-localisation whereby we work to create local jobs, local food and clothing, and local community support? How could such communities prompt and support the growth of the wisdom that is needed in our time of rapid change? From here on we will not refer to workplaces but rather work cultures which includes how we understand unemployment.

Wise work cultures would be those where people are supported, encouraged, and challenged to grow through the stages of adult mind development towards becoming a self-transforming mind. Wisdom in times of rapid change is the ability to evolve rapidly. This is not an attribute easily accessible to Imperial or Socialised minds. So, for those people to cope better with change they need to develop their modes of thinking. For the Imperial mind this means developing their communion. Of course, people who are truly psychopaths will have no interest or ability to develop in that way (Gillespie, 2017), but others might be encouraged on that route. In contrast the socialised mind needs to develop agency and ability to self-direct their identity development. Usually, people are able to think in new ways, but they need permission, encouragement, and practice to shift their old habits.

Although Kegan (2013) presents his four categories as a hierarchy with the Socialised mind above the Imperial mind it is hard to see how a person would progress from Imperial to Socialised. They would be simply exchanging a lack of communion for a lack of agency. The progress for both Imperial and Socialised levels would be to move to the self-authoring level which integrates both agency and communion. Change is more easily accessed by the Self-authoring mind, but the pace of change is still a challenge. What could be offered is support and challenge to grow into the Self-authoring mind with empathy to attenuate the risk of narcissism and a return to the level of the Imperial mind. The developed mind is as much about feeling as it is about thinking. Wise work practices put such support and challenge in place.

In her work with global corporations and with community groups, Margot Cairnes (1998) has found that the process of growth from socialised to self-authoring and onto self-transforming is facilitated by the adoption of a group purpose. Having people commit to something that is greater than themselves – this includes a mission, but it is broader than that. It is a mission translated into observable measurable results. Thus, personal growth is in the service of achieving for the whole. The growing trend towards B Corporations where companies undergo a strenuous accreditation process and commit to using their business to make the world a better place (Page, 2021), shows the growing willingness of organisations to think past the bottom line and their individual egos.

The self-transforming mind is the most flexible and resilient, but this level is not easily obtained and often requires years of mental practice such as meditation. If Kegan (2013) is right very few people will reach that state of enlightenment so we cannot rely on that small section of the population to help us.

Nevertheless, we can encourage personal development which might lead to self-transformation for more people.

In this time of rapid change, we cannot wait for life experiences to teach us, so what can we do to speed up our mental development? In this section we sketch out some strategies: education; collective activities, religious or spiritual practices, nurturing those with mental health problems, and addressing addiction to our screens.

5.1 *Education*

Wilber's (2000) observation that self-authoring level dominates in the social sciences and academia suggests that education, especially in the arts and social sciences, is one path to raising levels of consciousness. However not all courses will be equally beneficial. We also need to look at mass education and schooling and ask how we can use the many years that children and others spend in the current system to concentrate not just on learning skills but in supporting and challenging everybody to lift their level of thinking thus preparing them for the world of very rapid change. One example is the Preparing for Success Program (Figure 10.2).

Currently workplace education is usually direct training for a particular task or to fulfil occupational health and safety requirements. However, workplaces could provide stimulating education, which could provoke fresh ideas and a safe place for self-reflection. In Wilber's (2000) terms they need to move from monological instruction to dialogical conversation where monological thinking is looking out at the world and analysing it as separate to the self, whereas dialogical thinking is operating in relationship to the world. This would be the difference between traditional scientific method and action research where the researcher is seen as an active part of the system. Sufficient to say, as the world becomes more interconnected and changes speed, we need to learn very new ways of conceptualising it, researching it, and working with it skilfully. This is still considered radical, but wisdom would suggest that what is currently radical makes good sense in the emerging world order. For example, in their strategic leadership work, the World Economic Forum draws maps of how everything is connected to everything else.[4] Although AI can help us access this highly networked world, to deal with it cognitively and emotionally (that is, wisely) we need to grow our brains, that is, our capacity for wisdom.

Both Kegan and Wilber (2013) talk about the role of transpersonal (trans-logical) thinking as part of the route to the transformative mind. Trans-logical thinking is that thinking that happens when we are in a meditative (or transcendental) state. This can occur through personal meditation practices

Preparing for Success Program

Students in the Preparing for Success Program (PSP) at Southern Cross University have found the courage to take their first step in realising their dreams of becoming who they really want to be as a professional in the workplace. They have typically left school early in year 10 (15–16 Years old) and have worked in low paying or unfulfilling jobs as waiters, bank clerks, or mechanics. Somewhere in them they have always felt they could do more with their lives but have not had the opportunity or the self-confidence to pursue their dream career. The PSP provides the pathway into university and equips them with the skills, knowledge and self-confidence to start a university degree with a strong belief in themselves and their ability to navigate and succeed in their new academic context. And succeed they do. Students who do the PSP have higher success and retention rates in their first year undergraduate study than their counterparts who did not do the PSP. The curriculum and pedagogy are set up to encourage students to actively engage with their learning via self-access, self-paced online learning resources that encourage independent learning and flexibility in how and when they learn.

The tutors employ a number of strategies to foster interaction in class, which can be online or on campus. They use the Socratic method of questioning, supporting students to speak up and have their views heard by accepting all views and modelling expectations and appropriate language. Students learn how to accept feedback and use it to their advantage by examining their mindset and if necessary, changing from a fixed to a growth mindset. In one subject, students watch a short video on climate change from Sir David Attenborough and another from Donald Trump and compare the evidence presented to come to their own informed view. The tutors encourage questions and challenge students' understanding and perspectives, modelling how to evaluate and use evidence to support diverse viewpoints and argue a case.

The tutor will often start a topic asking students how the issue relates to their own lived experiences, and then move on to explore the topic from different vantage points. In this way, students build a trusting relationship with their tutors and with each other so that they can take risks, reflect on past beliefs and their new ideas, thereby growing emotionally and intellectually. No longer do they feel disenfranchised: "I thought I'd be mindlessly scrubbing toilets for ever," said one student in a recent focus group.

Now their view of their place in the workplace has changed to reflect their strengths and talents as they go on to become midwives, nurses, researchers, and teachers. They have been empowered to be active agents in their own lives with the self-awareness and emotional maturity to be able to critically reflect and analyse issues from different vantage points. Many of them are committed advocates for higher education as they spread the message about the pathway program and how it has transformed their lives and those around them.

Dr Suzi Syme, Developer of the Preparing for Success Program, Southern Cross University

FIGURE 10.2 Preparing for success program

or group visualisations in community or in the workplace. For example, in his highly successful program U.Lab which has been completed on line by 130,000 people around the world, Scharmer (2021) makes good use of meditation, mindfulness and visualisation as a way of thinking and growing into the emerging future.

5.2 *Collective Activities for Personal Development*

There are models of a more collective approach to personal development. In China it is commonplace for workers to come together to practice Tai Chi to improve both physical and mental health. Such daily rituals might be resisted in western workplaces. A more culturally appropriate approach might be to draw on our traditions of community service and volunteering. Australian Institute of Health and Welfare (AIHW, 2017) figures show that over 31% of people engage in formal volunteering. Informal help is likely to be even more widespread. Volunteering can bring high levels of life satisfaction despite other forms of disadvantage (Australian Bureau of Statistics [ABS], 2014). From prospective studies which follow the lives of people who volunteer for selfless reasons, it was seen that they have longer happier lives (Melina, 2011; Konrath et al., 2012). Although some volunteers are conscious of moral or religious duty, many are not. People who engage in volunteering or service to the community often have a sense that "What comes around goes around". They see themselves as part of a larger system and understand that a place where people help each other is a place that is fairer and safer for everyone even if they personally never expect to have to ask for help.

Currently employers encourage volunteering to varying degrees from requiring intense work commitment which allows no time for other activities through to recognising community service, organising staff group volunteering, and making community service a part of their paid work. Often companies are motivated to corporate social responsibility by their desire to improve their standing in the community. At its most cynical, such activities can be a strategy for an otherwise undesirable activity to be accepted by a community. It is part of the company's "social licence to operate". However, if volunteering were seen as a way of helping people move up the levels of adult development it would be valued for its inherent contribution to individual volunteers, the community and the benefit of the employer.

5.3 *Religious or Spiritual Beliefs and Practices*

Many authors who write about personal development, especially at the level of self-transformation draw on supernatural elements such as a belief in God, trusting in a higher power, transcendent practice such as meditation, prayer and transcendent experience (Wilber, 2000). Similarly, Scharmer (2021) writes about the future as integrating science, spirituality, and profound social change. We would argue that religion and spirituality can be practiced at any level. The Imperial mind might say "I know I am right, and God is on my side". The Socialised minds attend church because others around them do. The Self-authoring minds have considered a range of positions and decided that religion or spirituality are an important part of their identities. All such practices however offer the opportunity for self-reflection and potentially provide a wider gaze whereby the self is part of a larger whole. This wider gaze is an essential step for reaching the level of the Self-transforming mind.

Such broad perspectives are not the sole prerogative of religion and spirituality. For example, people can have a wide appreciation of the glory and complexity of the natural world and their place within it without any supernatural beliefs. A broader perspective can provide an inner sense of equanimity regardless of what is happening around them. They can then calmly see reality as it is and make wiser decisions. They may have lost their identity before so loss of identity through rapid change is no longer a source of fear and anxiety but rather part of the process of life. This does not mean those with a Self-transforming mind have no emotional reaction to change, rather, they can quickly and appropriately process that reaction, learn from it and operate accordingly.

5.4 *Nurturing Those with Stress or Mental Illness*

The first author, Margot Cairnes, belongs to the Mental Health and Wellbeing group of Resilient Byron, a community group that aims at supporting Byron Bay Residents to support each other and increase sustainability in the area. Problems faced in the mental health area include loneliness, anxiety, depression, family violence, addiction, and diagnosable illness. These have all increased with the increased stress and isolation from COVID 19.

Work cultures could also provide greater support for those stressed out or suffering from mental illness. In many cases a period of mental ill health may well be a great opportunity for people to grow into the next stage of development, because when we totally lose our sense of self and our perspective we have to remake ourselves and our world view. Unfortunately, all too often, what is offered is a pill or a quick series of therapy sessions to temporarily or artificially stabilise people. We do not deny the need for such treatment when people are in crisis, but real change is likely to need a longer period of nurturing. As therapist Moore (2012) suggests, depression is simply the soul crying out to be noticed and nurtured.

5.5 *Dealing with Addiction*

Addictions keep us in familiar but self-harming patterns of behaviour; they are a major constraint on personal development and our ability to move to higher levels of consciousness. It is instructive to look at the different ways in which addictions are addressed. In Australia, addiction to smoking has been greatly reduced in recent years through health campaigns, availability of programs, nicotine patches, increases in cost of tobacco through taxes, and restrictions on both advertising and availability. In contrast, opportunities for gambling have greatly increased, especially with online services. For alcohol, there are some advertising and availability restrictions but further efforts to reduce availability meet with great resistance by the liquor industry arguing for the value of their products to our economy. There is also a great deal of knowledge about overcoming addiction from long-term programs such as the 12 Steps developed for self-help by Alcoholics Anonymous and now used for many other self-help groups.

Addiction to our screens is another matter. As Greenfield (2014) argues, we are being infantilised by being manipulated into an addiction to our screens. Recognition of the problem is the first step, but it is hard to see how we can overcome the problem. Abstinence is not a practical option when so much of our work and social life is managed electronically. It would be difficult but not impossible to develop programs to identify and delete or prosecute material that uses known addictive manipulations. This could involve using the knowledge developed in psychology for advertising against the platform developers and advertisers.

6 Conclusion: What Direction Will We Take?

The list of potential interventions is of course not complete. It is an important part of our ability as humans to be creative and inventive. With the fragmentation of conventional workplaces there is the risk that individual people will be left to their own devices. This outcome is unfair. While many might grow through their adversities, others will suffer with flow-on effects to dependents and others around them. This is not wise.

The questions then arise, will education, health services, and work reinforce the trend to infantilise the masses into subservience or will we choose to fully develop our humanity. Will we seek out meditation, martial arts and other self-transcendent practices; will we congregate together to build growth inducing and humanity sustaining communities, which support individuals to go up the levels of adult mind development? Will we think past our narcissism and work together to be of service to others, will we realise that we are part of greater whole and that the well-being of us as a human race depends on us growing our humanity and supporting each other to be creative, community beings? As we work from home, will we learn to connect as humans with those around us or will we seek to become clones of machines living in a machine world where AI can do most of the doing better than we can?

Wisdom for work now has to be evolved.

The three interconnected social changes discussed above; the increased use of AI technology, high levels of unemployment or insecure work and addiction to screens appear to be here to stay and accelerating. Wisdom then demands that we accept this fact and look for ways of using our innate human capacity to capitalise on change and become masters at working with it.

Notes

1 https://dictionary.cambridge.org/dictionary/english/wisdom
2 https://www.weforum.org/strategic-intelligence/
3 While the theory of the 'triune brain' is now being questioned by neuroscientists, it is still widely used by therapists and psychiatrists because it has huge practical application.
4 https://www.weforum.org/strategic-intelligence

References

Actuaries Institute. (2020, December 16). The rise of the gig economy and its impact on the Australian workforce. *Actuaries Digital.* https://www.actuaries.digital/2020/12/16/the-rise-of-the-gig-economy-and-its-impact-on-the-australian-workforce/

Australian Bureau of Statistics (ABS). (2014). *General Social Survey: Summary results, Australia.* https://www.abs.gov.au/statistics/people/people-and-communities/general-social-survey-summary-results-australia/2014

Australian Institute of Health and Welfare (AIHW). (2017). *Australia's welfare – 2017* (Cat. no. AUS 214). Author.

Bakan, D. (1966). *The duality of human existence: Isolation and communion in Western man.* Beacon.

Cairnes, M. (1998). *Approaching the corporate heart* (Rev. ed., 2006). Zaffyre International Limited.

Cameron, C. D., Hutcherson, C. A., Ferguson, A. M., Scheffer, J. A., Hadjiandreou, E., & Inzlicht, M. (2019). Empathy is hard work: People choose to avoid empathy because of its cognitive costs. *Journal of Experimental Psychology: General, 148*(6), 962–976.

Clifford, C. (2017, December 18). 9 of the most jaw-dropping things Elon Musk said about robots and AI in 2017. *CNBC.* https://www.cnbc.com/2017/12/18/9-mind-blowing-things-elon-musk-said-about-robots-and-ai-in-2017.html

Davies, J. B., Sandstrom, S., Shorrocks, A. R., & Wolff, E. N. (2006). The global distribution of household wealth. *UNU-Wider.* https://www.wider.unu.edu/publication/global-distribution-household-wealth

Doige, N. (2010). *The brain that changed itself.* Scribe.

Erikson, E. H., & Erikson, J. M. (1998). *The life cycle completed: Extended version.* W. W. Norton.

Forsyth, A. (2020). Australia's $130 billion JobKeeper payment: What the experts think. *Over60.* https://www.oversixty.com.au/lifestyle/retirement-life/australia-s-130-billion-jobkeeper-payment-what-the-experts-think

Gates, W. (2019, March 26). A.I. is like nuclear energy – 'both promising and dangerous'. *CNBC.* https://www.cnbc.com/2019/03/26/bill-gates-artificial-intelligence-both-promising-and-dangerous.html

Gillespie, D. (2017). *Taming toxic people: The science of identifying and dealing with psychopaths at work and at home.* Macmillan.

Graves, C. W. (1966). Deterioration of work standards. *Harvard Business Review, 44*(5), 117–126.

Greenfield, S. (2000). *The private life of the brain.* Penguin Books.

Greenfield, S. (2014). *Technology & the human mind* [Video]. YouTube. https://www.youtube.com/watch?v=oc7ZYj4CCdM

Harari, Y. N. (2017, September 20). *How technology will turn men into gods* [Video]. YouTube. https://www.youtube.com/watch?v=FzitBZAptoQ

Huy, Q., & Vuori, T. (2015, September 22). Who killed Nokia? Nokia did. *INSEAD Knowledge.* https://knowledge.insead.edu/strategy/who-killed-nokia-nokia-did-4268

International Labour Organization (ILO). (2021). *ILO Monitor: COVID-19 and the world of work* (7th ed.). https://www.ilo.org/global/topics/coronavirus/impacts-and-responses/WCMS_767028/lang--en/index.htm

Kegan, R. (2013, July 11). *The further reaches of adult development* [Video]. YouTube. https://www.youtube.com/watch?v=BoasM4cCHBc

Kegan, R., Lahey, L., Fleming, A., & Miller, M. (2014, April). Making business personal. *Harvard Business Review.* https://hbr.org/2014/04/making-business-personal

Kegan, R., & Wilber, K. (2013, January 20). In over our heads: Development as a lifelong journey. *Integral Life.* https://integrallife.com/over-our-heads/

Konrath, S., Fuhrel-Forbis, A., Lou, A., & Brown, S. (2012). Motives for volunteering are associated with mortality risk in older adults. *Health Psychology Journal, 31*(1), 87–96.

Krantz, M. (2020, March 19). $325 billion in the bank: Nine companies ready for any crisis. *Investor's Business Daily.* https://www.investors.com/etfs-and-funds/sectors/sp500-companies-stockpile-325-billion-cash-financial-mayhem-cornavirus-stock-market-crash/

Kurzweil, R. (2017, November 17). *Top 20 predictions from Kurzweil – future technologies* [Video]. YouTube. https://www.youtube.com/watch?v=WhxhOLm1bjE

Leonard, R. (1997). Theorising the relationship between agency and communion. *Theory and Psychology, 7*(6), 823–835.

List of countries by foreign-exchange reserves. (2021, April 27). In *Wikipedia.* https://en.wikipedia.org/wiki/List_of_countries_by_foreign-exchange_reserves

MacLean, P. D. (1990). *The triune brain in evolution: Role in paleocerebral functions.* Springer.

Megginson, L. C. (1963). Lessons from Europe for American business. *Southwestern Social Science Quarterly, 44*(1), 3–13.

Melina, R. (2011, September 12). People who volunteer live longer, study suggests. *Live Science.* https://www.livescience.com/15978-volunteers-live-longer.html

Moore, T. (2012). *The gifts of depression: Care of the soul.* Little Brown.

Nitro Analytics. (2020). *The future of work: Six trends & takeaways for companies navigating the new normal* (Part 2). https://cdn.gonitro.com/express/pages/resources/library/ebooks/future-of-work/Nitro+Future+of+Work+Report+-+Part+2.pdf

Orlowski, J. (Director). (2020). *The social dilemma* [Film]. Exposure Labs.

Page, R. (2021, March 24). Explainer: What is B Corp status? *IDG Communications.* https://www.cmo.com.au/article/687119/explainer-what-bcorpstatus/#:~:text=Growing%20demand&text=Across%20Australia%20and%20New%20Zealand,in%20registrations%20to%20the%20BIA

Pickett, K., & Wilkinson, R. (2009). *The spirit level: Why more equal societies almost always do better.* Allen Lane.

Rubens, T. (2014). *Classic liberal-individualism and the contemporary Western world.* https://conwayhall.org.uk/ethicalrecord/classic-liberal-individualism-and-the-contemporary-western-world

Schaef, A. W., & Fassel, D. (1988). *The addictive organization.* Harper & Row.

Scharmer, O. (2021). *u.lab: Leading from the emerging future.* https://www.edx.org/course/ulab-leading-from-the-emerging-future

ValueWalk. (2019, November 11). *The ten companies with most cash in the world.* https://www.valuewalk.com/2019/11/top-10-companies-with-largest-cash-reserves-in-the-world/

Wiggins, J. S. (1991). Agency and communion as conceptual coordinates for the understanding and measurement of interpersonal behaviour. In W. M. Grove & D. Ciccheti (Eds.), *Thinking clearly about psychology: Essays in honor of Paul E. Meehl* (pp. 89–113). University of Minnesota Press.

Wilber, K. (2000). *A theory of everything: An integral vision for business, politics, science and spirituality.* Shambala Press.

CHAPTER 11

Realising Positive Futures Where There Appears to Be Little Hope

Janice Orrell and Anjali Habel-Orrell

Abstract

This chapter explores the role of education in helping to realise positive futures for those who live and work in contexts where there seems to be little hope. Hope and hopelessness, and in particular, the damaging impact of inciting hope without action or care are a particular focus. This chapter is premised on the view that a challenging role for education is to construct learning environments in which a sense of purpose, hope, optimism and care prevail. To illustrate the pervasive complexities and tensions at the intersection of education, hope and despair, two contrasting narratives are told and analysed. Both narratives are set in non-formal education programs for women in India. The participants in both of these programs could be described as being at the bottom of the pyramid (BOP) in terms of personal power, economic security and the ability to have agency in their lives. The contrasting conditions of these programs illustrate how education has the potential to be a powerful agent for fostering hope and optimism as well as a very real responsibility in situations where there is little reason for hope. We then illustrate how these conditions not only occur in developing countries, but are evident in our own, Australia. This chapter asks; in the midst of the lived experiences of powerlessness, and hopelessness, what agency and wise practices might education adopt to provoke hope, optimism and aspirations for a life where all can thrive and what changes are needed for this to occur.

Keywords

hope – hopelessness – wise practice – agentic education – integrity of care

1 Introduction: The Idea of Wise Practice

In this chapter we will generate a vision of a positive future that is grounded in wise practice. We begin this exploration with the belief that this vision must

 | DOI: 10.1163/9789004505544_014

include consideration of the needs, rights and wellbeing of all, especially for those living and working in circumstances where there is seemingly little hope. Wise practice is best explained by distinguishing it from the notion of 'best practice' that describes successful activities that are shared for others to emulate. Best practice is a model or a process that has a static positioning, thus it fails to account for diverse histories, cultural contexts, goals and needs that ought, and do, shape practice. Wise practice, by contrast, embodies principles, values and ethics that promote a concern for justice, inclusiveness and egalitarianism. Wise practice includes a weighing-up and a balancing of competing values and acquiescing to reciprocity and compromise in order to achieve a common good. Higgs, in Chapter 1 of this volume, describes wise practice as "having connotations of goodness and socially acceptable judgements, decisions and actions. It is embedded in humanity, being associated with wellbeing of others" (Chapter 1, Section 2).

Society is structured around both the powerful and the powerless, in which the latter are largely unable to confront the issues and structures that are barriers to their experience of hope and their realisation of aspirations and that maintain their oppression and prevailing sense of helplessness. A life in which there is oppression, marginalisation, poverty and no power or support to imagine or rightfully aspire towards attaining a more positive future, is most likely a life that is deprived of hope. Hope and hopelessness and the potential agentic role of education has been chosen in this chapter to examine how those involved in the education of the marginalised and poor might contribute to the realisation of more positive futures for those whose life experiences and survival are challenging and difficult.

In this chapter we explore the lives, conditions, restrictions and possibilities that have led to situations of hopelessness and consider what wise actions are needed to promote hope, optimism and feasible aspirations for the future. We use storytelling to recount our own lived experiences of hopelessness as teachers and community developers in both India and Australia to examine the active role that education can and should adopt to generate hopefulness and wise action to alleviate social and economic impoverishment. The intent is to use these stories to identify the nature of the wise decisions that have been made, or that ought to have been made, to address the challenges faced and to bring about change. Interestingly, what we, as writers, are able to discover by the end of this chapter, is that despite being a mother (Janice) and daughter (Anjali) with a 40-year age gap, there is an obvious synergy in our experiences as teachers. We were both challenged by poverty in the education contexts in which we found ourselves. Furthermore, within these contexts where hopelessness prevailed, we both attempted to find wiser practices than those we had been taught to use, to help those we were teaching to thrive rather than just survive.

Following these narratives we engage in a theoretical exploration of the relationship between education, hope, and what mindsets are needed to ensure justice, equality, hope, optimism and wise practice. In doing so, we will use aspects of the narratives that illustrate dualities in the mindsets of hope and hopelessness, social responsibility and indifference to identify what might be catalysts for change.

2 Lived Experiences of Hopelessness

Hope and hopelessness prevail world-wide and are found where power that is exercised, either wisely or irresponsibly, has a profound impact, either in fostering optimism, joy and inspiring aspiration or in perpetuating the conditions that lead to generational despair and hopelessness. This chapter will narrate two stories in which education features as an intentional strategy for liberation in poor, marginalised communities. These stories are in villages and narrate lived experiences of Indian women from remote communities who are engaged in non-formal literacy education.

2.1 *Janice's Indian Stories: Story 1. The Risk of Hoping for a Better Life*

I can still picture it clearly to this day even though it happened 36 years ago. It was 1984, on a hot South Indian day, where days are only distinguished one from another by either being hot or hotter. I was with a class of 20 literate village women from small, remote villages who had been recruited to become literacy animators (teachers) to poor and illiterate women in their own villages. My role was to help them develop their confidence and ability to teach. A European Christian organisation was building schools for young children in the region and had started the village women's literacy classes as a means of helping the women to be more mobile in their community. The assumption was that the women needed to learn to read and count so they could read bus destinations and thus catch the correct bus to get to town for medical treatment and shopping and then identify the return bus. They would also need to gain numeracy skills so they could shop without fear of being robbed of their meagre funds. Without an understanding about money and having numeracy skills, the women would just hold out their hand full of coins for the shopkeeper, honest or not, to help themselves. The literacy classes, led by local women who were trained as animators, were scheduled to occur in the evenings after the local women had returned from a day's labour in the fields as agricultural coolies. The classes commenced only after the women had stood in long queues to collect water from the well or a tap and prepared an evening meal for their family and food for the following day.

The teacher preparation class was held in a central township and the women who were to become literacy animators had walked several kilometres before travelling several hours on crowded buses to reach it. The atmosphere in the class was relaxed and the women were pleased to be with one another. We sat on the floor of a wide veranda that circled an old mission house and the women chattered amongst themselves about their lives and their villages. So we could all get to know one another I asked the women to draw what their village was like and to include representations of the problems they faced in their village.

The intention was to give everyone a chance to talk, to make the problems they experienced concrete for themselves and others and for me to learn about their lives. The task also demonstrated a more interactive way of teaching in non-formal settings and provided an example that they could reproduce in their own village classes. I had observed that their experiences of learning to teach as village animators were highly didactic in which they sat huddled on the floor while a teacher, usually a man, stood over them lecturing about the 'non-formal method'.

When they had finished drawing, each shared their story with the group, often shedding tears as they spoke. Some stories were so sad that it was difficult not to cry along with them because they revealed so many heart rending, life challenging problems that they faced on a daily basis. Their drawings were of hard labour for little pay; fear of sexual assault while they worked; having to balance taking a day off work to take a sick child for medical treatment against losing their percentage share of the harvesting bonus for bringing in a whole crop in time; being unwanted and unloved in their families because they were girls; and their struggles in collecting enough water at the end of each day. These were low caste or Dalits (outside the caste system) women, therefore, they were the last to get access to the village wells or taps; that is if they could get access at all. Often the water had run out by the time they reached the top of the queue.

Next, I asked the women to imagine and draw what it would look like in their village if they could change just one thing to make life better. I encouraged them to think about what value there would be in helping the women in their village to gain literacy and numeracy skills. I also raised questions for them to consider and include in their drawings such as, in what ways could the women they taught collectively engage in action for change that would improve their lives and that of their children. I thought that by drawing what potential changes would look like, it would help make their aspirations concrete and real.

I had no sooner described this activity when suddenly a mature woman in the group chastised me quite vehemently,

> It is a bad thing that you dare ask me to do that. You should not encourage us to have hopes and dreams, that only brings us hurt and disappointment because it can never happen.

This was such a shock to me and not what I had anticipated at all. I felt sad, confused and foolish. Why had I not considered the possibility that these women might feel safer in accepting rather than confronting their life circumstances. I felt challenged seeing the raw pain of hopelessness in these women's lives that were so constrained by poverty and immutable traditions that imposed such a sense of powerlessness that they feared and rejected experiencing hope.

My Reflection: This experience was a rude awakening for me that forced me to reconsider my assumptions and responsibilities in the way I taught, especially in marginalised communities. I was not unfamiliar with poverty. My first teaching position some 15 years earlier than this event, when I was just 19, had been in a remote rural mill settlement, deep into the Kauri and Jarrah forests in Western Australia. There was 20 miles of forestry tracks to get to a clearing with small circle of houses around a two teacher school with a general store with a petrol bowser next door to the mill and a boarding house for single men who were mill workers. Many of the children had never left the settlement to go to a country town and their families were very poor; poorer than I had ever seen. Little grade 4 girls took care of babies at recess and lunch times while their mothers worked in the timber mill. I witnessed these children struggle with grief and loss caused by the cot deaths of their tiny siblings who had been in their care. I knew they slept two or three to a bed in winter frosts because it would be warmer than sleeping alone under a single thin and worn blanket.

This experience in India taught me that while I could recognise poverty, I did not understand how it might shape the thinking of those in its life path or how it should shape my thinking and responsibility as a teacher in such environments. I cared about the young children I taught in the Australian forest mill settlement, and tried to make learning fun, creative and relevant, but nothing that I did as a teacher was deliberately focused on how the education they received might go some way to contribute to changes in their generational histories of poverty, hard work for minimal pay and limited life chances and choices. My time there was limited, just as it was for the teacher before me and those to follow. We came, we observed, we cared, but we left soon after, often after just one year. This was no way to establish trusting relationships. That takes time to grow.

Fifteen years later in India, despite my changing world view as a feminist educator with a commitment to social justice, I still did not understand my responsibility as a teacher of poor and powerless women any better. I cared about the struggles I could see they experienced as women in remote, isolated villages, but I knew little about them personally, and they did not know me. We were not engaged in a relationship of trust and oneness. I was a participant observer, recruited to meet with them for a few days once a month and occasionally visit their villages to observe their night classes in their remote villages in order to give feedback to help them become effective literacy teachers and inform those funding it of any progress made. I willingly took on this role because I had always believed that education brought hope and fostered aspiration as an act of changing ways of thinking, being and doing. It had been that for me and it had given me fulfillment. Yet here I was, being warned not to speak of change as it would only cause disappointment and harm, not hope and optimism and, once again, I would soon leave and move on.

Reflecting on this experience, I recall a verse in Emily Dickinson's poem, "'Hope' is the thing with feathers":

> 'Hope' is the thing with feathers –
> That perches in the soul –
> And sings the tune without the words –
> And never stops – at all – (Emily Dickinson, in Franklin, 1999)

Reflecting on that challenging moment I could only disagree with Emily Dickinson. It is possible to imagine that many of these women were quite hopeful as small children, but as they matured, as life handed them too many disappointments, hope, and even the desire for hope, faded. I was clearly being confronted with the evidence that hope can and does stop. These women's experiences were living proof that hope was to be avoided in order to avoid despair. I learnt that we, as educators, need to exercise caution before we exercise our drive to inspire aspirations for change. First, we need time to develop a personal relationship so that we and they have an opportunity get to know each other and come to understand what matters most to the other. Being in relationship provides some security to trust that there might be on-going support in any action for change. Without making haste slowly, we risk causing painful disappointment to the very people we hope to liberate.

Over time, my episodic engagement with these women over two years taught me that these women did have some kind of hope, even if they were small collections of immediate and feasible hopes. Hope for a good harvest. Hope that they would be given their rightful daily wage without the additional cost of sexual favours for the foreman. Hope for a new sari when the old becomes too shredded from hard labour in the fields. Hope for a child. Hope for a son. Hope for a safe marriage, not for themselves but for their daughter and a happy one for their son. These hopes had the possibility not to be false hopes. Strikingly absent was their hope for kindness and care from those who had the resources to make changes that would improve their life chances. Neither did they hope for respect for their humanity or hope for justice when their rights as human beings were infringed. Optimism that their future or that of their children could be any better did not exist. Like the mill workers in my home country, these women were poor and disconnected from the sources of empowerment in life. They were, however, only too aware of the realities of their lives and tacitly chose to protect themselves from further disappointment by rejecting any encouragement to aspire for change.

2.2 *Janice's Indian Story 2: Education for Liberation and Empowerment*

This next story follows on from the previous one, only because I, as an author in this chapter, was a participant in both. The context and the outcomes are very different, however, and they have both been chosen for this chapter because their stark differences illustrate that education can have a powerful role in situations where despair prevails in generating hope where there is hopelessness, and aspirations where beliefs are held that one's fate is earned.

The setting for this story is 1986–2021 in an Indian Hill Station established by British expatriates over 100 years before, sitting over 2500 metres above sea level in the Western Ghats in Southern India. The township (which is little more than a big village) is surrounded by jungle, as well as teak, eucalyptus, coffee, tea and cardamon plantations. Throughout the hills, are dotted tiny, remote villages many without roads, electricity or water supplies. Some are many hundreds of years old and only accessible on narrow, dusty, and steep foot tracks, often cut off by rushing streams in monsoon times. In summer, tourists flock to the central township to escape the heat of the plains and children of rich expatriate families attend the many private schools enjoying the safety that the high cooler hill station provides from malaria, cholera and typhoid.

There is a significant social and economic contrast between the lives of the tourists and expatriates and the life circumstances of the young women in the outlying villages. These villages are home to Dalits (non-caste, untouchables) and Indigenous people who are scheduled tribes, who for hundreds of years, have lived in and with the forest. With the encroachment of plantations ever higher up the mountains, along with the settlements of expatriates, the tribal communities, much like Indigenous populations around the world, have lost their homes to encroaching agricultural development, and are forced to live on rocky outcrops, having lost much of their traditional knowledge of health and wellness that they had gained from living in and with the forests.

The local young girls in these remote villages, and even many in the township, have had no more than one or two years schooling, if they had any at all. Any brief educational experience was often unhappy and of little relevance to them. Dalit and Tribal children were considered the bottom of the heap because they were outside the caste system and were often ignored by the village school teachers, who openly favoured the caste children. As a result, these marginalised children left school early, mostly unable to read, write or manage tasks that required basic numeracy, such as shopping. Due to their lack of numeracy, they were often duped of their meagre funds by the street traders. Furthermore, while the boys might learn basic skills 'on the job' such as car mechanics and forge a skilled career without formal education, there was no second chance for girls. From a very young age the girls were encouraged to abandon school so they could care for their younger siblings while their mothers worked as agricultural coolies or hiked high into the hills to collect 2–3 metres long heavy headloads of wood from the surrounding forests that they then carried 20 kms or more back into town to sell. These girls would be married very young in order to "protect their honour" leaving no possibility of returning to education or obtaining skills training. This life of unrelenting hardship and marginalisation was generational, with little or no hope of change. In 1985 I learned that there were marginalised communities of people in these hills, namely, the Tribal, Dalit and recently released Tamil bonded labourers from war ravaged northern Sri Lanka. It was clear that the educational needs of these young girls and women had failed to attract the attention of the government social programs or NGOs (Non Government organisations).

The focus of this story is the introduction of a Grihini program of non-formal education for girls and young women that began in 1986. Grihini, is a generic term used for non-formal educational programs for young women in India described by an Indian philosopher and theologian Dr Jessie Tellis-Nayak (1982). The target group of young girls in this program was between the ages of 12 and 24. They were recruited from the neglected and marginalised community described above as they are the least likely to engage in local government programs because they are wary and distrustful of people with power. The trigger event was the release from bonded labour of the repatriated Tamils from Sri Lanka that brought a local like-minded group together to assess the health, economic and social needs of this group. Since their release, the repatriated community was living in poverty. They had been given land to build a village of very basic housing (huts) but they had no work. Coinciding with the needs assessment was the discovery of Jessie Tellis-Nayak's (1982) book on Grihini education in India, as well as the receipt of an unsolicited donation from the

USA of US $4500 and an offer of rent free accommodation from a local Jesuit College. The combination of these three factors was the basis of a project to establish a non-formal residential education program for young Dalit, Tribal and repatriated Tamil women. Following six months of research, reflection and collaborative planning, as well as visits to other women's education programs that Tellis-Nayak had referred to, a live-in Grihini education program began for girls and women between the ages of 12 and 24 years.

The Grihini curriculum was designed using Freire's (1982) notions of pedagogy of the oppressed and the importance of oneness with the communities. From the outset the program was driven by a set of core values of respect, equality and inclusiveness upon which the program was based: Its goals were to:

1. Build student self-esteem and a sense of empowerment
2. Develop a social consciousness, dispositions of community concern and the capacity to become agents of change
3. Improve village literacy
4. Improve financial literacy and instil habits of saving
5. Develop income generation skills
6. Develop an awareness of the value of women's support networks within and between villages
7. Achieve a change of attitude in families towards young women
8. Develop an awareness of the need for environmental protection
9. Inculcate conscientisation through song, dance and drama
10. Improve women's health through exposure to alternative lifestyles with opportunities to practice them
11. Improve knowledge in the villages of available services and support programs and the law.

Key founders and influencers of the program and its vision and values were a group of Marxist Jesuit men who had become one with the Dalits and Tribals, eating and sleeping amongst them. These men were supported by a small number of educated Indian women who became Akka (big sister) to give the girls care and counsel. Their daily animators (teachers) were women from local communities who had gained an education and were literate and numerate or who possessed relevant skills such as kitchen gardening, tailoring, cooking and handicrafts. Alongside this were expatriates from Australia who sourced funds and visited on an annual basis to act as critical friends in the incremental evolution of the program.

The content of the teaching was relevant to the girls' lived experiences and helped them to understand their basic health care needs and their rights as citizens. There was also a focus on providing care and emotional and social support to the girls. For the first time in many of these young girls' lives they had the opportunity to experience fun, joy and learning achievement that enhanced their health and well-being and their self-esteem. Most importantly, those who taught them, the Jesuit priests, the local 'Akka' or animators, were one with the girls and their communities, respecting them and knowing that their poverty was not a deserved fate, but due to unjust inequities in their society. The women animators' capabilities were complemented by Jesuit priests who had expertise in Indian law and human rights. Literacy and numeracy were not taught as separate skills but were developed within the domains of social awareness learning. The focus of literacy classes were the everyday assumptions about the place of women, class and caste in Indian village society, the purpose of marriage and employer/employee relations which were critiqued and challenged.

Importantly, the curriculum not only focused on developing literacy and numeracy (in the local language of Tamil), but also used instructional strategies that fostered a critical understanding of their circumstances as poor women from marginalised communities as well as their legal rights as citizens of the democracy of India. Being set in India that is a country of diverse cultures and strongly held faiths, each morning the day began with prayer based on the understanding that it didn't matter which God they prayed to so long as that God affirmed them and affirmed others. Following this, they would listen to the early morning Indian news on the radio. This exercise developed their capacity to listen critically and after each broadcast they would recall what they had heard and discuss it in relation to their own experiences.

The residential program engaged the girls in growing some of their own food, gather wood for cooking, and cooking the food. Fostering learning through doing was possible because of the residential nature of the program and confronted ill-founded myths about nourishing foods that were plentiful in the region but not eaten by locals because of misbegotten taboos. For example, papaya was plentiful and a great source of Vitamin A, but no women would eat it because it was thought to induce miscarriage. There is a meme of truth in their concerns. Nutritional research has found that if eaten in the first trimester of a pregnancy papaya is problematic and could promote a miscarriage. Their local, experience-based knowledge of health had been over-generalised so that they perceive eating papaya as a health risk to all females at all times. In Grihini, health and nutrition were learnt in the preparation of meals and care of the forest and environment and was learnt as they gathered wood for cooking and during kitchen gardening. Social awareness was developed through song, dance and improvised dramas in which the girls enacted the trials and challenges they confronted in their villages and explored alternative responses that acknowledged the roots of their oppression and considered new and different ways to confront it.

These engaging and reflective approaches to learning developed personal and social consciousness that visibly improved the students' self-worth and self-esteem. Soon the thin, tearful, and shy young girls who arrived at the program, all too fearful to speak or have eye contact with others, who suffered from hook worm anaemia and toxicity from decaying teeth, developed into healthy, happy, alert and assertive young women who had a positive self-worth. By the time they graduated from the program six months to 10 months later they had gained a sense of their own rights and dignity and responsibility for their families' wellbeing. In addition, they took seriously their responsibility to contribute to the advancement of their community as well as ensuring greater rights and justice in their collective lives. A notable event occurred at one of the first graduation ceremonies when one of the fathers threw himself on the floor of the stage at his daughter's feet and begged her forgiveness for the hard life she had experienced before coming to Grihini and promised her greater respect. There wasn't a dry eye that day. To this day, the girls leave the program having hope and aspiration for a better life. Some go back to school and complete the government high school year 10 and 12 exams and go on to further study to learn nursing, social work and childcare, gaining employment in these fields. A subsequent five-year evaluation revealed that when interviewed about the value of the programs many families reported how their Grihini graduate daughters had persuaded the men in their families to stop drinking the highly toxic local arrack (locally brewed alcohol).

The acceptance of these Grihini graduates in their villages was not quick, but after initial scepticism, village elders realised that these graduates brought valuable knowledge and skills to their communities. Within a year or so the families and village leaders began to recognise the value of having literate, assertive young women who knew how to care for their children in ways that reduced infant mortality in the early childhood; who knew what they were due as workers in the fields and; who knew what services their community was due from their government. They discovered what their entitlements were for their communities and the ways to access them. There are records of tangible achievements due to the efforts of Grihini Graduates, such as getting roads put through to their villages, more taps for water as well as access to electricity. The young Grihini graduates soon began to be included in village decision-making. Importantly, the graduates came to understand the power of collective action. In one instance, they came together from many villages and lobbied as a forceful group to persuade the local council to permit women to have the puta (title deed) to the land on which their houses stood, in their own name. This was important because the men often left the mountain to look for work on the plains and often failed to return. In such case without the puta the women could lose their homes. Evaluation studies after 20 and 30 years of the program demonstrated that the graduates ensured their children and later grandchildren went to school and learnt to read. In one tribal village the graduates collaborated to build a small meeting hall and then weekly, contributed funds to a common pool to employ two teachers to come to their village after school and assist their children do their homework. These graduates had learnt first-hand the power of education.

With so many children, girls and boys, now attending the village schools, the question was raised, was the Grihini program necessary? The external evaluations of the program at 20 and 30 years (Benjamin, 2006; Muthu, 2017) both affirmed that the local women unanimously declared that program was still wanted by the village women. While they believed that their daughters should go to the government schools to get their high school certificate, they firmly believed that the girls would also gain from the type of education that Grihini provided, namely, the personal development, the social and political awareness education and the technical skills development that would help them to seek employment with a future and further education

Janice's Reflection: For some time, those leading and working in and for the program have felt assured of its success in meeting its intentions. The question is, what is it about this program that has meant that it could achieve acceptance in very remote and marginalised villages who were often deeply wary of outsiders? At the start of the program in 1986 those developing the program had wondered if the parents might need to be paid to let their daughters come. This was never necessary. Very quickly there were 3 applicants for every enrolment place. Now, 35 years later, there are over 2000 graduates from 150 remote mountain villages and still more come seeking the program. Why is this? We believe it is because they found there was reason to hope for something better than what many generations before had expected their lives to be like. The longer the program continued, the more many villagers experienced tangible evidence that change was possible, but also understood that change took bravery and action. The following tweet seems to underscore our belief.

> Without education there is no hope, without hope there is no future and future is an amalgamation of education and hope. (Ali, 2013)

So what was so different about Grihini in comparison to the previously described Indian Women's Literacy Program. To address this question the core features of the Grihini program are contrasted with aspects of the program in the first story.

2.3 *Articulation of Core Values, Purpose and Goals*

The first core attribute of the Grihini program was the early articulation of values, purpose and goals. In the six months of prior planning for Grihini, a key

feature was the deliberate development of shared values that would underpin all activities of the Grihini program. They were that Grihini would:
- Be a program based on caring relationships not a project
- Be flexible in its operations and open to change.
- Contain itself to a manageable size and its operations low cost and simple
- Have clear goals and purposes underpinned by respect, equality and critical reflexivity.
- Utilise existing resources and expertise to avoid needless duplication and expose students to people and places they would ordinarily not have.

In contrast, Story 1 (the Women's' Literacy Project's) sole objective was to assist the women to attain basic literacy as a skill. There were two people involved in instigating the project. They were the European chief engineer for the school building program who was very fluent in Tamil and who well understood the local culture and context, and a local educated Indian woman, Rangini, who was the administrator for the school building program. Rangini was an enthusiastic and committed coordinator of the literacy project in a voluntary capacity after work hours. I was recruited as a recently arrived expatriate who had a background in education and literacy and women's liberation from a Western perspective to provide support and ideas for improvement of the program. While there was a spirit of collaboration, and equality among the three of us, there was no deliberately articulated mission and goals for the program. There was also no statement about the core values to guide the design and delivery of the program or underpin the responsibilities of those who worked in the program, namely the field assistants and the animators.

The village animators were theoretically guided, supported and supervised by the field assistants, most of whom had two-year community college certificates as health workers. Apart from my attempts to model and guide the field assistants and animators in adopting more interactive teaching techniques, they lacked an established program of learning for them to develop their knowledge and skills in education, literacy or social awareness. In fact, their collective lack of commitment to the program's success was apparent with the occurrence of a crisis that resulted in the suspension and restart of the program. During my early observation period, I discovered that there were no records of progress in literacy development. However, there were detailed records of village women's debts to the pyramid sales of overpriced cotton saris, run by the field workers and the animators making them significant profits. The remote village women were too afraid to go to town to shop for such items and the people who should be supporting them, were exploiting them. Added to this, through making unannounced visits to the villages at night, Rangini and I discovered that classes only seemed to occur when we negotiated visits to the villages to observe classes. Following these two discoveries, many field workers lost their positions and new ones were recruited.

Try as I might to bring some change, the large evening literacy classes in the villages consisted of women sitting on the floor chanting the alphabet and followed by group out-loud reading of words and sentences that bore little relevance with their lived experiences. This didactic and rote method is typical in reading classes in local primary schools. At one stage I tried to introduce a booklet written in Tamil that contained drawings of women's bodies and information about women's health, pregnancy and childbirth because I thought this was relevant to their interests. Despite the fact that many women have delivered babies in the village, much of the content was a surprise to them. However, the village leaders declared the book to be pornographic and demanded that it be removed. I also tried putting together a newsletter written in Tamil that connected the women between villages and that had news and other content that lent purpose to learning to read. However, there was little support to maintain this initiative when I left. A year later the program folded.

2.4 *Research, Reflection and Evaluation for Program Evolution and Enhancement*

Story Two (the Grihini program) was based on the foundation team's study of literacy programs in India (Tellis-Nayak, 1982), visits to and observation of other Grihini programs and a six-month period of reflection, planning and preparation. In this time local village women who had specific skills and knowledge that aligned with the program were recruited, brought into the planning group and mentored. A core requirement for selection was their disposition of respect towards Tribal and Dalit communities.

The program also evolved over time based on regular internal reflection and review of teaching the class content and the students' progress and engagement. These reviews occurred weekly amongst the teachers, monthly with the students and three monthly with their families. In the early days of the program the parents would join with their daughters in an environmental care program that was part of the curriculum. The intent was for the program to work *with* the students or the villages rather than doing things *to* them. In addition, outsider education and development experts were commissioned to evaluate the impact and worth of the program for the target group every ten years and were invited to present their findings to the teaching and management team to consider its future direction. Thus the program evolved over time from its original design, while remaining true to its core values.

Once again, in contrast, the Village Women's Literacy Program had not been developed from an understanding of the context or of practices in other programs. In the Literacy project, individuals with no connection with the delivery of the classes, were hired to write booklets, that contained simple pictures and letters of the Tamil alphabet, as well as common words and phrases that were presented in increasing difficulty. These booklets were basic and boring, especially when women learners came to class after a long day in the fields, many still with more household responsibilities to attend to. Motivation was not high as they were tired and they failed to perceive any real purpose other than the social interaction with other women. These women were at a stage in their lives where they had priorities other than their own education. The only source of feedback to the founders of the project was from the field workers and animators. Their motivation was to maintain their paid positions, so their feedback on the achievements and impact of the project was positively biased.

2.5 *Equality among All Stakeholders*

From the outset, all those involved in Grihini were considered equal. The facilitators and educators were keen to establish that they were one with the village people, visiting them in their homes and eating with them. This sense of equal status of all was so fundamental and entrenched in the program that even among the original founders it was difficult to find anyone who would claim the title of leader or 'director', to the extent that it sometimes became problematic when grants or accreditation were sought and a lead person was needed to be nominated on the application form. No egos were involved. Everyone had equal rights and a voice that had a right to be heard, no matter what their role or status as student, staff, teacher or parent. All ate the same meal together. Students and core women staff all slept together in the same room. The target community was engaged and their opinion was sought.

In the Village Women's Literacy Project the leaders were respectful of one another, but the directives for the program came from a higher source in a European country. This really left those trying to administer the program with little autonomy or capacity to enact innovation and agency that took account of local needs. Furthermore, the project had not been negotiated with village leaders. These conditions left the people for whom the program was designed with little opportunity to perceive the possibility for change let alone engage in action for change and autonomy.

2.6 *Sustained Contact and Engagement*

There are several features of the Grihini program design that were deliberate choices from the start and have remained. One is that the program would be a residential one so that the students could be exposed to other environments and relationships and envisage possibilities for life outside their village. This meant that the students were younger and had less responsibilities to manage. The residential nature of the program supported the opportunities for novel exposures. The exposures included listening to Radio India at the beginning of each day to learn about their country. They also watched selected socially educative Tamil films that exposed them to new ways of understanding and confronting challenges that the girls were familiar with and had field trips that took them off the mountain, often for the first time in the girls' lives.

The second feature of the program that was determined from the outset was that relationships with and between the Grihini graduates should not be episodic, but should be maintained over years after they had completed the program. Two to three times every year, graduate reunions have been held that have attendances from 200 to 300 women each time and who would bringing their children and other village women with them. These reunions last for several days with food, games, music, dance and drama performances as well as classes with in-depth problem-solving small-group discussions. Often large group decisions were made based on these discussions which sometimes resulted in collective action for change.

In the Village Women's Literacy program there was little chance to develop sustained critical reflection on the conditions that caused problems because the women were living with them every day and had tacitly come to accept them as a strategic path for survival. The woman who scolded me, pleaded that we should not make them hope for things to be different, as it would only bring disappointment. The literacy classes themselves became rituals that centered on rote learning the alphabet and Tamil script writing. Absent from the class agenda was any attempt to build trusting relationships between the women or with the field assistants that might help generate any aspirations for change or provoke any risk taking that could empower and bringing about change.

2.7 *Hope and Empowerment*

Literacy skills alone are not enough. Grihini was deliberate in empowering students and graduates to control their lives. They learnt skills that enabled them to generate a small income when daily wages through coolie work was not available or when they chose to withdraw their labour to force the plantation owners to pay them the legal daily wage. Their animators regularly visited the villages taking raw material for handicraft for those wishing to continue using and developing their new handicraft skills. When the animators visited the graduates, the women gave contributions to a small Grihini banking system from which they could borrow money in hard times, rather than go to loan sharks or banks that charged high interest rates and causing debts that lasted generations. The women always repaid their loans because they understood that repayments were needed to keep the system functional. However, there came a time when the Indian government established a similar banking scheme for supporting women, therefore, as a matter of principle, Grihini ended its banking system rather than duplicate government programs.

Grihini graduates became valued as workers. They had learnt to be good at managing their time and were sought for employment in Balwadis (village childcare), in similar women's non-formal education programs, in offices and local manufacturing mills. Some used their wages to gain further education in nursing, social work, education and the arts. The evaluations at 20 and 30 years into the program identified that the graduates married later and as a result only had children once their bodies had matured. These statistics are in contrast to the early marriages that their mothers and grandmothers were forced to endure as well as their multiple pregnancies that were unable to be sustained because of young age and poor health.

2.8 *Flow Impact of Hope, Aspiration and Success*

Importantly, we should ask about hope in the Grihini context. Is there a difference? The first generations of Grihini graduates did develop a sense of hope and their aspirations were, and still are, for their children to have better lives with less hardship. They also aspired to improve the condition of their homes and villages, by demanding better services and working together to maintain the hygiene of their village. The graduates are reputed to halt the use of toxic arrack (alcohol) and tobacco by the men in their families. These achievements are not hearsay, but findings from external evaluation reports and direct observations and reports from the graduates themselves. Visits from Grihini staff to the villages always draw large crowds of graduates who bring other non-Grihini women. They actively display their willingness to take on ventures to improve their village life and to create opportunities for employment for their youth. The external evaluations report that those who have graduated from the Grihini program, say proudly 'I am Grihini'. It has become a valued personal identity. They have learnt that change is possible.

3 Education, Hope and Hopelessness beyond India

These conditions of hopelessness and despair and aspects of the successful strategies are not only found in developing nations such as India. We will now draw on our own experiences as educators in Australia to illustrate this.

3.1 *Anjali's Stories: Teaching beyond the Three Rs to Motivate Aspirations and Hope*

More than 30 years later, my experiences as a teacher in a number of low socio-economic areas in Australia have not differed greatly with those of my mother, Jan, in her early teaching career. I will recall four situations at four different schools which illustrate how the entrenched hopelessness experienced by children, the conditions which foster it, and the strategies employed to overcome it all resonate with the work of Grihini, in story 2. These stories demonstrate that these problems so easy to identify in a country such as India are also present in Australia in many forms that often go unnoticed. They also underscore the need for wise, rather than best practice, because these problems do not need formulaic responses. They require wise practice that always calls for contextualisation, discernment and social justice.

3.1.1 Story 1: Finding a Reason for Learning

When on placement in a remote school I was shocked by the low literacy and numeracy levels of the students. Many of the older students did not attend school regularly, and of those that did, most of these were there because of the no school, no pool policy. Some had come to escape the challenges of their home lives, to be fed, given a change of clothes, toothbrush etc., but were unable to perceive any value in gaining an education. There were few models for them to emulate. For many, school seemed to be about survival and what they could get in the moment rather than long-term thinking about the possibilities that would flow from any positive educational outcomes. Of course there were younger students, and a few older ones who were interested and engaged in the curriculum, but for many it seemed that school was a social place to be for a few hours that wasn't home. It is possible that I am being unfair here, but there was nothing in my education as a teacher that prepared me for this situation. I heard students saying:

> Why do I need to learn this? I will have a baby and get 'sit money'.

It was disheartening to hear that these girls had given up on their education. Encouragingly, I saw the staff at this site engage powerfully with students by providing access to essentials that were missing, using stories and teaching in the students' first language, and being assisted and sometimes led by the support workers who were a constant part of the community. The teachers formed an identity as caregivers as well as educators with each other, with students and with the wider community. Their attention to well-being and connection, which in turn led to student engagement, was one of the best examples of wise and caring teaching that I have seen since then.

As teachers didn't often stay for more than a few years in these communities, it was important to utilise local members of the community to help build relationships and continue the learning beyond the classroom. An effective strategy that worked the well with younger students was to use puppets and songs. They loved the characters and singing in both English and their first languages and this brought them joy. I found it was easier to get across concepts through song, storytelling and art, as this was the way that learning traditionally happened in this community.

When it came to working with the older students, it was important to make the learning situated and relevant. A maths lesson on its own was uninteresting. A maths lesson about how they could spend money at the tuck shop or local store was much more engaging.

My Reflection: My challenging experiences as a teacher in this community aligns with two of the earlier stories, namely the one set in the Village Women's Literacy program in India and the other in the Western Australian mill town. Hope for larger things seemed missing from general conversations, but hope for smaller things, putting effort into learning was relevant to ensure arriving first at the shop before they ran out of your favourite treat made learning worth achieving and was achievable. The use of storytelling and art to form connections, and the need for people to stay in communities and effect change from within rather than create a program from outside was more effective than one that was required to fit within existing structures and regulations imposed from the outside.

3.1.2 Anjali's Story 2: The Importance of Care and Personal Engagement

During one of my first teaching positions a young girl was put into my class. She had arrived from overseas days before and spoke no English. She was from a large family and her elder brother came to school but was in a different class. She spent the first days crying non-stop, clinging to the class partitions, running to her brother's class, and (I assume) asking for her mother. As it was a very multicultural school, some of the other staff spoke her first language, and at times I was able to speak to her through them, but this not always possible. The first time I was able to speak meaningfully to her on my own was by sitting by her and drawing pictures of our faces. We told each other our names and the words for the different facial features, each in our own languages. This was the start of connection, and soon after I was able to teach her with the rest of the class. Throughout the course of the year, she blossomed into an entirely different child. She became confident, even cheeky, she made friends, began to learn English well and became a vibrant and cheerful part of our class community. Although I moved schools, and she returned to her home overseas, I still get messages from her family checking in with progress and asking how

I am, once again underscoring the power of personal connection to breaking through fear, language barriers and educational divides.

In the early years access to literacy is critical, and in the early years of education there are always children who had not had exposure to a great amount of early literacy. For me some of my more memorable interactions were partly due to poor socio-economic situations in the local area, and partly my lack of understanding on how to work within that.

On returning to school at the end of the first holidays I asked: "what did you do?". I was met with several very similar replies:

> I went to visit dad (or my uncle or brother etc.) in prison.

I realised that I needed a different approach, but I had no response to this. This wasn't my world, these were not my lived experiences and I needed to adapt. If prison was normal and finishing high school was not accepted as a norm, I was unsure how to help the children find purpose in what I was asking them to do. One day I was asked "what are those wiggly lines?". They were the words in a book. This child had no concept not only of how to read, but also no understanding that words could be written and read and used to entertain and communicate. It was overwhelming. I met this with play, with lots of stories, with music and hands on activities. I formed connections with some of the most challenging students, talked to them about their lives. My year 6 and 7s kept journals that were just between me and them (unless of course I thought they needed to be shared for someone's safety). Some stories were unbearably heart-rending. But the thing that I learned the most was that they wanted someone to listen. Someone to hear them. Often that was not someone at home, it was the staff. We were who they were connected to. We had to be in relationship with them and care enough for them to learn to trust us, and in turn learn to learn. So I responded in writing to their journal entries.

In another school I had a child in my class who had extreme health issues which meant he was unable to attend school until year five (I met him in year seven) and he was unable to read. When it came time to assess his reading, I would have to get out the pre-readers, or the junior primary books. "That's for babies, those are baby books!". He knew he was behind and he was scared and proud and ashamed that he did not know how to do the classroom work. "Why do I have to learn to read? The people at Centrelink will fill in the forms for me". I asked him if he wanted to drive a car one day. His reply was: "Yes, obviously!". I asked him how he planned to do that if he couldn't read the rules, or the road signs or sit the test. "It's fine, my friends will just drive me". It was difficult to think what might motivate him to learn to read. We started just with talking and building a relationship. He was interested in his scooter, video games, and chess. We made a deal, every time he attempted to read, we'd shoot hoops or play a game of chess. With that in place, we moved to reading the small books, away from the other students. From there he chose a book he was interested in. It was far beyond his ability, but we got through it. Every day we would read a small section and every day we would play chess. Every time he got frustrated, we would take a break, talk, set a small goal based on a tangible relatable purpose rather than a need for compliance, and then choose one of his rewards if he met it.

My Reflection: These stories illustrate the complexity of learned situational hopelessness in children. For me, personal connections between teachers and students have been the key to inspiring the kind of hope that can lead to learning what matters most, aspirations that are feasible and change. As a teacher I need to feel hope and have aspirations for my students' futures and engage with them as individuals to inspire them to form aspirations. Despite the fact that my education as a teacher included a focus on special education, it did not really prepare me to confront these challenges. Fortunately, I was exposed to teachers who were models of wise practice who showed me how to think, care and act beyond the protocols, curriculum and regulations to find solutions for my students' empowerment to engage in their education with a purpose in mind and some hope and optimism for their future.

4 What Is Hope?

It seems reasonable to expect that those who lead and deliver education to less powerful and marginalised groups should aim to create environments that inspire optimism, hope and aspirations for a better future. But hope alone is not enough. Hope needs to be accompanied by action. Optimism and hope inspire expectations and aspirations that should then become the basis for action and change. Shaping environments that inspire hope, however, are dependent on the willingness of those in positions of leadership, power and influence to take responsibility for making wise decisions for action and change. When instigating aspirations for change it is important for these enablers, to reflect critically and evaluate the impact of their actions, so that the outcomes directly benefit those they seek to help. Education is one of the functional social organisations that has the capacity to shoulder this responsibility.

Hope is embodied in the thoughts, desires, expectations and aspirations for positive outcomes. Freire (1992) describes hope in his book, *Pedagogy of Hope,* as "an ontological need and without it there is hopelessness" (p. 2). Hope does not necessarily depend on a specific outcome, merely on the belief that a possibility for something better exists. Hope can bring inner peace and importantly, hope can become the motivation for engagement and action. Hope can also promote self-belief. Freire describes impoverished contexts where hopelessness prevails as sites of paralysis and immobility in terms of action for change and as environments where fatalism prevails.

By contrast, where hope exists, there is a greater likelihood for taking actions that will lead to a realisation of expectations. Hope promotes optimism and combats negative thoughts and pessimism. Hope can be a catalyst for action for change, but action without hope is pointless. Action for change is important in realising expectations, however, if expectations of change are not met, then there is a risk that hope will fade. Hope is a necessary motivation for action and change, but naïve hope is not enough. Wisdom must accompany hope and must embody critical consideration of feasibility, and is central in generating trust, empowerment and transformation.

5 The Responsibility of Education for Engendering Hope, Optimism and Aspiration

We will now consider the nature of wise thinking and practices and their capacity for fostering aspirations that will contribute to positive futures. In particular we will focus on the role of education and its capacity to foster hope and optimism in contexts where there is little hope. Such contexts have been explored through relating lived experiences of the authors and others and now we will turn to theory to attempt to resolve the question:

> What kind of awareness, actions, knowledge, and decision-making is required of leaders and those with access to resources and power to realise positive futures that generate hope and optimism for all people who live and work in inadequate circumstances?

The media, through film, TV and books, have long provided us with entertaining and heart-warming examples of creative, innovative teachers or educational organisations that have recognised conditions of hopelessness for individuals and groups in one form or another and have chosen to create environments that encourage and support the marginalised and forgotten, to inspire in them a sense of hope and optimism. These models of wise practices demonstrate how educators and the marginalised, together in partnership, have achieved significant changes that have provided hope and fostered aspirations for an enhanced quality of life and expectation about their future as individuals and for their communities. The weakness is, however, that so many of the individual stories of change have been born out of personal disposition rather than from deliberate action of powerful organisations that adopt a disposition towards their public responsibility to make human and financial resources available to liberate the dispossessed.

To address this exploration of the role of education in situations where there is little hope, the next section of this chapter will now examine the theoretical notions of hope and its place in education. To limit these narratives as mere examples would reduce our findings to notions of best practice rather than wise practice. To achieve success and fulfillment in education within environments that are overcome with social, emotional and economic challenges many argue the need to foster 'grit' or 'resilience' (Duckworth & Gross, 2014). For the privileged in society who find themselves challenged by hopelessness, the notion of resilience building might seem reasonable. Medicine, nursing, social work, health professions, policing and media have developed programs for building the resilience of their professionals to cope with the stressors of everyday practice as well as the challenges that accompany working in contexts that manage significant social and health related crises (see, for example, Chisholm-Burns, 2019; Jackson et al., 2007; Janssens et al., 2021; Pearson et al., 2019). We argue that to insinuate that the solution to hopelessness and marginalisation resides in inculcating personal attributes such as resilience in situations of poverty, marginalisation and hopelessness is unfair.

Hicks (2016) argues that it is far easier and less disruptive to the social order to expect that those experiencing hopelessness should be the ones to change, to "toughen up and confront their challenges" (p. 65). Hicks describes this expectation as a 'blind spot' in which those of us who have the resources to enable positive change and inclusion, opt for "denial to save us from having to face up to a problem and take responsibility or think about the consequences of our actions or inaction" (p. 65). This stance ignores the contextual factors that maintain the inequalities that perpetuate the conditions that contribute to marginality and hopelessness in society. In confronting communities and individuals who lack the power and resources to change their circumstances it is more just to consider issues of equity and inclusion and shift the gaze and responsibility for action from individuals to systems and organisations of power (Shaw et al., 2016; Yeh, 2017).

The issues raised by our earlier narratives are not restricted to developing nations. Yet we find individuals and corporations in developed nations recognise and are more open to contribute to the betterment of marginalised communities in developing nations, rather than the social and economic inequities of their own nations. This is because such inequalities in their own nations are largely what sustain their own privileged positions. It is not easy to overcome the tendency for citizens and corporations in developed nations to more easily observe inequalities in other nations. Yet it is easy to agree that promoting optimism, hope and aspiration for all is central to achieving the well-being of a democratic society. Fundamental to a just, thriving democratic society is deliberate action to ensure adequate access to education that is founded on an ethos of care and engages with agencies that ensure the provision of social supports that empowers the least powerful.

Fostering an environment in which hope can thrive requires trust, which is fundamental in establishing conditions for hope. Fisher and Tronto (1990) describe caring as "… a species activity that includes everything that we do to maintain, continue, and repair our 'world' so that we can live in it as well as possible" (p. 41). Tronto (2000) proposed a theory *of integrity of care* that embodies five interdependent elements that are important factors in caring, both by individuals and within organisations. These are: *Caring About*, which is an observable attentiveness and awareness in perceiving the need for care of those individuals and communities who are being marginalised and experiencing hopelessness. *Caring For,* which recognises that awareness of individual's or communities' needs alone is not enough, and must be accompanied by a willingness to take *responsibility* to act and engage in the process of making change. *Care Giving* is the willingness to act that must be accompanied by the acquisition of appropriate knowledge and *competencies* for taking action to ensure that the care given is adequate to meet others' needs wisely. *Care Receiving* embodies an integrity of care that involves a willingness to *critique the impact of one's actions of care giving* on those being cared for. It is not unusual for recipients of care to reject the actions because they feel diminished by a sense of dependency. Care givers, by contrast, often gain enhanced self-esteem through their provision of care. Mindfulness and sensitivity to this impact of care is a cornerstone to the integrity of care. Finally, *Caring with* embodies the ethos and integrity of care and calls for *solidarity and oneness* (being in relationship) with the recipients of care.

Zembylas et al. (2014), in their exploration of Tronto's theory of integrity of care, underscore that caring is not just a disposition, but is a laborious activity that is "crucial for human life" (Tronto, 2000, as cited in Zembylas et al., 2014, p. 203), involving thought, emotions, wise action, and work. Furthermore, it is not merely about individual responsibility, but also an important organisational competence. Optimistically, the possession of an ethos of care is not innate, but can be learned (Gherardi & Giulia, 2016). Where and how this ethos of care might be intentionally learned is an important question that does not readily find an audience in this time of economic rationalism, performativity, measurement and accountability (Moss, 2015; Sims & Hui, 2017). Tronto's theory of the Integrity of Care identifies mindsets of those individuals or organisations that possess an awareness of the need for care, and yet fail to take action as *privileged irresponsibility*.

It would seem that the most powerful argument to begin the process of change to a more caring and hopeful society is to recognise that it is the mindsets, that is, ways of viewing rights and responsibilities, amongst those who are privileged that are important in achieving wise practices if we are to craft more inclusive and positive futures. Krawczyk and Targowski (2019) have argued that "the future of society depends on the wisdom of the elite who are wealthy and the powerful" (p. 180). Wisdom in this case, is having knowledge and a deep inner awareness of contexts and of individual circumstances where hope seems lost. Wisdom is dependent upon possessing the capabilities to support right judgements and right choices if society is to achieve solutions to poverty, marginalisation, pessimism and hopelessness.

Krawczyk and Targowski (2019) perceive that there are critical conditions that influence the mindset of those who have the available resources to enable change and those who have not. These conditions pertain to both individuals and to organisations and communities. The first is their access to resources and power, the second is their awareness of, and connectedness to, the realities of societies, the third is seeking or longing for change. These three conditions give rise to four observable and distinctive mindsets that should be considered in any realistic, feasible (and we could say) wise endeavour that seeks to contribute to the well-being of a more democratic, just and inclusive society. Krawczyk and Targowski's (2019) four distinctive mindsets that either inspire or impede hope and change are:

Hopelessness:	Poor and disconnected from the realities of society and hope
Indifference:	Rich and disconnected from the realities of survival
Socially responsible:	Rich and aware of the realities and aspire to make a difference
Hopefulness:	Poor yet still have hope and longing for better times (p. 180)

Krawczyk and Targowski's and Tronto's notions of social responsibility of those who are privileged, reminds those of us in education who seek to lead change initiatives, that we must do so with a mindfulness about exercising care, that requires critical awareness and wisdom. Activists for change need localised knowledge, capabilities and dispositions that do not set them apart from those for whom they feel a concern. In addition to a disposition towards and ethos of care, they need competencies that stretch beyond pedagogical knowledge to enhance social literacy. This realisation was an important watershed moment in engaging in women's education where there is entrenched poverty and marginalisation in remote Indian villages and in schools in our own nation that are in marginalised communities.

There are many social institutions other than education that are positioned to develop pathways to more positive futures for those experiencing hopelessness, but we chose education, because we believe that at its best, education, has the capacity to create environments that can unveil possibilities for positive futures, and in doing so foster optimism, hope and positive self-regard, particularly in places and situations where these do not flourish. This belief is not surprising, as we, the authors of this chapter, are educators whose working lives have been confronted by communities, people and environments that taught us about the ways that inequality, powerlessness and poverty in society foster feelings of oppression and marginalisation and hopelessness.

The role of education is to unveil opportunities for hope no matter what the obstacles (Monchinski, 2010). There is a need for those who work in education in all its forms to understand the potential role and responsibility for enabling hope that will inspire action. If we can promote hope and optimism in education, it can encourage engagement in learning and promote persistence in the face of challenges. Yet, despite its obvious importance, it would be very hard to find hope and optimism mentioned in a teacher education or school curriculum. It is also questionable that it achieves the focus of attention of leaders of education at all levels of the education systems. Public discourses and polices disclose far greater attention to national and international rankings and comparisons in educational attainment and potential for economic gains through science and innovation. We need to ask why is this important element of care and equality in profession-based education so absent in our discourse as educators and educational leaders?

As educators we should choose to make becoming alert to hopelessness and inequality central to our work. This should occur with all our students, whoever and wherever they are, not just the poor and marginalized. Those of us who educate future teachers and future educational leaders must ensure that it occupies its rightful place in the curriculum and continuing professional education. Awareness of inequality, powerlessness and hopelessness is an important consciousness not only for individuals, but also for communities and organisations. As already stated, awareness and disposition is not enough, it must be accompanied by the development of specialised competencies for wise action and engagement in critical evaluation of the impact of the actions taken. While education alone does not hold the responsibility and wisdom to address social inequality and provide hope, it is, however, the social domain in which many are able to exercise their greatest influence (Noddings, 2003, 2005).

6 Conclusion

We envision that the responsibility for achieving a democratic and socially just society is on the shoulders of those who lead, including those who educate. To shoulder this responsibility, they need to understand what personal and organisational dispositions and competencies are at the heart of wise action (Monchinski, 2010). Educational leadership has a responsibility to be aware of the realities of the inadequacies and insufficiency that the current system of education is for many. Educational leaders need to demonstrate a willingness to take responsibility to provide resources for change while subjecting their decisions and action to critical scrutiny in regard to their impact on those for whom they seek to provide care. Furthermore, they need to do so in a democratic relationship with them and respect the powerful knowledge these communities possess from their experiences of poverty and marginalisation. Tronto's theory of integrity of care provides a useful insight into what is implied and needed.

Krawczyk and Targowski's (2019) four mindsets framework identifies that the reason that some groups of people have little reason for optimism and hope is due to their poverty and disconnection from social justice and support. As a result they experience hopelessness and fail to recognise the possibility for change. These communities are the most critical groups with whom leaders need to actively engage to foster their well-being if we are to have a democratic society. For these communities, gaining hope and optimism are critical in order to develop aspirations for change and engage in the processes for change. Education as a system must shoulder some responsibility to enable this. For the other group identified, who are poor but hopeful, they need the support of change agents and resources, because they will engage in action and change when they experience trusting relationships. The achievements of this latter group can also provide evidence for the former and provoke them to risk having hope and to exercise courage to seek help in confronting the barriers to their thriving.

We acknowledge that throughout all nations there are many programs that already act as catalysts for significant change in poor and marginalised communities. Successful programs demonstrate all the features of Tronto's integrity of care. Unfortunately, the programs are largely the result of the personal dispositions of groups of individuals, many quite isolated, who are doing remarkable things to contribute to the improvement of the lives of individuals and communities. Many enable communities to become agents of their own empowerment. Sadly, the wise practices that are generated in these programs rarely become public knowledge or public models for dissemination and contextual modification to new situations. We have been fortunate enough to meet many such agents of social equality in both India and Australia and understand first-hand what significant changes to the lives of many that wise care enacted with integrity can achieve. Unfortunately, we fear that it may be a long time to wait for national leaders, as a group, to be motivated to collectively take wise action in this regard. However, education as a system and educators as individual practitioners have power, opportunity and resources to undertake wise initiatives that engender hope and inspire aspiration for individuals and for communities. If as a system, education chose to collaborate with national and international initiatives, especially those supported by the goals and initiatives of the UN and WHO, wide scale enhancement to inclusion and equality could be achieved.

References

Agha Rizwan Ali [@AghaRizwanAli]. (2013, January 8). *Without education there is no hope, without hope there is no future and future is an amalgamation of education and hope* [Tweet]. Twitter. https://twitter.com/agharizwanali/status/288691603185491968

Chisholm-Burns, M. (2019). Building resilience to combat stress, burnout, and suicidal ideation among pharmacists. *American Journal of Health-System Pharmacy, 76*(18), 1364–1367.

Duckworth, A., & Gross, J. (2014). Self-control and grit: Related, but separable determinant of success. *Current Directions in Psychological Science, 23*(5), 319–325.

Fisher, B., & Tronto, J. C. (1990). Toward a feminist theory of care. In E. Abel & M. Nelson (Eds.), *Circles of care: Work and identity in women's lives* (pp. 35–62). SUNY Press.

Franklin, R. W. (Ed.). (1999). *The poems of Emily Dickinson.* Harvard University Press.

Freire, P. (1992). *Pedagogy of hope: Reliving pedagogy of the oppressed.* Bloomsbury Revelations.

Gherardi, S., & Giulia, R. (2016). Caring as a collective knowledgeable doing: About concern and being concerned. *Management Learning, 47*(3), 266–284.

Hicks, D. (2016). Educating for hope in troubled times: Climate change and the transition to a post-carbon future. *British Journal of Educational Studies, 64*(1), 129–130.

Jackson, D., Firtko, A., & Edenborough, M. (2007). Personal resilience as a strategy for surviving and thriving in the face of workplace adversity: A literature review. *Journal of Advanced Nursing, 60*(1), 1–9.

Janssens, K., van der Velden, P., Taris, R., & Van Veldhoven, M. (2021). Resilience among police officers: A critical systematic review of used concepts, measures, and predictive values of resilience. *Journal of Police and Criminal Psychology, 36*, 24–40.

Krawczyk, H., & Targowski, A. (2019). *Wisdom in the context of globalization and civilization.* Cambridge Scholars.

Monchinski, T. (2010). *Education in hope: Critical pedagogies and the ethics of care.* Peter Lang.

Moss, S. (2015). Accountability versus blame. *Journal of Perioperative Practice, 25*(1–2), 9.

Noddings, N. (2003). *Happiness and education.* Cambridge University Press.

Noddings, N. (2005). *The challenge to care: An alternative approach to education* (2nd ed.). Teachers College Press.

Pearson, M., McMahon, C., O'Donovan, A., & O'Shannessy, D. (2019). Building journalists' resilience through mindfulness strategies. *Journalism.* https://doi.org/10.1177/1464884919833253

Shaw, J., McLean, K. C., Taylor, B., Swartout, K., & Querna, K. (2016). Beyond resilience: Why we need to look at systems too. *Psychology of Violence, 6*(1), 34–41.

Sims, M., & Hui, S. (2017). Neoliberalism and early childhood. *Cogent Education, 4*(1).

Tellis-Nayak, J. (1982). *Education and income generation for women: Non formal approaches.* Indian Social Institute.

Tronto, J. (2000). Age-segregated housing as a moral problem: An exercise in rethinking ethics. In M. U. Walker (Ed.), *Mothertime: Women, aging and ethics* (pp. 261–279). Rowman & Littlefield.

Yeh, C. (2017, April 14). Forget grit. Focus on inequality: Why is grit at the centre of the national ed. debate? *Education Week.* https://www.edweek.org/leadership/opinion-forget-grit-focus-on-inequality/2017/04

Zembylas, M., Bozalek, V., & Shefer, T. (2014). Tronto's notion of privileged irresponsibility and the reconceptualisation of care: Implications for critical pedagogies of emotion in higher education. *Gender and Education, 26*(3), 200–214.

CHAPTER 12

Yarning and Wisdom

Simon Munro and Diane Tasker

Abstract

Knowledge and cultural understanding of Aboriginal and Torres Strait Islander cultures can be accessed through artefact-based learning and the use of Yarning, conducted in dialogue with Aboriginal people as custodians of that knowledge. Participation in the symbolic and material nature of Aboriginal and Torres Strait Islander knowledge transmission through artefact-based learning can challenge existing perspectives and lead to real cross-cultural systemic change.

Yarning together to write this chapter: The evolution of this chapter would not have been possible without the, sometimes, momentary, and other lengthy conversations (Yarns) between co-authors Simon Munro and Diane Tasker. For Simon, having a Yarn in his Aboriginal culture of the Kamilaroi and Anaiwan is about seeking and being curious about the anabranches of another person's life. (This term is used symbolically to convey curiosity about the many stories that make up a person's life. It means a stream that leaves a river and re-enters it further along its course.) The off-topic information creates a familiar environment where almost, anything is okay to talk about. There is no doubt that the coming together of this chapter is a result of the many invisible Yarns that occurred between the authors. This chapter encodes a great deal of personal experiences and lived journeys that many readers will connect with. Yarning and Wisdom is evidence that change in how Aboriginal and Torres Strait Islander voices are emerging hand in hand with non-Aboriginal and Torres Strait Islander brothers and sisters. Everyone can connect with a Yarn irrespective of their heritage.

Keywords

artefact-based learning – cultural consciousness – yarning – wisdom

Acknowledgement of Country

We wish to acknowledge the traditional peoples of the respective lands where this chapter is being written, the Kamilaroi and Anaiwan nations of Northern

 | DOI: 10.1163/9789004505544_015

and New England Tablelands of NSW and the Dharug and Gundungurra nations of Blue Mountains. Not only are the traditional people of Australia the custodians of their knowledge but also of the land we are privileged to share and practice business on. We would especially like to pay our respects to the Elders, both past and present of this country, and extend that respect to all Aboriginal and Torres Strait Islanders that may read this chapter.

Acknowledging Localised Culture and Content

It is important to acknowledge that any cultural content of the writing in this chapter is drawn from the Kamilaroi and Anaiwan nations as mentioned in the acknowledgment of country. While specific localised Kamilaroi and Anaiwan knowledge has been applied here, the chapter's outcomes and recommendations pertaining to the application of the Bora model of artefact-based learning may be transferable to other Aboriginal and Torres Strait Islander communities and learning environments (Duncan & White, 2015). This should only be considered after thorough consultation and partnership with appropriate Aboriginal and Torres Strait Islander authorities from the respective communities expressing interest in participation of any outcomes and recommendations detailed in this chapter. Our perspective and opinion on the topic of Yarning is not indicative of the broader opinions current in other locations throughout Australia and its territories.

1 Introduction

Aboriginal and Torres Strait Islander wisdom and wise living practice have sustained a cultural identity that is recognised as the oldest living culture around the world. When Geoff Bardon (1989) encouraged the painting of the traditional iconographic designs drawn in the sand in the small community of Pupunya Northern Territory, it began a wellspring of interest in Aboriginal and Torres Strait Islander art and artefact making that would captivate people and draw their interest into this unique aspect of cultural expression (Johnston, 2007).

Having worked in the arts (as a practicing artist and assistant art gallery director) Simon's observations of those attending and appreciating the many forms of Aboriginal art and art theory is well informed. Often the discourse is fluid and migrates from the brush stroke on the canvas to matters of social and political persuasion. This is where 'The Yarn', wisdom in living and understanding the finer detail of human interaction occurs. Perspectives and opinion can be constructively challenged and changed in such art spaces. The precedent can then set to deepen awareness of Aboriginal and Torres Strait Islander people and their histories of living and surviving in pre-colonial to post-colonial Australia.

Aboriginal and Torres Strait Islander art and artefact making through 'Yarning' illuminates broader notions of identity and assists in keeping culture alive by creating spaces where Aboriginal and Torres Strait Islander culture can be valued. Aboriginal and Torres Strait Islander people and their communities take comfort and feel safe in environments where elements of their culture exist. Simon introduces an interesting scenario to better explain to non-Aboriginal and Torres Strait Islander people, the unsafe feelings that many Aboriginal and Torres Strait Islander people feel in the numerous (white founded) domains within today's Australia:

Imagine yourself as a White European person entering a crowded room of people of colour; people who are the descendants of those responsible for the murder, rape, dispossession, and oppression of your forefathers. Imagine that you speak a variation of their language. Although they are polite, they don't really engage well with you. Imagine that the only evidence of your ancient culture is a few paintings hanging on a far wall in the room. There is no rational reason why you should feel unsafe, but you do. You remember the oral stories told to you by your old people, who speak of being cautious around 'coloured people'. Do you feel safe?

For Simon, as a person of Aboriginal heritage growing up in Australia, being the only person of colour in most domains is commonplace for him and many other Aboriginal and Torres Strait Islander people. Simon recounts that his life journey has been built on a heritage, which was pushed and shaped into something it was not meant to be, by a dominant force – European culture. If only, non-Aboriginal and Torres Strait Islander people had had a greater awareness of the invisible struggle for identity and social justice that occurred in Simon's life then perhaps his life may have had fewer heartaches, fewer occasions of being called 'nigger' or 'coon' and more opportunities toward equality. Simon's experiences motivate him to connect with people across cultural boundaries, seeking to connect with people through Yarning and storytelling about his Country and Aboriginal culture.

2 Yarning Is about Taking People on a Storytelling Journey

Although Yarning conventions and artefacts may seem like a combination better left in a community art class or a guided walk and talk through a museum, our chapter demonstrates through practice of our bora model and associated artefact-based learning through Yarning, that there can be a deeper experience which better addresses the void of understanding existing between Aboriginal and Torres Strait Islander culture and white Australia.

Growing up Aboriginal in Australia can be a complex experience because the requirement to move from Aboriginal to non-Aboriginal domains requires a range of acquired skills to sustain parity of participation in the dominant non-Aboriginal culture. Simon argues that moving between cultures requires a set of cross-cultural, skills, which can only be acquired through a person's life journey. These skills are intrinsically learnt in the home and community life as an Aboriginal person whilst others come from being a participant in predominantly non-Aboriginal domains (education, social environments, work domains and sport). For better or worse, Simon recalls that there is a wisdom that comes from the duality of this lived experience and that lies in being able to develop a cross-cultural understanding of how to exist within the two worldviews; this is a person's real experience of bi-culturalism.

We must pay respect to a silent participant in this chapter, Simon's father Eric Stephen George Munro (Eric); so we will tell a story about him. Eric was born in 1941 in the small rural town Tingha, NSW, Australia. He was a keen inland fisherman and so for family, holidays meant camping and fishing. Only now, sorting through the memories of Simon's lived experience as Eric's youngest son can we become aware of the subtleties of Eric's teachings through Yarning and demonstration of what he had to share with Simon. Eric's way of teaching transcended the formalities of a classroom and the many well-established teaching theories and approaches (pedagogies) we turn to when validating our education systems today.

For instance, at the age of 10 maybe 12, Simon recalls being able to tell by the drag of the fishing line, what kind of fish or turtle was being hauled to the bank during regular family fishing trips. This was possible through the patient instruction of Eric taking the time to expertly hold the attention of a child's mind that would otherwise have been occupied with throwing stones in the water to see how high a splash he could make. Securing the curiosity and attention of young minds is a skill that many trained teachers will attest to never being able to master but it was a skill that Eric did without obviously trying. Simon's gaze was directed to follow the line of Eric's bony finger; pointing out over the water where the line met the water. The trace of the fishing line in the water gave the identity of each fish away and so the knowledge acquired by Eric was forwarded on through Winanga-li, instruction (hear), personal observation (listen) imitation (know) and practice (remember). This particular Yarning convention will be explained further in Figure 12.1.

Winanga-li Yarning conventions

Hear

This Yarning convention places importance of allowing time to hear the emotion and feeling that accompanies storytelling and involves two different parties hearing each other's voice as well as changes in the pitch or tone of voice. Hearing also involves being aware and respectful of differences that accompany variations in language. Yarning is a way to talk about things that are culturally and personally important. "Information is embedded within the story or 'Yarn' being told, with the onus on the listener or receiver of the 'Yarn' to hear and make meaning of the information being imparted" (Lin et al., 2016, p. 378).

Listen

This Yarning convention requests that the Yarn not be constrained by strict timeframes enabling both parties to listen and respect the nature of storytelling. Paying attention to the speaker's voice and waiting for their story to be told is a vital aspect of the Yarn. Sometimes, that may involve waiting for a story to begin. Establishing a relationship, building trust, and beginning to understand each other's story is enshrined in the notion of listening. Yarning conventions like listening have the potential to establish reciprocal interest between people and assist both to know and understand where the other "is coming from" (Lin et al., 2016, p. 380).

Know

This Yarning convention is about being willing to engage or 'to know' different ways of knowing and learning and it is a key element of Yarning conventions. Being willing to build our awareness of other ways of knowing and learning and cultural experiences is central to bring about social justice. Having awareness and sensitivity toward Aboriginal and Torres Strait Islander people and knowing what is important to their identity we are making the previously invisible visible and valuing diverse cultural identities.

Remember

This Yarning convention is about putting into action what has been heard, listened to and known. Remembering is demonstrating a sound application of Aboriginal and Torres Strait Islander ways of knowing and learning and being able to move that knowing into social, cultural, educational, and vocational action. Remembering helps avoid misrecognition and misrepresentation of Aboriginal and Torres Strait Islander culture and its people, change.

FIGURE 12.1 Winanga-li Yarning conventions

FIGURE 12.2 Coolamon with rail spikes (Munro et al., 2019)

> Simon remembers … if I close my eyes today, I can still hear the lake wash on the banks and the distant sound of crows and pelican. The glow of other campfires around the lake pepper the dark blanket of my closed eyes like amber jewels and construct a memory like no other learning experience in my life but fishing was so much more than 'just fishing'. Unbeknownst to me at the time, the catching of fish and other animals such as rabbits was not just about the liking of a particular meat. For Eric's family, it was about supplementing the poor wages and disadvantaged state of home with something that was otherwise difficult to pay for. I'm thankful for the lessons.

Eric Munro and his father before him (Walter Munro) demonstrated that in the face of adversity, change and understanding was the responsibility of both Aboriginal and non-Aboriginal people. Expressing and achieving change can be a complex and multi-layered process and there is often pain with change. Simon thinks of his father as a traveller between cultures. He recalls his father being a railway worker in the white man's world from the age of 18 through to retirement and the cultural teacher and custodian of traditional knowledge in the Aboriginal world. Through his art and artefact making, the duality of Eric's life is bought to life in Simon's work 'Coolamon with Rail Spikes' (Munro et al., 2019). See Figure 12.2.

The juxtaposition of both materials presents us with a metaphor of an uneasy harmony demonstrating a limitless possibility to evolve as humans (one species) and the numerous cultures we represent; to change if we are willing and curious enough to Yarn. Yunkaporta (2009) defines Yarning as a dialogue, meeting, or discussion. A deeper understanding of Yarning reveals an interconnected and complex system of knowing and learning that requires culturally unique wisdom in application and surpasses superficial notions of 'just talking or having a Yarn'. For instance, Aboriginal and Torres Strait Islander ways of knowing and learning are linked to each community's' unique storylines, song, dance, initiation, survival, food, medicine through complex understanding of the metaphysical relationships with the natural environment and each other.

Ironically, the use of the term 'Yarning or have a Yarn' can be found to have its origins in English language use as the idiom 'to spin a Yarn' or tell a long, often fabricated and entertaining story. As early as the 1800s. 'Spinning a Yarn' was applied by colonial European explorer Thomas Mitchell in Australia who observed the length of time Aboriginal people took in dialogue as 'spinning a Yarn' (Mitchell, 1848, p. 289). Of course, Mitchell and others like him were a product of imperial thought at the time of Australia's colonial evolution where the Aboriginal way of communicating could be misrecognised and misrepresented as 'spinning a Yarn' instead of a form of language that needed understanding.

With the loss of traditional languages in many Aboriginal and Torres Strait Islander nations, an adaptation had to occur for traditional knowledge and customs to survive. During the forced transition from traditional language to what we now know as Standard Australian English language, traditional language conventions such as storytelling migrated and influenced Standard Australian English to create the Aboriginal and Torres Strait Islander variation now known as Aboriginal English. As a variation to Standard Australian English, Aboriginal English is now spoken within many Aboriginal communities across Australia and its territories. Although Aboriginal English is now an acknowledged spoken dialect of Standard Australian English it is often misinterpreted as bad English when spoken in professional, vocational, social domains and formal education (Eades, 2013).

Because Yarning can vary from one Aboriginal and Torres Strait Islander nation to the next, it is wise practice to be mindful that it is not straightforward (in literature or in conversation). An important element of having a Yarn within the Aboriginal and Torres Strait Islander context involves engaging in an orientation exchange, grounded in establishing tribal or kin affiliation and geographical origins (Eades, 2013). This exchange is reinforced by Aboriginal and Torres Islander thought that a Yarn is like a conversation, but it has also always been used to create and transmit knowledge between people (Yunkaporta, 2019). Yarning in the cultural context here, is intended to stoke curiosity between Aboriginal and non-Aboriginal individuals. It also establishes a sense of connection and belonging through the reciprocity that occurs when people engage in dialogue. Understandably, there is a requirement for a depth of cross-cultural articulation of Yarning conventions (See Table 12.1) by Aboriginal and Torres Strait Islander communities for those outside the cultural context to develop deeper intercultural understanding.

TABLE 12.1 Standard Australian and Aboriginal English forms of introduction

Standard Australian English introduction (orientation) in dialogue using Yarning conventions. (Aboriginal to Non-Aboriginal participants)	**Yarning introduction (orientation) in dialogue using Aboriginal English. (Aboriginal to Aboriginal participants)**
Participant 1: Hello, I'm Simon Munro from Tamworth or Kamilaroi country. **Participant 2:** Hello Simon. I'm Michael Smith I'm from Newcastle. **Participant 1:** Newcastle hey, I studied at the Uni down there in the late 90s. What part of Newcastle do you live? **Participant 2:** Around Jesmond, close to the Uni. Where did you live when you were down there? **Participant 1:** Jesmond, Birmingham Gardens and then New Lambton. Where you raised down there? **Participant 2:** No, my family are originally from Moree. Are you related to the Munro's out there? **Participant 1:** Yes, related to all that crew out there. I don't get out there much but am related on my dad's side. **Participant 2:** Would you know Lyall Munro? **Participant 1:** Yes, he's my great uncle.	**Participant 1:** G'day there brother/ sister I'm a Munro from up Tamworth way on Kamilaroi country. **Participant 2:** Arrh, a Munro hey. Are you related to the mob out in Moree? **Participant 1:** Yes, related to all that crew out there. Don't get out there much but related on my dad's side. **Participant 2:** Your dad from Moree? **Participant 1:** Nah, Anaiwan country up Tingha way. We are all related to the Blairs up that way too. **Participant 2:** Blairs hey. Are you related to Stella? **Participant 1:** That's my grandmother, dad's mother.

Complementary to Yarning, collaborative dialogical inquiry and appreciative inquiry methodologies have been used to explore notions of Yarning cross-culturally and establish understanding, creating a platform for change through the revitalisation of cultural conventions:

> Understanding the importance of Yarning and the transfer of oral knowledge within communities and across generations gave me a real insight

> into what I might be able to bring to my practice when communicating with the Aboriginal community. There is no doubt I will make changes that I hope are positive for all. I feel like this is just the start and I would love to continue to enhance my knowledge of Aboriginal culture. (Munro et al., 2019, p. 7)

Growing up Aboriginal in Australia, Simon recalls how the conventions of Yarning and speaking Aboriginal English were intrinsically practised within family and community. He had not thought of Yarning or having a Yarn as anything more than a natural way that communication occurred with family and community. However, the same Yarning conventions of practice now occur within vocational domains with his colleagues but with the knowledge of being able to switch from Aboriginal English to Standard Australian English, depending on the context and person with whom he might be conversing. This can be viewed as a form of bilingualism.

In Table 12.1 are two examples of such interpersonal discourse: 1) Discourse using Standard Australian English with Yarning conventions and 2) Discourse using Aboriginal English with Yarning conventions. Both examples demonstrate an orientation phase of personal information exchange before anything else (Eades, 2013).

3 Making Artefacts: An invitation to Yarning on and about Country

For many people outside Aboriginal and Torres Strait Islander cultures, the metaphysical nature of the Aboriginal worldview can be a difficult concept to grasp. For many non-Aboriginal and Torres Strait Islander people, art and artefact making may be viewed solely as a creative process but Aboriginal and Torres Strait Islander people view these processes as key to unlocking and building awareness and understanding of their culture and people. For Aboriginal and Torres Strait Islander culture art and artefact making is a holistic experience with the natural environment and every living and inanimate thing in it. Through movement and sacred rituals, Aboriginal people maintain access to the Dreamtime and play a dynamic and ongoing role in the world of the Ancestors (Davis, 2014, p. 184).

Everything is about the land. Aboriginal learning through Yarning about the stories of artefacts will be a journey of acquiring a new knowledge and physical skill, using non-linear approaches to learning, exploring a new landscape. Yarning is a legitimate method in Indigenous research (Bessarab & Ng'andu,

2019) and Yarning Circles have been called a means of social media activism (Carlson & Frazer, 2018).

New knowledge and awareness of cultural differences emerges through participation in the processes of Yarning through art and artefact making. Important to this process for non-Aboriginal and Torres Strait Islander people is being willing to defer to the appropriate experts (Aboriginal and Torres Strait Islanders) who have retained the knowledge and connectedness to the origins their art and artefact making has metaphysically. Patrick Dodson (1997) describes this as follows:

> To understand our law, our culture and our relationship to the physical and spiritual world, you must begin with land. Everything about Aboriginal society is inextricably interwoven with, and connected to, the land. Culture is the land, the land and spirituality of Aboriginal people, our cultural beliefs or reason for existence is the land. You take that away and you take away our reason for existence. We have grown that land up. We are dancing, singing, and painting for the land. We are celebrating the land. Removed from our lands, we are literally removed from ourselves. (p. 137)

Metaphysical thinking and understanding of concepts inherent in Aboriginal and Torres Strait Islander culture will be knowledge that most non-Aboriginal and Torres Strait Islander people have only ever engaged with through media outlets and social and cultural myth. How can non-Aboriginal people come to truly know and understand Aboriginal and Torres Strait Islander culture, if they cannot enter the same physical and metaphysical space with them? Surely wise cross-cultural practice needs to include the sharing of this space and knowledge?

4 Using the Bora Model of Artefact-Based Learning through Yarning

Using our Bora model (Figure 12.3) of art and artefact-based learning through Yarning we present a process whereby an invitation is extended to Aboriginal and Torres Strait Islander and non-Aboriginal and Torres Strait Islander participants to safely engage, share stories and build genuine beneficial awareness of each other. The word Bora is taken from the traditional Gamilaraay language of the Kamilaroi people otherwise spelt buurra (Duncan & White, 2015). It originally referred to the site and ceremony of initiation of young aboriginal men in

Eastern Australian tribes but is used in this context to refer to cultural education processes. When practiced authentically with willing participants, the impact of participation in our Bora model of artefact-based learning through Yarning can be profound. This was demonstrated in a Coolamon-making artefact workshop conducted with University of Newcastle Department of Rural Health (UON-DRH) educators in Tamworth NSW, Australia, 2016. In this learning project, the face value of the artefact, often viewed as a museum piece, was explored using Winanga-li-influenced Yarning conventions with the facilitator (Simon, who is of Aboriginal heritage), storytelling his lived experiences of how he acquired the knowledge of the Coolamon (harvesting and other uses) from his family and community based Aboriginal custodians of the traditional knowledge.

Aboriginal art and artefact making is well documented as a primary mode of teaching and learning within Aboriginal communities, but it also has great potential to increase non-Aboriginal and Torres Strait Islander understanding of Aboriginal ways of knowing and learning (Mbantua Gallery, 2007). We argue that part of wise living practice is knowing about the diversity of people we share space with. We propose that participation in the recreation of an artefact with 'Yarning' in our Bora model of learning will build greater awareness and knowing of Aboriginal perspectives (Lave & Wenger, 1991). To varying degrees, participants came to the workshop with a basic understanding of the Coolamon. This general awareness was that the Coolamon had been an Aboriginal and Torres Strait Islander artefact used by Aboriginal communities for gathering food. Participants' pre-knowledge of the Coolamon provided a platform for the introduction and revitalisation of Aboriginal ways-of-knowing-and-learning to explore broader uses of the Coolamon such as a vessel to carry water, for digging and a cradle for young babies.

> The experience [Coolamon-making workshop] left a physical change as well as a mental change. The importance of learning and discussing Aboriginal culture, artefacts and Yarning. The use of the artefact as a medium to touch, feel and hear the stories portraying both a physical use but also a spiritual sense of how important artefacts are for Aboriginal people. Previous cultural experiences have not delved into this sense of storytelling and physical engagement with the culture, which was captivating for both my mind and my senses. (Munro et al., 2019, p. 7)

The use of a Bora ring as a model of artefact-based learning was adapted from Hall's (1976) Iceberg model of culture, which introduces the notion of a deeper existence of culture from what we see on the surface. Bora ring sites

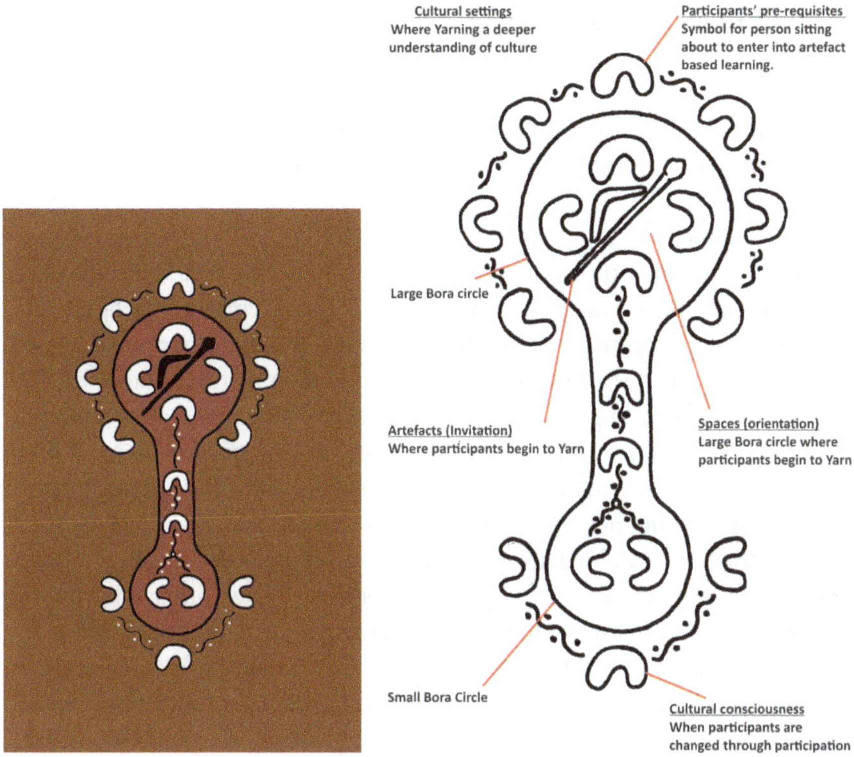

FIGURE 12.3 Bora model

traditionally (in pre-colonial Australia) consisted of two circles set out on the ground and connected by a pathway between them. Typically, Bora sites comprised a smaller ring around 10–15 metres in diameter and a larger ring with a diameter of between 20–30 metres. This varied according to localised practice and other materials used. The larger ring was a more public space, while the smaller ring was sacred and restricted to male participants who were either the instructing male elders or the initiates (Fuller et al., 2013).

Our adaptation of the traditional purpose of the Bora represents an extended invitation to initiates (Non-Aboriginal and Torres Strait Islander participants) into a space where they will be instructed in using the artefact as the central element to construct Yarning discourse around. This involved five phases:

1. Participants' pre-requisites
2. Spaces (orientation)
3. Artefact (invitation)
4. Cultural Settings
5. Cultural Consciousness

5 Participants' Pre-requisites

For the workshop participants, simply attending the workshop was evidence of 'Willingness to engage' and 'Curiosity for new knowledge'. At this phase the artefact becomes a genuine object of interest and curiosity for each participant.

5.1 *Spaces*

Space takes on an entirely different meaning when we consider those spaces to be most important only when people are in them (community, family, colleagues). Having a sense of community through authentic partnerships with Aboriginal and Torres Strait Islander people and their communities is the first step to creating learning spaces. As with traditional Bora sites, where temporality was for a specific purpose (ceremony), establishing spaces that are fluid to the point of being temporary is important to decolonising the notion of formal spaces of where and how education should be conducted. The process of 'getting together and 'catching up about each other' is essential. Ideally, the space should be symmetrical to allow participants to face each other, allowing the Yarning dialogue to flow without anyone having to turn around or talk to the back of someone, without seeing their face. A symmetrical space also allows for the artefact to be placed central to the Yarning dialogue amidst the convention of storytelling.

5.2 *Artefacts*

It is important to acknowledge that artefacts of all kinds, both material and symbolic, play an important role in revealing the essence of those who are connected to, create and continue to create them. The artefact itself is the starting point of a vast topography of knowledge that can orientate all people to Aboriginal ways of knowing and learning. Similar to Hall's Iceberg model what lies in the smaller bora circle (below the waterline and invisible) of Aboriginal and Torres Strait Islanders culture is what most outside of the Aboriginal and Torres Strait Islander culture often fail to make time and space to explore and understand (Jordan et al., 2008). For instance, out of the 2019–2020 Australian bushfire season emerged interest by those outside Aboriginal and Torres Strait Islander culture in the previously invisible wisdom of fire stick farming. From natural disaster and witnessing flora and fauna being pushed to the brink of extinction the revitalisation of an ancient and wise practice emerged. Fire stick farming offers ecological, social and cross-cultural benefits to prevent this. It is a timely reminder through the wisdom of cultural practice (symbolic and material artefact knowledge) that fire stick burning (the symbolic artefact) is a symbol of co-ownership, obligation and an expression of a collective commitment to upholding the sustainable use (and care) of the natural environment (Bliege Bird et al., 2008). Fire stick farming like many other elements of Aboriginal and Torres Strait Islander cultural expression is only known in contemporary Australia because of the culture's adaptive instinct to survive amidst colonial and post-colonial influences. Through engagement with the artefact or an artefact activity, a natural curiosity into the invisible culture of Aboriginal and Torres Strait Islander people can emerge. Yarning about the face value of the artefact moves participants from the orientation circle of the Bora and onto a path of being invited into the smaller circle.

As experienced with the Coolamon project, collaborative participation and the sharing of cultural knowledge is facilitated by Yarning conventions in this phase. Many would associate the physicality of the artefact to disciplines of archaeological and museology as a way to preserve and remind us of how human existence was, sometimes thousands of years ago. However, if we step outside this westernised ethnographic mindset, we start to see the artefact as embodying a continuity of culture, which explores and reveals issues relating to identity and ethnicity, the nature of knowledge, the flow of benefits derived from archaeological research, the indivisibility of tangible and intangible heritage, and different ways of knowing the world (Watkins & Nicholas, 2014). Our Bora model of artefact-based learning offers participants an opportunity to engage with Aboriginal and Torres Strait Islander ideologies. The artefact becomes a tool to decolonise westernised (Smith, 1999) approaches to perceptions of Aboriginal and Torres Strait Islander people and their learning conventions. Learning, no matter how it is variously defined, is something that, functionally, 'happens' as a direct response to some unique interaction, event or 'stimulus', and so the artefact and Yarning conventions become that stimulus (Falk, 2009).

6 Cultural Settings and Perspectives

Aboriginal and Torres Strait Islander nations in Australia have maintained an intimate relationship with the environment, by being embedded in it. Irrespective of the effects of colonisation there is still an understanding of being connected and related to all living things. David Suzuki states,

> I find it interesting that through a sense of total involvement and immersion in the world, Aboriginal people have a sense of wonder and awe and kinship with the rest of life that some of the leading ecologists and other

> scientists are only now beginning to see. We must begin to have greater respect for Aboriginal perspectives and realise that these two very different ways of knowing have things to tell each other. (cited in Campbell, 1993, p. 35)

Our bora model of artefact-based learning provides a cultural setting to learn about what Nakata (2006) has identified as the entanglement of different perspectives and knowledge systems. The bora model takes participants on a Yarning (storytelling) journey to change perspectives. Finally, I could see the link between the strong belief of connection to Country, knowledge transfers from elders and the art of Yarning to the ways of learning many in the Aboriginal community experience. The traditional way of knowledge being handed through the generations is fascinating.

> Use of the Coolamon as a way of facilitating this discussion was unique but a great idea. I felt somewhat in awe of the significance of this artefact in Aboriginal culture but was also keen to create a piece of work that I hoped could generate discussion within my own family. Whilst I am no artist, I was happy with what I created and now have it proudly displayed in my home. The Coolamon was more than simply an artwork. Learning about the significance of it within Aboriginal culture and the means by which it is created was a great experience. (Munro et al., 2019)

> Understanding the importance of Yarning and the transfer of oral knowledge within communities and across generations gave me real insight into what I might be able to bring to my practice when communicating with the Aboriginal community. There is no doubt I will make changes that I hope are positive for all. I feel like this is just the start. (Workshop participant)

7 Cultural Consciousness

Becoming 'conscious' is defined as "having knowledge of something" or "being aware of and responding to one's surroundings" (Collins English Dictionary, 2019). Of note, a Kangaroo Skin Cloak-making workshop and Coolamon-making workshop (Figures 12.4, 12.5, 12.6) produced a cultural consciousness that evoked feelings of being changed through participation. By participating in an art and artefact-learning workshop, it was hoped that participants would

FIGURE 12.4 Workshop Kangaroo skin cloak

FIGURE 12.5 Kangaroo skin cloak

FIGURE 12.6 Coolamon

experience a decolonising of perspectives toward Aboriginal and Torres Strait Islander knowledge, transmission and reception:

> At the beginning of the artefact workshop, I saw the Coolamon as purely a carrying vessel used by Aboriginal people, made from tree bark. I thought it was quite ingenious after hearing of its potential uses. However, by the end of the day I saw the Coolamon as much more than a tangible object. (Coolamon Artefact Workshop, Educator Participant Reflective Writing, 2016)

> I heard stories from past, present and hopes for the future
> I listened

I grappled with confronting knowledge
about my family's past and present colonial settlement
I remembered the stories I heard
I wondered how colonial settlement impacted on Aboriginal peoples.
What role did my family play in the past?
(Coolamon Artefact Workshop, Educator Participant Reflective Writing, 2016)

Artefacts of all kinds, both material and symbolic, play an important role in revealing the essence of those who are connected to, create, and continue to create them. The artefact itself is the starting point of a vast topography of knowledge that can orientate all people to Aboriginal and Torres Strait Islander ways of knowing and learning.

From Simon's perspective, it seems easier to represent and recognise Aboriginal and Torres Strait Islander culture through hanging an artwork on the wall or changing the bricks and mortar to suit. Changing tradition, bias, perspectives, general attitudes, social and cultural voids of understanding is a greater challenge. For many (Aboriginal and Torres Strait Islanders and those outside of the culture) with consciousness toward the historical and current social injustices upon Aboriginal and Torres Strait Islander people, a spectrum of emotions can arise. Anger, denial, manifestation of explicit and implicit discrimination at one end. Hopelessness, economic and social exclusion, transgenerational trauma, and oppression at the other. Simon has journeyed the tightrope of this spectrum and come to personally believe hope, patience and opportunity to change perspective waits at different places on the spectrum. In the context of this chapter and our proposed Bora model of artefact-based learning through Yarning offers an opportunity.

8 Conclusion

Being curious about difference can help people to share knowledge and wisdom about a different culture through Yarning and artefact making. Aboriginal art and artefact making with the accompanying gentleness of Yarning can have a powerful impact on participants, bringing together, different cultural ways of knowing and learning. Our bora model and artefact-based learning may, in part, allow those who are willing and curious to explore a way of knowing and learning that can take them on a deep, visceral and personal fishing trip of their own, similar to that Simon was able to experience with his Dad when he was a child.

References

Bessarab, D., & Ng'andu, B. (2010). Yarning about yarning as a legitimate method in Indigenous research. *International Journal of Critical Indigenous Studies, 3*(1), 37–50.

Bliege Bird, R., Bird, D., Codding, B., Parker, C., & Jones, J. (2008). The 'fire stick farming' hypothesis: Australian Aboriginal foraging strategies, biodiversity, and anthropogenic fire mosaics. *Proceedings of the National Academy of Sciences, 105*(39), 14796–14801.

Campbell, N. A. (1993). A conversation with David Suzuki. *The American Biology Teacher, 55*(1), 31–36.

Carlson, B., & Frazer, R. (2018). Yarning circles and social media activism. *Media International Australia*, 169(1), 43–53. doi:10.1177/1329878x18803762

Collins English Dictionary. (2019). Conscious. In *Collins English dictionary*. HarperCollins.

Davis, W. (2017). *Light at the edge of the world: A journey through the realm of vanishing cultures*. National Geographic Society.

Dodson, P. (1997). Reconciliation in crisis. In G. Yunupingu (Ed.), *Our land is our life: Land rights—past present and future* (pp. 137–149). University of Queensland Press.

Duncan, B., & White, H. (2015). *Speaking our way: A collection of Aboriginal languages within the Northern Tablelands of NSW*. Northern Tablelands Local Land Services.

Eades, D. (2013). *Aboriginal ways of using English*. Aboriginal Studies Press.

Falk, J. H. (2009). *Perspectives on object-centered learning in museums*. Taylor and Francis.

Fuller, R. S., Hamacher, D. W., & Norris, R. P. (2013). Astronomical orientations of Bora ceremonial grounds in southeast Australia. *Australian Archaeology, 77*, 30–37.

Hall, E. (1976). *Beyond culture*. Anchor Books/Doubleday.

Johnston, V. (2007). *Papunya painting: Out of the desert*. National Museum of Australia Press.

Jordan, A., Carlile, O., & Stack, A. (2008). *Approaches to learning: A guide for teachers* (pp. 68–79, 83). Open University Press.

Lave, J., & Wenger, E. (1991). *Situated learning: Legitimate peripheral participation*. Cambridge University Press.

Lin, I., Green, C., & Bessara, D. (2016). 'Yarn with me': Applying clinical yarning to improve clinician-patient communication in Aboriginal health care. *Australian Journal of Primary Health*, 22(5), 377–382.

Mbantua Gallery. (2007). *Indigenous art–securing the future: Australia's Indigenous visual arts and craft sector* [Submission 24]. Parliament of Australia. https://www.aph.gov.au/Parliamentary_Business/Committees/Senate/Environment_and_Communications/Completed_inquiries/2004-07/indigenousarts/ submissions/sublist

Mitchell, T. L. (1848). *Journal of an expedition in the interior of tropical Australia: In search of a route from Sydney to the Gulf of Carpentaria*. Longman, Brown, Green and Longmans. http://purl.library.usyd.edu.au/setis/id/mitjour

Mundine, J. (1989). Aboriginal art in Australia today. *Third Text, 3*(6), 33–42. doi:10.1080/09528828908576212

Munro, S., Brown, L., Croker, A., Fisher, K., Burrows, J., & Munro, L. (2019). *Yearning to Yarn: Using Aboriginal ways of knowing and learning to support clinical placement experiences of Aboriginal health professional students.* Report prepared for the Centre of Excellence for Equity in Higher Education's Excellence in Teaching for Equity in Higher Education. Centre of Excellence for Equity in Higher Education. https://nova.newcastle.edu.au/vital/access/services/Download/uon:35662/ATTACHMENT02?view=true

Nakata, M. (2006). Australian Indigenous studies: A question of discipline. *The Australian Journal of Anthropology, 17*(3), 265–275.

Smith, L. T. (1999). *Decolonizing methodologies: Research and Indigenous peoples.* Zed Books/University of Otago Press.

Yunkaporta, T. (2009). *Aboriginal pedagogies at the cultural interface* [Unpublished doctoral dissertation]. James Cook University.

Yunkaporta, T. (2019). *Sand talk: How Indigenous thinking can save the world.* Text Publishing.

CHAPTER 13

Recognising the Practical Wisdom of People from Refugee Communities

Jeanette Lawrence, Mardi Stow and Giovanna Citta

Abstract

This chapter focuses on the processes of recognising and respecting the distinctiveness and wisdom residing in refugee communities. Recognising the distinctiveness and equality of refugees facilitates their movement the distinctiveness and equality of refugees facilitates their movement from the margins of society and social inclusion. Professional workers with experience in trauma recovery are well placed to recognise the practical wisdom of people from refugee backgrounds. We illustrate the collaboration of professionals and refugee advisors to develop mental health literacy programs for recent refugees from Syria and Iraq. Recognising and adapting to the practical wisdom of refugees, professionals facilitate cascading levels of social inclusion and community engagement.

Keywords

recognition – respect – marginalisation – practical wisdom – refugees

1 Introduction

People do not usually choose to leave their homelands and travel through refugee camps and other dangerous places looking for sanctuary. Neither do people usually choose to remain at the margins of the society in which they settle. Officially invited in and provided for through humanitarian programs, refugees often find the welcome mat is muddied by protectionist discrimination or, more widely, by benign neglect of what they can contribute to society. Refugees are people who have survived violence, trauma and displacement, and demonstrated their willingness and ability to contribute to the social and economic life of countries that invite them to resettle (Hugo, 2014; Refugee

 | DOI: 10.1163/9789004505544_016

Council of Australia, 2010; Victorian Foundation for the Survivors of Torture [VFST], 2020). It is unprofitable as well as inequitable to leave refugee communities marginalised with 'one foot inside the door'. In this chapter, we focus on recognition of the practical wisdom and expertise residing in refugee communities, and how recognition of their distinctiveness facilitates their greater involvement in society. We first address the marginalisation of refugee groups politically and socially, and how facilitating their movement from the margins of society depends on close attention to their equality and distinctiveness, analysing the processes of recognition and respect. We show how professional service workers are well placed to recognise the experience of refugees and to facilitate their social inclusion and engagement. We present an illustrative case of inclusive collaboration within a society-wide mental health literacy project that draws on the practical wisdom of professional workers and advisors from refugee communities from Syria and Iraq resettling in Australia.

2 Living at the Margins of Society

As survivors, refugees have already navigated ways through multiple hardships only to face fresh challenges in procuring the secure housing, employment and education they hope for as they finally settle (Hutchinson & Dorsett, 2012; VFST, 2020). They especially look forward to a place of belonging for their own and future generations (Correa-Velez et al., 2015; Hamas & Vasta, 2009; Slee, 2019; Wille, 2011).

Major countries of settlement provide extensive community-based programs to assist new arrivals to make transitions into their service networks, especially for the health and education services families lacked during transit. Despite being assigned case workers to assist them through bureaucratic procedures and link them with community services, some families and individuals fall through service nets because of risk factors such as uneven provision of local services or lack of cultural understanding on the part of providers (Byrow et al., 2020; VFST, 2020). The Victorian Government's limited success in disseminating Coronavirus information to refugee and other disadvantaged communities is a recent example of the fall-out of unintended miscommunication to marginalised communities.

Marginalisation manifests itself at multiple levels of social life and in multiple ways ranging from systematic discrimination to lack of attention. Acts of exclusion reach across individual lifespans and across generations, feeding inter-subjective feelings of not belonging, of being alien and not valued (e.g., Correa-Velez et al., 2015; Kate et al., 2019; Mowat, 2015; Slee, 2019). In Dobson's (2004) terminology, marginalisation is a special kind of social exclusion

– 'inclusive exclusion' that occurs where humanitarian ideals and government provisions co-exist with competition for resources and scrabbles for power (Kate et al., 2019). Marginalised people live inside society's boundaries, but their lives are anything but free ranging and unfettered.

Not only are marginalised refugees disadvantaged by reduced access to formal and legal institutions but they are also frequently denied a voice in society-wide initiatives. Even when they have attained political citizenship, they do not always enjoy its benefits, especially when the exercise of citizenship rights calls for persistent representation in the face of discrimination or inattention in the public domain. As Mowat (2015) pointed out, incidents of marginalisation can be so varied that any moves to counteract its effects depend on taking account of people's subjective experiences by working with marginalised groups in genuine partnership.

3 Moving from the Margins

It is natural for people to want to move from the margins and to feel at home where they live (Slee, 2019). When functioning at its best, a democratic multicultural society gives new members room to negotiate a place for themselves in the social mix, while government provides the essentials and local communities make adjustments to their specific needs and efforts.

Historically, waves of refugees have become integrated into Australian society through mixing and familiarity in work and educational settings and through inter-cultural marriage (Jupp, 2011). Successive cohorts of refugees and immigrants from Europe, Asia and the Middle East have negotiated bi-cultural identities for themselves as Australians without destroying their ethnic roots (e.g., identifying themselves as Vietnamese-Australians or Australian Greeks). Although formal participation in social and political life does not automatically wipe out discrimination and prejudice, familiarity softens excluding attitudes over time, especially when there is a more recent and unfamiliar group still at the margins.

Authentic engagement requires that new and mainstream cultures both make adaptations, as one South Sudanese group explained: "it is a two-way process from the Australians and the refugees themselves" (Wille, 2011, p. 91). One-sided adaptations (by the new people) do not promote inclusiveness, but instead, promote a subtle form of exclusion practised within a discourse of inclusion. Ponzoni et al. (2017) nicely labelled this disjunction, "the doubleness of inclusion and exclusion" (p. 234): an idea that resembles Dobson's (2004) 'inclusive exclusion' where the official rhetoric is inclusive but everyday activities keep new people out of decision-making processes. In contrast, mutual adaptations (made by the new and the old) enable new people to move from the margins into the centre of activities, by an intentional reciprocity that leads to reformulation of operational problems and changes norms and routines to make them more inclusive. For example, a newly arrived person's difficulties with the dominant English language may be reformulated away from being an individualised problem to a systemic problem that the organisation tackles in its operational system (e.g., by investigating the extent of the problem and assigning resources to using interpreters or bilingual workers). In their efforts to be effective as well as equitable, policymakers need to be alert to the vulnerabilities of particular cultural groups without allowing those vulnerabilities to interfere with the right of each cultural group to be treated as the equal of others (Hamas & Vasta, 2009).

Clyne and Jupp (2011) pointed to the continuing relevance of multicultural principles defined for Australian Society by the Galbally (1978) Committee. These principles laid down that: all migrants should have equal access and have their general and special needs met by all programs and services; be able to maintain their culture without prejudice and disadvantage; and be consulted as clients of services with a view to quickly helping them to self-reliance. The relevance and urgency of these guidelines has not diminished although their implementation has vacillated with political will and priorities.

Unbalanced emphasis on refugees' vulnerabilities leads to expectations of deficiency and lack whenever they are considered without a corresponding emphasis on their strength and agency (O'Higgins, 2012). The dynamics of generating and retaining balanced and informed attention to the characteristics of people at the margins hangs on the processes of recognition and respect. The activity of recognising the strengths and vulnerabilities, the similarities and differences, of refugee people generates the means of enabling their movement in from the margins.

4 Processes of Recognition and Respect

Recognition and respect are two closely related psychological processes commonly understood to describe people's responses to each other (Assmann, 2013; Dickert, 2009; Lawrence et al., 2013). These concepts are used in everyday talk, and taken together, they describe how one person or group perceives and values another. Recognition has captured political attention in being associated with the identity of particular groups in multicultural societies, as it was raised in Charles Taylor's (1994) influential philosophy of political recognition (e.g., Assmann, 2013; Gutmann, 2018).

4.1 *Recognition*

Recognition describes the process by which a person notices and attends to someone. Recognising involves more than seeing them. It has the sense of intensity and depth in the attention given them. Psychologically, the person we call the Recogniser notices the Recognised Person when with close attention they notify and mark the Recognised in a particular manner. In thinking and saying, 'I recognise you', the Recogniser marks the Recognised as a particular person with noticed markers.

Recognition like respect is a response to the characteristics and actions of someone else: the Recognised One (Dickert, 2009; Dillon, 1992). The Recogniser is not absorbed with themself, but is paying close attention to the other, noting what one does in the specific situation. Of course, the Recogniser also is involved in the same situation: concretising and personalising the personalised observation.

There may be considerable variability within a cultural group in how members express their attention or lack of attention to particular people, but there is a generally accepted understanding of what it means for one person to be recognised and another not. Positive recognition marks out a person as having some characteristics or qualities that call out a favourable personal response, for example, a perceived similarity to oneself. Negative recognition marks another person's characteristics as calling out an unfavourable response, possibly, difference from oneself. Negative recognition may indicate failure to notice someone's critical markers or a 'false recognition' (Igor, 2019) or 'misrecognition' (Taylor, 1994).

People who are marginalised may be actively misrecognised by people's negative intentions, or by people's failure to attend to their characteristics, needs or situations, and thus, overlook them. Both forms of non-recognition have psychological significance for the way people relate to each other and depend on reciprocal feedback in the development of people's identity and self-esteem. Thus, Gutmann (2018) recently reasserted the contemporary relevance of Taylor's vision of the oppressive effects of non-recognition in a democratic society. She drew on Taylor's linking of dignity and identity to emphasise taking full account of people's varied situations, especially in the case of those whose group identities would otherwise be neglected (Blacks, women, gays). From this perspective, in direct opposition to overlooking the situations of marginalised people, a genuinely multi-cultural approach should base the social inclusion and treatment of refugees on their right to equal citizenship (UN High Commissioner for Refugees [UNHCR], 2018); and also on recognition of their exceptional refugee experiences (Dobson et al., 2019; Hamas & Vasta, 2009). While Taylor's position is criticised as supporting identity politics that disrupt social cohesion and equality (Assmann, 2013), his insistence on the ethical obligation to respond to group distinctiveness that includes prior hurts and injustices fills out the case for special notice and respect of those groups with particular needs. According to Dillon (1992), special attention and dignity can be grounded in care and protection needs as reasonably as in exceptional achievement. Awareness of the multiple reasons for singling out a particular individual or group as warranting special notice goes hand-in-hand with responding to and registering their worth with respect.

4.2 *Respect*

Respect describes the valuing, worth-ascribing dimension of responding to another person. Activated by noticing, respect adds the valuing dimension of positive regard. Philosophers Dickert (2009) and Dillon (1992) argued that there are both general and specific reasons for responding to a person with positive regard and appreciation of their value. Respect for shared humanity is the universal principle behind treating people with dignity as well as equality. In addition to that common ground, some people are seen as deserving dignity and special treatment because they are celebrities, heroes or outstanding achievers. Other people whose dignity has been denied, deserve its restoration and value the sense of being valued as much as basic provisions. Violation of basic humanity cannot be recognised or noticed without appreciation of the need for dignity and special care (Dillon, 1992; Lawrence et al., 2015). But that is not all that matters for refugees. Respect for refugee survivors also appropriately acknowledges their achievements.

Exclusive attention to the vulnerability of refugees skews the reality of people who at the same time as being wounded and victimised also are coping with new situations with agency and tested skills deserving of special attention and valuing. Refugee women, for example, who may be under-valued or over-looked demonstrate everyday exceptional skills as they manage families and networks; renegotiate traditional connections and practices; and generate new meaning in their lives (Lenette & Ingamells, 2014). Spitzer (2007), for example, found how women from Chilean, Somali and Chinese groups used culturally specific ways of making sense of their new Canadian context, developing hybrid identities and places of belonging. Pulvirenti and Mason (2011) discovered how refugee women in Australia used their past experiences of violence as reference points for interpreting and managing current instances of family violence.

Young refugees also negotiate the contingencies of daily life with largely unacknowledged or misrecognised agency. For example, unaccompanied young asylum seekers in the UK were concerned that social workers treated them only as vulnerable victims and ignored the organisational skills they used to manage the housing and travel requirements that would satisfy the social workers who were over-looking their social competencies (O'Higgins, 2012). Similarly, young refugee clients complained that their Australian counsellors did not recognise what they had and were continuing to achieve and did not consistently treat them as valued persons (Valibhoy et al., 2017).

When a member of the dominant culture, in contrast to overlooking the distinctiveness of a refugee group, recognises their right to be different as well as equal, s/he is taking the first step towards enabling that group to engage with society. By enabling their movement from the margins, s/he is opening-up both parties to an integration style of cross-cultural encounter. According to Berry's (2005) analysis of acculturation strategies, integration is the most positive strategy by which people from both entering and receiving cultural groups made accommodations and adaptations that do not ask the other group to violate their cultural ways. It is positively linked to the development of socially adaptive bi-cultural identities in either group, although historically, the Berry scheme has been applied to the acculturation of entering rather than receiving cultural groups. Mutual adjustments are required to change marginalisation to integration and engagement. As Berry commented in an interview,

> A person can only integrate or assimilate if others in the larger society are open and accepting of that person's culture. There is 'reciprocity' in acculturation: if the person is rejected by the larger society, then the larger society will be rejected by that person. (Interview by Emamzadeh, 2018, p. 2)

The South Sudanese men in Wille's (2011) Australian study understood this need for reciprocal adjustments, unlike conservative political and media figures whose negative representations of Sudanese youth show little accommodation by them, and little concern about the young people's disrupted sense of belonging and wellbeing (Macaulay & Deppeler, 2020). Such dismissive representations resist any suggestion that local communities may need to meet refugee communities halfway as they deal with resettlement problems. Ideally, social inclusion involves adjustments by the dominant culture of its local norms and routines so that marginalised groups can fit in without having to surrender all their norms and routines. In turn, marginalised groups need to be willing to make some, but not all, the accommodations. The specifics of reciprocal adjustment and compromise will vary over situations and time, as different indicators of social inclusion emerge in continuing interactions.

5 A Collaborative Partnership Built on Recognition and Respect

Client participation in program development is widely accepted as best practice in public health (Ocloo & Matthews, 2016; Pratt, 2019), especially when it ensures that community members are being empowered in the process and avoids token participation. Our illustrative case focuses on the inclusion of advisors from refugee communities (refugee advisors). They were central to the development of community programs to address a society-wide issue that has direct relevance to the life circumstances of refugee communities. The issue is the prevalence rates of depression, anxiety, PTSD and other forms of mental ill health that are usually high in refugee groups (Byrow et al., 2020). A community-wide initiative sought to promote equal access to mental health services by identifying and overcoming barriers for refugee communities that typically stigmatise and avoid dealing with mental health problems (e.g., Mechammil et al., 2019; VFST, 2020). Government and services are aware that a range of knowledge bases and skills are needed to design and implement interventions that can effectively communicate with the diverse cultural groups organised around schools, community hubs, churches, mosques, temples or sports clubs.

The programs were organised through school community hubs and were specifically directed to recently arrived refugees. Participants were members of Muslim and Assyrian-Chaldean Christian communities from Syria and Iraq for whom Arabic was the official language. Like most groups from the Middle East, irrespective of ethnic, regional and religious affiliation, they held stigmatising attitudes about mental health (Mechammil et al., 2019). Yet, mental health issues, although often prohibited topics of discussion, continue to be critical aspects of how well people recover from past traumas and cope with discrimination and social exclusion in resettlement. Without intervention, communities of recently arrived refugees are in danger of ignoring the psychological risk factors that disturb the wellbeing of people of all ages.

As part of the general initiative, the Victorian Foundation for the Survivors of Torture (VFST) as a trauma-specialist non-government organisation works in partnership with refugee communities to co-develop community programs. Consistent with its mission to promote the health and human rights of refugee people, VFST supports communities towards self-reliance by encouraging cohesive relationships and partnerships, harnessing and enhancing community skills and resources, and facilitating participation in decision-making and leadership to ensure community ownership (VFST, 2017). Program development becomes a consultative activity enabling greater participation by refugee individuals and groups.

VFST's contribution to the partnership included its organisational resources and personnel (especially its bi-cultural workers with experience in mentoring and program development and delivery), contacts with other services and its inclusion of refugee representatives in its negotiations with other services.

Refugee advisors contributed their refugee experience including their understanding of settlement difficulties, knowledge of cultural attitudes and practices, and involvement in cultural groups and organisations. Advisors were recruited into an advisory group that worked with professionals to co-design mental health literacy programs to be delivered through school and other local groups. They were recognised through a process of recommendations by VFST workers, screening interviews and stakeholder meetings. Advisors were invited to work in partnership to generate culturally sensitive strategies for engaging with key community groups; developing a program framework that would open conversation about mental health and wellbeing and facilitating participation in information dissemination by other community members. In each of these activities, advisors performed bridging roles to help draw refugee communities into the mainstream discourse on mental health ideologically as well as practically. By these activities, they constructed the means of taking up society's support to deal with this contentious matter within their communities.

Professional practical wisdom has a role to play in enabling the engagement of refugees in the development of programs that are aimed at supporting their communities. A knowing program developer has hands-on strategies for interpreting patterns of community lifestyles and for reading community preferences and sensitivities. In a landscape crowded with marginalised and newly integrated refugee groups, practical wisdom also involves knowing the limits of its own interpretive powers. The mental health initiative brought together the wisdom of professional and refugee practitioners.

5.1 *Practical Wisdom of Professionals*

Practical wisdom is identified as experiential, practice-focused knowledge and skill that experienced professionals use to link current problems and tasks back to situations and activities they have seen before and the solutions that did or did not work then that may be useful now (e.g., Fook, 2016; Higgs, 2019). As the personalised knowledge professionals construct in concrete situations, practical wisdom grounds decisions in practice and directs strategic action (Chu & Tsui, 2008; Eriksen et al., 2014; Higgs, 2019; Thompson & West, 2013). It has the potential to open up negotiations but also to close them down. Professional experts are able to respond to situational suggestions creatively by drawing on their own tried strategies and values. However, they are also capable of over-looking cross-cultural hints if they are locked into their own enculturated experiences. Along with the formal academic knowledge it supplements and sometimes modifies, professional practical wisdom is likely to fall short as a final arbitrator of strategies for working with refugee communities. Not all professionals can transcend the limitations of their own culture. Their engagements with other cultural communities are informed by cultural values and beliefs that, according to Eriksen et al. (2014), sit just below the surface of awareness and are infused with values, beliefs and attitudes, and also understandably, prejudices and biases. These personal dimensions of professional practice have the propensity to rise up to skew how a person approaches unfamiliar situations, but the Scandinavian mental health workers in Eriksen et al.'s (2014) study worked sensitively with their clients to resist such tendencies by considering new ideas and alternative perspectives. Being aware of one's own cultural strengths and limitations encourages culturally sensitive practitioners to step beyond personal attitudes as well as beyond formal training (Thompson & West, 2013).

In the mix of knowledge and skill needed to reach different community groups, experienced professionals are able to expand their practical knowledge as well as academic and technical knowledge by being willing to engage with the insights, rights and advocacy needs of particular client groups, such as disabled or homeless people, and in our case, different refugee communities. Wise professionals are able to fill out formal knowledge (Fook, 2016; Higgs, 2019), and strengthen their own contextualised practical understanding by seeking out the culturally embedded practical wisdom in refugee groups that is often left untapped (Watters, 2008). Costa et al. (2019) reported how Portugese professionals from a number of disciplines expanded their knowledge and competences by working with refugees with flexibility and adaptability. Through self-reflection and self-diagnosis, professionals described how they came to develop the empathy to put themselves in the place of refugees, to take sincere interest in the concerns of refugees and respect for their choices, and to assume advocacy roles. With such reflective openness to change personally and professionally, professionals are able to extend the scope of their own practical wisdom and practice. Similarly, in our work of program development, the practical wisdom of professionals and refugees complements and extends each other.

5.2 *Practical Wisdom of Refugee Advisors*

The practical wisdom of people from refugee backgrounds is both similar to and different from the practical wisdom of professionals. As for professionals, it is experiential: has been tried over time. Past situations provide benchmarks against which to assess new situations. In addition, the accrued knowledge of refugees has the distinction of being built up within hardships that have few if any parallels in everyday practice. Gains, especially educational and vocational gains have tested the aspirations, especially of women (Harris et al., 2015). Mistakes were costly, placing people and their dependents in jeopardy, for example, if they trusted exploitative people smugglers or corrupt bureaucratic systems. Nevertheless, the lessons learnt in hard situations provide opportunities to develop survival skills that transform people and their interactions with the social environment (Guyot, 2007). Their recovery and survival skills, of course, may not always match mainstream expectations, when they display agency by relying on their own initiatives instead of being vulnerable and dependent on social workers' arrangements (O'Higgins, 2012).

Having learnt from the past, refugees are survivors with ability to recover. They have a stake in achieving stability for themselves and future generations and concentrate on coping strategies that allow them to move forward by transforming the hurts of the past to protect themselves and their families from further damage (VFST, 2020). Programs to help refugees are likely to miss people's motivations to the extent that they do not incorporate the accrued strategies and wisdom developed by individuals, families and communities as working parts of systems of recovery (Marley & Mauki, 2018; Watters, 2008).

As with professionals, the practical, and cultural wisdom of refugees is contextualised in everyday life and cannot be replaced by textbook knowledge. There were no initial training manuals to prepare people for violence, torture and trauma. Neither could the life skills needed to settle and re-establish family life be anticipated. They differ for families and life circumstances, and add their own challenges to health and wellbeing, for example, negotiating new political systems and citizenship rules and dealing with new medical and educational provisions and regulations – all in a new language.

The wisdom of refugee people involves more than becoming contextualised within the mainstream environment. It also involves being flexible enough to work with the different patterns of belief and practice that run through seemingly homogeneous cultural groups. Both heritage and mainstream cultural systems are comprised of subcultures vying for identity and power within and between groups. Resettlement opens up gaps in relationships, for instance, gaps between genders and generations about roles and responsibilities. Individuals, especially young people who adjust to the mainstream sooner than older people often fall out with traditional elders, and women find new meanings that bring them into conflict with patriarchal authority figures (Guyot, 2007; Goodnow & Lawrence, 2015; Harris et al., 2015). Most ethnic and religious cultural groups are peppered with family and organisational subgroups whose beliefs and practices require sensitive attention when professionals suggest that people access mainstream provisions and services. Wise professionals tread lightly when suggesting change and adaptation to any seemingly homogeneous cultural group and are cautious when recruiting cultural leaders as representative informants. They are likely to have encountered, for instance, the reluctance of some deeply religious groups to discuss mental health issues with their religious leaders.

Perhaps the major difference in the practically wise professional and the practically wise refugee community representative is related to status and recognition. Professional persons enjoy a recognised role in community activities and programs. Refugee persons do not enjoy such an accepted role, regardless of their ability. Their place has to be achieved and be given intentional opportunities to inform practice. As Woolf et al. (2016) specified for clients of medical services, so refugee communities receiving services need opportunity for authentic engagement with service providers, where 'authentic' as opposed to 'token' engagement involves being a recognised stakeholder with the right to partnership, appropriate knowledge, and a voice contributing to how programs and services are developed and implemented.

6 Indicators of Refugee Practical and Cultural Wisdom

The advisory groups that were established to co-design mental health programs were seen to have the authority of stakeholders as well as the voice of community representatives (VFST, 2020). Professional workers were committed to working with them flexibly and adaptively. As programs for school-hub groups rolled out over the weeks of a school term (10 to 12 weekly sessions), bi-cultural workers reported back to advisory groups. The advisors came to recognise VFST's commitment to reciprocity and to realise their input was genuinely valued and acted upon. They realised that ownership of the project was a collaborative partnership. As one advisor observed, 'We shaped how the project looked'.

This sense of shared ownership was formalised with an honorarium specifically itemised in funding applications. The honorarium was a tangible marker of the power sharing that is crucial in health-based programs (Ocloo & Matthews, 2016; Pratt, 2019) and added to the advisors' confidence to suggest how the content and presentation of programs could be tailored for particular groups of school parents, specifically isolated young mothers and older women whose traumatic experiences in their homeland made them reticent to express their difficulties. Indicators of their ownership and valued input included the different levels of social engagement involved in the programs and their input on culturally appropriate naming, language use and activities.

6.1 *Social Engagement*

The project facilitated several cascading levels of social engagement. Through the partnership, the advisors were enabled to participate in program development and to become bridges back into the diverse community groups, which they represented (e.g., youth, sporting, women's groups from either Muslim or Christian communities). Expanding their own knowledge of mental health issues and services, they used their new knowledge and confidence to more boldly confront the mental health stigma and to encourage others to join in the programs and seek help for themselves and their families. These advisor actions enabled another level of social inclusion for women who participated in the weekly programs organised through school hubs. For some women with personal or family worries, the weekly sessions were followed-up with individualised meetings with bi-cultural workers. These opened up further opportunities for the women to connect with psychological, counselling and medical services or to access previously untapped childcare, housing and employment services.

6.2 *Naming*

When considering the naming and presentation of the project to Christian and Muslim communities from Syria and Iraq, advisors insisted that the label 'mental health' never be mentioned. As a stigmatised and threatening concept (Mechammil et al., 2019), it would embarrass people, suggesting they were 'crazy' or weak instead of addressing their common problems of anxiety, depression, or disturbed relationships or sleep. Intense and extended talk focused on concept development and a project title that would not be offensive to Muslim or Christian Assyrian-Chaldean or Syriac communities. The resulting 'Al-Rafahiya Al-Sehiya' meaning 'Healthy Well-being' title in Arabic (the working language of all groups), gave people a positive basis for discussing psychological comfort, and its absence, psychological discomfort. These concepts could be used within group and individual talk and in printed and survey materials.

6.3 *Language*

The language used publically is a major indicator of cultural distinction that was woven throughout the ownership and delivery of the project. Advisors intensified this linguistic ownership of the project by insisting that the programs be delivered by native speakers, who were also fluent in English. All program sessions and individual meetings were chaired by Arabic speaking bi-cultural workers. English speaking counsellors and visiting speakers were assigned to adjunct roles in weekly and individual meetings. Bi-cultural workers worked with advisors to assemble a set of cross-cultural flash cards of everyday activities to help stimulate talk in sessions, for example, having coffee with others, listening to music, playing games and nature settings.

Refugee groups are accustomed to having program material delivered first in English with interpretations in their language. Advisors alerted workers to the value of communicating with groups directly in their own language, especially when medical and technical concepts were involved. In the case of mental health concepts that are culturally difficult, native speaking bi-cultural workers would be able to observe cultural practices and introduce non-threatening terminology to people who may be grappling with psychological issues for themselves or family members.

As programs rolled out, conversations in Arabic sometimes spilled over into Assyrian-Chaldean for culturally homogeneous groups who were fluent in both languages. These women were amazed at this localised acknowledgement of their cultural background, considering the years when their Assyrian-Chaldean language was forbidden in any public discourse in their homeland and transit countries.

6.4 *Cultural Sensitivity in Activities*

Closely aligned to the use of people's languages was the cultural sensitivity to how people would interact in program sessions. Advisors were concerned that programs presented in English often rely on top-down, unidirectional transmission of information and ideas: a style contrary to a Middle Eastern style of free-flowing conversation and negotiation. Cultural wisdom proposed substituting discussion for presentation and simple activities for what advisors described as 'teaching' (meaning for them – didactic presentation). Participants were to be encouraged to be active contributors to program sessions rather than listeners. Bi-cultural workers accordingly included physical activities to convey new ideas, for example, using yoga breathing as a simple means of controlling intrusive thoughts. Flashcards with photographs of mealtimes were used to prompt talk, and group activities heightened trust and willingness to talk.

Overall, the mental health literacy project assisted refugees to adjust to new knowledge and service provisions. Its programs could be rolled out with due cultural sensitivity because of the mutual adjustments made in the collaborative practical wisdom of professionals and refugee advisors. Each party recognised and respected the other's expertise. Each made adjustments to the other's knowledge. Professionals recognised the appropriateness of advisors' practical and cultural wisdom about language and concept development and cultural sensitivity as refugees confidently expressed their ownership of the project. Advisors recognised the practical wisdom of professionals' program implementation skills and VFST's trauma knowledge and connections and influence throughout the service sector. Both took up opportunities to develop new insights to channel into their collaborative work of assisting refugee communities to identify and manage obstacles to mental health.

7 Conclusion

Our analyses point to the significance of recognising the practical wisdom of people who have survived the refugee experience and committed to their new country. Willing contributors to community life should not be left at the margins. We proposed recognition as the means of enabling refugees to move away from the margins and to engage with community services. The close attention involved in recognising groups at the margins of society foregrounds their distinctiveness as well as their rights to equal treatment in ways that are appropriate in a multicultural society. Social inclusion and engagement does not demand the surrender of cultural beliefs and practices. There is room for distinctiveness when old and new cultural groups are reciprocally adaptive.

At a deeper level of engagement, specifically in the provision of community services, recognition has further significance. As professional workers pay close attention to the strengths and vulnerabilities of refugees, they find themselves opening up to exceptional experiences of these recovering survivors. Attentive recognition of the practical and cultural wisdom of refugee advisors gives professionals access to new ways of thinking in program development. As well as honing the suitability of mental health programs for other refugees, a professional worker's close attention to the wisdom residing in community groups can fill some of the gaps in their own encultured understanding of the concerns of people from other cultures. It also gives professionals opportunities to expand their own practice by incorporating insights from beyond their own experience.

In ways that fit the equality and distinctiveness markers of a multicultural society (Hamas & Vasta, 2009), the partnership involving VFST and refugee advisors exemplifies how professionals and community advisors can collaborate in constructing initiatives that foster the social inclusion of refugee communities. The initial step into collaborative work usually entices wise practitioners into novel situations that ask them to make adjustments and to share power. Collaborative adjustments and power sharing may be costly and sometimes risky, for example, in budgeting and scheduling requirements, but they introduce new learning and development to the individual practitioner as well as to the work.

While the engagement of participants in community programs is unlikely to match the intensity of an advisor's engagement, when advisors and professionals do their collaborative work with appropriate contextualised wisdom and cultural sensitivity, they create pathways for others away from society's margins. The outcomes of reciprocally recognised practical wisdom cascade down to enable other levels of social inclusion in programs and consultations. They forge pathways away from marginalisation for people who may previously have been hovering at the edge of societal provisions, because of prejudice and ignorance in either mainstream or refugee communities or in both. The discernment and, noticing of professionals and community advisors contributes to the construction of pathways to services and willingness to use them.

Collaboration and power sharing are not achieved at once for all, but again and again as community members are included and heeded in decision processes. People are empowered as professionals work with them instead of for them, and according to Ocloo and Matthews (2016), this involves blurring professional-recipient boundaries around control and responsibility. Such blurring reduces the tendency to over-emphasise professional expertise that impedes the very take-up of the public services it seeks to promote (Hutchinson & Dorsett, 2012). Recognising the limits of one's own wisdom is associated with recognising the wisdom residing in refugee groups that can enhance and extend one's professional wisdom.

Accordingly, our analyses focused on a particular kind of recognition, which is oriented to the practical wisdom of professionals and refugee partners. Each form of wisdom warrants close attention and noticing. Close attention to the experiential survival and recovery of refugee people is the response of an organisation and its workers who have amassed knowledge of the refugee experience by working closely with refugees and learning from them. An organisation and its professional workers in genuine partnership with refugee advisors draws on previous instances of engagement and accrued on-the-ground experience of their specialised knowledge. Experienced wisdom may suggest where normal local practices should be modified when they do not accommodate a community advisor's insights or expressions. Social inclusion is promoted when people from different cultural backgrounds are given the means of understanding and mutually adjusting to each other. To recognise is the beginning of understanding and mutual adjustment, and the way from marginalisation into inclusion and authentic engagement.

References

Assmann, A. (2013). Civilizing societies: Recognition and respect in a global world. *New Literary History, 44*(1), 69–91.

Berry, J. W. (2005). Acculturation: Living successfully in two cultures. *International Journal of Intercultural Relations, 29*(6), 697–712.

Byrow, Y., Pajak, R., Specker, P., & Nickerson, A. (2020). Perceptions of mental health and perceived barriers to mental health help seeking amongst refugees: A systematic review. *Clinical Psychology Review, 75*. https://doi.org/10.1016/j.cpr.2019.101812

Chu, W. C. K., & Tsui, M. (2008). The nature of practice wisdom in social work revisited. *International Social Work, 51*(1), 47–54.

Clyne, M., & Jupp, J. (Eds.). (2011). *Multiculturalism and integration: A harmonious relationship*. ANU E Press.

Correa-Velez, I., Gifford, S. M., & McMichael, C. (2015). The persistence of predictors of wellbeing among youth with refugee youth eight years after resettlement in Melbourne, Australia. *Social Science & Medicine, 142*, 163–168.

Costa, A. L., Coimbra, S., Pinto, M., Teixeira, E. G., & Caramelo, J. (2019). Professionals' key knowledge, competences and practices to promote social inclusion of refugees. *International Journal of Inclusive Education*. https://doi.org/10.1080/13603116.2019.1678777

Dickert, N. W. (2009). Re-examining respect for human research participants. *Kennedy Institute of Ethics Journal, 19*(4), 311–338.

Dillon, R. S. (1992). Respect and care: Toward moral integration. *Canadian Journal of Philosophy, 22*, 105–132.

Dobson, S. (2004). *Cultures of exile and the experience of refugeeness*. Peter Lang.

Dobson, S., Agrusti, G., & Pinto, M. (2019). Supporting the inclusion of refugees: Policies, theories and actions. *International Journal of Inclusive Education*. https://doi:10.1080/13603116.2019.1678804

Emamzadeh, A. (2018). *Acculturation and migration: Interview with Dr. J. W. Berry*. https://www.psychologytoday.com/au/blog/finding-new-home/201803/acculturation-and-migration-interview-dr-j-w-berry

Eriksen, K. A., Dahl, H., Karlsson, B., & Arman, M. (2014). Strengthening practical wisdom: Mental health workers' learning and development. *Nursing Ethics, 21*(6), 707–719.

Fook, J. (2016). *Social work: A critical approach to practice* (3rd ed.). Sage.

Goodnow, J. J., & Lawrence, J. A. (2015). Children and cultural contexts. In M. Bornstein & T. Leventhal (Eds.), *Handbook of child psychology and developmental science* (Vol. 4: Ecological settings and processes in developmental systems, pp. 746–788). Wiley.

Gutmann, A. (2018). The power of recognition: When Charles Taylor parsed personal identity. *Philosophy & Social Criticism, 44*(7), 793–795.

Guyot, J. (2007). Child and youth participation in protracted refugee situations. *Children, Youth and Environments, 17*(3), 159–178.

Hamas, S., & Vasta, E. (2009). *'To belong or not to belong': Is that the question? Negotiating belonging in multi-ethnic London* (Working Paper No. 73). Compas Centre on Migration, Policy & Society, University of Oxford.

Harris, A., Spark, C., & Ngum Chi Watts, M. C. (2015). Gains and losses: African Australian women and higher education. *Journal of Sociology, 51*(2), 370–384.

Higgs, J. (Ed.). (2019). *Practice wisdom: Values and interpretations.* Brill Sense.

Hugo, G. (2014). The economic contribution of humanitarian settlers in Australia. *International Migration, 52*(2), 31–52.

Hutchinson, M., & Dorsett, P. (2012). What does the literature say about resilience in refugee people? Implications for practice. *Journal of Social Inclusion, 3*(2), 55–78.

Igor, H. O. A. (2019). Multiculturalism and recognition of the other in Charles Taylor's political philosophy. *Critical Horizons, 20*(4), 305–316.

Jupp, J. (2011). Politics, public policy and multiculturalism. In M. Clyne & J. Jupp (Eds.), *Multiculturalism and integration: A harmonious relationship* (pp. 41–52). ANU E Press.

Kate, A., Verbitsky, J., & Wilson, K. (2019). In different voices: Auckland's refugee communities' engagement with conflict resolution in New Zealand. *Journal of International Migration & Integration, 20*, 459–477.

Lawrence, J. A., Kaplan, I., & Dodds, A. E. (2015). The rights of refugee children to self expression and to contribute to knowledge: Respect and methods. *Journal of Human Rights Practice, 7*(3), 411–419.

Lawrence, J. A., Kaplan, I., & McFarlane, C. (2013). The role of respect in research interactions with refugee children and young people. In K. Block, E. Riggs, & N. Haslam (Eds.), *Values and vulnerabilities: The ethics of research with refugees and asylum seekers* (pp. 103–126). Australian Academic Press.

Lenette, C., & Ingamells, A. (2014). Mind the gap! The growing chasm between funding-driven agencies, and social and community knowledge and practice. *Community Development Journal, 50*(1), 88–103.

Macaulay, L., & Deppeler, J. (2020). Perspectives on negative media representations of Sudanese and South Sudanese youths in Australia. *Journal of Intercultural Studies, 41*(2), 213–230.

Marley, C., & Mauki, B. (2018). Resilience and protective factors among refugee children post-migration to high-income countries: A systematic review. *European Journal of Public Health, 29*(4), 706–713.

Mechammil, M., Boghosian, S., & Cruz, R. A. (2019). Mental health attitudes among Middle Eastern/North African individuals in the United States. *Mental Health, Religion & Culture, 22*(7), 724–737.

Mowat, J. G. (2015). Towards a new conceptualisation of marginalisation. *European Educational Research Journal, 14*(5), 454–476.

Ocloo, J., & Matthews, R. (2016). From tokenism to empowerment: Progressing patient and public involvement in healthcare improvement. *BJM Quality & Safety, 25*, 626–632.

O'Higgins, A. (2012). Vulnerability and agency: Beyond an irreconcilable dichotomy for social service providers working with young refugees in the UK. In A. Orgocka & C. Clark-Kazak (Eds.), Independent child migration – Insights into agency, vulnerability and structure. *New Directions for Child and Adolescent Development, 136*, 79–91.

Pratt, B. (2019). Constructing citizen engagement in health research priority-setting to attend to dynamics of power and difference. *Developing World Bioethics, 19*, 49–60.

Ponzoni, E., Ghorashi, H., & van der Raad, S. (2017). Caught between norm and difference: Narratives on refugees' inclusion in organizations. *Equality, Diversity & Inclusion, 36*(3), 222–237.

Pulvirenti, M., & Mason, G. (2011). Resilience and survival: Refugee women and violence. *Current Issues in Criminal Justice, 23*(1), 37–52.

Refuge Council of Australia. (2010). *Economic, civic and social contribution of refugees and humanitarian entrants*. Refuge Council of Australia. https://www.refugeecouncil.org.au/economic-literature-review/

Slee, R. (2019). Belonging in an age of exclusion. *International Journal of Inclusive Education*. https://doi:10.1080/13603116.2019.1602366

Spitzer, D. L. (2007). Immigrant and refugee women: Recreating meaning in transnational context. *Anthropology in Action, 14*(1&2), 52–62.

Taylor, C. (1994). The politics of recognition. In C. Taylor, K. Anthony Appiah, J. Hubermas, S. C. Rockefeller, M. Walzer, & S. Wolf (Eds.), *Multiculturalism: Examining the politics of recognition* (pp. 25–73). Princeton University Press.

Thompson, L. J., & West, D. (2013). Professional development in the contemporary educational context: Encouraging practice wisdom. *Social Work Education, 32*(1), 118–133.

UN High Commissioner for Refugees (UNHCR). (2018). *Global compact on refugees, Part II*. United Nations General Assembly Official Records, Seventy-Third Session, Supplement No. 12. https://www.unhcr.org/en-au/the-global-compact-on-refugees.html

Valibhoy, M. C., Kaplan, I., & Swarc, J. (2017). 'It comes down to just how human someone can be': A qualitative study with young people from refugee backgrounds about their experiences of Australian mental health services. *Transcultural Psychiatry, 54*, 23–45.

Victorian Foundation for the Survivors of Torture (VFST). (2017). *A framework for community capacity building*. Author.

Victorian Foundation for the Survivors of Torture (VFST). (2020). *Rebuilding shattered lives* (2nd ed.). Author.

Watters, C. (2008). *Refugee children: Towards the next horizon.* Routledge.

Wille, J. (2011). Agency and belonging: Southern Sudanese former refugees' reflections on life in Australia. *Australasian Review of African Studies, 32*(2), 80–100.

Woolf, S. H., Zimmerman, E., Amber Haley, A., & Krist, A. H. (2016). Authentic engagement of patients and communities can transform research, practice, and policy. *Health Affairs, 35*(4), 590–594, 1–18.

CHAPTER 14

Practical Wisdom of Shaping Futures for Communities at the Margins of Society

Collaborative Development and Evaluation of Community Programs

Agnes Dodds, Ida Kaplan and Jeanette Lawrence

Abstract

In this chapter, we propose a developmental approach to community programs that brings together program development and program evaluation in collaborative activity. Developers and evaluators interact throughout as a collaborative team, and by their interactions, coproduce knowledge. The approach expands the practical wisdom of program developers through their acquisition of an evaluative perspective, and expands the practical wisdom of evaluators through their acquisition of contextualised and cultural insights and knowledge construction. Dedicated service agencies build their capacity as they incorporate the wisdom and productions of collaborative teams and make evaluation a routine part of service delivery. Being interactive at its core, our developmental approach fosters participation. Working together, wise developers and wise evaluators are able to design and deliver programs that recognise and respond to community needs.

Keywords

practical wisdom – program development – program evaluation – collaboration

1 Introduction

Faced with the challenge of making a difference for marginalised and disadvantaged community groups, a dedicated social service agency usually develops programs to improve inclusion and access to services for community members. Such intervention programs are designed to respond to community needs and to reflect the agency's priorities, by drawing on the experience and knowledge of workers from social service disciplines (e.g., social work, psychology, education). Program developers engage with targeted community

 | DOI: 10.1163/9789004505544_017

groups to develop understanding of their difficulties and needs, offer programs sensitive to contextual conditions, and strengthen cultural authenticity and relevance by working in partnership with community bodies.

As a consequence of close involvement with client communities, the professional identity and practical wisdom of program developers is tied to the commitment and effort they invest in developing their programs (Harrison & Healy, 2016). Their experiential learning is deeply grounded in working to understand the contextual circumstances of client groups. Program developers are challenged to create intervention programs that offer practical solutions and to ensure that the programs offered fit to community needs with due cultural recognition and respect (Lawrence et al., Chapter 13, this volume).

In this chapter, we propose an integrated approach that brings together program development and program evaluation as a collaborative service-oriented activity. We add a further dimension to service delivery collaboration as the expansion of the practical wisdom of the collaborators, and a service agency's capacity to work with disadvantaged client groups. We outline the background to treating program development and evaluation as a collaborative co-production of knowledge and wisdom and present a model of integrated development and evaluation activities. The model demonstrates how this integrated approach expands the practical wisdom of program developers and evaluators; and how service agencies can build their capacity for providing community programs by encouraging an evaluative perspective in their service workers. Finally, we explain how an integrated approach serves disadvantaged communities and furthers social justice for disadvantaged and marginalised communities.

2 Background

The programs that workers design and deliver not only to respond to community needs are grounded in their professional values and identity, but also in contextual knowledge that they accumulate over time and service situations (Collins, 2016). Working to craft program offerings to appropriately address cultural needs and agency priorities take program developers into areas of contextualised learning and practice that go beyond their academic and technical training (Chu & Tsui, 2008; Higgs, 2019; Schwartz, 2011) into crafting their content and processes to fit community and agency conditions. Matching processes arise from the concentration of their accumulated knowledge and insights on situational specifics, and the tools for trying out possible matches are the tools of evidence gathering and interpretation that evaluate the appropriateness and effectiveness of their goals, design and delivery processes.

3 Program Evaluation

Whenever program effectiveness is at issue, someone is given the responsibility of evaluating it. That responsibility traditionally has been entrusted to an external evaluation consultant. These consultants are seen as knowledgeable, independent and skilled in gathering and applying evidence to assess program effectiveness (Stufflebeam, 2001). Although external evaluation results are intended to improve programs, they often are remote from the professional values and expertise of program developers, and may be used for managerial and accounting purposes rather than evaluation of how programs are delivered. As Chouinard (2013) pointed out, whenever program evaluation is used as a management or instrumental tool, it fails to respond to contextual needs and cultural sensitivities, and consequently may not advance program improvement. Ideally, evaluation should add value to programs that are offered to disadvantaged communities. Program evaluation involves the systematic collection, analysis, reporting and interpretation of information about social programs with specific goals, for example, the goal of inducting young people from refugee backgrounds into employment opportunities; or the goal of facilitating mental health literacy of refugee adults with stigmatised views of psychological ill health (The Victorian Foundation for Survivors of Torture [VFST], 2020). Improvement of programmatic interventions depends on evidence-informed judgments and astute application of such judgments to different aspects of a program.

Traditionally, evaluation activities were reserved as the province of expert evaluators who operated strictly apart from program development to produce independent assessments and reports. Evaluators' reports mainly addressed external accountability and funding requirements, and sometimes appeared long after a program concluded, and did not find their way back to the developers or the targeted community in time for the findings to be used productively.

A contemporary shift in the evaluation discipline has led to greater emphasis on making evaluation evidence and judgments available to the people who actually produce and deliver programs. Some contemporary approaches foreground specific features such as increasing client participation and empowering client groups to engage in partnership with service providers or take up program ownership (Cousins & Chouinard, 2012; Fetterman et al., 2015). Some shifts adopt a basic principle of integrating evaluation into program development, and ask evaluators to engage in a greater range of activities than the production of a final report (Patton, 2018). They are expected to guide a multidisciplinary approach to making value judgments that are more penetrating and encompassing than simply giving a final assessment of effectiveness.

Schwandt (2015) provided a perceptive overview of the evolving line of activities undertaken by a modern evaluator:

> As a program is underway, an evaluator charged with examining its implementation and progress towards stated goals makes judgments about whether implementation is going as planned, whether the program is reaching its targeted audience (the program beneficiaries), whether problems in the delivery of the program are severe enough to require attention, whether progress towards goals is reasonable, timely, and so on. These decisions are made on the basis of evidence and on appraising the quality, strength, and relevance of that evidence for each kind of decision. (p. 47)

In order to progressively contribute this evidence-based input, evaluators need to be in continual interaction with developers so that their questions, evidence and judgments can be targeted and timely. It is a moot point, whether evaluators are enlisted as permanent members of a program development team, or they train program developers to become their own evaluators (Donaldson et al., 2010). Whatever the position followed about this permanent/temporary embedding of evaluators, the collaborative task of the evaluator, put forward by Patton (2018), is centred on advancing the evaluative thinking of developers. Patton argued that engaging in evaluative thinking is akin to using critical and creative thinking in that it uses systematic evidence and induces questioning, reflective transformation of knowledge (Archibald et al., 2016; Buckley et al., 2015). It also is distinctive in always being contextualised and used in practice and always being directed towards making judgments about the suitability and usefulness of practices.

Schwandt (2018) added another, social feature related to judging the value of a program. Without diminishing the cognitive work of the individual, evaluative thinking, especially in an organisational setting, is a collective, collaborative social practice bound up with making sense in a particular social situation. Sense is made and judgments are formed as people engage in reflection that is coupled with continuous learning and a willingness to modify their views in the light of reasoned argument and evidence (Schwandt, 2018). This perceptive view is a reminder that collaborative work does not mean turning program developers into evaluators who engage in evaluative thinking to the extent of displacing their program development work. Evaluative thinking is an extra not a displacement.

By asking questions, pointing to specific instances and characteristics of content and delivery and responding to contextual conditions, evaluators are encouraging, educating developers to frame program making decisions by adding an evaluative perspective to their existing ways of thinking – exercising and refining both perspectives by working in an interdisciplinary team. Thus, evidence and questions about content and modes of presentation are likely to be posed in planning meetings instead of being kept exclusively for end-point reports. In negotiations, evaluators expose program developers to new information that asks them to inspect their previously accepted ways of operating and to reflect on fresh evidence and insights. In turn, evaluators are exposed to the contextualised community knowledge that program developers have accrued and refined from practical experience. Each collaborator is in a learning situation, and the overall project benefits from their interactions.

4 Organisational Program Offerings

This shift in evaluation emphasis is in line with an historical shift among community services organisations of awareness of demands for accountability, transparency and contextual relevance in community programs (Baulderstone, 2008). The developer/evaluator interaction enhances an organisation's ability to respond to those demands. Specialist organisations working with needy groups may have lagged behind corporations and government departments in realising the benefits of diverting precious resources from direct services to demonstrating the value of those services to funding agencies and participating community groups (Fetterman & Wandersman, 2005). Encouraging developer and evaluator collaboration gives organisations working platforms for demonstrating the value of their services by producing strong evidence that their programs are identifying contextual issues and building them into the programs.

Our approach to integrating evaluation into program development and design was initiated and worked out in the context of a specialist non-government organisation that provides services to advance the health, wellbeing and rights of people of refugee backgrounds in Australia: The Victorian Foundation for Survivors of Torture (VFST). It operates from a trauma recovery framework with a multi-disciplinary staff. Collaborative evaluation fits well with its organisational concerns to expand the skill-base of its staff and to assist refugee communities to build their skills and knowledge for interacting with government and other organisations (VFST, 2020).

A service organisation that addresses specific community needs is in the business of continually providing and improving targeted programs. Each individual offering of a program, then, can be treated as one iteration of an evolving package of activities where the emphasis is on the evolving features of a programmatic offering. An agency is able to accrue a bank of content and procedural materials to use reflectively and thoughtfully to adapt to specific purposes. This allows it to avoid two extremes of on the one hand being confined to strictly one-off programs with no systematic core or consolidation, and on the other hand, being dependent on a set package that is not contextually grounded or responsive. With an evolving motif, a program with a particular purpose, instead of being 'Offering 1 only' or 'Offering 1 repeated' will be conceptualised as 'Offering 1a, 1b, 1c' by which it can be revised and refined over several offerings (b, c), for example, changes in the number of sessions needed to introduce a particular concept or the method of presentation.

Working reflectively and progressively across programs also allows agency workers to draw on previously effective content and procedural materials and to adapt them to the specific needs of community groups. For example, a mental health awareness program for recently arrived refugees from the Middle East may form the basis of a similar program for recently arrived refugees from China, with adaptations to fit the new culture and context. Successful adaptation calls for refitting the previously effective program to community needs. However, discernment of cultural differences and contextual needs are dependent on the ability of professional workers to obtain and interpret information that guides their reflection and adjustments. Service providers are not typically trained or experienced in the systematic application of evidence. A developmental approach to providing programs for disadvantaged communities brings together the skills of service-oriented program developers and evidence-oriented evaluators.

5 Developmental Program Development and Evaluation Integration

Our approach is developmental in working with the goal of progressive creation and improvement across different offerings of an evolving program, by the integration of evaluation questions, decisions and actions throughout program planning, design and delivery phases. The developmental motif means that an individual component may change and change other related components (e.g., design changes to encourage more participant talk may lead in delivering greater reliance on small buzz groups in place of planned didactic presentations). Interim evaluation of the usefulness of such an adaptation then focuses on changes in talk across sessions that can be assessed in relation to other outcomes. Program design and delivery activities are coordinated with evaluation activities and the coordinated set progress together through their reciprocal interactions. By being connected to the program components, evaluation activities have a reciprocal interaction with program development activities. Program choices may suggest suitable evaluation evidence, for example, inclusion of observation of a novel physical activity. Evaluation questions may prompt program decisions and choices, for example, the choice of a new way of presenting particular content. By way of illustration, the content and procedures suggested by the development and evaluation of a program of mental health awareness for refugees from Syria and Iraq generated new ideas about the content and procedures for a similar program for refugee women from Afghanistan (e.g., using bi-cultural workers and Dari language, and modifying tools for evidence gathering in an on-line environment). Features of the program also were available for adaptation for a post-COVID job preparation program for refugee youths.

This developmental approach contrasts with traditional end-of-program or pre-and-post designs for assessing overall effectiveness (Patton, 2011). Developmental evaluation allows for the emergence of new content and procedures throughout. It occurs within an individual program as it is planned, designed and delivered and as changes are incorporated into the goals, design and delivery of this and successive program offerings.

The integration of evaluation decisions and activities with the components of program development is illustrated in Figure 14.1. The primary context is formed by community characteristics, including its needs and strengths, and the needs and strengths of the service agency. Other features of the context include funding bodies and stakeholders from specific community groups and organisations to which the program may make referrals (e.g., counselling, health and education clinics or practitioners).

The progressive and continued integration of program and evaluation decisions and activities in the delivery of service for specified community groups operate within this context. Major components of an individual program, with their progressive links are the goals, design, delivery, outcome and report of a single program's development. Each program rolls out under the direction of goals that are defined in relation to contextualised community needs and organisational orientations, priorities and capacity.

Program decisions and activities proceed from goals to design and delivery on to outcome and report and back into reflection or movement on to the next program offering. Evaluation decisions and activities occur throughout and match the progress through program development and delivery, as shown in the figure. These are illustrated as double-headed arrows to identify the reciprocity of the collaborative interactions at each point. Early evaluation questions prompt the incorporation of contextualised knowledge and concerns when setting goals and determining content and procedures on the basis of those goals. For example, evaluation questions may ask the most culturally

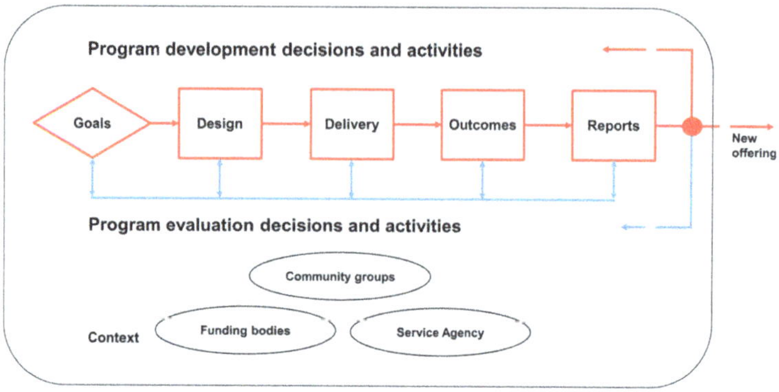

FIGURE 14.1 Developmental model of program development and evaluation

appropriate ways of using ethnic language and interactive style to advance participation goals when working with a reticent community group (Lawrence et al., Chapter 13, this volume). Design decisions lead into the delivery of goal-directed content and procedures in various sessions. Delivery is responsive to design decisions and also to situational variations that arise out of fresh evaluation questions that may not have been anticipated in goal setting or design activities. Data collection can be responsive to details as they emerge, sometimes unexpectedly and that responsiveness does not need to wait until a final report in which it may be overlooked (Patton, 2018). In one school-based program for refugee mothers, program developers became aware of mothers' distractions from program activities because of the extreme attachment needs of their insecure toddlers. A program developer and an evaluator moved quickly to gather relevant information and to modify existing child care arrangements to work on separation and attachment issues with the toddlers, and then to offer the young mother's family referrals in addition to program sessions.

Program outcomes are likely to be varied and to make particular demands on matching outcome measures to stated goals and also to content and processes. Some outcomes will be directly related to stated goals and their implementation, for example, changes in participants' mental health awareness. In such cases, outcome measures are planned from the start in coordination with goal setting and are constructed to yield evidence of effectiveness in achieving those expressed, specific goals. Other outcomes may have emerged, unanticipated, from progressive attention to evaluation questions and activities, for example, additional referrals in response to participant issues. Responsive outcome measures (e.g., rates and progress of referrals) will be used for reflective revision and forward planning.

Reports are made with attention to the interests of multiple parties. For stakeholders, reports address accountability, transparency and usefulness in relation to contextual conditions and ownership. For developers, evaluators and the service organisation, reports are framed to feed back into reflection and revision and to feed forward to the construction of further offerings and adaptations of the program.

At the end of the program, Figure 14.1 shows the different branching lines that take the collaborative team into reflection on their decisions and activities about program development and evaluation and forward to the next program offering. Reflection on how the program has developed may concentrate on any aspect of design and delivery and reactivate collaboration around the knowledge and insights featured in the evaluation processes. Evaluation decisions and actions also are open to reflection and revision in the collaborative space.

In summary, this developmental approach integrates program development and evaluation decisions and actions in relation to the cultural and institutional context. It works progressively under the direction of program goals and reflectively through the reciprocal interactions of program developers and evaluators. These cumulative processes promote the generation and use of information that improves programs and also assists the development of professional and cultural wisdom. For example, in the face of a drop in attendance in a second session of a six-week program, a developmental approach would seek relevant information at that point rather than at conclusion. In the context of community stake-holder consultations, developers and evaluators may be made aware of a disjunction between cultural expectation and presenter style: a preference for interactive versus didactic presentations. Reflection on evidence in relation to the goal of conveying usable knowledge, leads to modifications of presentation style and language, and checking with community advisors. Recording attendances then becomes cumulative evidence of the usefulness of developmental changes.

The processes of developing and evaluating a program in this way advances an organisation's ability to contribute to the community both through the specifics of programs that it provides and through building the practical wisdom and service capacity of its workforce. Such is the commitment of social workers to their constituent communities (Collins, 2016), that their professional development is locked into the processes of program development. The idea of a collaborative, working partnership with evaluators opens up particular avenues for building professional expertise and practical wisdom.

6 Advancing Practical Wisdom

Not all professionals become wise in practice. Time on the job gives no simple guarantee that professionals will acquire advanced practice knowledge, although they cannot proceed to strategic and flexible use of work experience without having a bank of more and less successful prior cases to assess and apply to current problems and tasks. The processes of acting wisely in practice start with multiple prior experiences in similar and different situations that the professional has integrated and distilled into a system of thinking. This experience-fuelled system of thinking suggests how to read the characteristics of a new situation, with professional values and confidence for trying new reflective use of situational feedback.

7 Practical Wisdom

When it is acquired, practical knowledge differs from formal, academic knowledge in being situated, contextualised, and experiential. This form of knowledge cannot be gained from books or formal, pre-practice training, but is constructed in living situations in response to presenting problems and prompts (e.g., Chu & Tsui, 2008; Higgs, 2019; O'Sullivan, 2005). According to Schwartz (2011), a wise person uses their practical skills with social perceptiveness. A practically wise person is alert to the situation – able to read and balance situational particulars and conflict aims, improvise; and is alert to the need to understand and adjust to other people's perspectives and needs.

Flexibility and openness to different ways of thinking is endemic to the inclusive developmental approach we have described. In the collaborative workspace, the injection of evaluation questions and evidence is part of the interaction. Integrated evaluation activities are able to expand the thinking of program developers – inducing an 'evaluative perspective' and making available the evaluation tools that support contextualised flexible and reflective thinking.

The collaborative work space also gives evaluators the opportunity to take up into their thinking specific situational factors that may not have been available to them apart from their interactions with situationally knowledgeable program developers. Cross-disciplinary coactions and negotiations encourage both parties to examine and articulate their professional assumptions that, when expressed and challenged, may be seen as unexamined and entrenched. Openness and negotiation by collaborative parties are essential parts of power sharing around the construction of new knowledge (House, 2015).

8 Co-constructed Knowledge

Developers and evaluators each contribute knowledge they have already distilled from their own discipline-based experiences. Their negotiations do not mean abandoning disciplinary and experiential wisdom, but bringing it into the work space while being open to expanding it with new ways of thinking brought by others. They each cognitively work over new ideas suggested in the negotiated work space in relation to their own existing ways of thinking and then contribute their new ideas back into the collaborative mix. Knowledge is co-constructed through the interactions in which they sometimes question and sometimes support each other's actions. By working together, they "coproduce evaluative knowledge" (Cousins et al., 2016, p. 4).

Interactivity was anticipated in an earlier analysis by Huberman and Cox (1990) who considered negotiated knowledge construction to be foundational to greater evaluation utilisation. At that time of growing dissatisfaction with end-on evaluation removed from program production, Huberman and Cox (1990) proposed that evaluators' clients would see evaluation activities as more useful if they occurred in a "sustained interactivity" (p. 159) of negotiation with their clients, throughout the total life of a program and beyond into knowledge dissemination and use.

The emphasis on interaction that 'co-produces' knowledge in the applied, evaluation domain aligns with developmental accounts that provide theoretical explanation of the processes by which people typically construct knowledge. A person's acquisition of knowledge and skill is never a solo achievement. They are developed in interactions with the environment and other people in it. What the social context allows culturally or linguistically, what it provides as tools, how it supports or constrains a person's attempts to understand something new – all contribute to each person's development of knowledge.

Developmental biologist Gottlieb (2007) saw the actions and acquisitions of all developing organisms as so organically and functionally intertwined with the environment that he referred to individuals' achievements as 'co-actions' stressing how each side of the interaction plays an essential role. Each developing person is understood to develop and acquire new knowledge and skill only as they coact in situ with other people and the environment (Valsiner, 2014). They generate and refine new knowledge and skill by taking up available information into current ways of thinking, turning over and refining both old and new thinking and developing something even newer (Lawrence & Dodds, 2017; Lawrence & Valsiner, 2003). New knowledge, thus, is 'co-constructed' by the dual processes of internalisation (taking up) and externalisation (expressing socially).

In terms of the collaborative interactions of developers and evaluators, the processes of taking up new ideas and interpreting and refining them in relation to prior disciplinary and experiential understanding and experience gives meaning to the idea of the expansion of the practical wisdom of each contributor. It is a generative, developmental change in which the changing person is an active participant in transformational and contextualised engagements.

While Huberman and Cox (1990) had a clear idea of the interactivity involved, their explanatory concept of a 'transfer' of knowledge fails to account for the psychological processes by which changes in people's thinking are made. They referred to evaluators 'transferring' knowledge into the program context. However, a 'transfer of knowledge' motif could easily give the impression of an automatic injection of new knowledge into the service providers' thinking, and neglect the active processing by each co-actor that they seem to be reaching towards. For instance, Huberman and Cox (1990) referred to the cognitive activity of program providers (called the local client); "the local processing of evaluative data is akin to the processing of information by individuals learning a complex skill … it involves a conceptual re-ordering" (p. 164). Re-ordering, reframing, reapplying information are among many knowledge generation activities by which the practical wisdom of program developers and evaluators is expanded.

9 Expanding the Practical Wisdom of Program Developers

Program developers step into the construction of knowledge whenever they embark on offering a new program. They need to keep the program in mind as a whole and to craft its parts around their stated goals. As they work collaboratively with evaluators, they find themselves prompted to think analytically and reflectively and to apply a new, evaluative lens to the various parts of their program. Evaluators prompt them to adopt an evaluative perspective that transforms prior knowledge, and to make use of evaluators' evidence-managing tools. Developers who follow the prompts and processes add an evaluative perspective to their existing framework for program development. In the process, they expand their practical wisdom by the addition of a different lens through which to see their experience. For example, when designing how a program will be rolled out (at the design phase, Figure 14.1), evaluation questions may ask developers to clarify how their proposed content and materials will follow their specific goals. The inter-disciplinary team may encourage them to enlarge the design by incorporating evaluation tools, such as, deciding to ask presenters to record their assessment of each session, noting how well that session expresses their goals, what in the session is useful and repeatable and what should be revised in the next session in order to more explicitly address goals.

Program developers who incorporate these aspects of evaluative thinking into their practice are engaged in knowledge transformation that expands their own expert knowledge with a newly acquired perspective and its associated tools. Weiss (1998) called this attaining an 'evaluative cast of mind' that is akin to an evaluative perspective:

> Helping program people reflect on the practice, think critically, and ask questions about why the program operates as it does. They learn something of the evaluative cast of mind – the skeptical questioning point of view, the perspective of the reflective practitioner. (p. 25)

O'Sullivan (2005) also understood that practical wisdom is developed, for social workers, by transforming available information into useable knowledge that they can apply flexibly to specific situational demands. In common with critical thinking, evaluative thinking emphasises socially-contextualised, evidence-based reasoning and it always involves making value judgments (Vo & Archibald, 2018). So taking up evaluative thinking is a means of shedding light on entrenched assumptions, that according to Archibald et al. (2016), is the Achilles' heel of program development: liable to trap the developer in a narrow, disciplinary focussed perspective that fails to take account of insights from outside the received view. Developers do not automatically turn to evaluative thinking. Their wisdom, situationally and experientially grounded, nevertheless may also be attached to unexamined beliefs and attitudes. Negotiations of the inter-disciplinary, collaborative process challenge them to question their assumptions and to move on from dialogue with evaluators to asking themselves evaluator-type questions about their work – "Will this serve my goal? What evidence will inform my activities?" In effect, they will be expanding their wisdom by adding an evaluative perspective on their program development work.

10 Expanding the Practical Wisdom of Evaluators

Evaluators embedded in a collaborative work space find themselves revisiting and transforming some of their practices and accepted procedures. They are not the prime movers of the main action of program development, but their contributions are critical to the coproduction (Cousins et al., 2016) of the expansion of developers' practical wisdom. They are in the business of information generation and refinement. The dark arts of statistical analyses may be greeted with suspicion, and evaluators may be expected to demonstrate how their evidence-managing wares are relevant to rolling out a particular program. Although evaluators too have their own version of hands-on, disciplinary experience, it is less public and inspectable than that of program developers. Traditionally, evaluation is taken for granted as a specialty with uncontested tools and evidence. Such an unchallenged position exacerbates evaluators' reliance on their own routinised expertise and exposes them to complacency (Donaldson et al., 2010). It is possible for an evaluator to overlook the nuances of developers' contextualised knowledge and thus to fail to include some unorthodox features of program specifics, for example, responding to the trauma of refugee experiences by using relaxing and fun activities as the backdrop for discussing trauma-related issues. In the collaborative work space, the evaluator comes to see the need to include light-hearted activities as part of program effectiveness. Just as evaluators prompt developers to adopt an evaluative perspective, so developers prompt evaluators to take up contextualised and cultural insights into their thinking. By interrogating prior assumptions, for instance, about what constitutes usable evidence, they too may engage in knowledge transformation that changes how they gather evidence from community groups whose experiences make 'validated' standardised rating scales uninterpretable.

A program developer may ask for fine-tuning and situational application of evaluators' techniques for managing evidence. They may alert the evaluator, for example, to the unfamiliarity and unwieldiness of quantitative ratings for some community groups, and how these may consistently provide ceiling-effect response in their attempts to express gratitude. In qualitative data-collection, wise contextualised developers also may alert evaluators to cultural sensitivity to some interview settings and questions (e.g., who may appropriately ask questions of elders or children, and how). It is here that Schwartz's (2011) concept of social perceptiveness is relevant. Turning over their long-standing assumptions of control and being willing to creatively use their skills to coordinate with developers' insights of community characteristics enlarges the body of useful evidence, for example, being willing to simply count how often people from a Middle Eastern background mention anxiety or depression in their talk, when developers raise the cultural stigma associated with mental health concepts. Expansion of the practical wisdom of evaluators relates to their willingness to frame interdisciplinary negotiations with co-constructed knowledge that draws on the contextualised, practical wisdom of their collaborators

> Can we adapt my standard approach to get a better fit to this community?
> Can I draw on this activity to test the value of what the program is doing?

While on-going collaboration expands evaluators' perspectives and wisdom, it comes at a cost, at least potentially, of independence and objectivity. Scriven, in contributing to a conversational debate about the historical shift to embedded evaluators (see Donaldson et al., 2010), argued that embedded evaluators might find themselves evaluating their own work in long-term interdisciplinary projects. Scriven's caution highlights the classic dilemma of weighing objective, independent expertise against transparency and relevance. Independent evaluation may avoid potential interference or co-option by a development team, but at the cost of usefulness for progressive checking and refining and certainly, at the cost of knowledge construction. For House (2015), the practical wisdom of an evaluator lies not in objectivity or transparency per se, but in the inspectability of decisions and the evidence supporting them.

11 Expanding Organisational Capacity

An agency's credibility rests on the capacity of its service providers to meet community needs and funders' criteria. Public accountability and reputation are bound up with an agency's ability to build up the capacity of its workers to a level where its services are timely delivered to meet community needs while reflecting the agency's values and goals (Forss et al., 2006; Mayne, 2008). An organisation benefits whenever its workforce is upskilled, and whenever it makes significant investments in building the capacity of its service providers as well as their clients.

As a working system, the organisation must incorporate the wisdom and productions of the collaborative team into its routine operations. While the collaborative coproduction of knowledge is foundational to the development of a creative organisation culture that resources and encourages new ideas, management is responsible for leading and nurturing that cultural development (Mayne, 2008). An organisation conveys its cultural priorities in its everyday operations and routines. Management needs to first understand the logic of evaluation, according to an analysis by Goswami and Lane (2017), and to build it into organisational routine that makes evaluation a mainstream operation. The take-up of an evaluative perspective into the operational routines of key workers provides a key to how evaluation becomes understood and becomes normal practice for programs, individual service providers, organisational units and the whole system. They bring their understanding of interactive, progressive evaluation to unit and agency-wide meetings.

An organisation committed to understanding and valuing evidence-based decision-making invests back into coproduction activities and facilitates its spread of evidence as well as its sustainability for the original collaborative team. For instance, an organisation that invests in system-wide IT data management undergirds professional capacity building and constructs the possibility of expanding the range of new knowledge across the organisation. Evidence is made doubly useful by the way it is systematised and distributed (Mayne, 2008). By encouraging program developers to acquire an evaluation perspective, the organisation strengthens the whole system through greater coordination and consistency of efforts. By encouraging the embedding and collaboration of evaluators, the organisation strengthens the evidence-base of its coordinated services.

Forss et al. (2006) argued persuasively that establishing and maintaining an evaluative culture demands dedicated staff with evaluation skills who can support program developers over successive program iterations. They carried out an exercise in evaluation capacity building in an UNESCO collaboration involving an external evaluation team that worked with its in-house evaluators and field officers. They found mixed responses through different levels of the organisation; "People do what they think is important and what is expected of them, and in the course of a day's work there is always more to be done" (Forss et al., 2006, p. 142). Their recommendations were to maintain a continuing partnership with evaluation specialists. But, specialised collaborators do not cancel organisational responsibilities to create an evaluation culture that raises the evaluation capacity of its program developers (Cousins & Chouinard, 2012).

It may be debatable whether an evaluation culture continues to be provided by embedded evaluators or whether, over time, having service providers with an evaluative perspective will suffice, but in either case, there are continuing needs for strong management support, champions and incentives to convince people working in the service sector that time taken away from direct services for evaluation purposes is profitable.

Dedicated agencies may view evaluation as a burden when it is cast as an exercise in accountability to funding bodies. Patton (2011) related how he has often been called out to help agencies produce evaluation reports at short notice to satisfy the demands of funding agencies. Accountability becomes a totally different operation when it is inclusive and part of the total development/evaluation package throughout. Patton argues that funding bodies also need to be sensitised to community voices and the progressive noticing of those voices empowers their sharing of ownership and their rights to be addressed as effective stake-holders.

12 Conclusions: Serving Disadvantaged Communities

How does this integrated, collaborative approach benefit disadvantaged communities? Does a disadvantaged community gain anything special from an agency's investment and promotion, and does society? Or does this approach only have vision of inward looking professional improvement?

Throughout we have emphasised the significance of contextual factors and the need to fit programs to the living circumstances of a targeted community. There is ample evidence of how misinformation and mismanagement arise when contextual details are overlooked for cross-cultural communities, for instance, in the roll-out of COVID-19 information and services. Ignorance of the extra hardship of lockdown rules for overcrowded and under-resourced households who could not understand the rules led to unnecessary anguish and disruption. The Lawrence et al. chapter (Chapter 13 in this volume) proposes recognition as the basis of understanding the needs and life circumstances of marginalised groups, including being attentive to how the practical wisdom already existing in the community advances program offerings. Wise professionals are attentive to ideas and signals from the community. In this chapter, we take up Schwartz's (2011) concept of the social perceptiveness and empathy with which wise practitioners recognise such input and are open to turning over and reflecting upon their own assumptions as they engage in negotiation. Bringing together the two analyses reveals the ways collaborative program development and evaluation pick up contextual leads and craft programs around those leads.

The contextual circumstances of interactions with marginalised groups are more than situational background details. They contain vital indicators of how well a program may work, and of what may work or not work. Contextual indicators, such as language preferences and culturally based fears and stigmas, need to be given foreground attention in program design and delivery. They cannot influence how a program rolls out if they are relegated to mentions in a final, possibly unread report. A collaborative, interactive work space provides tools for recognising and acting upon contextual details as they arise in living situations.

Matching program content and presentation in response to leads provided by the community continues to be a multifaceted enterprise. It requires contextualised understanding and experience to be able to pay close attention to the leads and to discern their meanings for those who wish to intervene. Such discernment is facilitated by the sharpness of evaluators' evidence tools coupled with the sharpness of developers' interpretive contextual understanding. Their combined close attention is not only perceptive, but effective in focusing on what to include and how to include it in program design.

It does not matter for community participants if the evidence gathering and interpreting tools are wielded by a wise program developer with an evaluative perspective or by a wise evaluator with a contextualised perspective. What matters for the community centres on the cultural sensitivity and evidence managing fineness; the respect with which such tools are used; and feedback to the community. Professional social perceptiveness is enacted by contextualised recognition.

Being interactive at its core, our approach fosters participation – and participation that thrives on negotiation. When community participation is built into program design, it can be expected to convey its inclusive values to community participants. Ultimately in the domain of service delivery, the usefulness of program development and evaluation, and the value of practical professional wisdom and organisational capacity will be judged in terms of how well they serve their needy communities. We have argued that practical wisdom is expanded for both developers and evaluators when they engage in sustained interactivity to coproduce knowledge. This expansion enhances the work of a service agency that supports and disseminates the approach. Wise practitioners and wise agencies benefit communities with due recognition and inclusivity.

References

Archibald, T., Sharrock, G., Buckley, J., & Cook, N. (2016). Assumptions, conjectures and other miracles: The application of evaluative thinking to theory of change models in community development. *Evaluation and Program Planning, 59*, 119–127.

Baulderstone, J. (2008). Changing relationships between the public sector and community service organisations: Insights from the South Australian case. *Public Policy, 3*(1), 1–16.

Buckley, J., Archibald, T., Hargraves, M., & Trochim, W. M. (2015). Defining and teaching evaluative thinking: Insights from research on critical thinking. *American Journal of Evaluation, 36*(3), 375–388.

Chouinard, J. A. (2013). The case for participatory evaluation in an era of accountability. *American Journal of Evaluation, 34*(2), 237–253.

Chu, W. C. K., & Tsui, M. (2008). The nature of practice wisdom in social work revisited. *International Social Work, 51*(1), 47–54.

Collins, S. (2016). The commitment of social workers in the UK: Committed to the profession, the organisation and service users? *Practice: Social Work in Action, 28*(3), 159–179.

Cousins, J. B., & Chouinard, J. A. (2012). *Participatory evaluation up close: An integration of research-based knowledge.* Information Age Publishing.

Cousins, J. B., Shulha, L. M., Whitmore, E., Al Hudib, H., & Gilbert, N. (2016). How do evaluators differentiate successful from less-than-successful experiences with collaborative approaches to evaluation? *Evaluation Review, 40*(1), 3–28.

Donaldson, S. I., Patton, M. Q., Fetterman, D. M., & Scriven, M. (2010). The 2009 Claremont debates: The promise and pitfalls of utilization-focused and empowerment evaluation. *Journal of Multidisciplinary Evaluation, 6*(13), 15–57.

Fetterman, D. M., Kaftarian, S., & Wandersman, A. (Eds.). (2015). *Empowerment evaluation: Knowledge and tools for self-assessment, evaluation capacity building and accountability.* Sage.

Fetterman, D. M., & Wandersman, A. (2005). *Empowerment evaluation principles in practice.* Guilford.

Forss, K., Kruse, S.-E., Taut, S., & Tenden, E. (2006). Chasing a ghost? An essay on participatory evaluation and capacity development. *Evaluation, 12*(1), 128–144.

Goswami, S., & Lane, V. (2017). Building evaluation capital in government: A Queensland departmental approach. *Evaluation Journal of Australasia, 17*(4), 39–49.

Gottlieb, G. (2007). Probabilistic epigenesis. *Developmental Science, 10*, 1–11.

Harrison, G., & Healy, K. (2016). Forging an identity as a newly qualified worker in the non-government community services sector. *Australian Social Work, 69*(1), 80–91.

Higgs, J. (Ed.). (2019). *Practice wisdom: Values and interpretations.* Brill Sense.

House, E. R. (2015). *Evaluating: Values, biases and practical wisdom.* Information Age Publishing.

Huberman, M., & Cox, P. (1990). Evaluation utilization: Building links between action and reflection. *Studies in Educational Evaluation, 16*, 157–179.

Lawrence, J. A., & Dodds, A. E. (2017). Developmental science, child development and the law. In L. Young, M. A. Kenny, & G. Monaghan (Eds.), *Children and the law in Australia* (2nd ed., pp. 83–102). LexisNexus Butterworths.

Lawrence, J. A., & Valsiner, J. (2003). Making personal sense: An account of basic internalization and externalization processes. *Theory & Psychology, 13*(6), 723–752.

Mayne, J. (2008, November). *Building an evaluative culture for effective evaluation and results management* (ILAC Working Paper 8). Institutional Learning and Change Initiative.

O'Sullivan, T. (2005). Some theoretical propositions on the nature of practice wisdom. *Journal of Social Work, 5*(2), 221–242.

Patton, M. Q. (2011). *Developmental evaluation: Applying complexity concepts to enhance innovation and use.* Guilford.

Patton, M. Q. (2018). A historical perspective on the evolution of evaluative thinking. In A. T. Vo & T. Archibald (Eds.), *Evaluative Thinking: New Directions for Evaluation, 158*, 11–28.

Schwandt, T. A. (2015). *Evaluation foundations revisited: Cultivating the life of the mind for practice.* Stanford University Press.

Schwandt, T. A. (2018). Evaluative thinking as a collaborative social practice: The case of boundary judgment making. In A. T. Vo & T. Archibald (Eds.), *Evaluative Thinking: New Directions for Evaluation, 158*, 125–137.

Schwartz, B. (2011). Practical wisdom and organizations. *Research in Organizational Behavior, 31*, 3–23.

Stufflebeam, D. L. (2001). *Evaluation models: New directions for evaluation* (No. 89). Jossey-Bass.

The Victorian Foundation for Survivors of Torture (VFST). (2016). *Integrated trauma recovery service model.* http://www.foundationhouse.org.au/wp-content/uploads/2018/08/INTEGRATED-TRAUMA-SERVICE-RECOVERY-MODEL_cr.pdf

The Victorian Foundation for Survivors of Torture (VFST). (2020). *Rebuilding shattered lives: Integrated trauma recovery for people of refugee background* (2nd ed.). Author.

Valsiner, J. (2014). *An invitation to cultural psychology.* Sage.

Vo, A. T., & Archibald, T. (2018). New directions for evaluative thinking. In A. T. Vo & T. Archibald (Eds.), *Evaluative Thinking: New Directions for Evaluation, 158*, 139–147.

Weiss, C. H. (1998). Have we learned anything new about the use of evaluation? *American Journal of Evaluation, 19*, 21–33.

PART 4

Future Possibilities

Introduction to Part 4

Joy Higgs

This part deals with future possibilities. In particular it talks about aging and youth, and leadership.

> Without the human community
> one single human being cannot survive.
> (The Dalai Lama, in Exley, 1999, n.p.)

> Really good leaders need to be able to transcend the here and now in a number of ways. To be transcendent in a secular, (post-)modern world, a good leader:
>
> – Can go beyond what the rules of reason might dictate.
> – Respects and draws upon experience to gain reason personal insight.
> – Sees possibilities in the future, and is aware of possible long-term implications.
> – Can enter empathetically into the lives of others to better understanding.
>
> Implied in these leadership qualities is a profound humility in the sense that one can forgo personal needs and 'natural' reactions. In essence, this kind of comportment is a openness that allows us to better see things as they are. (Rooney et al., 2010, p. 181)

> Without leadership we have no one to steer our path
> Yet with poor leadership we are led astray
> What knowledge and wisdom do leaders
> Need to learn to guide us towards sensible paths?
> (J. Higgs, personal communication, May 30, 2020)

> Listen to the children
> They have wisdom too.
> Linked to their imaginations
> And seeking to give hope to others.
> Finding a way to give meaning to their lives.
> (J. Higgs, personal communication, May 30, 2020)

 | DOI: 10.1163/9789004505544_018

All over the world, millions of young people – inspired by Greta Thunburg, the teenage girl who began a lone protest in front of the Swedish parliament – are engaged in civil disobedience to draw attention to climate change. (Figueres & Rivett-Carnac, 2020, p. 2)

A New Kind of Leadership

Ardern's strength is her ability to speak on behalf of those without a voice. [p. 243] … After Christchurch, Arden's instincts were better than anyone's and the way she carried herself was an exemplary way to lead a nation in mourning. Internationally, Ardern was held up as an embodiment of compassionate leadership. And rightly so. … Ardern's strength has always been embracing communities – ones that she was not personally a member of – wholeheartedly [p. 243]. … There are many kinds of leaders in the world. … [some] will be remembered for one or two things they did exceptionally well. Most will be forgotten entirely. … [Ardern] will be remembered for her humanity and empathy… (Chapman, 2020, p. 250)

The current financial and on-going ecological crises have taught us that without practical wisdom, organisations and leadership cannot be sustainable. In response to this situation, the handbook of practical wisdom presents a critically informed understanding of wise practices, contributing to more integrative organizational and leadership studies and practice. The focus on integration emphasizes the interdependencies of practical wisdom in relation to members, groups and cultures of organizations in their socio-cultural spheres. (Küpers & Pauleen, 2013, back page)

What do we mean by Professional Wisdom? (Swinton, 2011, pp. 154–156)

Professionalism

The traditional professions were characterised by the acquisition of systematic and valuable knowledge (knowing), the practice of application of this knowledge through techinical skill and training (doing), and the value placed on on putting this knowledge and skill to work in the service of helping others (helping). (Donovan, 2000, as cited in Swinton, 2011, p. 13)

A professional is one who professes an intent to practice in quite specific ways. … it finds itself enshrined within particular ethical codes and assumptions, and embodied in the various skills and practices that fall within the boundaries by particular professions. (Swinton, 2011, p. 154)

Wisdom

Basically, wisdom has to do with the process of accumulating knowledge, experience and intuitive understanding over a lifetime, and developing a capacity to apply such things within a lifetime that one considered to be lived well. (Swinton, 2011, p. 155)

Professional Wisdom

At a basic level, professional wisdom relates to the accumulated body of authorititative, historical, relective and practical knowledge that is gained by a profession over time and which requires it in the development of its theoretical and practice developments. (Swinton, 2011, p. 154)

Wisdom and Imagination

If we have no imagination we could have no sense of the world. (Swinton, 2011, p. 156)

Although a sigificant proportion of the knowledge base of a profession is grown by scholars in the academy, it is not *professional* knowledge unless and until it is enacted in the crucible of the 'field'. Professions are ultimately about *practice*. The field of practice is the place where professions do their work, and claim for knowledge must pass the ultimate test of value in practice. While the theoretical is the foundation for the entitlement to practice, professional practice in itself is the end to which all the knowledge is directed. … In spite of the importance of both theory and practice, professions are not simply conduits for taking knowledge from the academy and applying it to the field. The process of judgement intervenes between knowledge and application. … And human judgement always incorporates both technical and moral elements, negotiative between the general and the specific as well as between the ideal and the feasible. (Shulman, 2004, pp. 533–534)

Wisdom and Capability

> A capable leader is first and foremost, a capable and confident human being. While knowledge and competencies are necessary ingredients, capable leaders also instil a deep sense of values and confidence in all those they touch through their leadership. Their sense of self-efficacy is contagious, thereby creating a learning culture in which those involved believe that they can be whatever they want to become. (Duignan, 2006, p. 123)

References

Chapman, M. (2020). *Jacinda Ardern: A new kind of leader.* Nero.

Duignan, P. (2006). *Educational leadership: Key challenges and ethical tensions.* Cambridge University Press.

Exley, H. (1999). *Wisdom for the new millennium.* Exley Publications.

Figueres, C., & Rivett-Carnac, T. (2020). *The future we choose: Surviving the climate crisis.* Manilla Press.

Küpers, W., & Pauleen, D. J. (2013). *Handbook of practical wisdom, leadership, organization and integral business practice.* Gower Applied Business Research.

Rooney, D., McKenna, B., & Leisch, P. (2010). *Wisdom and management in the knowledge economy.* Routledge.

Shulman, L. S. (2004). *The wisdom of practice: Essays on teaching, learning, and learning to teach.* Jossey-Bass.

Swinton, J. (2011). The wisdom of L'Arche and the practices of care: Disability, professional wisdom and encounter-in-community. In L. Bondi, D. Carr, C. Clarke, & C. Clegg (Eds.), *Towards professional wisdom: Practical deliberation in the people professions* (pp. 153–157). Ashgate.

CHAPTER 15

Leadership in Uncertain Futures

David Giles

Abstract

The world is changing in complex and uncertain ways and the breadth and rate of these frenzied changes is exhausting for personal and professional lives. These rapid changes include natural disasters through to opportunist, ideological and pragmatic discourses. In short, the context of our being, doing, knowing and 'leading' has shifted in an irreversible manner. Today's leaders must enact their role 'within' and 'beyond' the context in which they find themselves, motivated and convinced by the reality that 'the status quo is never an option', leaders must move beyond formulaic styles of leadership toward relational and nuanced ways of 'being in' leadership.

Keywords

relational leadership – relational sensibilities – leadership formation – appreciative inquiry – life-centric

1 The Pressure with-in Complex, Changing, Uncertain Times

The world is changing in complex and uncertain ways (Wheatley, 2005). These widespread and mostly unpredictable changes can be seen and felt in a paralysis emanating from the pace and enormity of change, concerns for wellbeing, and the unrelenting pressure for change on a daily basis. Indeed, the breadth and rate of these frenzied changes is exhausting for our personal and professional lives (Ball, 1998).

It is not only the breadth and complexity of change across our organisations, which poses significant challenges for those in leadership, but the pace, scale and enormity of change, along with the inability to resist change is unprecedented. As Lao Tzu says, "resisting change is like trying to hold your breath, even if you're successful, it won't end well" (Schwan, 2019, n.p.).

As a consequence, organisational leaders need to manage their 'own' feelings of burnout and change fatigue while lessening the characteristics and

 | DOI: 10.1163/9789004505544_019

realities of burnout and fatigue for staff under their leadership. During these times, individualism can take precedence over community, and survival can take over from sustainability. One wonders whether the scope and pace of change has been advantageous to the organisations and their associated communities. In short, the impact of change on collegial and organisational relationships appears to be unrelenting.

1.1 *Paralysis, Creep, Limbo*

Widespread uncertainties resulting from ever-present change can be experienced as a form of *paralysis* within, and amongst, organisational decision-makers. The paralysis involves an extreme lack of personal confidence alongside an inability to 'read' the changing context of the organisation. Paralysis typically involves a leader's hesitation about making any kind of decision. This paralysis leaves many leaders in a type of 'organisational limbo' where the organisation feels 'rudderless', lacking direction, and with an absence of leadership that has the organisational members feeling vulnerable. The urgency and apparent hopelessness has those within the organisation scanning and searching for leadership that can make wise decisions as a matter of urgency.

The paralysis can also be associated with a 'mission creep' (Giles, 2019). A 'creep' occurs when the solutions being suggested by leadership to the immediate concerns involves a pragmatism that 'is the easy way out' and is highly likely to be contrary to the original mission and purpose. In this way, the organisation has 'crept' away from deeply held shared understandings of the organisation's future for the sake of short-term survivalist actions. Mission creep can often be birthed during times of organisational limbo, but more often, is seen more fully in hindsight as the creep involves an incremental movement away from one's core mission.

Being in a paralysed state of being involves a condition of being overwhelmed by current pressures and demands of the moment so much so that a reaction is more likely to be forthcoming than a well-considered decision. Further, the busyness and perceived issues cramp the opportunity for strategic thinking. While in this state of paralysis and limbo, the purpose and mission of the organisation can be reconsidered by leaders in an overly pragmatic manner and at inappropriate times.

The paralysis within an organisational context extends to the *wellbeing* of those 'in' leadership as well as those in differing roles who are 'with' organisational leaders. What is critical here is the importance of the *wellbeing* of those within the organisation as well as to the organisation as a whole in its own right. How wellbeing is supported and grown in an organisation has a lot to do with how the organisational leaders understand the essence of an organisation. Traditionally, organisations have been likened to a 'machine' where production line thinking and priorities of efficiency and effectiveness are seen as the basis for future organisational development. Numbers and surveys provide data in support of decision-making. This traditional view of organisations as 'machines' has been challenged.

An alternative view of an organisation is to consider it to be a 'living system' (Wheatley, 2005), where relationships come to the fore. In this way, each person's wellbeing is inherently interconnected and influenced by others across the context. The essence of a living systems approach can be seen in the manner in which the organisation's development is constructed and in its priorities. Some important differences focus on the organisation's appreciative and life-centric formation, where problem-solving of what is going wrong gives way to 'solution finding' that involves an appreciative 'eye' (Cooperrider et al., 2000). Relationships come to the fore in addressing what gives 'life' to the organisation and what is 'working' that might be leveraged for further endeavours. The message here is that what we focus on becomes our reality.

1.2 *Increasing Pressure on Those Who 'Provide' Leadership*

The context of our being, doing, knowing and 'leading' has shifted in an irreversible manner and continues to do so. There has also been increasing pressure and tension for those who 'provide' leadership, whether they are leaders, administrators, or managers. Leaders have been facing new pressures, increasing complexities, and broadening uncertainties with, at times, serious consequences for both the individual responsible for providing leadership, and the organisation as a whole. Leaders in these times,

> … need, more than ever, to critique their practice. Leaders need to remain cognizant of the changing context of … [the organisation] and work towards shared, on-site understandings of who and what their organisation is becoming. Such understandings must take into account the *characteristics* of an increasingly complex context …, namely:
> – uncertainty, unpredictability
> – ambiguity, uncertain meanings
> – volatility, rate of change
> – health and wellbeing versus performance …
> – professional trust versus de-privatization
> – standards versus standardisation
> – certainty versus dynamic change. (Giles, 2019, p. 153)

Today's leaders must enact an aspirational role 'within' and 'beyond' the context they find themselves in. Motivated and convinced by a reality that "the status quo, in terms of care and growth, is not an option" (Giles, 2019, p. 77).

While different 'practices' might be reconsidered in response to immediate challenges, the 'purpose' of the organisation should remain unchanged and act as a signpost, pointing to what it would take to achieve the purpose with an enduring sense of alignment for the 'life' of the organisation. Take for example, the following purpose statement.

> The purpose of the organisation relates to the fullest formation of the individuals and the organisation, such that greater synergies emerge that enables a collective interdependence where,
> - the purpose of the organisation has a *relational* intent,
> - the organisational processes are inherently *relational* and experiential,
> - the participants are *relational* beings,
> - the organisation is a *relational* entity,
> - the *relational* culture is more than the sum of the *relationship*. (Giles, 2019, p. 131)

This 'purpose' of an organisation need not be changed when challenges abound. Contextual and practical changes need not affect the purpose unduly: rather the 'purpose' statement should provide an intentionality that supports the stability and alignment of the organisation's short and long term future. Regarding the purpose statement above, it is not difficult to see the relational nature of our practice as organisational leaders so
- When is leadership not *relational*?
- When are organisations not *relational* entities?
- When are the members of an organisation not *relational*?
- When is an organisational culture not *relational*?

The enormity of change has been seen in many social contexts, as well as being expressed within recent ideological changes. These rapid changes also include natural disasters through to the cajoling of opportunist ideological and pragmatic discourses. Ideologically, the systematic and ideological advancement of neoliberalism over the last 30 years is being called into question as the primary and privileged basis for our lived experiences (Ball, 1998; Connell, 2013; Fullan, 2001).

2 Leadership beyond Packaged Formulas

Leaders must also move beyond formulaic styles of leadership toward relational and nuanced ways of 'being in' leadership. In doing so, there is a need to differentiate and demarcate the roles and meanings of leadership and management, alongside strategies and models of organisational development that seek to restore a greater sense of humanity through life-centric relationships in the workplace. This is a time when leaders need to prioritise and practise relational approaches as they read longer-term realities and the decision-making there-in.

2.1 *Deficit Understandings of Leadership, Management and Organisation*

The seriousness of the contextual paralysis described above also highlights critical differences between the role, function and responsibilities of leaders and managers. Those in positions of leadership have different priorities to managers and focus instead on the inter-relationships across the organisation and their role as guardian of the organisation's culture and mood. Bradberry (2018) contrasts the difference between managers and leaders as the former who lights a fire under people whereas the latter lights fires in people. A critical role for managers in this time of significant change is the creation of strategic options and the associated risk-management for presentation to those in leadership (Fullan, 2002). In this way management needs to serve the intentional engagement of leadership.

A similar difference can be found between *leaders and managers* in terms of their approach to organisational development. Typically, the approach to organisational development taken by managers is that of 'problem-solving', where the end goal is to lessen or remove problems within the organisation. The dominant methodology underpinning this form of analysis is Action Research, which spirals through Kolb's Learning cycles model (Stice, 1987). The Action Research approach has been described as a *deficit* model. Deficit problem-solving approaches start with questions, such as; what's wrong with the organisation? What needs to be fixed and what are the gaps to be filled? The question remains, when all the problems in an organisation are addressed, does that necessarily lead to a greater sense of 'life' in the relationships within the organisation?

3 Relational Leadership: A 'Life-Centric' Way of '*Being In*' Leadership

3.1 *Leadership Styles*

The prevailing discourse on different leadership practices is currently framed around styles of leadership, namely transformational, distributive, shared, instructional, servant and the like. Moreover, the leadership 'styles' accentuate the need for greater knowledge and skills as the basis of growth and development as a leader. Arguably, this form of development might be seen as largely a technicist approach with a skills-based emphasis on the 'what' and 'how' of being in leadership, but not the 'why' or purpose of the organisation and epitomises a deficit and problem based model that emphasises and maintains a strictly individual focus.

3.2 *Relational Leadership*

What is in common across the content in this chapter to date, and of paramount importance, are the dual phenomenon of relationships and leadership. The experiential nature of these phenomena have been theorised using phenomenological and ontological research approaches resulting in the phenomenological expression, 'Relational Leadership' (Giles, 2019). The phenomenological concern of 'Relational Leadership' is always holistic and unpacked as taken for granted meanings and shared understandings that lie beneath our everyday existence and are revealed as the essence of a leader's humanity.

In contrast to 'styles' of leadership practice, relational leadership is not a style but rather a 'way of being-in' leadership. Every leader, manager, and colleague has ways of being that are enacted *between* those relating. The term 'Relational Leadership' is also a reminder of what is critical to our practice as leaders. Indeed, it is said that leadership is always relational, and relationships are the essence of leadership. Four phenomenological themes, which shape the nature of 'Relational Leadership' have been articulated (Giles, 2019) and are presented here in three different ways, moving from an expansive statement for each theme through to two other more simplified statements:

1. Relational Leaders live 'towards' a deep moral and ethical commitment to critical, humane and connected inter-relationships,
2. Relational Leaders live 'out' a way that authentically models and embodies care-full relationships (individually and organisationally)
3. Relational Leaders 'attune' to the subtleties of the immediate, dynamic & relational context through refined relational sensibilities
4. Relational Leaders 'enact' a phronesis (practical wisdom, tacit knowing) which was context-specific and involved relational sensibilities (such as attunement, tact, nous, resoluteness, improvisation, moral judgment amongst other sensibilities)

The first phenomenological theme, "Relational Leaders live 'towards' a deep moral and ethical commitment to critical, humane and connected inter-relationships" can be stated as follows:

#1 Relational Leaders live 'towards' deep humane inter-relationships.
In summary, this first theme focuses on the purpose and direction with which a Relational Leader points a way forward for themselves and others in an organisation. The pointing is not static but rather a proactive stance, which is 'for the sake of' others. Relational Leaders show an authenticity and consistency that enables superficiality to be identified and dealt with. Equally important is the leader's thoughts on 'what' the organisation is, and what is the organisation becoming. The second phenomenological theme, "Relational Leaders live 'out' a way that authentically models and embodies care-full relationships (individually and organisationally)" can be stated as follows:

#2 Relational Leaders live 'out' a way of being that authentically embodies 'caring-full' relationships.
In summary, this second theme focuses on the holistic expression of those in leadership. How do the leaders 'walk the talk' and embody the change they wish to see? A Relational Leader's intentional engagement with those in the organisation shows a sincere and genuine care. The third phenomenological theme, "Relational Leaders 'attune' to the subtleties of the immediate, dynamic and relational context through refined relational sensibilities" can be stated as follows:

#3 Relational Leaders 'attune' to the subtleties of the immediate, dynamic and relational context.
In summary, this third theme focuses on a leader's critical discernment with regards to the dynamic and subtle organisational culture. The leader can show a 'with-it-ness' that is on top of pending change. In short, they value being able to lead with perspective. Such perspective involves greater stability in the face of change while also having an eye for opportunities that might arise.

#4 Relational Leaders 'enact' a phronesis (practical wisdom, tacit knowing) which is context-specific, and involves relational sensibilities (such as attunement, tact, nous, resoluteness, improvisation, moral knowing amongst other sensibilities). In summary, this fourth theme focuses on a leader's way of being in leadership and the extent to which the leader shows refined relational sensibilities. Relational sensibilities appear within our everyday experiences, sometimes by their presence and at times by their absence. Leaders need to grow a practical wisdom (phronesis) that is responsive and intuitive to what occurs in their current context.

The four phenomenological themes can be further reduced as follows: Relational Leaders have a 'way of being' that,

Theme 1	lives 'towards'	their being 'points'
Theme 2	lives 'out'	their being 'shows'
Theme 3	'attunes' to	their being 'feels'
Theme 4	'acts'	their being 'enacts'

3.3 *Critical Discernment*

In these complex and troubling times, leaders need a deepening 'critical discernment' to understand the organisational context and how relationships are mattering to those in leadership alongside the mood across the organisation. The critically discerning process does not work from a 'deficit' model of thought nor a quest solely for reasons of effectiveness and efficiency. Such 'measures' are limited in terms of their ability to engender hope within individuals and organisational cultures. The critical discernment process adopts an 'appreciative' 'life-centric' lens, which seeks the 'life' within our daily experiences. Such an exploration would include the identification of individual and organisational strengths, opportunities and aspirations.

Two sensibilities central to a deepening critical discernment of an immediate context of leadership are 'being attuned' to what is mattering, and 'nous;' that is, a sensibility which seeks to 'read' relationships and the game-playing nature of being in relationship. These sensibilities are integral to the development of a leader's practical wisdom and professional learning. Critically important in this process is the need for organisational leaders to affirm the 'special character' of their organisation, that is, what does the organisation stand for? What is unique about the organisation? What sets the organisation apart from other organisations? What is the organisation known for?

3.4 *"Only Dead Salmon Go with the Flow"*

What lessons might be learned about Relational Leadership from observations of the life cycle of a Salmon. There-in lies a useful metaphor for our daily activity during times of change. Consider the spawning season of Canadian salmon as an analogy for the different ways leaders experientially grapple with their immediate context.

From the outset, salmon return to their origins during the seasonal spawning. During this time, one of the most obvious characteristic of salmon's behaviour involves the need, requirement and commitment to swim 'up-stream', against the flow, and to the final destination for procreation. Simply going with the flow does not bode well for the continuity and community of life within the many interdependent relationships. The salmon instinctively move towards life and hope. In the effort to swim upstream, against the flow, salmon are constantly under pressure to turn back from engaging with the issues of the day, and just go with the flow. Similarly, salmon don't have the option of remaining 'in' the status quo, given the flow they are immersed in. In fact, for the salmon, ***the status quo is not an option!*** *But manoeuvring up-stream is a matter of swimming 'against the flow' for sustained periods of time.*

Two examples of the interplay occur between swimming up-stream and going with the flow. The first example relates to the nature of employment offered to new employees. The second example relates to the re-building of an organisational culture after a period of dysfunctional organisational leadership. It should be noted that these examples are set within the context of a dominant managerialist priority. Managerialism has a 'go with the flow' priority of ensuring quantitative and objective measures are seen as the means to increasing the effectiveness and efficiency of an organisation. Employees' wellbeing is less of a concern. Completion of tasks is priority as employees have a designated space for the requirements of the job. Overseeing the employees is typically a line manager.

In contrast, life-centric organisational leaders take responsibility for building creative, innovative and humane organisational cultures where synergies foreshadow opportunity, and emergent and latent strengths are proactively sought. Equally important are the inter-relationships and aspirational thinking that reside within the organisational community. Life centric 'up-stream' concerns also acknowledge the need for the completion of employment-related tasks. The difference here is the concern for 'how' the tasks are completed, and the ability to contribute to the direction of the organisation. Relational Leaders must show a life-centric way-of-being that is sincere, authentic and aligned to a set of shared understandings. In addition, Relational Leaders must advocate, and 'be' an advocate for those in their care. Leading in this manner is contrary to managerial imperatives.

In most organisations, the employment of new staff is often a contestable activity. It is during these times that the direction and priorities for the organisation are re-stated. These are times that require respectful arguments and advocacy for greater alignment to the mission and vision. At a pragmatic level, leaders need to advocate on a matter of principle, that a lessening proportion of fixed and casual staff will positively enhance the organisational mood. The trend has been in the opposite direction where casual, fixed term positions are becoming the norm. Casual fixed term appointments provide no incentive to contribute beyond watching hours.

Similarly, the opportunity for organisational members to participate in the direction of the organisation is paramount. There is no need for exclusive membership at these times. Equally, the process adopted for the task of re-visioning an organisation can be a matter of going up-stream or going with the flow. The membership of these occasions is critical and directly permission dialogue. As a welcoming activity, questions that follow can be used to generate an inclusive occasion (Giles, 2019):

- How long have you been associated with this organisation?
- On a good day, what keeps you in the organisation?
- Over the time that you have been associated with this organisation, what positive characteristics is this organisation known for?

Following these starters, the staff might engage with the idea of the organisation's special character using the following questions (Giles, 2019):

- What is our special character?
- What do we collectively stand for?
- How do we provide a unique contribution to our sector?
- What are we known for by our stakeholders / community?
- What do we want to be known for?
- What are we becoming collectively, or is this just a collection of individuals?

An important message from the scenarios above is that planning is required to go up-stream, resisting going with the flow.

Leaders need to critically consider the overt and covert games people play with leadership and those outside of organisational leadership. Equally important to any analysis by leadership is a deliberative re-alignment with the organisation's sense of purpose and lived values. Such activity provokes any organisational wanderings in the form of mission creep. Relational leaders need to have a way of being that points to, embodies, and charts a path ahead for the organisation as a whole; who are we becoming? In this regard, relational leaders' ways of being act as signposts for opportunities and aspirations that act as shared understandings to be considered in the short and longer term.

The development, or formation, of an organisation is two-fold; personal development and organisational development. Personal development relates to growth within the individuals who make up the organisation, whereas the organisational development focuses on the growth of the organisation as a whole including the organisation's operational systems and processes. These processes of personal and organisational development should not be mutually exclusive. It would normally be expected that both the personal and organisational development would align to the mission and vision of the organisation. For example, an organisation's new strategic initiative would need to take into account the personal professional qualities of existing staff as well as particular needs and upskilling that might be necessary to support the organisation's agenda. These needs would not come as a surprise to the individuals involved, particularly if the strategic initiative was the outcome of some corporate planning activities.

4 Relational Approaches to Professional Development

The framing of leadership as a relational way of being in leadership opens exciting professional development opportunities, which serve life-centric priorities rather than confronting deficit practices. These new priorities and initiatives are yet to be fully realised in organisations but would include the exploration and application of solution-focused approaches along with appreciative inquiry and other strengths-based practices.

Informal and formal programmes of professional learning and development should be central to everyday activity and innovation. What is noticeable is the need for a relational orientation, commitment to each staff member, and the contribution to the life-long learning of each person, regardless of position. The relational orientation can be seen by the proactive involvement of senior leadership in the workplace. Sensing the life and mood of the organisation first-hand, enables a *knowing* and a starting place for the support, encouragement and guidance available to staff.

Unlike professional learning and development programmes being taught '*to*' organisational members, members enjoy experiencing new learning '*with*' their leadership and peers. For the purposes of professional learning and development, organisations can adopt and utilise research approaches such as Appreciative Inquiry (AI), Strengths-Opportunities-Aspirations-Results (SOAR) inquiries, and life-centric and strengths-based approaches (Cooperrider & Srivastva, 1987; Cooperrider & Whitney, 1999).

5 Relational Approaches to Organisation Development

A major criticism of a deficit approach to leadership and organisational development comes from an alternative and competing ideological approach variously labelled as 'solution-focused', 'appreciative', 'life-centric' or 'strengths-based'. An alternative approach to organisational development starts with questions such as, what's working in the organisation? What characteristics of the organisation's positive core can be identified within the member's experiential narratives of high performance events?

The process and outcomes of an alternative, strengths-based, qualitative approach to organisational development starts with the gathering of life-centric stories from participants. Life-centric stories can be moments when the participant felt 'alive', had a sense of 'life', were at their best, lost track of time, or related to a peak performance. These stories are then analysed for patterns in the words alongside exploration of 'taken for granted' understandings that exist between the lines.

Following more generic analyses, the focus of the analysis moves to the identification of 'strengths', through to an articulation of 'opportunities' that exist within the strengths. Finally, these opportunities become the basis for the construction of carefully shaped 'aspirations'. The final task concludes with analysis, report expectations and targets being set.

5.1 *SOAR*

These various elements of the SOAR strategy from within an Appreciative Inquiry are summarised in Figure 15.1.

The SOAR strategy comes from the suite of strategies within an Appreciative Inquiry research approach. SOAR is a robust strategy that enables greater relational and contextual insights and understandings within an organisation. The SOAR strategy comprises four phases: Strengths, Opportunity, Aspirations, and Results. The starting place for an inquiry is the 'Strengths' of the individuals and relationships within the organisation. 'Strengths' are sought which range from very overt through to 'taken for granted' influences within the modus operandi of the living system known as the organisation (Wheatley, 2005). Importantly, strengths are evidenced in achievements. 'Opportunities' explore the possibilities and strengths that have yet to either be realised or endorsed for further consideration. Opportunities are identified from the list of strengths. This involves discussion of the strengths and their possibilities and potential.

It needs to be understood that the creative outcomes of these opportunities needs to be explicitly linked. Describing strengths and opportunities is linked

SOAR Strategy

Strategic Inquiry		**Purpose-full Intent**
(***Critical Discernment***)		(***Intentional Engagement***)
Strengths		Aspirations
Opportunities	→	(measurable) Results

FIGURE 15.1 SOAR strategy within an appreciative inquiry (adapted from Giles, 2019)

to a process of 'critical discernment'. This process forms the platform for the 3rd and 4th phase of the SOAR process, namely Aspirations and Results. 'Aspirations' are deliberate statements of purpose and intent. Like other phases, the Aspirations arise from the list of opportunities previously identified. Aspirations are constructions, or co-constructions, that shape the vision and the 'work' of an individual, individuals, and the organisation. These statements are invariably life-centric and share a commitment that gives greater meaning to each person's endeavours. The phase of 'Results' is two-fold, involving the time-lines for meeting selected aspirations while also resolving the evidence by which organisational members realise they have individually and corporately reached the aspiration. The final two phases, aspiration and results, constitute what is referred to as 'intentional engagement'. On the basis of a critical discernment process, professional endeavours can continue with an intentionality and engagement that is built upon a growing wisdom of the particular context and its complexity.

A critical question remains; which of these two approaches, Action Research and Appreciative Inquiry (AI) would present compelling reasons to work relationally, for shared understandings, towards an agenda that deliberately grows individual and organisational strengths and talents? In our uncertain world, there is mounting pressure on leaders to raise standards through greater risk taking. This pressure for innovation is said to be a matter of pioneering and innovative practices that are invigorated by a push for entrepreneurial outcomes. It needs to be stated that any such endeavour needs to be viewed as influencing inter-relationships. The enduring strengths and talents of staff are integral to the sustainability of the intentional, appreciative and life-centric model for professional learning and practice.

5.2 *Characteristics of a Completed SOAR Inquiry*

There are a number of 'taken for granted' and understated characteristics of a SOAR inquiry both in terms of the process and product. The primacy and depth of the critical discernment should not be understated. Critical discernment involves reading the relational games within an organisation to understand the times we live in. At times, and in the rush of completing these strategic processes, the significance and influence of the times we live in can be minimised and overwhelmed by what has been taken for granted.

Another characteristic of a SOAR inquiry is its increasingly purpose-driven process. While the purpose of the inquiry is to identify life-centric characteristics of the organisation, the pursuit of such involves a combination of systematic activity and intuitive contemplation in search of taken for granted understandings. The focus of the inquiry becomes further refined and specified as new meanings are uncovered from within the understandings. The complexity of the context of inquiry deepens. This can be seen, when the positive and appreciative lens opens in-depth the understanding of the role of relational sensibilities in the development of practice-based wisdom.

Leadership inquiries can take on a life of their own as opportunity opens the influence of creativity and innovation. In a similar manner, the SOAR approach to inquiry is always holistic and the energy of its positively life-centric approach also engenders deprivation of professional practice to lessen such a need for professional secrecy. In times of creativity, secrecy is antithetical to the spirit and intent of a SOAR inquiry.

6 Concluding Comments

There is no doubt that we live in a world experiencing unprecedented changes. It is not surprising that all too often our language slips into deficit thinking and at worse, a sense of hopelessness. Easy solutions are few and far between. If we are seeking easy solutions, we are running the risks outlined in this chapter namely, paralysis, organisational limbo, mission slip and deficit thinking. What is needed is a new and different organisational discourse that is hopefull, appreciative, strengths-based and relational. Such a new and different discourse would have critical implications for professional development and organisational development. Relational leadership, for example, calls for experiential and phenomenological approaches to underpin development endeavours that utilise descriptive and interpretive journaling.

References

Ball, S. J. (1998). Big policies/small world: An introduction to international perspectives in education policy. *Comparative Education, 34*(2), 119–130.

Bradberry, T. (2018). *The seagull manager*. Travis Bradberry.

Connell, R. (2013). The neoliberal cascade and education: An essay on the market agenda and its consequences. *Critical Studies in Education, 54*(2), 99–112.

Cooperrider, D. L., Sorenson, P. F. J., Whitney, D., & Yaegar, T. F. (Eds.). (2000). *Appreciative inquiry: Rethinking human organisations towards a positive theory of change*. Stipes.

Cooperrider, D. L., & Srivastva, S. (1987). Appreciative inquiry in organisational life. *Research in Organisational Change and Development, 1*, 129–169.

Cooperrider, D. L., & Whitney, D. (1999). *Collaborating for change: Appreciative inquiry*. Berrett-Koehler Communications.

Fullan, M. (2001). *Leading in a culture of change*. Jossey-Bass.

Fullan, M. (2002). The change leader. *Educational Leadership, 59*(8), 16–20.

Giles, D. L. (2019). *Relational leadership in education: A phenomenon of interest and inquiry*. Routledge.

Schwan, S. (2019). Impact of holding your breath during organizational change. *Evolving Strategies LLC*. https://evolvingstrategies.com/resisting-change-is-like-holding-your-breath-if-you-persist-you-die-lao-tzu-the-founder-of-taoism-any-change-effort-is/

Stice, J. E. (1987). Using Kolb's learning cycle to improve student learning. *Engineering Education, 77*(5), 291–296.

Wheatley, M. J. (2005). *Finding our way: Leadership for an uncertain time*. Berrett-Koehler.

CHAPTER 16

Wisdom and the University

Two Rival Modes – and a Resolution of Sorts

Ronald Barnett

Abstract

Extracting from Heidegger, paths to two modes of wisdom in the university can be discerned, a mode of being-in-the-world and a mode of inspecting the world. For Heidegger, it was the first of these that offered an authentic mode of being. However, it is the second of these that more easily attaches to the university, that mode of being that stands off from the world so as forensically to analyse a portion of it. A balanced view might suggest that the two modes should be brought together. However, each has its pathologies. The one leads to wisdom of the craftsperson, embedded in a set of traditions but this is an interior wisdom, trapped in a locale. The other leads to a separation of humanity from humanity itself and from Nature and from that has flowed the instrumentalism of modernity. More is required than simply a coalescing of the two rival modes. Suggested here is wisdom founded on a unity-with-Nature but which is sufficiently spacious to include our earlier two rival modes. This would amount to an *epistemic wisdom* but which exhibits the property of emergence, forever responsive to the expectations being always heaped *upon* wisdom. Wisdom asks the impossible of both universities and their members, for the category of wisdom continues to expand and to exceed the available resources for its realisation. This wisdom is in a state of perpetual becoming, its burdens never to be fully redeemed.

Keywords

wisdom – university – Heidegger – Nature – epistemology – epistemological displacement – epistemic wisdom – ideology – becoming

1 Introduction

The topic I have been invited to address is that of wisdom and the university and perhaps I can start with an assertion: we have no adequate way of conjoining

 | DOI: 10.1163/9789004505544_020

'wisdom' and 'university'. We do not even possess a satisfactory way of framing the matter. With few exceptions – and Nicholas Maxwell (2014) is the standout exception – the matter of wisdom and the university is not one that has much troubled philosophers or educational theorists. But even the idea of wisdom as such has not received much attention in Western thought and key questions are entirely open: is it a particular range of beliefs or even knowledge of the world? Is it a state of mind? Is it a disposition, or set of dispositions? Is it a certain class of actions? Is it a way of being in the world? Is it a synonym for the spiritual?

In Chapter 1 of this volume, Joy Higgs has done us contributors a service in laying out a schema for comprehending wisdom and within which to place our offerings. That schema consists of four elements – Dasein (or being in the world); Agentia (purposeful action in the world); Sapience (deep insight into the world); and Eudaimonia (human flourishing). All four elements have to be present for us to be in the presence of wisdom, and this is crucial. No element is reducible to any of the others, and no element takes priority: each has an equal part to play.

However, when it comes to the university, we are immediately faced with a conundrum. After all, the practitioners and professionals of the university are single persons, so there are difficulties in carrying over that framework in fathoming wisdom in relation to the university. Might the idea of wisdom play out for the university as a social institution? What might it mean to speak of a university as being *wise*? *Can* wisdom be felt to be a unitary attribute of a complex institution – such as a university – with its many inner cultures? Does, therefore, the coupling of 'wisdom' and 'university' hold *any* water? These are the questions before us in this chapter, and I think that we can do no better than coming at them via the four-fold framework that Joy Higgs has given us.

My basic tack will be to distinguish two fundamentally opposed approaches to wisdom and the university – essentially wisdom in sheer being and a wisdom in understanding. However, I shall go on to muddy the waters, to observe that the idea of wisdom is all the time expanding and that, therefore, as in life generally, for the university, wisdom can be at best only a matter of perpetual internal struggle.

1.1 *Being*

Being is a particularly problematic concept in the present setting; and here, we have to delve briefly into Heidegger (for just the next three paragraphs). For Heidegger, *being* was – as Joy Higgs reminds us – intimately related to Dasein. Dasein possessed "historicality" (Heidegger, 1962/1998, p. 40). Dasein, therefore, is a matter of indwelling, of being in a certain place or possessing a certain disposition. It is the state into which one is 'thrown', in one's everyday existence. It is "not to be construed in terms of some concrete possible idea of experience" (ibid., p. 69). Dasein has an essential hiddenness, but it can be uncovered to some extent: "Dasein can discover tradition, preserve it, and study it explicitly" (ibid., p. 41). (The sense of wisdom having its place within tradition is important for our analysis here.) Dasein, in other words, can become "transparent to itself" (ibid., p. 42), and it is through such processes of self-reflection that the fuller aspects of Being can show themselves.

This sense of there being manifestations (plural) of being is portrayed vividly in Heidegger's famous example of the hammer, to which he repeatedly returns. In its everyday usefulness, the hammer is "ready-to-hand" (ibid., p. 98ff.). This usefulness is not theoretical but it is far from being blind. In its 'being used', in its usefulness, it "withdraw[s]" from the user (ibid., p. 99). Dasein is in the world, not apart from the world. The matter is different when we take up an enquiring attitude towards things in the world, whether a hammer or Nature, when we give the world our "circumspective concern" (ibid., p. 106). Then, entities in the world – such as a hammer – become "present-at-hand": then, we may analyse them in "going through them" (ibid., p. 101).

In this phenomenological structure – as set out by Heidegger – we have a distinction of fundamental import for our present inquiry. It is that which is ready-to-hand that Heidegger associates with authenticity: "… only in … 'coming before us' is the current world authentically ready-to-hand" (ibid., p. 106); and "… in its readiness-to-hand, it must … withdraw in order to be ready-to-hand quite authentically" (ibid., p. 99). *Here we reach the crux of the matter*: "Being-in-the-world … amounts to a non-thematic circumspective absorption … for the readiness-to-hand of a totality of equipment" (ibid., p. 107). That term 'absorption' is crucial here.

The issue before us is wisdom and the university and we need to tease out how this conjunction – 'wisdom' and 'university' – might have meaning, if at all. And we have just alighted on Heidegger's analysis of being in which he distinguishes between (1) being as immersed in – *absorbed* in – the immediate world experienced through traditions and taken-for-grantedness; and (2) being as standing off from, and inspecting, the world.

In effect, in this distinction Heidegger is opening *two paths to wisdom* but is declaring in favour of one as being authentic, namely that form of being – in which entities are ready-to-hand, with which one just *is*. And we can sense a form of wisdom not far away, the wisdom that comes as a result of being deeply inside a form of life. It is the wisdom of the elders.

However, for the university, it could be said that wisdom is to be found in *systematic* reflection, in careful analysis, in inquiry with sound methodologies, in critique. In other words, wisdom in the university is located in the kind of being that is taken up towards the *present-at-hand*, in taking up an analytical stance towards the hammer and in seeking to understand its properties and its performance characteristics. Something along these lines might be felt to be implicit in the idea of the university forged in liberal democracies over the last two hundred years; namely, the university as a site of critical reason.

However, the logic of Heidegger's analysis of being is that we should not go in that direction at all in trying to fathom the meaning of the university and wisdom. Rather, the 'authentic' way has to lie in the university as a site of 'absorption'. It would not be fair to say that Heidegger is leading us towards an unreflective university but his analysis does lead to the value of the university – and its wisdom – as residing in its traditions, in its embodied life, in its community; in other words, in what its members live in its being absorbed.

Two ideas of wisdom and the university are therefore emerging here: wisdom as lived-in and wisdom as emergent through an uncovering of the world. In the first, there is a sense that wisdom is naturally contained within the life forms, the social forms, the traditions and the lifeworld of the university. Universities have tendencies to be long-lived; many have been in existence for hundreds of years. Most universities seek to develop and enshrine their own traditions, marked by symbols, ceremonies, styles, modes of address and styles that endure over the generations. Cultures have evolved over time, characterising each discipline and each department. Universities, too, take on institution-wide organisational cultures.

The upshot is that there accrues, for any individual member of a university, a way of being in that situation in a particular university. Bourdieu (1990) called it a *habitus*; it is not a bad term at all for it intimates a sense of a complex form of being that is habituated; taken-as-read; a lived-in mode of being; the mode of being that is akin to Heidegger's ready-to-hand. One simply knows what to do and how to do it in different settings in the university and in academic life more broadly. One has imbibed the customs and the habits have been formed.

What kind of wisdom is here? Here, there is the possibility of a practical wisdom – *phrónêsis*. It is not simply a matter of carrying out the actions that are expected, akin to wielding the hammer in certain ways. It is rather the wisdom that can be said to inhere in the work of the craftsman (Sennett, 2008), with the care, perspicacity, diligence, foresight, practical judgement, timefulness (in using one's time sensibly given the tasks in front of one; being-in-time indeed), a sensitivity to the rhythms that are part of good work in the field in question (Lefebvre, 1992/2004), awareness of audience or relevant others and so on and so on. This wisdom, therefore, is not just a matter of being in the world but of *Being* in the world; that is to say, of being reaching for and sometimes accomplishing its possibilities in the world.

However, as intimated, Heidegger's account of being suggests another and quite different sense of wisdom; a polar opposite in some way. This is the wisdom opened for us by Heidegger's idea of the hammer being present-at-hand; the idea of a hammer not only in use but as an object of circumspection. In this mode of Being, one stands off from an object or a situation or a matter and holds it before one, such that it becomes a topic for understanding. And the university has become a social institution that holds within it all manner of paths towards such an analytic understanding.

Note how radically different is this form of wisdom. Whereas in practical wisdom, one is bound into the moment, even as one deploys a huge array of resources to accomplish a work of excellence, here wisdom is to be derived precisely by effecting a distance from the world. One stands off from the world in order to understand it. Indeed, even though it has been much impugned in some quarters over recent decades, essential to the idea of objectivity (Archer & Outhwaite, 2006) in the university lies an assumed value in displacing oneself from one's natural proclivities, one's own beliefs and opinions, and instead reaching into and participating in the formation of a world of knowledge that stands independently of mind as such (Popper, 1975).

We have, then, two polar opposites wrapped up in the idea of wisdom in the context of the university. On the one hand, the dedicated, skilful, care*ful*ness of living in and living out the full traditions of the university, committed to the demands of a discipline and to the nurturing of student as persons; of their very being. This is a wisdom born of working with one's immediate resources, of having a care for one's work, of its nuances, its finessing, its crafting. In this wisdom, one sees deeply into situations out of one's embodied understandings of presenting situations and possibilities (Dall'Alba & Sandberg, 2020; Tanaka, 2011), caught and expressed in the moment. The student's act opens up a panoply of responses and a 'right' response is created; it is not simply produced. This crafting acts not so much in executing one's own reasons for the wisdom is there, in the response. The response does not follow the reasoning but *is* the reasoning. This is a *wisdom-in-action.*

The other form of wisdom could hardly be more different. This is a wisdom that steps out of a situation and cognizes it, inspects it and, moreover, seeks cognitive resources to understand it. More still, in its fullest form, this wisdom seeks to displace and even ultimately to *subjugate* the understandings of the lived-in wisdom. It is here that we find a way of cashing out the idea of emancipation born of the Frankfurt School of Critical Theory and also Freierian libertarian Marxism. Through the intellect – even if ultimately to be coupled with practice and so to form 'praxis' – human being can supplant itself. The hammer could be inspected and analysed from *numerous* points of view: it could be recognised as an instrument of oppression, or as literally an instrument of instrumental reason (the gas chambers were hammered into place) or as a means of critique (in the geologist's work in determining the effects of climate change). A way opens here, not merely of seeing into things but seeing *through* things and carried on the wings of multiple cognitive frameworks.

We have here, therefore, within higher education and the university, two completely opposed ideas and forms of wisdom. Note that Heidegger would give the palm to our first form, that of the wisdom that comes from living-in the traditions and modes of experience of the university. This is the mode of wisdom that Heidegger would term 'authentic'. This has to be understood for what it is: in being confined in this way, without its supplement, we have here a Fascist form of wisdom. This is not a term ever to be used lightly. (It is instructive that Heidegger not only became Rector of the University of Freiburg but also a member of the Nazi party and delivering a scarcely designed apologia in his [2018] Rector's address.) For Heidegger, the favoured form of Being was that of a surrender to an in-the-moment and non-critical form of being, sophisticated as he made it out to be.

There IS value in this form of wisdom, a wisdom of the skilled and experienced professional who intuitively brings into the moment a wide array of epistemic and personal resources and deploys those resources to effect. But by itself it is limited and dangerous (confining one to one's traditions). And it is not the wisdom that might naturally be associated with the university. That wisdom would be closer to the 'present-at-hand' mode of being, which Heidegger tends to downplay. This mode of being offers the promise of an opening of new ways of seeing the familiar: the sun was thought to revolve around the Earth and is then understood as a modest star on the fringes of a galaxy; a table is understood as a mass of electrons flying around atoms in excitation; a person on the street is understood as standing in a set of hidden social class relationships; animals and glaciers are understood to be keeping company with human beings in an emerging Ecocene (Boehnert, 2018). This inquiring mode of being naturally critiques and transforms one's fundamental mode of being.

Two points can be derived from this analysis. Despite what has been said, neither mode of being *in itself* offers a route to wisdom. Being-in-the-world and being-as-inspection-of-the-world have to be brought together. Putting it crudely, practice and theory have to be unified. And many programmes of study in higher education have sought to do just this, putting their students into practical settings, to come into the 'habitus' and live the arts-and-crafts of being a doctor or an engineer or a social worker; *and* – in different pedagogical settings – to gain theoretical frameworks through which to interrogate one's lived and embodied experiences.

But the matter of wisdom lies still on the table. The question is whether educators are losing sight of – or never possessed – sight of the possibilities for a wisdom that rests on the highest and emancipatory forms of critique. Does the geology student acquire the wherewithal and the dispositions for critiquing the ecological aspects of the policies of petroleum companies? Is the medical student sufficiently attuned to the practices of big-pharma, not least as they play out across the world? Is the social theorist able to critique the ideological tendencies of some sociological theorising? Is the student in the university's business school being equipped to stand back and critique the value structure of an individual corporation in which she or he might find themselves subsequently working?

1.2 *Agentia*

Our analysis of being has posited one mode of being as being-in-the-world. Being-in-the-world is not in itself the exhibition of agency. Agency accrues when a person is self-willed and is not merely acting out a part already prescribed. Agency requires self-understanding and self-reflection; not merely thought-in-action, important that that is but also pre-thought, thought outside the event, such that frameworks of understanding are brought into the action.

In sociological theory, agency is conventionally placed against structure and the relationship between structure and agency has been a conundrum that many has sought to resolve (or dissolve) and there is a natural tension between the two. However, agency can be seen as having point and substance precisely in situations that are structured. Agency has no anchor, no pivot, no exemplification in simple societies, still less on a desert island. It has expression, literally, when human beings come to realise their powers within the complex structures in which they are embedded. No structure, no agency.

It is much more than a matter of being self-directed, for automata can be said to be self-directed. In agency, the mind puts itself into action; again, literally so. The mind puts itself into *its* actions. Mind lives recursively in its actions (Arendt, 1958). And actions have their place and point in structures of several kinds, whether institutional, discursive, cultural or economic. Actions, therefore, gain their authenticity in bearing the imprint of a particular mind at work within the structure(s) in which an action has point.

This agency is clearly linked to the mode of being that we termed 'lived-in'. In agency, a human being invests her or himself into an action; the action is willed by the human being, and so becomes a human action. But, and crucially, this agency is a bridge between the two kinds of being that we identified in the previous section. Not only is being inserted into the action in question – it is lived-in the sequence of actions that constitute a practice – but it becomes an authentic action when it is also imbued with the analytic inspection-of-the-world – that other mode of being that we encountered earlier. The surgeon is in the moment, living out the traditions of craft and care that have evolved over centuries in medical practices, but also living out of the considerable frameworks of understanding and analysis acquired over many years of training in a university (or more likely in universities, plural).

However, even when, say, professional practice exhibits this extraordinary combination of practical and theoretical capabilities, still we are not in the presence of practical wisdom. For that, a self-monitoring capacity is required that enables the surgeon to stand back from the possible operation and to move into a different judgemental space, to consider the ethical appropriateness of the operation. Even though all the equipment is to hand, and the surgeon and her team have all the necessary surgical resources and skills, and the family wish it to proceed, a *wise judgement* may be that, in the patient's interests, the procedure should not be attempted. A few more months of life may be possible but the quality of life so rendered would be likely to be poor. Wisdom in this case would also extend to sharing the decision-making among the team and the relatives but the decision requires leadership, and so *wise professionalism* frequently calls for *wise leadership*.

Let us recap. In this essay, we have been gradually widening the dimensions of wisdom. In summary, we may say that Heidegger cannot provide us with a full basis of wisdom, even within Heidegger's own terms. In Heidegger, we have two modes of being, a being-in-the-moment and a being-out-of-the-world, in order to inspect the world. Each of these modes of being can provide a heightened form of human being, and each tends towards its own kind of wisdom: a wisdom in the hands of the craftsperson and a wisdom of far-sightedness, offering us quite new frameworks for comprehending the world, and even overturning the world.

Each of these forms of being can be carried into the world, in a form of action, and so provide a form of agency. The first is that of the painter who knowingly sets about, with some passion to transform not just the way we think of painting but of the world. The great painters, Picasso, Monet, Bacon did just this. The second is that of the great thinker who carries their thinking into the world. One thinks of Karl Marx or Bertrand Russell or – as a more recent example in the field of critical theory – Roy Bhaskar, who founded the School of Critical Realism and promoted it across the world. Interestingly, and perhaps importantly, these individuals tend to be on the margins of academic life, if not fully outside it.

In making these observations, we are already extending our analysis beyond Heidegger. Heidegger did not – so far as I know – draw on the concept of wisdom as such. Heidegger spoke of such matters as existence, thinking, dwelling, being, concern, and authenticity but not of wisdom; or, at least, very little. Surely, this was no accident. The lack of wisdom in Heidegger reflects the rather closed and limited conception of being in his oeuvre. Wisdom, after all, implies breadth of being, and not only of being able to inspect the world but to place any such analysis against the broadest of horizons.

As implied in Maxwell's (2014) work, wisdom is bound up not only with a concern over what is of value in life, but also with the capacity to go on interrogating what is of value in life. A university that takes this point seriously will attend to its pedagogies but it will also establish an institutional capacity for this value interrogation: what might be of value in life and how can the university respond?

As we go on examining this matter of wisdom in the context of the university, so it continues to unfold and to widen. Action, thought, depth, breadth, inquisitiveness, far-sightedness, a displacement of self against large horizons of space and time, a criticality, objectivity, personhood, and capacities for reflection on what is valuable in life at both the personal and the institutional levels, thought, action, disciplinary frameworks: all surely now have to be part of the conjunction of 'wisdom' and 'university'. We have so far considered only two of Joy Higgs' four moments of wisdom: the more we inquire into wisdom, the more elements come forward asking for attention. This is a point to which we shall return: that *the concept of wisdom is not only elusive but is eternally expanding*. We shall never exhaust its meaning since tomorrow it will have widened still further.

1.3 *Sapience*

As Joy Higgs observes, knowing – the essence of sapience – extends far beyond knowledge. And that introduction provides many elements to fill out this idea, including appreciation, mindfulness, self-awareness, discernment, criticality and epistemological fluency.

I want to push at the boundaries of this panoply of components and I shall begin by picking up the idea of epistemological fluency. We learn that this idea 'refers to having a command of the language', being on the inside of the discourse of a 'practice community' and so possess 'the means and tools for communicating with colleagues' drawing on the 'shared understanding embedded in … [a] profession'. This is all a vital part of what it is to be a practitioner imbued with the care and concern that are part of Heidegger's first mode of being, the being-in the world, being-in a community. But I want to suggest that this is not in itself anything like a sufficient condition of wisdom. Nor is it sufficient to add the other mode of being to which Heidegger points us – albeit with rather little enthusiasm, namely, being-as-a-will-towards-inspection. To put it sharply, even adding to epistomological fluency both the capacities for criticality and a disposition of criticality, our conceptual framework would still not pass muster.

The problem is that epistemological fluency, even filled out with the idea of criticality, could still leave our practitioner trapped in her or his practice community. An immediate rejoinder might be that wisdom requires the capacity to step outside of one's immediate professional framework and so one should possess interdisciplinary resources. In that way, one can inspect not just presenting situations – through the language, concepts and frameworks of one's profession – but one can interrogate that very framework. The lawyer can inspect her activities and the legal profession coupled with concepts and frameworks of *social* justice, societal equity and so forth. The engineer can interrogate his activities and profession coupled with concepts of ecology and sustainability. The doctor can analyse her activities and profession through theological concepts of the sacred, spirit, meaning (of life) and becoming. Inter-disciplinarity has potential to become *critical* inter-disciplinarity.

A view from outside – that such inter-disciplinarity can afford – could constitute a resource on which the idea of the whistle-blower can gain purchase. This is crucial since unless our concept of wisdom can embrace the whistle-blower, it will be deficient. The whistle-blower, after all, is precisely a person who can step outside a situation and size it up from a distance, and do so by bringing in extra-mural resources, of knowledge, values, goals and operational perspicacity. In particular, the whistle-blower draws on cognitive frameworks not ordinarily available within her or his profession's understanding of a presenting situation. (The whistle-blower does not have to shout: the Dalai Lama *is* a whistle-blower.)

Let me cut to the chase. What is required is not so much epistemological fluency but epistemological *displacement*. Wisdom requires knowledge but, more than that, wisdom requires understanding. More than that too, wisdom requires the capacity to distance oneself from one-knowledge frameworks. One needs to displace oneself epistemologically.

But what then – epistemologically speaking – is this space of displacement? It is the space that is afforded one when one has at one's disposal a range of cognitive resources, of doubting, of imagining, of seeing matters from different points of view (perhaps historical, or in having a sense as to how matters might seem in other countries), of values (perhaps of justice or of wellbeing or of the public good), and of a sense of ever-lasting contingency (for matters can normally be other than they are). It is to see a situation from *afar*.

This space of wisdom, therefore, is no definite space and has no boundary or definition. There can be no blue-print wisdom, no recipe for reaching a position of purity or utter neutrality or of a pre-suppositionless visitor. A position of wisdom entails a reflexivity such that it is understood that any position, any utterance, any claim can be contested. Wisdom cannot imply any kind of finality; and it is understood that this is the case. It indicates, too, that at the institutional level, a university must have space – institutional autonomy – in which to attain such reflexive wisdom.

It may be felt that at least the idea of multi-disciplinarity can provide the resources necessary for this epistemological displacement but, while helpful, it is neither necessary nor sufficient. It is not necessary because epistemological displacement can be achieved through practical experience or, say, through having access to a set of values counter to those in the epistemic community in question. But it is not sufficient for ultimately, in epistemological displacement, what is called for is the capacity to take up a different *attitude* to the world. Let us briefly delve into this important matter.

For the past two hundred years, and with ever greater force, the Global North has been developing and exporting to the rest of the world a particular ontology. The world is held separate from the knower and it is the task of the knower to "hold a mirror up to Nature" (Rorty, 1980), and to produce accounts of the world that correspond to the world, even though – following Kant – it is understood that the world does not readily disclose itself. It is on the basis of such a sense of the relationship of knower to the world that the Earth has come to be regarded as separate from 'humanity' and so available for exploitation. Ecological destruction owes much to the instrumentalism built into the epistemology-ontology relationship characteristic of the Global North (Code, 2006).

It follows that epistemological displacement calls for the power to disinvest oneself of this epistemological framework and the capacity to appreciate that human beings are part of the Earth that they wish to understand. Here we have *an inkling of a new kind of wisdom*, and it contains several components. It requires, in the first place, a movement into a new relationship between knower and the world, between epistemology and ontology. In this relationship, as intimated, the world is not out there, waiting to be inspected and analysed by the knower who has somehow managed to move to a distant place that provides a disinterested view of the world. Now, it is understood that oneself as a would-be knower is immersed in the world even while trying to be distant from the world.

Traditional communities are much more immersed in Nature, not seeing themselves as standing off from Nature; and some today seem to want to return to such a position of unity-with-Nature. But, of course, there can be no retreat to the position of traditional epistemologies. The epistemological cat is out of the bag and cannot be put back. Somehow, both modern and traditional epistemological positions – and relationships with the world – have to be held together, uncomfortable as that may be, as one shifts in perpetuity from one foot to the other, continuing to see the world now as out there and *now* as in one and one in it.

There is talk these days of an ecology of knowledges (de Sousa Santos, 2014), the implication being that the epistemologies of the Global North and of the Global South should be brought together into some kind of unified knowledge ecosystem. Quite apart from the difficulties that the idea presents at the systems level, practical suggestions being rather thin on the ground, what is largely omitted from consideration is the extraordinary demand that this idea places on the individual, of living – as it were – both in the Global South and in the Global North simultaneously; both in Nature and apart from Nature. But this is what wisdom has to demand in the C21; and it is an idea that radically expands the idea and the practice of wisdom. It is – again – the Dalai Lama option: to engage with the technologies, knowledge frameworks, social institutions, media and state violence of the twenty-first century, *and* all the while holding fast to the habitus of Buddhism, with its sense of an enveloping universe and the displacement of self that it offers.

A further part of this wisdom is that Nature has star billing. Nature is there, and commands our respect, as possessing inherent value. There are, though, two codicils here. Firstly, the sense of Nature called for is not of cuddly entities but, again, of intricately layered phenomena, with its layering and their differential force, in which entities exert power over others (Bhaskar, 1975/2008). Secondly, and to reiterate, Nature is not out there, but enfolds human beings even if they have also managed in part to effect a little autonomy from it. The point is crucial for it takes us, as Bruno Latour (2004) has observed, towards a politics of Nature. Especially when put into the company of the new realisms, the questions have repeatedly to be pressed: "Who speaks for the glaciers? Who speaks for the rain forests? Who speaks for the rhinos?".

This *epistemic wisdom*, then, makes heavy demands upon those few animals called human beings. The question arises now as to what it is to be human: indeed, have we ever been human? It is evident that what it is to be human is all the time expanding, and with it too, the idea of wisdom. We have just observed the problematic idea of an ecology of knowledges. Hazy as it is, it opens to a sense of the wise person living both in a world of cognitions and in a world of enveloping spirit (Stiegler 2014; White, 2013). Secondly, as intimated, the world itself – and its key institutions such as universities – has to become wise, by enfolding these two forms of knowledge into each other. It is, in short, to live in two worlds simultaneously (Niblett, 1974).

2 Flourishing

In turning to the final (fourth) domain of wisdom identified by Joy Higgs, I want to bring together the threads of the argument and to weave a picture of the wise university. The idea of flourishing presents us with a perfect vehicle for this final set of suggestions, for flourishing speaks to fullness, to an integrated set of possibilities, and to a realisation of as yet unfulfilled promise.

The question has to be asked: is flourishing possible in the late capitalist society of the twenty-first century? Suppose that it is not. Then we would have a gap between concept and the world: our concept of flourishing would exceed the possibilities that the world offers. This was the situation that Adorno (1966/2014) wrestled with as a steady stream in his work, that our concepts exceed their manifestations in the world. That universities fail to flourish and to exhibit the wisdom that is associated with flourishing is not just a contingent matter but is explicable. To continue with Adorno (2008), to suggest that universities do or even could flourish would be to engage in an ideological negation: the very idea would compound the real situation (negation upon negation). What, then, is the status of any attempt to undo this negation: would it, could it, amount to a positive resolution of the matter or would it plunge us into a further (negative) negation, of acting out practices bearing the label 'flourishing' but which insidiously – and ideologically – reinforce the existing negative state of affairs?

The Rector tells the world that, in his university at least, teaching and research are complimentary to each other, when academics in most of its departments know full well that the reverse is the case; that research and teaching are in mutual combat with each other. Moreover, they experience the tension – between research and teaching – on a more-or-less daily basis. They can be 'bought-out' of their teaching to conduct research but not vice versa; monies can be found to support academics who wish to present papers at conferences but not to engage in cross-university workshops on teaching; rewards flow for papers published in leading journals but not for high satisfaction scores from one's students. How to account for this state of affairs? And what would wisdom look like? The second question can be tackled only on the basis of an answer to the first question.

We account for this situation – as intimated – as a set of ideological negations (Zizek, 1999, 2008). That there is a tension between research and teaching is a negation of the idea that the two functions in a university are integrated; and this negation is exhibited in the practices of the university. The Rector then tells the world that the two functions are well integrated, so providing a negation of the negation. This is NOT a positivity but a further and even deeper negation, an ideological negation. Furthermore, the Rector knows that matters are otherwise; but still declares matters to the contrary. This is not really a false consciousness but an attempt at mystification. Things are wrong, and the Rector knows that things are wrong, but still exacerbates the problem, organisationally and discursively.

What, then, does wisdom look like in such a situation? It cannot be simply to declare that there is a gap between the idea of the university and the practices, for that leaves everything as they are. Nor can it be simply to put in hand institutional policies and practices that seem fundamental but leave everything largely as they are. After all, our university has its eye on being in the top one hundred universities in the rankings.

The lesson here is that again there is an inevitable and necessary gap between the idea of wisdom and the possibilities for its realisation in practice. Moreover, this gap will keep on expanding. On the one hand, the real of the university – the deep forces that act upon the university – are all the time intensifying. On the other hand, the sense of what wisdom could mean for the university in the best of all possible worlds, both the human world and the world of Nature, keep expanding! Now, we have to be sensitive to matters of epistemic injustice, of global injustice, of colonialism, of gender inequalities as well as the myriad of forms of human suffering that have been with us for decades if not centuries; and now, too, we have to take account of Nature, with a capital 'N' as it were, pressing its claims upon us, in all *its* forms. Moreover, we are now aware, perhaps more than ever, of the whole world, the whole universe, being in motion, and exhibiting contingency, entanglement and haphazardness. This is a world without stability but with unequal power and fortune among its entities. In short, *the horizons of, and for, wisdom are continuously expanding.*

3 Conclusions

Can the university be wise? Can those who work in it exhibit wisdom? Yes, but not in a facile way. Wisdom is *neither* a state of being as such, *nor* even a movement to a particular state of being – either that of a university as an institution or of individuals associated with it. It is not like reaching the summit of a mountain, with a sense of a particular destination having been reached, even after an arduous and treacherous journey. Nor does it even represent an ascent – to use one of Newman's (1873/1976) terms – to a lofty viewpoint, from which to see the world clearly and unencumbered.

In the early part of this essay, we identified two rival modes of wisdom, a warm agentic living-in-the-world wisdom and a cold analytic wisdom. Quickly, we saw limitations in that typification of wisdom, which came to be seen as more intricate, subtle and vibrant, as we drew on the four-fold schema of Joy Higgs. *Epistemic wisdom* seems to call for far-sightedness and for forensic depth; for epistemic generosity towards other knowledges and for a careful craftsmanship within a field. *Agency* seems to call for the capacity precisely to act and to act in the light of reasons; but also at times to desist from action. *Flourishing* beckons but to where? What is it for a university to flourish – by whose reckoning? And by which set of values? And *being* calls one both to live faithfully according to the traditions of the academic calling but yet to have the nous and the courage to critique those very traditions.

This complexity is the way of the world, that it calls upon universities and their members – including their students – to live, uncomfortably as maybe, in manifold states of being, and more or less simultaneously; and these demands that wisdom places – on universities; on its members – are all the time expanding. But note the implication. *Wisdom asks the impossible of both individuals and the university.* The more we dwell on it, so the category expands. *Of the demands that wisdom places on the university and its members there is no end; and there can be no end.* But then, we glimpse an opening.

Wisdom has to be that state of being in which one is sensitive to the unending demands *of* wisdom. The wise university, the wise academic, the wise student, has a concern for wisdom, sensitive to its unceasing, ever-widening and impossible character. Can the university, can its curricula, be sensitive to those who never enter a university? Can its research and scholarly endeavours be conducted against a horizon of sheer otherness? Can its members – students, academics, administrators, even secure the spaces that wisdom calls for?

Wisdom is a state of perpetual *becoming*, not just in the world but also for-the-world and from-the-world (Deleuze & Guattari, 2013). But now, more than a state of being, wisdom becomes a category that can be given some substance. For the world *is* the world, the total world; everything in heaven and Earth. The English philosopher Bertrand Russell (1912/1967) depicted himself as a citizen of the universe. In caring about wisdom, the Earth calls; the universe calls. For there can be no boundaries to wisdom.

It is fitting that attention should be turning nowadays to wisdom for wisdom is manifestly a concept for our age. Those earlier questions impose both upon the university (as an institution) and upon the pedagogical situation: Who speaks for the glaciers? Who speaks for the rain-forests? Who speaks for the rhinos? This is the context in which the wise university and its members have to place themselves and their endeavours. This wisdom displaces itself not at all into the transcendent (Levinas, 1999) but into the Real of the world. It is a terrible responsibility for its burdens can never be fully redeemed. Perhaps this is not much of a resolution to our dilemmas here but that is how matters are.

References

Adorno, T. W. (2008). *Lectures on negative dialectics: Fragments of a lecture course, 1965/1966*. Polity.

Adorno, T. W. (2014). *Negative dialectics*. Bloomsbury. (Original work published 1966)

Archer, M. S., & Outhwaite, W. (Eds.). (2004). *Defending objectivity: Essays in honour of Andrew Collier*. Routledge.

Arendt, H. (1958). *The human condition*. University of Chicago Press.

Bhaskar, R. (2008). *A realist theory of science*. Verso. (Original work published 1975)

Boehnert, J. (2018). *Design, ecology, politics: Towards the Ecocene*. Bloomsbury.

Bourdieu, P. (1990). *Homo academicus*. Polity.

Code, L. (2006). *Ecological thinking: The politics of epistemic location*. Oxford University Press.

Dall'Alba, G., & Sandberg, J. (2020). Bodily grounds of learning: Embodying professional practice in biotechnology. *Studies in Higher Education*. https://doi.org/10.1080/03075079.2019.1711047

Deleuze, G., & Guattari, F. (2013). *What is philosophy?* Verso.

de Sousa Santos, B. (2016). *Epistemologies of the South: Justice against epistemicide*. Routledge.

Heidegger, M. (1998). *Being and time*. Blackwell. (Original work published 1962)

Heidegger, M. (2018). *The self-assertion of the German university: Address delivered on the solemn assumption of the Rectorate of the University of Freiberg*. Reproduced in M. A.

Latour, B. (2004). *Politics of nature: How to bring the sciences into democracy*. Harvard University Press.

Lefebvre, H. (2004). *Rhythmanalysis: Space, time and everyday life*. Continuum. (Original work published 1992)

Levinas, E. (1999). *Alterity & transcendence*. Colombia University.

Maxwell, N. (2014). *How universities can help create a wiser world: The urgent need for an academic revolution*. Imprint Academic.

Newman, J. H. (1976). *The idea of a university*. Clarendon. (Original work published 1873)

Niblett, W. R. (1974). *Universities between two worlds*. University of London.

Popper, K. (1975). *Objective knowledge: An evolutionary approach*. Clarendon Press.

Rorty, R. (1980). *Philosophy and the mirror of nature*. Blackwell.

Russell, B. (1967). *The problems of philosophy*. Oxford University Press. (Original work published 1912)

Sennett, R. (2008). *The craftsman*. Allen Lane.

Stiegler, B. (2014). *The re-enchantment of the world: The value of spirit against industrial populism*. Bloomsbury.

Tanaka, S. (2011). The notion of embodied knowledge. In P. Stenner, J. Cromby, J. Motzkau, J. Yen, & Y. Haosheng (Eds.), *Theoretical psychology: Global transformations and challenges* (pp. 149–157). Captus.

White, R. (2013). *The heart of wisdom: A philosophy of spiritual life*. Rowman & Littlefield.

Zizek, S. (1999). *The sublime object of ideology*. Verso.

Zizek, S. (2008). *The ticklish subject: The absent centre of political ontology*. Verso.

CHAPTER 17

Towards Practice Wisdom in Politics

Developing a Leadership Framework through Dispute Resolution Values and Skills

Rachael Field and Laurence Boulle

Abstract

Dispute resolution values and skills can usefully and positively inform and support practice wisdom in the day-to-day discourse and decision-making activities of political life. This chapter argues that all politicians, elected and aspiring, should receive compulsory dispute resolution training to increase their practice wisdom and thus positively influence their engagement in politics through the development of a new leadership framework based on the skills and values that inform dispute resolution theory and practice.

Keywords

politics – practice wisdom – dispute resolution

1 Introduction

Political discourse in Western liberal democracies is a powerful forum for and tool of civic leadership; informing public perspectives on the exercise of governmental power and authority, and helping the electors and citizenry to understand key issues of decision-making in public policy and governance. In recent years, however, the citizens of many countries around the world have made clear that the state of politics and of political discourse has become toxic, unsatisfactory, and unsatisfying to them. (Brooks & Geer, 2007). Reactions against the negative tone and nature of political debate are strong and insistent, with calls for more respectful, fact-based and substantive approaches to political communication. There are concerns about the heated, adversarial and aggressive nature of political discourse and behaviour, and apprehension about what are deemed to be low standards of conduct, with flow-on effects in terms of compromising the quality of political decision-making. The public

 | DOI: 10.1163/9789004505544_021

has become tired and resentful of political infighting and public relations informed discourse, and are critical of the inward, individualistic and self-focussed lenses of privileged politicians.

Concerns about the standards of political discourse and decision-making highlight the importance of holding politicians to account for the quality of their conduct and leadership in the public domain. It brings into question the efficacy of democracies, challenged as they are by neoliberal ideologies and their focus on adversarialism and 'winning'. In our view, there is currently an absence of practice wisdom evident in the actions and rhetoric of politicians and a failure on the part of those engaged in the political sphere to model appropriate and ethical engagement. A new positive political leadership framework is called for.

This chapter argues that there is potential to transform the current political paradigm by using the notion of practice wisdom to inform a new political leadership model based on dispute resolution values and skills. First, the context of political discourse and decision-making in Western liberal democracies is explored and the negative nature of that paradigm is explained. Second, the key elements of dispute resolution values and skills are considered and their relevance to practice wisdom in the context of political activity is established. The chapter concludes that all politicians, elected and aspiring, should receive essential dispute resolution education and training so that their engagement in the political sphere reflects high levels of practice wisdom through a new, more positive leadership framework.

2 Current Political Paradigms in Western Liberal Democracies

Citizens in Western liberal democracies enjoy the privileges and protections that this long-established system of government represents: legal systems and procedures guided by the rule of law, transparency and publicity in political processes, defences against abuses of political power and cross-checks and balances that keep the arbiters of power publicly accountable (Held, 2006). These forms of democracy are more complex than simply 'majority rules' systems with principles relating to both the substance and procedures of democratic governance (Lijphart, 1999, 2008). They also have features such as a breadth of political inclusion, absences of arbitrary action, relative equality among citizens and the protection of liberty and autonomy within a context of collective responsibility and accountability (Tilley, 2007).

Democracy in Western societies, informed by liberal ideals, is also the claimed go-to societal structure for providing stability, order and peace (Horowitz, 1993). As Diamond (2008) notes, democracy makes peace possible because it provides balance and equilibrium through the recognition of diverse identities whilst also providing legal protections for group and individual rights. That is, the political institutions at the centre of democracies empower citizens by providing for their participation in political processes and by devolving some decision-making power to them, while also encouraging and enabling bargaining and accommodation (Diamond, 2008). Thus, a peaceful and ordered society is possible in such democracies because a network of accessible, fair and, usually, open and accountable institutions and procedures are in place.

It follows that political systems in democracies should be focussed on orderly and structured decision-making through procedures that are fundamentally grounded in negotiation, accommodation and compromise. These desiderata should be collective endeavours, with participants not limited to individual politicians, but extending to the members of their parties as well as various interest and campaign groups, lobbyists and the electorate itself. Political rule through such democratic deliberation, negotiation and accommodation as part of political discourse can be contrasted with autocratic or totalitarian systems of government.

It might be expected, then, that the political paradigm in liberal democratic systems would be positive, accountable and respectful. However, whilst citizens of Western liberal democracies might be privileged to live within the protections and freedoms they offer, there are challenges to the efficacy of democratic principles' operation in the real world of political life in 2021. It is beyond the scope of this chapter to canvass all these challenges, so our focus is on two impactful ideologies that detract from the likelihood of positive contemporary political paradigms. First is the global ideology of neoliberalism and second is the ideology of political adversarialism. These ideologies endanger the efficacy and sustainability of contemporary politics according to the normative tenets enunciated above.

2.1 *The Ideology of Neoliberalism*

Neoliberalism is a "socio-economic theory that rejects governmental intervention in the domestic economy and promulgates materialism, consumerism, and the commodification of many public goods" (Saunders, 2007, p. 1). Neoliberalism in practice, it is argued, has had a negative impact on political procedures and discourse around the world. As a dominant and pervasive ideology it presents many economic, cultural and sociological challenges for the contemporary world (Chomsky, 1999; Davies, 2016; Giroux, 2000, 2015, 2018; Hall et al., 2015; Harvey, 2007; Saad-Filho, 2019; Saad-Filho & Johnston, 2005; Springer et al., 2016).

With a focus on the 'free market', the core elements of neo-liberalist approaches include reductions in the role of the state and governing spending alongside increases in privatisation and deregulation and greater emphasis on the role of the private sector. Other core factors include increased preoccupation with market competition and productivity, efficiencies in production and the promotion of free trade (Goldstein, 2007). It is undeniable that neoliberalism has had a rapid impact globally, and that it has strongly influenced the political paradigm in which political discourse and decision-making take place. Economic ways of thinking have come to dominate the polity in western societies and rent-seeking behaviour,[1] albeit inconsistent with market thinking, is regarded as a standard contemporary practice.

Some of the impacts of neoliberalism on the political sphere include:

- The fiction of scarcity which permeates thinking in political economies
- An over-commitment to efficiency in the husbandry of scarce resources
- A focus on competition as the only way to promote efficiency and productivity through the discipline of the market
- The privatisation of the means of production with an emphasis on profit motives and
- The deregulation of commerce and industry

to make way for the supposed disciplines of private enterprise. Evidence that market ideology has been extrapolated to the global level can be seen in the liberalisation of finance and investment that has enveloped the world in past decades, and the preponderance of trade and investment treaties, global administrative bodies and international supply chains. Transnational corporations have become the 'citizens' of this global leviathan, able to shift investment capital, dividends, executives, marketing, tax liabilities and coal in virtually passport-less ways.

A corollary of these developments in both national and global environments is the shrinking of the state and the narrowing of the scope of domestic politics. As has been often lamented, local democracy, domestic policy and international globalisation are all possible, but not all three at once. It is the domestic political sphere that is often a casualty in terms of the loss of the commons and public goods, the compromise of political efficacy and an emphasis on short-term thinking. These imperatives have arguably increased adversarial contestation in the political domain.

2.2 *The Political Ideology of Adversarialism*

Adversarialism is an inherent, though not a necessary, aspect of many Western liberal democratic political traditions, with oppositional two-party political systems dominating relevant systems around the world. However, as Russell (2005) notes, adversarialism in the form of politicians' "tribal loyalty to their own side, and hostility to the proposals of their opponents" is more and more "out of step with the public mood" and is therefore an ideology "that is increasingly unsuited to the modern environment" (Russell, 2005, pp. 17–18; Brooks & Geer, 2007). Nevertheless, the competitive, combative ideology of adversarialism in politics continues to pervade our corridors and halls of power, one political commentator noting: "Australians play politics like they play sport, ruthlessly, and to win" (John McTernan, Communications Director to Australian Prime Minister Julia Gillard, quoted in Hayes, 2013, para. 17).

Political adversarialism focuses on partisan, limited, one-dimensional and binary 'right' and 'wrong' perspectives on issues, rather than taking bi-partisan, expansive, creative and responsively integrated approaches that are focussed on rational analyses of the merits of policies and proposals. An increasingly educated and sophisticated citizenry is rejecting the adversarial model as both infantile and alienating (Russell, 2005), and satisfaction surveys of politicians around the world indicate that reform and change are long overdue (Jones, 2020; Russell, 2005). Indeed, adversarialism in politics can be said to "undermine the integrity of government" (Russell, 2005, p. 19) and compromise the democratic principles that it should be the job of politicians to serve and protect. As Russell (2005) acknowledges:

> There is a widespread belief that politics is in trouble. Barely a day goes by when we are not reminded that trust in political institutions is low, and that people are turning away from the mainstream political parties. We have become accustomed to the idea that people feel let down by politicians of all parties. (p. 3)

One of the many manifestations of this trend is the drastic decline in membership of mainstream parties over past decades.

2.3 *The Imperative for Cultural Change in Political Discourse, Decision-Making and Leadership*

Refreshing and renewing the political paradigm, informed as it currently is by neoliberal ideology and adversarial practices, calls for a recalibration of how politics is practised, experienced and perceived. Systemic and procedural changes are required in reforming the dynamics of political engagement that feed the present paradigm, such as changes to electoral systems, election frequencies and pre-selection processes. But while structural reforms are essential, they will not be sufficient of themselves. What is also required is a shift in political culture away from the dominance of neoliberal and adversarial ideologies towards good governance focussed on higher levels of collective problem-solving and consensus. This will necessitate "a conscious effort from politicians" (Russell, 2005, p. 5).

In a difficult contemporary political context, the importance of a strong leadership framework for politicians cannot be overstated. The presence of leadership in the political and operational dimensions of government implies strong structures, clear strategic directions and responsible communications. Political leadership requires the taking of ownership and responsibility for the alignment of policies and resources through effective and timely decision-making (Kellerman, 1986). In the context of global challenges in the form of pandemics, financial crises, wealth inequalities and climate change, the citizens of nation-states are looking more and more to political leaders for rational and considered approaches to governance, and for practice wisdom in their performance.

As we have noted, however, while positive and effective political decision-making and discourse is a critical feature of democratic governance, the current paradigm evidences a contrary emphasis on competition, adversarialism, incivility and toxicity. As Russell (2005) notes: "Politicians and the media fail to communicate the very essence of politics – that it is about negotiation and compromise, difficult choices, and taking decisions together as a society" (p. 4). People around the world are calling for political leadership and respectful, fact-based and more substantive approaches to political communication and action. Yet they are witnessing, on the contrary, heated, combative and aggressive behaviour on the part of politicians and low standards of conduct in government, with flow-on damaging effects in relation to public regard for the quality of political decision-making. There is a clear and concerning absence of practice wisdom in political actions and accompanying discourse.

Ubiquitous concerns about standards of conduct and culture in politics in political discourse and decision-making highlight the importance of holding politicians to account for the quality of their leadership, language and demeanour in the public domain. They bring into question the efficacy of democratic systems, challenged as they already are by neoliberal ideology, the focus on adversarialism and 'winning' the ultimate prize; access to the levers of state power. In our view, the current absence of practice wisdom, evident in the actions and rhetoric of politicians, has resulted in leadership and systems failures, as well as a breakdown in the modelling of appropriate and ethical engagement in the political domain. A new positive political leadership framework is required; one that enhances the development of practice wisdom in our politicians through the influence of dispute resolution values and skills. As Russell (2005) has said:

> Only a conscious effort by the political classes to create a new and more honest politics, that seeks to build on the social advances we have made, will have any real chance of success. Only by having a frank conversa-

tion with people as citizens, rather than consumers, can politics hope to survive. (p. 5)

3 Practice Wisdom

Practice wisdom, which includes phronesis, denotes a type of wisdom or acumen, in the context of practice or practical action that constitutes a form of inductive and intangible professional knowledge (Chu & Tsui, 2008, Higgs, 2019; Samson, 2015). Practice wisdom implies good judgment as well as excellence of character and a moral compass, and it is therefore related to ethical intent and the legitimacy of practice (Carr, 2019). Practice wisdom includes knowledge that arises out of concrete experiences drawing on reflective practice (Litchfield, 1999), embodied and analytical reasoning (Chu & Tsui, 2008; O'Sullivan, 2005), and professional values (Klein & Bloom, 1995). Practice wisdom goes beyond knowledge obtained through education and training processes. It brings together life experiences, normative belief systems and professional expertise (Higgs, 2012).

While there can be claims to its intuitive nature, in reality, practice wisdom has foundational bases in experience, professional theory and knowledge, as well as reflection. DeRoos (1990) refers to the development of practice wisdom as 'evolutionary epistemology', an accumulated integration and synthesis of knowledge and ideas from multiple sources that are always in development as an influence on practice decisions. Samson (2015) argues that practice wisdom involves 'knowing-in-action' and 'reflecting-in-practice' in order to arrive at new professional knowledge that also assists practitioners to recognise and respond to personal and professional limitations (Thompson & West, 2013).

Practice wisdom supports discernment, good judgement and appropriate decision-making. The argument of this chapter is that the demands of political leadership in contemporary liberal democracies call for our politicians to embody practice wisdom in their discourse, in their conduct and in their decision-making. We are persuaded that whilst the current political paradigm reflects an absence of practice wisdom, as considered above, practice wisdom for politicians can be developed and nurtured through training in dispute resolution values and skills. In this way, the moral compass of politicians in their daily labours can be enhanced because they will be better able to practice creatively, fairly, justly and with good judgment within the new leadership framework. The intentional support of developing practice wisdom in politicians will enable their practices to be informed by a deeper self-understanding and an appreciation of their own professional purpose and identity, which will positively influence their approach to political work and better enable them to help others and build community. As a result, the standards of political conduct will be improved and public concerns about political honesty, integrity, collaboration and respect will be addressed.

4 Dispute Resolution (DR) Values and Skills

What then are the key value propositions and quintessential techniques of DR that might be taught to politicians to develop their practice wisdom and support higher standards of political conduct and discourse? We start with identifying some of the principles of DR as these inform the application of DR skills. DR values are meaningful beliefs or philosophies, grounded in a range of ethical, ideological, social or aesthetic perspectives, that can be "used as standards for evaluating ideas and behaviour" in DR contexts (Wolski, 2009; Seligman & Katz, 1996). Such values include commitments to fairness, equality, justice and integrity. They also include beliefs in accountability, innovation and resilience, and the merits of generosity, effective communication and collaboration. Further, DR's aesthetic values include regard for factors like creativity, peace, serenity and fun (Seligman & Katz, 1996; Wolski, 2009). Larry Krieger's empirical work on values in legal DR contexts identified the most meritorious principles as including patience, decency, fairness, humility, courage, caring, integrity, willingness to work hard for worthwhile goals and helpfulness to others (family, friends, clients or community) (Krieger, 2005).

These values of DR effectively illustrate what DR practitioners, institutions, and systems represent; they are key indicators of what the DR discipline and profession, comprising conciliators, mediators, facilitators and other brokers, stand for, and as such they strongly and significantly influence the behaviour, discourse and decision-making of DR practitioners. Such values sit at the centre of both the personal and professional identities of DR professionals and inform their sense of practical purpose, integrity and occupational satisfaction. They therefore constitute a strong framework within which DR practitioners build and extend their practice wisdom towards levels of mastery and artistry (Lang & Taylor, 2000). They guide judgments on what is acceptable behaviour and decisions on appropriate courses of action.

The values of DR offer a positive and constructive normative framework that supports a more prominent place for non-adversarial, problem-solving oriented, collective and collaborative approaches to political discourse and activity. A more significant role for these dispositions of DR within political leadership and practice is merited if the challenges of neoliberalism and adversarialism are to be overcome and if cultural reforms to political discourse and conduct are to be attained. We propose that educating politicians about this ideology will serve to strengthen their practice wisdom and create a new framework for productive political culture.

Ideology alone, however, is somewhat empty without concrete skills and strategies to bring it to life. Therefore, we next consider some of the pivotal skills of DR and their practice that could positively inform a new leadership framework for politicians. Whilst there is potentially much to discuss in terms of the positive and productive nature of DR skills, our focus here is limited to a brief discussion of communication skills and positive negotiation techniques.

It is self-evident that effective communication is important to successful political discourse and engagement in political activity. Indeed, communication is an indispensable ingredient in all forms of personal and professional endeavour, informing and supporting the development and implementation of practice wisdom across diverse disciplines. Effective communication skills can help to ensure that communicative interactions with others are clear, positive and balanced. Communication strategies can be used to reassure the targets of professional discourse, to form connections and alliances with them, and to create positive communication environments.

Politicians can improve their discourse techniques by adopting DR approaches to communication that identify four broad responsibilities in communications with others (Boulle & Alexander, 2020):

1. Taking responsibility for effective and appropriate communication practices
2. Working intentionally to ensure communications with others are as accurate, explicit, comprehensible, constructive and appropriate as possible
3. Adopting a commitment to continuous learning and improvement of effective communication techniques and
4. Fostering environments, which encourage effective communication (pp. 175–180).

These responsibilities require commitments away from the positional, restrictive, self-serving, judgmental and public relations discourse which has prevailed for some time.

How can such responsibilities be practically brought into effect? In our dispute resolution practice, scholarship and training experience, five key elements of communication are prominent as critical to the practice wisdom of DR professionals:

1. Listening
2. Acknowledging
3. Reframing
4. Summarising and
5. Questioning

We briefly consider each of these DR communication tools in turn, followed by a short discussion of positive negotiation techniques.

Effective listening (Boulle & Alexander, 2020): Politicians do a lot of talking, but would be well served to bring greater practice wisdom to their professional endeavours by listening more actively and effectively. In an ideal world, careful and attentive listening would be part of all discourse in both professional and personal contexts. Factual and content-related messages would be heard accurately, and emotions, concerns, interests and underlying needs, hopes and priorities could be accommodated and responded to. Effective listening involves being able to engage attentively in the moment of communication, grasping facts and information analytically and picking up on affective content, narrative patterns and the themes being conveyed. However, conscious listening is not always an intuitive response in communication situations, which is why education as to specific listening strategies is important for DR practitioners, and we contend, for politicians also.

Acknowledging (Boulle & Alexander, 2020): Acknowledgement is an important part of effective communication because it is critical to human engagement. Feeling heard is a humanistic imperative, common to dispute resolution procedures and parliamentary question time. When a person's emotions, needs, interests and priorities are acknowledged, they feel heard and recognised, they feel respected and understood (even if not agreed with) and they feel as though what they are experiencing matters and is valued. When people feel heard and understood, they are more likely to be able to cooperate, collaborate and engage in constructive problem-solving. This is why acknowledgement is a critical key to effective DR, and we believe if politicians utilised the skill of acknowledging more often in their political discourse, as an element of practice wisdom, the culture of politics could be altered very positively. Whilst it is not hard to show acknowledgement, it is easy to forget to engage in this practice. Enacting our capacity to acknowledge others requires a commitment to (at least) two things; first, a willingness to respect and engage with emotions; and second, an ability to empathise with others. Any training of politicians in DR skills would necessarily address these two components.

Reframing (Boulle & Alexander, 2020): Reframing is a responsive communication strategy that is closely related to active listening. Communication often occurs within a fixed or static frame of reference; this is particularly prevalent in political communications. However, if politicians were trained in the DR skill of reframing, they would be open to looking for alternative frames of reference and to thinking differently about matters at hand. The basis of reframing is the fact that the language used in communication contexts affects perceptions of the issues being communicated, and perceptions can impact on behaviour. By working intentionally with the type of language used, it is possible to change perceptions and behaviour in constructive ways. Reframing then is a form of translation exercise through which the tenor of communication can be made more positive and conducive to collaborative problem-solving. Politicians skilled in reframing will be able to use different words, concepts and terms, and altered emphases and intonations, to provide new frames of reference for difficult communications. For example, reframing can be used to;

- Detoxify language by removing accusations, judgments and verbal stings and barbs
- Focus on positive issues by removing references to negative and judgmental factors
- Focus on interests and needs by removing references to positions
- Focus on the future by removing references to the past and
- Mutualise problems by avoiding one-sided definitions and reframing to dual-sided formulations

The practice wisdom of master DR practitioners lies in sophisticated reframing skills, and we believe such skills are also invaluable for politicians in a new framework of quality engagement and leadership within a more constructive political culture.

Summarising (Boulle & Alexander, 2020): A periodic summary of progress in communications is a useful DR skill for ensuring that there is an accurate and balanced account of what is being communicated and that communications have been heard properly and understood. Summarising involves brief restatements or recapping of important features of preceding discussions. It is a potentially powerful intervention in communications because it can achieve a range of positive objectives. For example, summarising can:

- Provide a neutral and organised version of a sequence of discussion
- Emphasise vital issues which might otherwise be overlooked
- Simplify convoluted exchanges,
- Signpost progress in communications
- Affirm common directions
- Provide acknowledgment of understanding
- Establish a bridge to future discussions
- Assist with establishing trust and respect.

Experienced DR practitioners have sophisticated skills in using summarising for effective communications. We believe that politicians could also benefit significantly from education in such skills in support of their practice wisdom development, particularly when engaging with 'adversaries' in the media and other public fora.

Questioning (Boulle & Alexander, 2020): The skill of asking appropriate questions is critical for constructive communications and collaborative problem-solving. DR practitioners use questioning throughout every aspect of their practice. Politicians, however, tend to err on the side of making statements rather than asking clarifying questions, and when they do ask questions they are often of an accusatory or cynical nature, connoting judgment of those being questioned. There are many different categories of questions, each having different objectives and uses. Three positive types of questions that DR practitioners commonly use include:

- *Open questions*, which support general disclosure and the exchange of information in an open-ended way. Open questions are useful when seeking a non-specific and non-defensive response in communications. They form part of dispute resolvers' dictate to 'be curious'.
- *Focused questions*, which facilitate the disclosure of more detailed facts or information about a specific issue or theme. Focussed questions are useful when there is time pressure or there is a need to (re)-focus on particular issues.
- *Clarifying questions*, which are appropriate at all times when active listening and reframing are called for. Clarifying questions assist with verifying or correcting understanding in communications and are useful if greater precision on a point is needed.

Effective questioning is also used by DR practitioners for reality-testing, that is, acting as an agent of reality to test whether proposals and solutions put forward in communications are realistic and viable, cogently assessing the risks, options and choices available in the situation. Politicians with practice wisdom would also be able to harness this skill for more effective political discourse in a range of communication contexts relevant to their professional practice. While political actors, unlike dispute resolution interveners, are not impartial in their question, appropriate effective questioning would add lustre to their activities and redound to the benefit of the political system as a whole.

Engagement in positive negotiations: Dispute resolution practitioners adopt constructive, efficient and productive approaches to negotiations, in order to positively manage and influence bargaining efforts. We believe politicians can benefit from the practice wisdom of DR in reforming the culture and ideologies of modern-day politics and its discourse.

Constructive negotiations are very different to the adversarial, combative and divisive approaches currently found in the discourse and activity of politicians, whether in parliamentary debates or electoral campaigns. DR experts bring refined, systematic and supportive approaches to negotiation efforts that allow a focus on mutual problem-solving and collaborative decision-making, even where there are issues of significant disagreement or contention such as refugee policy or aged care funding. DR professionals have a range of skills in their toolbox that assist with defusing positional and argumentative approaches, and diverting them to interest-based and problem-solving modes of negotiation. Such interventions shift the focus from positions to interests, needs and priorities. Strategies employed include separating the interpersonal aspects of disputes from substantive aspects, looking for and identifying areas of common ground, and using objective criteria to generate and develop options. In this way DR practitioners act as catalysts for creative problem-solving, future thinking and forward-looking outcomes. If politicians were to be trained in such DR skills for the benefit of enhancing the development of their practice wisdom, then the curriculum would need to focus on developing negotiation practice strategies.

5 Conclusion

The influence of adversarialism and neoliberalism on the culture of Western democratic politics has resulted in public dismay and dissatisfaction with our ruling bodies, including legislatures and governments. Politicians have lost touch with the mood of the populace, which is generally seeking constructive, collaborative approaches to collective problem-solving for effective governance over oppositional bickering and partisan divides. Politicians demonstrate low-levels of practice wisdom, thus hope in the efficacy of political discourse and activity is being lost.

Structural and systemic reforms are part of the answer to a sustainable political future in Western liberal democracies globally, but so too is reform of the culture and conscience of politics. Paradoxically governments have required of other disciplines, especially courts and legal procedures that they move from negative adversarial combat to positive collaborative practices, but have not included themselves in the changed mind-set.

Responsibility for reform falls squarely on politicians themselves. As Russell (2005) has said: "a concerted effort by all those engaged in the political process to change their behaviour is now essential if faith in politics is to be restored" (p. 6). Politicians need to remember what politics is for and why constructive approaches to politics in contemporary times are a necessary, indeed critical, aspect of good governance. Parliamentary systems have ameliorated some of their adversarial excesses through committee systems, but these constitute only a small part of political materiality.

We are persuaded that the discipline and practice of DR has much to offer any future reform efforts in politics. If politicians were to be educated in the values and skills of DR, we believe there is hope for the development of real practice wisdom in the political sphere. Our proposal is that all politicians, elected and aspiring, should be required to engage in DR education and training and on-going continuing professional development as part of the growth of their political practice wisdom. Managers, lawyers, judges and countless other professionals in recent years have coped with such requirements. This proposal offers a new political leadership framework, one that will positively shape a wise future in global politics.

Note

1 "**rent-seeking** n. *Economics*[:] the fact or process of seeking to gain larger profits by manipulating public policy or economic conditions, esp. by means of securing beneficial subsidies or tariffs, making a product artificially scarce, etc. [...]" (Oxford English Dictionary, online edition, subscription or participating institution membership required).

References

Boulle, L., & Alexander, N. (2020). *Mediation skills and techniques* (3rd ed.). LexisNexis.

Brooks, D., & Geer, J. (2007). Beyond negativity: The effects of incivility on the electorate. *American Journal of Political Science, 51*(1), 1–16.

Carr, D. (2019). Wisdom, (moral) virtue and knowledge. In J. Higgs (Ed.), *Practice wisdom: Values and interpretations* (pp. 15–28). Brill Sense.

Chomsky, N. (1999). *Profit over people: Neoliberalism and global order.* Seven Stories Press.

Chu, W. C. K., & Tsui, M. (2008). The nature of practice wisdom in social work revisited. *International Social Work, 51*(1), 47–54.

Davies, W. (2016). *The limits of neoliberalism: Authority, sovereignty and the logic of competition* (Rev. ed.). Sage.

DeRoos, Y. S. (1990). The development of practice wisdom through human problem-solving processes. *Social Service Review, 64*(2), 276–287.

Diamond, L. (2008). *The spirit of democracy: The struggle to build free societies throughout the world.* Times Books.

Giroux, H. A. (2000). *Impure acts*. Taylor & Francis.

Giroux, H. A. (2015). *Against the terror of neoliberalism: Politics beyond the age of greed*. Routledge.

Giroux, H. A. (2018). *Terror of neoliberalism: Authoritarianism and the eclipse of democracy*. Routledge.

Goldstein, N. (2007). *Globalization and free trade*. Infobase.

Hall, S., Massey, D., & Rustin, M. (Eds.). (2015). *After neoliberalism? The Kilburn Manifesto*. Lawrence & Wishart.

Harvey, D. (2007). *A brief history of neoliberalism*. Oxford University Press.

Hayes, D. (2013, August 28). Election 2013: The view from up above. *Inside Story*. http://inside.org.au/election-2013-the-view-from-up-above/#sthash.QTM9xBuJ.dpuf

Held, D. (2006). *Models of democracy*. Polity Press.

Higgs. J. (2012). Realising practical wisdom from the pursuit of wise practice. In E. A. Kinsella & A. Pitman (Eds.), *Phronesis as professional knowledge* (pp. 73–85). Sense.

Higgs, J. (Ed.). (2019). *Practice wisdom: Values and interpretations*. Brill Sense.

Horowitz, D. (1993). Democracy in divided societies. *Journal of Democracy, 4*(4), 18–38.

Jones, J. (2020, August 4). US satisfaction at 13%, lowest in nine years. *Gallup*. https://news.gallup.com/poll/316736/satisfaction-lowest-nine-years.aspx

Kellerman, B. (Ed.). (1986). *Political leadership: A source book*. University of Pittsburgh Press.

Klein, W. C., & Bloom, M. (1995). Practice wisdom. *Social work, 40*(6), 799–807.

Krieger, L. S. (2005). The inseparability of professionalism and personal satisfaction: Perspectives on values, integrity and happiness. *Clinical Law Review, 11*(2), 425–445.

Lang, M. D., & Taylor, A. (2000). *The making of a mediator: Developing artistry in practice*. John Wiley & Sons.

Lijphart, A. (1999). *Patterns of democracy – Government forms and performance in thirty-six countries*. Yale University Press.

Lijphart, A. (2008). *Thinking about democracy – Power sharing and majority rule in theory and practice*. Routledge.

Litchfield, M. (1999). Practice wisdom. *Advances in Nursing Science, 22*(2), 62–73.

O'Sullivan, T. (2005). Some theoretical propositions on the nature of practice wisdom. *Journal of Social Work, 5*(2), 221–242.

Russell, M. (2005). *Must politics disappoint?* Fabian Society.

Saad-Filho, A. (2019). Crisis in neoliberalism or crisis of neoliberalism? In A. Saad-Filho (Ed.), *Value and crisis: Essays on labour, money and contemporary capitalism* (pp. 302–318). Brill.

Saad-Filho, A., & Johnston, D. (2005). *Neoliberalism: A critical reader*. University of Chicago Press.

Samson, P. L. (2015). Practice wisdom: The art and science of social work. *Journal of Social Work*. https://doi.org/10.1080/02650533.2014.922058

Saunders, D. (2007). The impact of neoliberalism on college students. *Journal of College and Character, 8*(5). https://doi.org/10.2202/1940-1639.1620

Seligman, C., & Katz, A. N. (1996). The dynamics of values systems. In C. Seligman, J. M. Olson, & M. P. Zanna (Eds.), *The psychology of values: The Ontario Symposium, Volume 8* (pp. 53–76). Lawrence Erlbaum Associates.

Springer, S., Birch, K., & MacLeavy, J. (Eds.). (2016). *Handbook of neoliberalism*. Routledge.

Thompson, L. J., & West, D. (2013). Professional development in the contemporary educational context: Encouraging practice wisdom. *Social Work Education, 32*(1), 118–133.

Tilley, C. (2007). *Democracy*. Cambridge University Press.

Wolski, B. (2009). *Skills, ethics and values for legal practice*. Lawbook Co.

CHAPTER 18

Carving out New Spaces for Journalists and Political Leaders to Make Better Nations

Janice Orrell and Lauren Novak

Abstract

Now, more than ever, Australians need journalism that we can trust so that we, as citizens, can make informed and confident choices when voting for who governs us. Creating an informed and trusting voting public is highly dependent on the type of political news available. This, ideally, should be accurate and evidence-based rather than built on opinion or filtered by personal biases. In recent times, with the move to online publishing and uptake of social media, the ability of journalists and media outlets to produce this kind of journalism has faced new and increased pressures which have changed the way they go about their work. These changes have shifted the way political journalists interact with politicians, who are also operating in new ways – bypassing traditional media to find alternate channels to communicate with the public and dismissing unfavourable mainstream coverage as "fake news". In this chapter we seek to understand the scope and impact of these changes on political news communication through an examination of current academic commentary. We then compare these observations with the lived experience of political journalism by interviewing a small but diverse group of working political journalists and a political scientist. We explore what kind of relationship is needed between politicians and journalists to enable the types of journalism that will support a healthy democracy, and what changes are needed to encourage wise practice in political reporting.

Keywords

journalism – media – politics – political journalism – Fourth Estate – democracy

1 Introduction

The focus of this chapter is the public communication, or news coverage, of political matters to inform citizens about what those who govern them are

 | DOI: 10.1163/9789004505544_022

doing to meet public needs and shape national futures. Our starting premise is that the quality of political communication is key to political involvement, which, in turn, is essential for a democratic society (Nygren & Johansson, 2019). Key in determining the quality of political communication and news coverage is the interplay between politicians and political journalists.

Until recent times, journalists largely mediated the communication between society and its leaders through mainstream, mass broadcast media. To gain accurate information to share with the consumers of news media journalists depend on networking to build relationships and communication channels with politicians. An important dimension of journalists' relationships with politicians is forging and sustaining these connections without compromising their obligation to produce balanced reporting that informs the public with honesty and integrity and without bias. However, the advancement of social media, the rising power of politicians' press secretaries, shrinking resources and the increasing concentration of media ownership globally, have impacted on the interplay and interdependency between politicians and journalists. Mainstream media is no longer the public's only means for accessing information because the internet and social media, in its multiple forms, have provided new channels for consuming news. Politicians too, are increasingly utilising alternative ways to transmit the information they want the public to know, which gives them greater control over how it is framed and disseminated.

Academic discourse on this subject tells us that good political journalism is essential for a healthy, robust democratic society (Albaeck, van Dalen, Jebril, & de Vreese, 2014). In this chapter, we seek to explore how the contemporary changes we have noted above have impacted on citizens' access to political news (for better or worse), and how those changes have impacted on the practices of political journalists and politicians. Could they be more effective in carrying out their respective social obligations? What changes are needed to encourage wiser approaches to developing a politically informed public? To answer these questions, we will examine the roles, responsibilities and practices of these two key players, including the ideals and standards of political journalism and political practice and the realities of operating in both fields.

This chapter has three distinct sections. The first will consider academic discourse through a selected review of contemporary media research in regard to the principles, responsibilities and practices of politicians and political journalists, the interplay between these roles and the impact this interplay has on quality news coverage. The second section is grounded in an acknowledgement that there will always be a difference between espoused ideals and the lived experiences and practice realities with which journalists must contend. Based on this assumption, we consulted three Australian political journalists and a political scientist, who is also a media election commentator and a university teacher of both journalists and politicians. All four were invited to respond to a series of questions regarding the realities of political reporting and for journalists interacting with political leaders. Our goal is to uncover what might be wise practices to ensure a politically informed and engaged public, as well as what changes might be needed to enable wise practice to occur.

2 Academic Discourses on Political Journalism and Politics

In this section of the chapter the role of journalists and politicians will be examined, as well as the ideals and standards of their practice. We will also consider what research has revealed about the interplay between these two key players and the impact on providing media coverage of government plans and actions.

2.1 *The Role and Standards of Journalism*

Journalism, in particular political journalism, is often referred to as the "Fourth Estate". This term is derived from historical European constructs that referred to the different sites of power as Estates. The English used the construct to denote the differing authority domains of the Clergy (The First Estate), the nobility (The Second Estate) and the elected parliamentarians or commoners (The Third Estate). Alternatively, other European nations have used the construct to refer to the separation of powers, namely, legislative, executive and judicial. Now, the "Fourth Estate" has come to refer to the press and news media in acknowledgement of the power of the press to influence opinion and choice amongst the electorates or voting public. The use of the term is an acknowledgement of the media's key role in contributing to informed public debate, which is essential for democratic societies (Nielsen & Kuhn, 2014).

There are various statements that spell out the ethics and ideals of Journalism that, for the most part, are very similar. For example, we considered the International Federation of Journalists' (IFJ) *16 Principles on the Conduct of Journalists* (IFJ, 2019) and the *Australian Media and Arts Entertainment Alliance (MEAA) Journalists Code of Ethics* (MEAA, 1944). Both of these Codes of practice have adopted principles that are based on the premise that journalists should have a respect for the facts and the right of the public to the truth. Journalists are guided to act in particular ways; namely, that they are expected to distinguish factual information from commentary and criticism, not suppress essential information, use fair means of gaining information, respect personal privacy and grief, rectify any errors, maintain secrecy of a source of information gained in confidence and not contribute to prejudice. Journalists should not act as agents of government or seek personal advantage by either dissemination or non-dissemination of any public interest information. Journalism is charged with a responsibility to, first and foremost, inform the public over its other responsibilities, such as to its employers or other authorities (IFJ, 2019).

2.2 *The Role and Standards of Political Representation*

Codes of conduct for politicians also exist, but vary widely between political parties, states and parliamentary systems. Brenton (2009) who, as an Australian Parliamentary Fellow, researched the lived experiences of both upper and lower house parliamentarians argued that:

> While representative democracy is often poetically described as government 'of the people, by the people, for the people', (however) it is not only 'the people' who are represented: political parties, ideologies, states, business, unions, the environmental movement (etc.) are also represented. (Brenton, 2009, p. 71)

Brenton further argues that the notion that the politician is a representative of 'the people' is further contested because it is not possible for each elected politician to represent the diversity of 'the people' and their differing needs and conflicting interests. Pitkin (in Brenton, 2009) is reported as describing good representation as "delegates reflecting constituent concerns" (p. 74). However, Pitkin (1967, p. 143) acknowledged that most representatives are forced to "act within an elaborate network of pressures, demands, interests, or the binding of the member to a party program, which a constituency endorses" (Pitkin, 1967, in Brenton, 2009, p. 74). As a result,

> A parliamentarian evolves as more a representative of a party than of a constituency or of national interests, because they are called upon to be responsive to party concerns and cultivate relationships with party colleagues and leaders. (Pitkin, 1967, p. 143)

However, to honour the electorate's trusteeship also requires independence from party discipline. This tension between party interests and electorate interests constitutes the challenge of most politicians.

As well as the expectation of electoral representation, politicians are called upon to consider the moral ethics that are involved in the position they hold and how this should guide their practice and decision-making. Political ethics is the practice of making moral judgments about political action (Thompson, 2019, p. 168). What should, or to what extent, might the ethical principles that govern political office align with the ethical principles of a moral life more generally (Hampshire, 1978; Thompson, 1987). In other words, "to what extent are politicians permitted to take actions that would otherwise be wrong?" (Thompson, 2019, p. 168). The complexities, dilemmas, contradictions and challenges that are experienced in public office suggest it would wise for political parties to provide the kind of induction that would assist new politicians to develop their ethical imagination and help them face the complex decisions and compromises they confront as parliamentarians.

2.3 *The Interplay between Political Journalists and Politicians*

In this chapter we are attempting to examine the dynamics of the relationship between political journalists and politicians, who we have already established often have competing priorities in their roles. Nielsen and Kuhn (2019) argue that the interplay between political journalists and political leaders is so symbiotically bound that it is not possible to understand political journalism without also understanding politics. It is undeniable that the Third and Fourth Estates hold mutual and aligned interests. "Journalists rely on politicians to produce news and politicians need journalists to communicate their ideas and arguments … in order to be politically successful" (Matthes, Maurer, & Arendt, 2019, p. 345). However, these researchers question the dependability of the espoused respect and mutual trust between politicians and journalists, suggesting that it is "sometimes an uneasy relationship" (p. 345). Nygren and Johansson (2019) describe the interdependent relationship between politicians and journalists as focused on power, attention and influence.

> Political elites need media attention in a complex society with an abundance of information and a deficit of attention. Media can give the political elites access to the public sphere and the attention of citizens … but there is the question of how this attention is framed – and how politicians and politics are framed. (Nygren & Johansson, 2019, p. 10)

Understanding this interplay will shed light on the influential potential of these two key actors on public opinion and voters, which is a critical factor in a democratic society. A consistently held view amongst media theorists is that the relationship between these two political estates or powers is highly institutionalised, interdependent and strategic (Matthes, Maurer, & Arendt, 2019; Nygren & Johansson, 2019; Van Dalen, 2019). Ideally, both estates are committed to a shared culture of respect for the role of the other and seek to maintain a productive relationship (Van Dalen, 2019; Nygren & Johansson, 2019).

Nielsen and Kuhn (2014) who regard political journalism as "a key part of democratic politics and the very heart of the journalistic vocation" (p. 1) cited Macaulay in 1828 and Carlyle in 1841, both famed and feuding English academic historians, who eyed the English reporters' gallery with interest and respect, identifying it as the Fourth Estate, the Fourth Power. Despite their personal differences these two political commentators were in agreement, perceiving political journalism as an authoritative and powerful force for shaping public opinion in all acts of lawmaking and for safe-guarding public debate and democracy through publication (Nielsen & Kuhn, 2014, p. 1).

Nielsen and Kuhn acknowledge that there are national differences in the relationships between the Third and Fourth Estates. Their viewpoint, and ours, is focused on media and politics in Western democratic nations. They also note that the relationships in the modern era "are shaped by social, economic and technological factors largely external to the profession itself and, in part, by dynamics internal to journalism and its institutionalised relationship with the political world" (p. 15). Davis (2007) argues that undoubtably both journalists and politicians depend on each other. "Journalists are the public 'watchdog' that observe political elites, inform and also entertain the public, while politicians answer the demands of their electorate to explain their strategies and plans with the help of the news media" (Matthes, Maurer, & Arendt, 2019, p. 346).

While we are primarily examining the interplay between politicians and journalists, it is important to note that citizens' use and experiences of the media affects this dynamic (Schrøder & Phillips, 2007). A prevailing assumption is that journalism plays a central function in regard to citizens' democratic literacy and civic engagement. Citizens make choices about what news to consume and this in turn affects their decisions about which politicians to listen to and vote for. All this is now taking place in an environment of mediatisation of politics (Mazzoleni & Schultz, 1999), tabloidisation of the media and the emergence and uptake of the Fifth Estate (social media), that has no limits, no code of practice, and no boundaries. What impact do these conditions have for ensuring an informed democracy?

Returning to the direct interplay between politicians and journalists, researchers such as Matthes, Maurer and Arendt (2019) point to an inclination among politicians to regard the news media as hostile to their own views and argue that there are consequences for both politicians and journalists in carrying out their roles that flow from this perception of hostility. They suggest that biased perceptions of political reporting among politicians leads to suspicion, cynicism and concealed plans. In particular, unfavourable and negative media portrayal of politicians' policies and personal behaviours leads to avoidance of contact with political journalists and the uptake of other means to convey their information to the public audience.

The perception of biased reporting is regarded as the cause of Hostile Media Phenomena (HMP) or Hostile Media Effect (HME) (Vallone, Ross, & Lepper,

1985). HMP is a plausible explanation for the way in which highly involved and committed individuals perceive the news media to be more hostile compared to individuals who are less involved and committed (Matthes et al., 2019). These researchers also found that it is politicians at extremes of the radical left or established conservative viewpoints that are most likely to express HMP. Dedicated experts and campaigners for action such as for climate change, animal rights, immigration, anti-immigration, refugees and racism, for example, have also been found to be more likely to perceive the slant of media reports as relatively unfavourable and hostile to their position. Furthermore, it has also been found that HMP is not only provoked by issues of content but by the source of the reporting, such as, reporting derived from a low-ranking news outlet or by attributes associated with the individual journalist who is reporting (Matthes et al., 2019).

As is clear by now, the relationship between the Third and Fourth Estates is ultimately one of competition for power in the control of information and access to the public's attention. Nygren and Johansson described that ultimately, the dimensions of relationships between these two powers are either symbiotic and mutually balanced or adversarial and steeped in conflict. Symbiotic relationships are publicly observable in press conferences, debates, public performances such as televised "Meet the Press" events and journalists referring to what politicians are saying. Less obvious and hidden symbiotic behaviour is "positive leaks (to journalists) about good news to get the news before (their media) competitors" (p. 18). Adversarial dimensions of the relationship are observable in journalists' close scrutiny of politicians, and political actions initiated by journalists such as campaigning on issues for which they have a personal commitment. Less obvious are "negative leaks from the political sphere about competitors and cover-up of scandals and trying to hide negative information" (p. 18).

Given the central role of these powers in developing an informed, democratically literate society it is important they exercise their power wisely. Wise practice, in contrast to common practice and best practice, involves a concern for the greater good of society rather than self-interest and a weighing up of alternatives in decision-making to ensure feasibility, while maintaining the integrity of one's core values and ethical principles. Wise practice is grounded in wisdom, and scholars (while they have diverse conceptions of how wisdom might be defined) agree that the acquisition of wisdom requires time and effort and a combination of education, practice, apprenticeship, personal experience, and deliberate reflection about life matters (Balts & Smith, 2008, p. 117).

To gain some insight into the 'wisdom of experience' in transforming the principles and ideals of political journalism into practice in the current changing climate, we will explore, just how feasible is it to abide by these tenets in practice while meeting the demands of the 24-hour news cycle, or meeting diverse electoral needs and party allegiances. Like Mellado and Van Dalen (2014) we recognise possibility for the gaps between rhetoric, principles and practice, thus we ask what are the possible implications for modern democracy and the democratic processes?

3 The Lived Experience of Political Journalism

The following section provides an introduction to the three journalists and the political scientist who contributed to our exploration of the lived experiences of political journalism and politics. Following the introduction, we will provide a thematic narration of their reported experiences. The narration will address the preparation, development and work of political journalists and politicians. It will also raise the question of diversity and inclusion in politics and political reporting, as well as the impact of prevailing industry conditions for journalists. The narration will also address the nature of the interactions between the stakeholders; including, interactions with their audiences.

3.1 *The Interviewees*

The interviews were conducted with three respected Australian political journalists and a political scientist. Each has had diverse experiences within various forms of media, including print, television, online and radio, with a focus on political interests. A set of questions were put to each of the participants in this project to examine the issues that currently impact on the relationship between politicians and political journalists, and the preparation of each for their role in informing the public. These questions reflected on the demands of communicating with each other and the public and what might be the hallmark standards of good political journalism. While those interviewed cannot be said to be representative of the diverse scope of political journalists, they are all well respected within their profession. They represent a wide range of experiences within media and journalism and offer their personal perspectives on the current state of political journalism and politics, the interplay between media and politicians and with the public consumers of political media.

The profiles of these journalists and the political commentator follow:

– *Phillip Coorey*

Phillip Coorey is the political editor for *The Australian Financial Review*. Phil started his working life as a scientist, working in a laboratory, before undertaking a journalism cadetship at *The Advertiser* in Adelaide. He was later appointed as a political reporter. In 2003, Phil was made New York correspondent for News Corp Australia, before going to the Australian federal capital, Canberra, as political editor for The Advertiser. In 2006, Phil moved from News Corp to Fairfax Media, taking on the role of chief political correspondent at *The Sydney Morning Herald.* During his seven years at the paper, he gained a reputation for being a journalist with key contacts on both sides of politics, who broke major political stories. He won the Paul Lyneham Award for Canberra Press Gallery Excellence in 2012 and 2013. In 2012, Phil moved to *The Australian Financial Review*. He regularly appears on the ABC's Insiders program.

– *Sarah Malik*
Sarah Malik is a Walkley-award winning Australian investigative journalist and television presenter. She began her career studying a double degree in Arts, majoring in Journalism and Law. Sarah is currently a presenter and writer for SBS Voices. She has also covered stories relating to refugee, asylum and migration policy, domestic violence and gender inequality, surveillance and technology and intersections with gender and race. Sarah's writing has been featured in the *New York Times, The Sydney Morning Herald, Daily Life, The Saturday Paper* and *The Guardian*. She has also appeared on, presented and produced programs for ABC Radio National and Al Jazeera English.

– *Tory Shepherd*
Tory Shepherd is a freelance journalist and author. She writes for publications including *The Advertiser, Guardian Australia, Crikey* and *Cosmos Magazine* and is a regular on ABC radio and television. Tory studied anthropology before joining *The Advertiser* as a cadet in 2006. While at News Corp she covered health and politics and started a weekly opinion column, which she still writes. She is a Churchill Fellow, a Walkley Judging Board member, and the author of *On Freedom.*

– *Haydon Manning*
Haydon Manning is a retired Australian Political Scientist and currently Adjunct Professor with the College of Business, Government and Law at Flinders University of South Australia. His areas of interest include voting behaviour and electoral politics, political parties, South Australian political history and political satire. Haydon taught a range of topics including "An Introduction to Government and Democracy"; "Parties, Voters and Elections in Australia"; "Environmental Politics" and "Government, Business and Society". Haydon is a frequent commentator on South Australian and national politics

through columns published by mainstream Australian newspapers, and websites including *InDaily*, *The Conversation* and *On Line Opinion*. He also provides commentary on state and federal politics and was formerly Co-Convenor, Electoral Regulation and Research Network, South Australia and the Coordinator of the Copland Leadership Program run by the Committee of Economic Development of Australia (CEDA) South Australian branch.

4 Wisdom Gained from Media Experience

4.1 *Preparation and Career Development of Political Journalists*

In many newsrooms the role of political journalist is among the most coveted titles for a reporter. Political reporting covers crucial aspects of the lives of citizens, from health and education to the price we pay for our power or water supply, and how safe our communities are. Given this broad and important impact on the lives of consumers of news, political reporting is often given high prominence in newspaper front pages, website leads and the first items in television or radio bulletins. In addition to this prominence, the access afforded to political journalists – to decision-makers and power players, right up to the leader of the nation – makes the role an appealing one for many. The interviewees speak of conventions that have long been that the title is earned over time, after gaining news reporting and other life experiences. However, they explain how, in more recent times, changing industry conditions have also changed the career development of political journalists and particularly those who cover national affairs.

4.1.1 Phil Coorey

On his first day as a journalist, the *Financial Review's* Phil Coorey was told to keep his opinions to himself and just report the facts. That was 30 years ago and he argues that a lot has changed since then about the way journalists are prepared for their role.

> My first day as a cadet journalist, the old guy (our mentor) … the first thing he said: "No one gives a shit who you are and what you think!" That was the first rule. But no one teaches them that anymore. The current crop of new reporters are a lot smarter, a lot more informed, but they're a lot more opinionated. Now they are using the personal pronoun, writing opinion pieces. I mean you have to be 100 years old and get to know enough. Only a couple of decades ago you had to earn that right to have an opinion. I came to journalism with a Bachelor of Science, having worked in pathology and I recall being viewed as 'a bit of a freak'. They

> called me Professor. I find the profession of journalism is now full of a lot more people who have some sort of background profession … understanding of science, economics, law … rather than just coming straight out of school and not having any real understanding of how the world works. I always think it is a mistake to go straight to Canberra. I started in state politics and local government rounds. I think it (having other life, work and study experiences) makes you better qualified to write about topics on complex policy issues if you have some sort of knowledge, or the ability to theorise and analyse critically. One of the changes one notices is everyone wants to be a celebrity now. Also, in general, younger journalists I think are more prone to go on Twitter and express opinions.

4.1.2 Tory Shepherd

Tory Shepherd began her journalism career as a cadet reporter at *The Advertiser* in Adelaide. She observed:

> Journalists, are woefully underprepared for the mental health challenges they will face. MEAA (Media, Entertainment and Arts Alliance) and the Walkley Foundation do a good job of offering additional support and training, but the only way to have consistent improvement in journalist training is for employers to commit to giving it on the job. Some new journalists have the privilege of being mentored and guided through their early years by senior journalists with ethics and empathy. But too many are thrown in the deep end, and this will only get worse as newsrooms are worn evermore thin.

4.1.3 Sarah Malik

Sarah Malik graduated from the University of Technology, Sydney, with degrees in Law and Journalism and began her career as a cadet reporter for the Australian Associated Press.

> I definitely would advocate newsroom experience developing a career in political reporting. Just being edited and edited and edited and developing that humility, realising your work is always a work in progress, and to take that humbly. It's a long slog and you have to build up to it and there will be competition. There are ranks and having those mentors that are up the ladder from you, who can offer you that helping hand, that is so important.
>
> I didn't really have anyone that looked like me that I could look up to when starting in journalism. I guess the answer is really being mentors for other people. So, a lot of we, journalists of colour, we are those mentors.

> We are those pioneers stuck on the mid-low levels. That's when I wonder how can I move forward? It's really hard to do that when the jobs are shrinking. It makes it really difficult to get that mentorship and training from older people who are more experienced. I did a law degree, and I would make a lot more money in law.

4.1.4 Haydon Manning

From outside of newsrooms, Associate Professor Haydon Manning observed that

> There is such a difference between the younger journalists and the more mature. There is less of them today that come to a story with a degree of depth and background perspective on its history. Frequently, I've tried to offer the message that maybe you're being a bit harsh, because you don't understand the relevant history or understand the pressures for a leader or whatever politician it might be in the news. The fact is many have not been in the job very long and they're thrust into reporting on very serious topics without sufficient reflection on the history that is behind the topic they're addressing and, arguably, a reluctance to do solid research. Journalists need to respect the fact that they may not have a sufficient level of historical knowledge, particularly during elections, knowledge of actually how the electoral systems work.
>
> Whenever I give a community talk, if you ask people to explain how the votes are counted, you know, the only people who tend to know in any community group, are those students and other individuals who have been scrutineers for a political party. Otherwise, we all vote, but we actually don't know how it's counted. People have often written to say I'm wrong about what are the chances of some insider to win. Journos often don't understand, but they're not alone. In fact, most journos are great.

Manning also emphasised that preparation for this role would ideally go back as far as childhood and university education.

> Apparently, civics and citizenship education is happening better in high schools, so that the study of the institutions of government in Australia are actually understood. Obviously, that's going to be beneficial for those students who go into journalism. It's not going to happen, but I'd like to think that anyone appointed to being a political journalist would only be given that job if they'd studied politics. To join the national press gallery is clearly coveted, but you have to do your apprenticeship to prove yourself.

4.2 *Preparation and Career Development of Politicians*

To the voting public, it might seem logical that a politician who is responsible, as Health Minister, for the nation's health system would have some sort of background or training in healthcare. However, this is not at all how the Westminster model of government works. Instead, we vote for people who argue they have the leadership skills to manage a portfolio, such as health, and take advice from the experts. As our interviewees have noted, it is most common for a politician to have a background in law, or to have risen through the political system as a political party operative or adviser.

4.2.1 Haydon Manning

> It would be lovely to have a Minister of Education or Minister of Health who had a rich background in that field, but they don't. Most of them have got a law background. The people who put their hands up for office are too often unfairly chided for being lazy, overpaid, etc. People are ignorant of the amount of work they do now. Talking to these individuals, you get to understand what they go through being a politician, or even just getting pre-selections. They went out to 250 card carrying Liberal Party homes, to have a cup of tea and eat their cake and convince them that they were worth voting for. There are untold stories about what it takes, to get pre-selection, and then go through election campaigning, even though it is a safe seat. Yeah, they earn their keep. I admire most politicians for the effort they put in. Most of them are good ones who would earn a lot more doing something else. And it's even worse now. I think we're in real strife to attract people, and particularly women. It's the realm of social media and the constancy of not showing weakness in the public eye. There is no private life allowed. Any mishap you suddenly become the news.

4.2.2 Phil Coorey

> We have fewer people in politics now with expertise. Younger politicians are coming in now, they're not very expert at anything, including life. I think that's dumbing down our polity a lot. They're coming from a law degree, staffer role, candidate pre-selection, politics. John Howard (Former 25th Prime Minister, of Australia 1996–2007) used to sort of lament this, the rise of the professional politician, he called it. Even Mick Young (Former Labor Minister) sheared sheep before he came into the Parliament. Everyone talks romantically about Ben Chifley (16th Prime Minister of Australia 1945–1949) who was a train driver. But if Ben Chifley had the kinds

> of opportunities which he created, he probably would have become a barrister. In addition to law backgrounds, small business owners remain common among new MPs, particularly in the Liberal Party. I think across the board there is a lack of diversity in politics or a large lack of experience. If I had a rule, I don't reckon you should be allowed to come into politics unless you're in your forties and you've spent two years in the private sector.

4.2.3 Tory Shepherd

> Politicians certainly aren't prepared, as there is no set method of preparation. Regardless of professional background, many of today's politicians lack scientific literacy, critical thinking skills, basic logical progression skills and the ability to interrogate their pre-existing biases. They are also unprepared in a mental health sense for the extraordinarily weird world of Canberra, so resilience support would also help.

4.3 *Recognising and Attending to Diversity in the Media*

Intersecting with the series of challenges already canvassed in this chapter is the effect of a lack of diversity among the ranks of political journalists in Australia and to a slightly lesser extent, Australian politicians. Our interviewees acknowledged this lack of diversity, predominantly in terms of race and class, although both politics and political journalism continue to be more male-dominated fields.

4.3.1 Sarah Malik

Working at SBS Voices, Malik has experience in one of Australia's more culturally and linguistically diverse newsrooms. Nevertheless, she noted:

> The majority of newsrooms and leadership in Australia, in arts organisations as well as in newsrooms, in front of the camera and behind the camera, is largely white. The fact that our multicultural history is not being reflected in our media is really concerning. It's not just about 'Oh it's lovely to see different kinds of faces', it's necessary to be reflected in your country and in the mainstream media of that country. That's part of creating a feeling of 'I belong here, I deserve to have a voice, I can participate in this democracy'. I feel like the media's role is not only to make leaders accountable, but it's also to reflect and represent society and all its different voices, not just in the political sphere but also in feature articles, human-interest stories, with the faces you see on TV and in the newspapers.

> The lack of racial and cultural diversity among the journalists covering politics in Australia really has an impact on the kinds of stories that we read and the perspective that we're thinking about. There are all these untold stories out there that are not getting told because our shrinking media sphere is not diverse. I do feel like Australia is becoming more of a conservative place because people are not exposed to difference and differences of opinion. We saw with the Black Lives Matter movement, so many stories of journalists of colour talking about their challenges in these white-dominated media organisations and having their perspectives whitewashed or diluted or dismissed for not fitting into the white normative structures. We often see certain minority communities purely through the lens of disadvantage and I think the fact that we counter this by platforming these voices is important on all levels. When a woman who happens to be Muslim, for example, writes about her cat or parenting, it is just as valid as your white lady talking about her cat or parenting in the lifestyle section of *The Sydney Morning Herald*. It's about normalising and creating spaces for all of us not just on issues related to our identity (but that too if it's one that needs to be expressed). When you have different kinds of journalists in the mix, they're going to have different life experiences. When we have that diversity in our political ranks, in our journalism ranks, we're going to be able to identify stories that are otherwise overlooked. We can't just want new voices and then shut them down as biased and activist.
>
> When those voices speak up in ways that challenge the norm, or notions of objectivity, they are restructured around the status quo, that is an invisible white, male, upper class, norm. Being a minority in the public sphere, already subjects you to so much abuse online, so without structural support within organisations that is taking these threats and the mental health risks seriously and actively supporting staff from marginalised backgrounds, it just makes people feel like this kind of career is not worth it.

While her discussion has largely focused on racial and cultural diversity, Malik also noted the impact of a homogenous class among Australia's media.

> Media is generally dominated by white people, but also middle to upper class people. Because it is run on networking and unpaid internships … I think that only middle to upper class people will be able to afford to have careers in media. We need to have more working-class journalists to really reflect on society in all its dimensions.

Malik cited the example of the 2016 US election that saw Donald Trump and the rise of white nationalism, that was underestimated by most pundits, pollsters and reporters. In order to achieve greater diversity, Malik said the industry must consider quotas.

> There needs to be reserved spots for people of different backgrounds and make that a very specific part of the promotion process. This amount of the senior leadership is going to be diverse, or it's going to feature this many women of colour. That's really important because otherwise we don't really see change. Otherwise, the dominant groups always just dominate.

4.3.2 Phil Coorey

> There is a lack of diversity in the parliamentary press gallery covering politics across Australia and we do need more diversity but it's not reasonable to only validate reporting by people with a lived experience of the issue at hand. There seems to be a view of political journalism you can only write or report about something if you have direct experience in it.

He cited an example where the *ABC Insiders* program experienced backlash for hosting a discussion on the Black Lives Matter movement without including an Aboriginal commentator.

> If there's a lack of diversity on the couch on Insiders it's because there's a lack of diversity in the parliamentary press gallery. It's not the fault of the ABC. That show draws its panel from the press gallery primarily. A journalist should be able to analyse objectively. We're not there to talk about our life experiences, we are there to analyse objectively what the government is doing and why.

4.4 *Evolving Industry Conditions*

As noted earlier in this chapter, there have been huge shifts in the conditions under which political journalists operate in a media industry which is contending with a now 24-hour news cycle and constant demand for new content, a proliferation of new online and social media channels, changing consumer appetites and new attitudes and approaches by politicians to their roles. Competition for revenue and cuts to resources have had a huge impact on how newsrooms operate and this has affected how journalists are prepared for their role and go about it on a daily basis.

4.4.1 Phil Coorey

As traditional news organisations we have become less resourced. We all have three times as much in a day to do as we used to. You just can't do as much in-depth as you used to. And at the same time as we've become less resourced, those people in politics trying to spin you have become significantly more resourced. The worst thing in the world of social media is when people just abuse you all the time because you're just objectively reporting something. Or they're sitting at home just watching TV and they saw an interaction involving a journalist and they formed an entire opinion on you and your organisation. There is a tendency to generalise from the outside. People tend to regard the Canberra press gallery as some sort of homogenous block in which everyone operates the same way. In fact, it couldn't be more different. It's easily the most competitive field of journalism in Australia. From my perspective, I don't operate any differently than I always have and that is independent of anyone else.

I am still what is quaintly called mainstream media which involves adhering to a basic set of ethics where you've got to try to report objectively, in that you have got to try to represent both sides of the story. And that hasn't changed for me but I find the industry has become increasingly polarised where journalists and their organisation take sides. These days, the hardest line to take is the middle line, because you're expected to have a view. The worst thing that has happened to journalism is social media. Many journalists, especially the younger ones, play for hits on Twitter rather than just stick to their job of reporting. I am gobsmacked constantly by the number of journalists who overtly use social media to comment and, in the process, display their bias. As for those members of the public who frequent social media, many don't understand what we do and what objective reporting is. They just want their perceptions reinforced. The misunderstanding is to think we're actually reflecting our view in the reporting. Journalistic principles shouldn't change, even if the medium and the pace does. I still do what I always do, which is to treat everyone with respect, regardless of who they are. So that hasn't changed; its just becoming harder.

4.4.2 Tory Shepherd

Most senior Australian journalists would say that conditions changed at the time when they moved to Canberra's new Parliament House (my main experience is Federal Parliament). That's when interactions became far more stage managed, rather than incidental, and when press secretaries began muscling up. Since then, there have been other major changes, particularly the move to online. That has led to a demand in more copy, faster. But it also means politicians speak directly to the public, controlling their own messages. US President Donald Trump is a prime example of this.

There is an increasing emphasis on the number of online hits that articles get, which distorts journalism overall and encourages sensationalism. It also encourages a rush to publish, which has an obvious effect on accuracy. That shift to online has also meant people can curate their news feeds and see only the stories they want to see. This means audiences are creating bubbles for themselves and not necessarily consuming diverse media.

4.4.3 Sarah Malik

Audiences are not getting different kinds of views if they are curating their own news feeds via social media. There are these social media algorithms that are just highlighting the most clicked news stories, not even the most factually accurate information. The digital age has caused a lot of change. Social media is so variable in its quality and its focus, and it's unpredictable. It's this rupture and this cost cutting that's affected media in modern times. And I think that's come as a shock to people who've always been comfortable in the industry. I can't imagine having a job in the same media outlet for 25 years, but that's what it was like for the journalists in the golden era. It is enormously difficult with less media organisations, more redundancies, more closures, less diversity in media. It's a hard industry to be in.

4.4.4 Haydon Manning

[t]he worst thing about all of this is, more than ever, we need quality from the major political journalists to counter the realm of social media and the realm of fake news. Social media is making it less attractive for decent citizens to put their hand up for being elected to political office, because there is no private life allowed. There is a need to respect the seriousness of the job they're doing in a democracy, which is at risk of being eroded by social media.

4.5 *Interactions between Stakeholders*

Despite the increasing tendency of politicians to use social media to bypass traditional journalists, there remains a strong two-way reliance between political operators and reporters. In this section we examine three key relationships involved in producing political news; between politicians and reporters, between reporters and the public (their audience) and between politicians and the public (their voting pool).

4.5.1 Tory Shepherd

> There is a symbiosis in this relationship, but the dynamics of the relationship vary widely depending on the desires of the actors and their approach to their work. There are many different systems of interaction between the Australian media and politicians, ranging from 'gotchas' to friendly fluff pieces, to transactional deals. There are also plenty of admirable interactions, as longer-form interviews would attest. Some journalists operate on a transactional basis; politicians might get a softer run in an exclusive drop to a paper, for example. In some cases, it can effectively be blackmail; journalists might run a nasty line if they're 'off the drip' of information from a politician. And politicians can play games such as freezing out particular journalists. Many politicians try to alter or kill stories by threatening or trying to intimidate journalists, or by calling people higher up the food chain in the news organisation. To change this takes a courageous journalist but if those in charge refuse to play politician's games, they can nullify the process.

4.5.2 Sarah Malik

Malik raised concerns about interference by politicians pressuring newsroom leaders. She cited a letter of complaint written by Prime Minister Scott Morrison about a story aired on the ABC, and Australian Federal Police raids on journalists as examples.

> It's really important that whatever non-corporate media we have left is free in terms of its editorial to be able to do its coverage as fearlessly as we can without feeling like it must constantly justify its existence and its funding or be called by politicians who are upset by its coverage.

On counteracting the influence or interference of politicians, she said:

> You really appreciate the journalists who can really persist and kind of keep at politicians. It just takes strength and conviction and really being honest and truthful, even if it's difficult. That kind of courage in the work of people I admire really moves me and it's something that I aspire to and want to emulate.

Malik also referenced former US President Donald Trump's use of Twitter, in particular, to highlight how politicians are bypassing the journalist-politician dynamic to instead speak directly to the voter.

> I think a lot of politicians are using social media now to go directly to the public. They speak to people through Twitter and they seem off the cuff. Journalists are no longer an exclusive conduit for information; blurring the line between media and social media, public and private, global and local, and physical and online newsroom and forcing change in how politicians and journalists communicate and convey information. There's value in being a bit more upfront and open, speaking in more, kind of, a human way to people but this appearance of openness has also been commodified. I think we all realise that media and social media are now a big part of their job but it moves with breakneck speed, are less controlled and has less checks. And although it has opened space up for diverse voices that had been previously shut out from legacy media, it can also be taxing on mental health.

4.5.3 Phil Coorey

Coorey's emphasis was on respect when it comes to interactions between politicians and journalists.

> There's this view that you've got to yell at them or abuse them to make a point. And people are constantly trying to spin you rubbish or sell you stuff that's not quite right. They're going to try and use you as much as they use anyone else. As a political journalist, you're in the middle of that constant tension. I still do exactly what I always do, treat everyone with respect, regardless of who they are. I need to be able to talk to a member of minority parties as much as I need to be able to talk to the Leader of the Greens or the Prime Minister or a Labour backbencher. They all need to trust me so they can talk candidly off the record. If you want to be a successful political correspondent you've got to be able to talk to all sides. The best thing that anyone can call you is fair. Some journos, especially TV interviewers, think they've got to be tough and they'll ask all sorts of

> rhetorical questions, trial accusations, rather than listen. One of the first things I was taught when I was a journo was when you're interviewing somebody, just let them graze and talk, and then they spill the beans. I just want to get information out of it.

Coorey argued there should be a core set of principles that guide journalism, despite varying topics or interviewees.

> A journalist should try to adhere to principles regardless of the boiling sea you find yourself in. You've got to be civil. You've got to be polite, use their title, none of this first name business, whether they are talking to a backbencher or a Prime Minister. There's a core set of principles that don't change. The kinds of questions you ask might change but the way you do it, the way you relate to politicians is based on some sound principles and they don't change. My advice to any young journo is keep your personal opinion to yourself and just be a good news reporter and break stories and everything will look after itself. If a politician announces a policy that I find utterly horrid personally, I still just report the policy. I separate those two, but it is a bit of a dying art.

4.5.4 Haydon Manning

Manning raised the approach of so-called "gotcha" journalism as "one of the biggest problems" with interactions between journalists and politicians.

> It is often about embarrassing the person the journalists are interviewing rather than soliciting the story. I think that's one of the biggest problems is the relationship between the journalist and the elected politician or minister being interviewed. Too often, the journalist comes at the subject exceptionally, unnecessarily cynical, or worse, with a keenness to employ gotcha journalism. Before there was some level of mutual respect, certainly going back to Menzies and Whitlam's (Former Australian Prime Ministers) eras. But 'gotcha' journalism is a way of turning around and saying 'Look at me' to the audience and to their employer. The focus is on the fact that the politicians have contradicted themselves, they've stumbled, foot in the mouth, rather than this is a serious issue. This entrapment reinforces reticence on the part of the minister to being interviewed. Really what politicians are trying to be is so cautious it shows in their tone and their tempo. They are trying to be careful because they don't want to do something that gets misinterpreted. The irony is

> that the more media training they have, the more 'tricky' they seem when they're speaking. The problem is the Minister being interviewed has been so straightjacketed by all the media training they've had, they're being ultra-cautious such that it's undermining authenticity.

5 Discussion

We have a number of key observations from these narratives. It was very clear that the ideals and codes of 'Ethical practice for Journalists' described in the review of academic literature earlier in this chapter align closely with the ideals held by our interviewees. The values they reported underscored the importance of exercising a disposition of respect for the politicians they interviewed. They also had clarity about reporting news versus opinion. They all expressed personal objections to egoistic gotcha journalism that entrapped the interviewee and reporting that became personal attacks on individuals. In regard to the impact of social media on their work, all expressed some measure of disappointment, yet Sarah Malik also appreciated that it has made political news more accessible to some communities, particularly those living at the margins, such as migrants, refugees and Indigenous communities. Tory Shepherd also raised the potential for adverse mental health issues as a result of the inherent conflict in the work of political reporting and dealing with the public backlash aimed at both reporters and politicians. She posited that it was ultimately the responsibility of media management to ensure that there was adequate education and support for journalists to help them maintain their wellbeing and develop resilience. She also argued that politicians should have similar support.

There were sustained discussions about the issues of equality, inclusion and the potential for the marginalisation of individuals and communities that are culturally and linguistically diverse. Malik underscored the importance of the media itself being culturally diverse, as well as its content. Without such diversity whole sections of Australian society perceive themselves as being at the margins, not really Australian, as they cannot identify with a reporter or what is being reported. Malik argued that it is not enough to say, 'there should be greater diversity among journalists' and hope that it will evolve. She called for deliberateness from media management, by using quotas and mentoring for journalists of colour, and for deliberately seeking greater Indigenous representation amongst the political press. She argued that with greater cultural representation amongst media personnel, news stories will be more diverse and more representative of the community's experiences and interests. At the same time, Phil Coorey argued that all journalists have a responsibility to engage at a deeper level with the impact of political, economic and social issues on minority and marginal groups in the community, without limiting the reporting to their lived experience.

Despite agreement on these ideals, a problem arises when they 'butt up' against reality. There is always a gap between ideals and practice and this gap has been the subject of considerable research (Mellado & Van Dalen, 2014). It is important to remember that there are economic and work environment factors that impact on journalists' ability to align their practice with their ideals.

In these narratives the interviewees identified a number of work-related factors that impeded the way they could carry out their role. The advent of the 24-hour news cycle and the shift to online publication are at the centre of many of the new pressures. Time to research before interviews or publication has diminished alongside an expectation to produce more news reports in less time, due to reduced staffing and the 24/7 demand for content. There are some realities that cannot be changed. Newsrooms are not going to suddenly increase staff numbers to the level they previously enjoyed. Editors and media executives are not going to suddenly find untapped resources that will bring in huge revenues again to return income to the levels received prior to the internet's permanent impact on the way news is produced and disseminated. The competitive pressure to get more people to read or watch a journalist's coverage, in preference to that of their competitors, won't go away, nor will the ability of the public to 'talk back' through social media or online comment sections. Politicians will continue to find their own channels to speak directly to their audience. It used to happen on soap boxes in parks and at street corner meetings but now it happens virtually and in real time.

However, some realities raised by our journalists can be managed more wisely:

- *Diversity in newsrooms*: New strategies for hiring practices can be developed to increase the diversity among journalists, such as Malik's suggestion of using quotas. These have been used to good effect in some sections of politics – although there remains resistance in others. Increasing diversity has the snowball effect of encouraging more diverse applicants to put their hand up for roles in media because they can now see journalists and media leaders who are from their communities. It is also important for journalists to be given the time to better inform themselves through ongoing professional education that seeks to gain insights into diverse cultural viewpoints, and by identifying more diverse sources to contribute to their reporting (people with lived experience or from culturally diverse backgrounds etc). But this will only occur system-wide if media leaders acknowledge its importance and make the necessary time and resources available (Kim, 2001).

- *Quality over quantity*: Accurate and insightful reporting is grounded in a deep understanding of the factors at play with regard to specialist issues, including their foundational history. This was raised by both Coorey and Manning. In fact, Manning suggested that all journalists and politicians should have a background in political science to understand how the electoral system works. This is an argument that has been further developed by Nyhan and Sides (2011). They have posited that engaging with political science can bring fresh angles to the news and identify stories that deserve coverage, help counter spin from political operators and provide insights into trends and historical comparisons. The journalists we interviewed emphasised the value of having some members of a newsroom who are specialists in a certain field. However, they lamented the cuts to resources that have seen a loss of this specialised expertise that has not been replaced. Instead, less experienced journalists who command lower salaries are hired. To recapture this expert knowledge base takes time, but would add immensely to the quality of reporting and provide a valuable resource for a newsroom. Feasibility is an issue here as we have noted earlier how journalists, in the current climate, do not have the time to commit hours to research before an interview, as Manning might like. That said, there is a point of compromise to argue for incrementally building specialisations, putting the case to media employers that consumers will pay more for or be more loyal to reporting that is more in-depth and informed, and marketed that way.

5.1 *How Might Journalists and Politicians Develop Wiser Practice?*

Journalistic compromise and adaptation, while also adhering to core principles of practice, requires wisdom and a well-developed ethical imagination for confronting the unexpected. Wisdom also entails consideration of, and contribution to, the common good – a core principle of journalism (IFJ, 2019) and journalistic integrity in practice, which is demonstrated by many journalists who produce honest and respectful reporting of the truth. As we have learned from our interviewees, this integrity of practice sometimes comes down more to a personal disposition, rather than consistently-required corporate competence.

Equally, politicians, quite apart from their interactions with journalists, are called upon to maintain their electorate's trust while navigating their parliamentary duties and party expectations. They must make decisions regarding public wellbeing and the common good while balancing personal career aspirations; all while remaining authentic to their core morals and values. This complex management of expectations while trying to establish and maintain a positive and trustworthy public image is not easy for the uninitiated. We have raised questions earlier in this chapter as to whether politicians are sufficiently inducted, mentored and supported by experienced political leadership to do this. Without such support it is easy to see why naïve and inexperienced politicians develop defensive or avoidance behaviours around seasoned, questioning journalists.

So where might wisdom come into play in fostering a less defensive, more resilient political class and more respectful reporting by political journalists? In the first instance, induction to their roles, mentoring by experienced representatives and support in fostering resilience would help both journalists and politicians. This fostering of wellbeing is a responsibility of the leaders of newsrooms and political parties. Should they take this responsibility seriously, it would constitute a positive and wise improvement.

For politicians particularly, the fear of being found to have 'got things wrong' is a major limitation to wise practice, that is heightened by instances of journalism which perceives that the key role of the Fourth Estate is to shine the spotlight on politician's mistakes and biases. There is little to wonder at politician's tendency to defensiveness and avoidance of the press when press conferences are bogged down in 'gottcha' questioning designed to bolster a journalist's ego or the entertainment value for their readers or viewers. We are not suggesting that journalists should turn a blind eye to error, poor policy, or bias in politicians. However, our interviewees argued there is a more respectful way to uncover important details which focuses more on the issue and less on the person. Respectful, professional journalism does not seek personal aggrandisement, but involves listening with respect to what is said, understanding the issue and focusing on what it means for the public good and what will be done. All too often spectacles are made of individual politicians' failures. This can prompt political elites to respond defensively, by dismissing media reporting as "fake news" or otherwise untrustworthy, or providing 'sacrificial lambs' by sacking lower ranking parliamentarians or public servants to redirect media attention.

By contrast, there are contemporary political elites who take a wiser stance. A recent example in Australia was at the beginning of the first wave of the COVID-19 pandemic when a decision was made to permit passengers to disembark from a cruise ship in Sydney, New South Wales (NSW), without requiring health checks for the virus. This decision was made despite there being a clear indication that many passengers were ill. The decision had drastic ramifications for many Australians, causing illness and death as the passengers proceeded to travel to all Australian states. When the point of error and those responsible were identified, the Premier of NSW, Gladys Berejiklian, remained willing to face the press, admitted the error, offered an abject apology, explained what would occur in the future, and refused to dismiss the staff responsible. She said, "we are all learning and we have learned valuable lessons from this error and it will not occur again". Whether or not it did, or does, recur is irrelevant. The point here is that what she gave was an honest, and rare admission of failure, an acceptance of responsibility without defensiveness, maintaining respect and support for her bureaucrats. Her opposition counterpart applauded Premier Berejiklian's response and management of the matter (Collins, 2020). Also on the public record are the wise practices of New Zealand's Prime Minister Jacinda Ardern and Germany's Chancellor Angela Merkel. Both have a record of, and are described as, being brave, positive and honest in the face of opposition and negative reporting and choosing to respond with an abiding, lifelong commitment to social justice, equality and a concern for the marginalised (Chapman, 2020; The Daily Telegraph, 2011).

Like politicians, journalists go about their craft in different ways. As Coorey said at the beginning of his interview,

> There is a tendency to generalise from the outside. People tend to regard the whole (media) system as some sort of homogenous block in which everyone operates the same way. In fact, it couldn't be more different. It's easily the most competitive field. From my perspective I (and my colleagues) don't really operate any different than I always have. I still operate by a basic set of ethics where you've got to try to report objectively, in that you have got to try to represent both sides into the story. And that hasn't changed.

Despite these values being enshrined in media codes of ethics (IFJ, 2019; MEAA, 1944) it is regrettable that these desirable wise practises are sometimes due more to personal dispositions of individual journalists than any requirement for consistency across the industry. We, the public, need to understand that there are significant differences in the ways that journalists regard their role as reporters of political news, and this influences the degree of integrity and ethical reasoning they exercise in their practice. Similarly, we need to recognise that there is diversity of intent, engagement and integrity amongst our parliamentary representatives. In the same way that we have canvassed the need for journalists and politicians to have better preparation and education for their roles, the public too has a responsibility to be informed and educated about how the systems of politics and media work. Our interviewees pointed out that the public are increasingly prone to make snap judgements about how journalists and politicians operate, and to provide that feedback directly through social media, email or comment sections of websites but this is often done with only a surface understanding of the systems within which they operate. Veteran journalist Margaret Simons noted this phenomenon in an examination of the public reaction to live press conferences held by Victorian Premier Daniel Andrews during the height of the 2020 COVID-19 pandemic lockdowns in that state. Live coverage of press conferences is a relatively new form of news coverage, driven by the 24-hour demand for news content to fill websites, radio air-time and subscription-service television news channels. "People are watching the news sausage being made, rather than just getting the finished product in the form of a tidy news bulletin. Many are disgusted by what they see – and mistake what they are seeing for the whole story …". Simons (2020) noted "Journalists were called out in aggressive, sometimes abusive, terms for perceived bias, repetition and silly questions" (para. 6). Simons references Jay Rosen (2006) who identifies these public critics as "the people previously known as the audience, but who are now themselves a social media commentariat and participants in the process" (Simons, 2020, para. 18). On reflection, she points out that, at the end of the day, the rabid public demand for information during the evolving stages of the COVID-19 pandemic has shown us "that a journalist's main worth is to get the facts and to find things out".

6 Conclusion

Gathering and reporting news about what political leaders are doing and planning, and how it will impact on the quality of civilian's lives, is a powerful and critical role in our modern world. The quality of this reporting has been under considerable scrutiny by media researchers asking whether it contributes to a politically literate voting public. Political news reporting is also challenged by political elites, based on their perceptions of hostile and negative styles adopted by some journalists. Political journalism in mainstream media has been criticised for reinforcing a loss of trust in political leadership and contributing to cynicism about politicians. Some politicians and academic commentators argue this is a result of negative journalistic reporting styles. Taken to extreme, political objections have coined new labels for some styles of journalism that they believe lead to this, such as "gottcha journalism" and "fake news" (Quandt, Frischlich, Boberg & Schatto-Eckrodt, 2021). This new way of framing political news that politicians find unfavourable does little to build trust in news agencies. A downside of this failing trust is that news consumers seek out even less reliable sources. In this process they build their own information 'bubbles' that provide limited perspectives on critical national matters and have potentially unwarranted influence on the democratic literacy and voting decisions.

Political journalism as a profession is underpinned by principles that are seemingly under pressure from significant changes in terms of media commercialisation, ownership and the means of gaining and communicating news. Thus, we would argue that to lay the responsibility for the negativity and cynicism regarding politics solely on political journalists is unwarranted and unjust. Journalists are just one cog in a complex and increasingly unbalanced interplay that not only engages political journalists and politicians, but also includes media owners, political party operatives, press secretaries and owners of blogs or alternative information sources who create, communicate and respond to political news.

Unequivocal principles have been espoused for the practice of journalism that are intended to guide ethical practices that reject the very notion of gotcha journalism, and news reporting not grounded in evidence and truth. The journalists we spoke to were clear that no matter what changes there were to their work conditions, the core principles should still apply. They also underscored the notion that the practice of political journalism was a privilege and needed to be developed over time, with mentorship from more senior and experienced journalists. Given the increasing pressures and changes in news media, adaptation and compromise have become necessary to be successful in producing political news that has the potential to contribute to a politically literate and engaged democracy.

We submit that adopting deliberate strategies to address the barriers to quality news media and greater inclusiveness is wise practice. Deliberateness, involves transparency, reflection and being aware of the consequences of actions or for not taking actions (Trede & McEwen, 2016, p. 7). This is because wisdom, in contrast to traditional, common or best practice, always has an element of social justice and equality (Walsh, 2015, p. 285). We emphasise the need for deliberateness in pursuit of a culturally diverse media. We also see that there is a need for greater concern for the wellbeing and resilience of journalists and politicians. Such concern includes the allocation of time and resources to ensure the best preparation for the key players, The pursuit of quality, equality, diversity, inclusiveness, wellbeing and resilience should not be left to personal dispositions. It should be a central concern of an organisational intelligence and competence (Zembylas, Bozalek, & Shefer, 2014) and requires deliberate buy-in of media and political leadership to become embedded in everyday practice.

References

Albæk, E., van Dalen, A., Jebril, N., & De Vreese, C. (2014). Do role conceptions matter? In E. Albæk, A. van Dalen, N. Jebril, & C. De Vreese (Eds.), *Political journal-*

ism in comparative perspective (Communication, Society and Politics) (pp. 72–93). Cambridge University Press. https://doi.org/10.1111/j.1745-6916.2008.00062.x

Baltes, P., & Smith, J. (2008). The fascination of wisdom: Its nature, ontology and function. *Perspectives on Psychological Science, 3*(1).

Brenton, S. (2010). *What lies beneath: The work of senators and members in the Australian Parliament.* Commonwealth of Australia.

Chapman, M. (2020). *Jacinda Ardern: A new kind of leader.* Black Ink.

Collins, A. (2020, August 17). NSW Premier Gladys Berejiklian apologises 'unreservedly' over Ruby Princess mistakes that led to coronavirus outbreak. *ABC News.*

Davis, A. (2007). *The mediation of power. A critical introduction.* Routledge.

Hampshire, S. (Ed.). (1978). *Public and private morality.* Cambridge University Press.

International Federation of Journalists (IFJ). (2019). *Global charter of ethics for journalists.* Adopted at the 30 IFJ World Congress, Tunis.

Kim, Y. (2001). *Becoming intercultural: An integrative theory of communication and cross-cultural adaptation.* Sage Publication.

Matthes, J., Maurer, P., & Arendt, F. (2019). Consequences of politicians' perceptions of the news media. *Journalism Studies, 20*(3), 345–363.

Mazzoleni, G., & Schulz, W. (1999). "Mediatization" of politics: A challenge for democracy? *Political Communication, 16*(3), 247–261.

MEAA. (1944). *Journalist code of ethics.* http://www.meaa.org/meaa-media/code-of-ethics/

Mellado, C., & Van Dalen, A. (2014). Between rhetoric and practice. *Journalism Studies, 15*(6), 859–878.

Nielsen, R., & Kuhn, R. (2014). Political journalism in Western Europe: Change and continuity. In R. Kuhn & K. Nielsen (Eds.), *Professional journalism in transition: Western Europe in a comparative perspective.* I.B. Tauris.

Nygren, G., & Johansson, K. (2019). The interplay of media and the political executive: Introduction and framework. In K. Magnus Johansson & G. Nygren (Eds.), *Close and distant: Political executive-media relations in four countries* (pp. 9–26). Nordicom.

Nyhan, B., & Sides, J. (2011). How political science can help journalism (and still let journalists be journalists). *Press, Politics and Political Science. The Forum, 19*(1), art. 2.

Pitkin, H. (1967). *The concept of representation.* Univerity of Califonia, Berkeley.

Rosen, J. (2006, June 27). The people formerly known as the audience. *PressThink: Ghost of Democracy in the Media Machine.* http://journalism.nyu.edu/pubzone/weblogs/pressthink/2006/06/27/ppl_frmr.html

Quandt, T., Frischlich, L., Boberg, S., & Schatto-Eckrodt, T. (2021). Fake news. In T. P. Vos, F. Hanusch, D. Dimitrakopoulou, M. Geertsema-Sligh, & A. Sehl (Eds.), *The international encyclopedia of journalism studies.* John Wiley and Sons.

Schrøder, K., & Phillips, L. (2007). Complexifying media power: A study of the interplay between media and audience discourses on politics. *Media, Culture & Society, 29*(6), 890–915.

Simons, M. (2020, August 17). Front row seat to COVID-19 reporting reveals uncomfortable truths. *The Age*. https://www.smh.com.au/national/front-row-seat-to-covid-reporting-reveals-uncomfortable-truths-20200814-p55lxq.html

The Daily Telegraph. (2011, August 24). Angela Merkel the world's most powerful woman. *The Daily Telegraph*. Retrieved May 18, 2021, from https://www.telegraph.co.uk/news/worldnews/europe/germany/8720698/Angela-Merkel-worlds-most-powerful-woman.html

Thompson, D. (1987). *Political ethics and public office*. Harvard University Press.

Thompson, D. (2019). Political ethics. In H. LaFollett (Ed.), *International encyclopedia of ethics* (pp. 168–177). Wiley Online Library.

Trede, F., & McEwen, C. (2016). Scoping the deliberate professional. In F. Trede & C. McEwen (Eds.), *Educating the deliberate professional: Preparing for future practices*. Springer International.

Vallone, R., Ross, L., & Lepper, M. (1985). The hostile media phenomenon: Biased perception and perceptions of media bias in coverage of the Beirut massacre. *Journal of Personality and Social Psychology*, *49*(3), 577–585.

Van Dalen, A. (2019, November). Rethinking journalist–politician relations in the age of populism: How outsider politicians delegitimize mainstream journalists. *Journalism*.

Walsh R. (2015). What is wisdom? Cross-cultural and cross-disciplinary syntheses. *Review of General Psychology*, *19*, 278–293.

Zembylas, M., Bozalek, V., & Shefer, T. (2014). Tronto's notion of privileged irresponsibility and the reconceptualisation of care: Implications for critical pedagogies of emotion in higher education. *Gender and Education*, *26*(3), 200–214.

CHAPTER 19

Wise Futures in Ageing Societies

Janice Orrell and Lilly Xiao

Abstract

Wise societies take seriously the evidence that populations worldwide are ageing. Age sociologists and gerontologists argue that past and current practices in caring for older adults are not appropriate indicators for the future, because each generational cohort is born into a unique point in history. Each cohort's accompanying life chances shape the uniqueness of their expectations regarding as well as functional and cognitive capacity in their later years. Thus, wise practice for aged care needs to be evidence-informed and based on an understanding that ageing is an ever-changing social construct. The United Nations and the World Health Organization have established goals to promote healthy, active ageing and age friendly environments globally, maintaining an overview across nations regarding emerging ageing demographics and the well-being of older citizens in each country. The UN and WHO gather and analyse trends worldwide to provide guidance for governments and service providers to assist them to translate the information into appropriate action in local contexts. It is questionable, however, whether individual Governments make adequate use of this guidance? Wise Government agendas should aim to combat ageism, enable autonomy, and account for cultural, gender, and sexual diversity as well as elderly citizens' socio-economic differences in life chances. Wise societies should seek active engagement of older people, respect their wisdom and value the contributions that older people have made, and continue to make, to their families and their communities.

Keywords

ageing – ageism – wisdom of age and experience – World Health Organization – age friendly cities

1 Creating Wise Futures in Ageing Nations

The goal of this chapter is to identify what dispositions, resources and actions are needed to foster societies that include and involve older adults in ways that

 | DOI: 10.1163/9789004505544_023

enable them to live their later years actively engaged in society, maintaining and using their functional and cognitive capacities to the full. The world-wide ageing demographic is a phenomenon that is not only the result of a global increase in longevity, but also of a complex interplay between advances in medical treatments that increase the survival of disabled persons, greater control of chronic diseases, decreased fertility rates and improvements in individuals' educational opportunities and health behaviours (Robine & Michel, 2004). Working towards a wise future in an ageing society should be one that recognises and values the past contributions older citizens have made to society, welcomes their potential to continue to engage and contribute to society, respects their wisdom of experience and heeds their concerns. Wise societies also willingly provide an environment of care and support when older citizen's capabilities begin to fade as they become increasingly dependent on the support of governments, communities and their families. Articulating these aspirations for shaping a wise future in an ageing society is easily captured in a global vision, government policies or organisational plans. It is more important, however, to question how these aspirations are fostered in practice and evaluate how actions have achieved the intended outcomes.

The World Health Organization (WHO) and United Nations are committed to addressing the challenges of ageing world populations and gather evidence of the current status and well-being of older citizens in all nations. In particular, they seek to reduce inequalities and poverty that are most profoundly experienced by the poor and marginalised as they age. Information gathered is promulgated globally to contribute to the effective execution of worldwide measures and the development of resources to assist local Governments to help create age friendly cities and communities. Multi-disciplinary collaboration in gerontology, sociology, psychology, economics and health care research provide evidence and critical perspectives to inform national policies, provision of aged care service and actions to address the implications of an ageing population. This body of research and commentary has identified major omissions in governments' policies and planning and point to many erroneous assumptions about ageing regarding the functional capacities and needs of older people upon which they are built (Jalland, 2015; O'Loughlin & Kendig, 2017).

Sociology of Aging research has produced evidence that contradicts common assumptions and negative social stereotypes of ageing (Dionigi, 2015; Gratton & Scott, 2016; Healy, 2004). These scholarly works uncover the impact of prevailing ageist stereotypes that ignore the value and benefits that can flow from adopting an approach that acknowledges reciprocal trans-generational sharing of economic support and wisdom between generations (Healy, 2004).

Many of these critical discourses call for a paradigm shift as the basis for reform and wise planning for the future (Minichiello & Coulson, 2005). There are also encouraging records of efforts by communities and agencies in the creation of age friendly environments that seek to listen to the voices of older people, encourage their inclusion and engagement in society as well as capture their wisdom of experience (see, for example, Parisi et al., 2009).

2 The Concept of Ageing

It is predicted that by 2050, 1 in 6 people will be over the age of 65, which is an almost twofold increase from 2019 (1 in 11) (United Nations Department of Economic and Social Affairs, 2019). The chance of survival beyond the age of 65 has already risen from less than 50% to more than 90% in the countries with the highest life expectancy. This means that in most developed countries the proportion of life spent post 65 has risen from a fifth to a quarter. While women still tend to outlive men, it seems that the gap is closing (Healy, 2004; Human Mortality Database, 2015; Sundberg et al., 2018) and "single women continue to be at a substantial disadvantage relative to men in terms of their vulnerability, poor health and housing security" (Gong & Kendig, 2016, p. 38). In contrast to governmental focus on ageing chronology, Novak (2012) outlines a more expansive approach to understanding ageing including the following four dimensions: chronological age (number of years), biological age (physical changes), psychological age (mental functioning and personality) and social age (role, relationships and perception). Ageing should be considered from a 'life course' perspective, as part of life, and with an understanding that it has a course that is unpredictable, different and variable across all nations and their communities.

The focus and concern about ageing citizens is not new. Four decades ago, Riley (1978) in his exploration of the *Sociology of Age*, made it clear that age and ageing, are social constructs, are being constantly defined and redefined and are neither stable across time, nor common across cultures and communities.

> Ageing is not inevitably prescribed. There is no 'pure' process of ageing, … the ways in which children enter kindergarten, or adolescence move into adulthood, or older people retire are not ordained. (Riley, 1978, p. 39)

Riley (1978) described the concern of *Sociology of Age* as the integration of "the ageing process as individuals move through the changing social structure with the changing social structural environments and their impact on successive cohorts of human lives" (p. 40). Riley elaborates further on the significance of the unique generational life course influences by drawing on Mannheim's argument classic essay *The Problem of Generations,*

> … each new cohort, starting its life course at a unique point in time, has unique characteristics because of particular historical events undergone or particular knowledge or attitudes acquired in childhood. (Mannheim, 1952, p. 309)

While it might be useful to consider past conceptions of, and responses to, ageing (Jalland, 2015; Novak, 2012) the past strategies are not an indication of what will be appropriate or wise for the future. Each generation has experienced significantly different life paths that influence their capacities and needs in older age. For example, the present post WW2 cohort of older adults, the baby boomer generation, who now are entering their 7th decade, have experienced very different lives in terms of social expectations and economic opportunities than those of their parents and grandparents. Older adults in modern, affluent nations, have had greater educational opportunities (United Nations Department of Economic and Social Affairs, 2019) than their predecessors and have been afforded an expansion of secure employment options. As a result, they are entering older age in better health than their parents and grandparents, possessing secure accommodation, reasonable wealth to be self-sufficient and not be reliant upon the public purse and, in many cases, they have the choice to continue employment beyond 65 and are active and socially engaged citizens (United Nations Department of Economic and Social Affairs, 2019).

What is considered chronologically old is also quite different across different societies and is strongly influenced not only by the historical contexts of each generational cohort, but also by the prevailing culture. Local and ethnic cultural values and expectations, local and global historical events and conditions and economic opportunities and status all have profound impact on biological, psychological and social dimensions of ageing in individuals (Fung, 2013). Depending on their global location and socio-economic status, there are many older people who have had challenging life paths that leave them in their later years living in marginalised circumstances in terms of poor health, unemployed or the need to stay in employment, without secure housing and dependent on families and social services for their survival. Typically, these are the elderly in poorer nations, the migrant groups in more affluent nations, Indigenous populations and people living with disabilities. Older single women are especially represented in these communities and have greater requirements for targeted support.

3 Older People's Social, Psychological and Economic Needs

From a psycho-social perspective, ageing is a complex process that includes both losses and gains. In 2002 the WHO released a landmark report, *Active Ageing: A Policy Framework*, to promote health and quality of life for older people by maximising their opportunities to participate in various activities across social, economic, cultural, spiritual and civic affairs arenas (WHO, 2002). Since this global initiative, a policy shift from active ageing to a wellness focused healthy ageing framework has occurred. This framework is based on evidence that older people are very diverse in terms of their health conditions, the environment they live in, and their values, preferences and expectations of health and wellbeing. Public health policies need to acknowledge and address this diversity amongst older adults in order to promote health and wellbeing for all.

3.1 *Social Needs of Older Adults*

There is an obvious concern for the physical health needs of older people, however, their social and emotional needs are also very important and are often overlooked. Bruggencate et al. (2018) conducted a systematic review of the existing quantitative and qualitative literature focusing on the social needs of older people to identify the characteristics of successful interventions that satisfy these needs and based on an assumption that satisfying social needs assists in helping older people in staying healthy. Importantly, they found that in growing older it is very important to have social connections and a sense of belonging in the community and this should not be a time for withdrawal from active participation. Older people themselves report that the challenge of ageing is coping with the changing of social networks which occurs when there is a health decline or a death or illness of a spouse or when relationships change within families, resulting in the loss of people they have known for a long time (Charles & Carstensen, 2010). Furthermore, older adults seek to engage in reciprocal relationships in which they felt they are contributing to the wellbeing of others (Bruggencate et al., 2018).

3.2 *Psychological Stressors*

The Bruggencate et al. (2018) review identified that older people reported that maintaining a sense of personal independence was high on their list of important factors in their lives and that they struggled with having to become dependent on others and found it difficult to adjust to these new circumstances (Vos et al., 2020). Charles and Carstensen (2010) argued that strong stable social networks are essential for psychological and emotional wellbeing through old age stating that "when life is controllable and social supports are strong, older people fare better than their younger counterparts" (Charles & Carstensen, 2010, p. 385). In contrast, they found that prolonged stress affects physical functioning such that "when stressors are unavoidable, and exposure is prolonged, physiological regulation suffers" (Charles & Carstensen, 2010, p. 385).

3.3 *Support for Chronic Health Conditions*

Despite older people valuing their independence, those with chronic health conditions often lack professional advice on how to obtain self-care services due to poor communication and a lack of information on services available to them and lack of coordination between the different services (Abdi et al., 2019). Abdi et al. found that not only was this gap in knowledge among older people themselves, but also found in older workers and older carers. Thus, Abdi et al. make the case that older people with long-term chronic conditions have unmet needs to assist them with their physical and psychological health as well as maintaining a social life. This is a significant issue that should not go unattended.

3.4 *Educational Needs of Older Adults*

The need for life-long education for the older adult is also yet to be realised. In societies that increasingly turn to interactive and communicative technologies, older adults are an important cohort for providing appropriate education related to technological tools and applications and technology services. New communication technologies assist older adults to maintain contact with friends and family who are at a distance and to access government and community services. The educational sector has done little to date to respond to the on-going education of older adults in the ever-changing 21st century. Older adults need targeted support from education systems in developing their technological skills and knowledge to enable them to maintain their employability and to assist them to engage with online communications with government and other organisations and to develop and maintain family and social networks in highly mobile societies.

3.5 *Employment Needs of Older Adults*

In both affluent and poorer nations many older people want or need to continue as workers beyond 65 years of age. Whereas in affluent nations older adults often continue working because they gain satisfaction from their work and feel that their accumulated life experiences enabled them to continue to have something to offer their chosen field of practice. Others have experienced life courses that have not enabled them to acquire financial resources or housing security and are concerned at the prospect of mounting costs to meet their increased ageing needs, despite receiving a pension that has failed to be increased in line with the rises in the basic cost of living. This is financially challenging in societies in which governments are expecting older citizens to prepare themselves for self-sufficiency in their later years. Governments in affluent nations are also concerned about the costs of supporting an ageing population and already report being unable to meet the current need for provision of social housing and as a result, have increased the eligibility age for receiving government age pensions, forcing many to continue working beyond 65, whether they want to or not, thus workforce participation has increased in recent years amongst those over 55. However, many older adults face heavy competition from younger applicants, and there remains considerable room for improvement in the range of employment options offered by employers (Podger, 2016). By contrast there are many poorer nations whose governments lack systems to provide older people with financial safety nets such as pensions and social housing. Older adults in these nations need the full support of their families, without which they must work well into old age, sometimes until death.

4 Contributions Older Adults Make to Society

The current cohort of older adults, particularly those in affluent nations, can, and do, continue to make valuable contributions to society. Contrary to a prevailing concern regarding the increased dependency of older people and the financial burden that such dependency might place on the public purse, older citizens make diverse contributions to the betterment of society.

4.1 *Older Adults as Carers*

Older adults are the major providers of help and support to other older adults and to the community generally which they do up to at least to the age of 75 years (Healy, 2004). They provide emotional, physical and economic care and support to their adult children, their grandchildren and their siblings and other relatives when they become frail and have chronic diseases. Increasingly, older adults have more living parents than children (Healy, 2004) for whom they also provide support and care.

4.2 *Older Adults as Consumers of Goods and Services*

Older citizens constitute a substantial source of economic benefit to their communities. In many countries citizens over 50 years of age own the greatest proportion of wealth. Their contribution as consumers is not only derived from those who are affluent and financially independent, but also those who receive government pensions who spend their money on their daily living needs and health care services as well as on leisure activities and entertainment. Older people are increasingly a source of new markets for consumer goods and services, however, the potential value of these new markets have yet to be fully recognised by most industries. There has been a failure in the business sector to recognise the emergence of older age markets and to transition from an established focus on the increasingly dwindling youth markets.

4.3 *Older Adults as Models of Good Citizenship*

Across all cultures older citizens are, for the most part, law abiding citizens whose dispositions and behaviours tend to become more deeply aligned with the core traditional values of their society and communities and they become more compliant with the dominant culture (Fung, 2013). As such, older people provide good role models as responsible citizens for younger people and it could be argued that their presence and engagement in society has the potential to enhance the quality of community life (Ranzijn, 2002).

4.4 *Older Adults as Volunteers*

In all societies and cultures there are unmet social and physical needs that governments, organisations and communities do not have the resources to pay workers to meet. It is in these situations older retired people are eagerly sought as volunteers by service organisations and are the principal source of intergenerational care across cultures. Volunteering in social organisations often plays an important role in giving meaning in older people's lives. Such unpaid caring and voluntary work adds up to a significant proportion of the GDP on a nation; around 7% on some measures but this contribution is rarely factored into governments' cost/benefit calculations (De Vaus et al., 2003; Healy, 2004; Ranzijn, 2002).

4.5 *Older Adults as Workers*

Healy (2004) identifies that "Mature workers today have greater capacity than previous generations to work beyond 60 or 65 because they are healthier and better educated and the nature of work is less physically demanding" (p. VIII). In 1999, an Australian government study found that there are advantages in maintaining older workers largely because the quality and efficiency of their work improves with age and experience; they are more loyal, possess valuable corporate knowledge, and are less likely to change jobs, thus reducing job turn over as well as recruitment and training costs (Healy, 2004). As a result, the government has encouraged adults to stay in the work force beyond 65 by increasing the age for eligibility for the pension. This change may be immaterial for some due to their fortunate economic status or even welcomed in particular fields of engaging and rewarding occupational work. However, enforced deferment of the pension and hence retirement, has failed to recognise that imposed working beyond 65 in occupations that are physically demanding, such as nursing and manual labour, can inflict significant and in some cases insurmountable physical hardship (O'Loughlin & Kendig, 2017). There are also contradictions among government policies. Policies that enforce deferred retirement for older adults are in conflict with recent political corona virus pandemic economic recovery strategy that promotes youth employment by providing financial incentives. These incentives influence employer recruitment decisions to form barriers to continued employment of older people. These ageist practices and prejudices create significant challenges for older adults seeking to maintain their independence, and to make employment choices that are appropriate to their physical and mental capabilities.

5 Ageing Populations and Ageism

> While older persons are often said to enjoy particular respect, the reality is that too many societies limit them ... The marginalization and devaluing of older persons takes a heavy toll. (Ban Ki-moon, 2016, cited in The Benevolent Society, 2017, p. 17)

National economists advise that confronting the phenomena of global ageing populations demands balancing the needs of dependent elderly with the long-term economic burden on governments and younger generations who must pay for a perceived increased consumption of health care provision and other supportive services.

> [In] Australia, older people can be depicted as a 'social problem' as a consequence of public concern about the costs to government of demographic change and an ageing population. (O'Loughlin & Kendig, 2017, p. 29)

This ageist perspective often observed in economic and political commentary is of particular concern given contemporary ageing populations because it polarises the needs of one generation against the other rather that validating them both.

Ageism, particularly in western societies, impacts at all levels and sectors of society. Unlike other isms, that refer to "the other", ageism is distinctive because we are destined in future life to become "the other" (Butler, 1980, p. 8). Agism could refer to discrimination and. prejudice against any age group, but Butler (1980) first coined the term 'ageism' in reference to old age and found that psychological studies had demonstrated conclusively that

> the adverse physiological effects of ageism, showing that older individuals who are presented with negative stereotypes of ageing over time experience detrimental changes, such as a decline in memory performance and a heightened cardiovascular response to stress.

He argued that the impact of ageism in government policy, in the practices of social institutions and in public attitudes and beliefs about ageing is considerable and deprives older people of the potential playing a significant role in our social and cultural life provides. The Benevolent Society's (2017) report on *The Drivers of Ageism*, found that ageism prejudices and discriminatory practices were evident at all levels and ages of society and perpetuated stereotypical beliefs as a self-fulfilling prophesy that amounted to "discrimination against one's future self" (p. 17). In their extensive survey, respondents aged 65 years and over reported experiences of ageism, that included being told a joke about older people, being talked down to, being ignored, being turned down for a job or denied a promotion at work because of their age.

There are two distinctive discourses on ageing, namely, supporting healthy ageing and economic concerns. The dominant focus is limiting the economic costs of aging physical, mental, and social decline. By contrast, the research and scholarly discourses of psychology and sociology generate evidence that older citizens can make a significant contribution to society due to their accumulated practical wisdom gained from life's experiences (Ardelt, 2011a, 2011b). The debate between public policy assumptions about ageing and the scholarly discourses focusing on ageing and wisdom seems to find little alignment. Central to these debates is a recognition that there is no recognisable pattern in ageing, just as there is no fixed pattern in child development. Therefore, policies and service provision must recognise the diversity in the functional, cognitive capacity of older citizens and in that consideration engagement and include them in the search for wise solutions. There also seems to be a failure at the policy level to consult with older citizens to give them voice in making plans, designing services and practices and setting priorities that would enhance their lives.

6 Wisdom in Old Age

> With age comes wisdom, but sometimes age comes alone. (Oscar Wilde, as quoted in Gide, 2012, n.p.)

Many societies associate ageing with greater wisdom (Baltes & Smith, 1990). The concept of wisdom is ancient (see Habel, Chapter 7, this volume) but the notion of what wisdom is in contemporary society, is diverse and variously related to intelligence, tacit knowledge, spirituality, emotional stability, and interpersonal acumen with little general consensus. Many have explored the relationship between ageing and wisdom, with agreement that age holds the potential for wisdom (Brugman, 2006). However, it is argued that personal resilience and successful coping strategies are more important attributes of wisdom than spirituality and higher intelligence and, while wisdom does not require religious faith, it potentially benefits from a spirituality that is characterised by humility, gratitude, altruism and compassionate love for others (Ardelt, 2008). Based on her psychological gerontology studies, Ardelt (2008) has synthesised the elements of wisdom as possessing three primary dimensions:

> *Cognitive:* the ability to understand situations thoroughly, knowing the positive and negative aspects of a situations, awareness of life's inherent uncertainty, yet able to make decisions despite this.
> *Reflective:* the ability to examine the phenomena from multiple perspectives with an absence of projections and blaming others.
> *Affective:* positive emotions and behaviours with an absence of indifference and or negative emotions towards others and remaining positive in the face of adversity. (Jeste et al., 2010, p. 669)

Jeste et al. (2010) report that research does not support a significant relationship between old age and wisdom per se, but rather only those older people who use their lifetime experiences optimally tend to acquire wisdom with ageing. Vaillant (2002) argues that wisdom increases only up to the fourth decade of life. Much of the acquisition of wisdom is dependent on an individual's ability to learn from their wealth of experience in a meaningful way. Those who have acquired wisdom in their later years have acquired greater capacity to deal with the challenges and uncertainties of life and tend to have been found to possess greater Subjective Well-Being (SWB) (Ardelt, 1997). This indicates that wisdom is more strongly related to life satisfaction, rather than aspects related to physical environment, sufficient finances and social engagement. Ardelt described wise older adults as able to accept the realities of life with a calm contentment and a reduced self-centeredness, increased altruism and ethical attitudes. She found that older adults seemed to put both positive and negative events into perspective, knowing, based on experience, that both would eventually change. Walsh (2015) concluded that wisdom in older age could be said to be characterised by "expertise in reducing suffering and enhancing wellbeing for both oneself and others" (p. 285).

7 The Role of Governments in Creating and Age-Friendly Futures

WHO has established goals to promote worldwide age friendly environments (Wrath, 2016) that require multi-sectorial action: health, long-term care, transport, housing, labour, social protection, information and communication. It also involves many actors – government (all levels), service providers, civil society, older people, their affiliated organisations, families and friends. Key WHO approaches relevant to all stakeholders to combat ageism include enabling autonomy and supporting Healthy Ageing in all policies at all levels.

Governments and service providers have a major role to play in setting a path for an age friendly society, setting in place policies that are translated into service delivery and the design and provision of age friendly environments. As policy statements are developed and enacted, it is important to scrutinise the underlying assumptions they hold regarding ageing as well as to identify what is absent, but should be considered, and what is inferred and invisible that should be made explicit. The meanings both explicit and tacit that we attach to age and ageing have power to shape the balance of attention paid to the care of older citizen (Gong & Kendig, 2016). To assess various responses to these relatively different needs, the Population Division of United Nations Department of Economic and Social Affairs compiles and analyses economic and social data regarding ageing populations using an Old Age Dependency Ratio (OADR) that they have devised to alert national governments to local needs and to provide guidance on how to translate relevant UN and WHO goals on health ageing into local action (United Nations Department of Economic and Social Affairs, 2019). Each nation makes their own decisions on how to respond to this data and advice.

According to the WHO (2015), 'Healthy Ageing' involves "developing and maintaining the functional ability that enables well-being in older age" (p. 28). Achieving healthy ageing for all citizens in a society regardless of their health conditions and financial circumstances requires consideration of two core factors, namely, intrinsic capacity and functional ability. Intrinsic capacity is the physical and mental capacities that an individual possesses; while functional ability is the health related capability that the individual demonstrates to fulfil activities they have reason to value (WHO, 2015). Under the healthy ageing framework, the role of the government is to provide an enabling environment including, but not limited to, physical and psychosocial environment, resources, information communication technology (ICT) and education and training programs to support life-long learning. The aim of healthy ageing is to optimise intrinsic capacity and maximise functional ability for older people.

Healy (2004) observed that government responses are largely based on 'demographic determinism' and fail to recognise the diversity of functional, economic and social capabilities of older citizens. Demographic determinism is based on a presumption of the inevitability of economic 'inter-generational transfer' that imposes the costs of caring for older citizens on younger generations (De Vaus et al., 2003). Reports from the Australian Treasury over the last two decades provide illustrative evidence of governmental reactive responses to the prospect of inter-generational transfer, in their advocacy for 'intra-generational self-sufficiency'. In other words, they advocate that all people should plan to fund their own retirement and older age across their lifetime so that that older citizens do not impose an economic burden on the public purse and on younger people through increased taxation to pay for aged care. Merely focusing on economic concerns risks excluding important issues such as the human rights of older people and fails to consider the past and current social and economic contributions of older citizens, or to account for the diversity of capacity and needs that exist amongst older populations (Australian Association of Social Work, 2013).

There are indications that the financial and social dependency of older people is rising more slowly than the increase in population ageing (United Nations Department of Economic and Social Affairs, 2019). This is largely due to the baby boomer, post WW2 generation, experiencing quite different opportunities than previous generations. Generally, they have had greater educational opportunities than their parents and grandparents, and more diverse and sustained employment opportunities. As a result, a larger proportion of this current ageing population are more likely to have secure home ownership and have attained greater long-term financial security. As a result, many older people do not put a strain on the public purse or their families and are living active, engaged lives beyond 65, either into retirement or by remaining in employment far longer.

8 Wise Practices to Promote Healthy Ageing at the Government Level

The WHO healthy ageing framework has implications for wise practice in government policy, resource and practice development in health and social care systems. First, older adults with a high level of intrinsic capacity need to be supported in preventing disease, maintaining healthy lifestyles and participating in meaningful social activities they value and enjoy. Health education and ageing-friendly environments, including ICT-enhanced environments, are crucial for this group to maintain health and wellbeing. Second, older adults who have reduced intrinsic capacity due to chronic diseases and age related functional decline require additional primary care interventions in the public health care system. The purpose of primary care intervention for this latter group is to enable them to perform effective self-care to slow down the progress of their chronic health conditions as well as to effectively engage with treatment and prevention regimes. Third, older people with a significant loss of intrinsic capacity due to complex health issues (i.e. the late stage of dementia and a terminal illness), a public health policy intervention needs to focus on providing comprehensive and integrated care services that combine social care, health care and support for informal carers in order to preserve older people's dignity, minimise pain and distress, prevent complications and promote wellbeing for them and their informal carers.

The use of ICT-enhanced care and services, for example smart homes, assistive devices, e-Health and mHealth, has improved functional ability and reach to older people in care services (Benoit-Dubé et al., 2020). Easy access to ICT devices has also generated a new learning curve for older people to master the ICT-enhanced care and services and new challenges for them to overcome (Rasi et al., 2021). Contemporary lack of support for older people to master these ICT tools and services provokes challenges with associated unintended negative consequences, for example enlarged inequity in the use of public funded health and social care services with ICT component (Turnbull et al., 2020).

Solutions for achieving healthy ageing in the context of ICT needs to be explored at the policy level. Accessible, public funded education and training for older people and/or their informal carers to master ICT-enhanced care and services are needed for all. Moreover, the co-design of products and care services with ICT components with older people and their informal carers needs to be mandated in the development and evaluation process (Latulippe et al., 2020). In a country with Indigenous population and populations from culturally and linguistically diverse groups, solutions in the use of ICT-enhanced care and services should be culturally safe and linguistically appropriate for older people.

9 Wise Practices to Promote Healthy Ageing at the Individual Level

The WHO healthy ageing framework also has implications for wise practice at an individual level, principally, by developing self-efficacy in self-care. Self-care is described as individual-initiated and performed activities for the purpose of maintaining health and wellbeing (Orem, 1991). Self-care emphasises the individual's responsibility to make lifestyle choice and behavioural changes in order to maintain health and wellbeing. Self-efficacy in the self-care context encompasses an individual's beliefs about their capabilities to maintain their health and wellbeing effectively. Older people with a high-level self-care efficacy possess accumulated mastery experiences in performing successful self-care through their life course, which they adapt into their current self-care situation and is demonstrated in good health and wellbeing outcomes. Engaging in life-long learning of self-care and chronic disease prevention and management through high-quality learning resources and programs help older people to gain current health-related literacy, knowledge and skills in self-care and, therefore, improve their mastery experiences.

Participating in peer support groups in chronic diseases management is an important way to learn from expert peers. Verbal encouragement from family members, friends and significant others will also enhance older people's belief that they are capable of achieving their self-care goals. Older people may experience setbacks in self-care, which will trigger emotional stress, frustration and feelings of hopelessness. Engaging in relaxation activities, talking to family members, friends and significant others and seeking health counselling services are important ways to manage emotional stress for older people. Novak (2012) argues that an important factor impacting on self-care is the meanings that we hold about ageing because they can become stereotypes that influence the of older adults, their, families and those around them and become constraints that are

> ... built into social structures, moulding the course of our lives and directing social change ... continually affecting the way we grow up and grow old, modifying the values attached to life and death, pressing towards social conflict or integration. (p. 49)

Dionigi (2015) also highlighted the pervasive nature of stereotyping ageing. They have an impact on older adults' views of themselves and other older adults as well as on their "cognitive and physical performances, including (their) ability to recover from disease, (their) health behaviours. It has been found that ageist stereotypes impact on individuals decisions to engage in cognitive, social, and physical activity, to seek medical assistance" (p. 7), as well as on how older adults are treated by others and by society as a whole.

10 What Should an Age-Friendly Society Be Like?

An age friendly society includes older adults in designing and developing healthy environments that work toward a more equal society. Societies that consult, engage and attend to the needs of all age groups have greater chances of fostering intergenerational understanding, empathy and satisfaction with life. Such societies share both the positive aspects of life and the challenges in confronting life's difficulties. Experimental projects exploring inter-generational interaction between kindergarten children and adults in aged care have demonstrated the benefits not only accrue for the children and the aged care residents, but also the families of both (Skropeta et al., 2014). Similar projects occur in primary schools where intergenerational engagement has welcomed the wisdom of older adults in tutoring and mentoring young children (Parisi et al., 2009). Instances of these projects and the measurement of their success in fostering social and emotional well-being have been published in academic publications, newspaper headlines, and TV programs, with many quietly becoming a way of being in enlightened communities.

Providing environments that seek to support healthy ageing is the responsibility of the whole community. Not to do so is tantamount to discrimination against our older selves. All levels of government and services need inclusive mindsets in both planning and designing physical environments that acknowledge the special needs of all age groups and all abilities in both cities and in remote and rural environments. This means that planning groups include in their membership diverse representation so that forward planning is not about 'doing to', but 'doing with' the elderly, disabled and marginalised. The inclusion of the voice of older people in creating age friendly environments captures the spirit of Charlton's (1998) book *Nothing about us without us* that argues for greater representation of the voices of people with disabilities. Not to undertake inclusive planning processes and representation is tantamount to 'privileged irresponsibility' (Tronto, 1993) on the part of leaders and managers of environmental and service provision planning. Tronto described privileged irresponsibility as that which occurs when those with power fail to notice the uneven distribution of resources and care, and ignoring the hardships experienced by those at the margins of society.

11 What Changes Are Needed?

We need to reconceptualise ageing by recognising that people are not defined by their age and that their needs are diverse. Public policy alone is not enough. Education of the wider community aided by the public media is needed to develop a critical awareness of the damaging impact of images and discourses that perpetuate negative stereotypes about ageing at a time when older citizens are being challenged by the potential onset of chronic illnesses, disability, frailty and dependence. The changes required in political and public thinking and the practices of service agencies regarding ageing and aged care are fundamental and should impact every aspect of life. Podger (2016) argues, that we need to stop thinking of demographics of ageing populations and of the changes as representing a crisis,

> These changes will be permanent, requiring fundamental and ongoing re-conceptions of the life-span of individuals and the age profile of societies, affecting family and community relationships as well as individuals' planning for lifetime wellbeing. We need perhaps to consider the idea of 'multiple beings' over the life-span with individuals choosing more and different roles at different ages. (p. 303)

Action and effort are needed to project more positive and more realistic conceptions and images of ageing, such that retired people can recognise themselves as they mostly are, namely, wise, caring, empathetic, resilient, active, engaged and contributing economic and social benefits to society. Let that become the new self-fulfilling prophecy. Society at large needs to be aware that older adults' needs are diverse and reasonable and that they have a right to expect caring support once they can no longer manage alone. This awareness should bring with it sensitivity to the unique needs of diverse communities including multicultural differences (Xiao et al., 2017), the imposts of remoteness and living in rural communities, and to the particular legal, social and emotional challenges experienced by Lesbian, Gay, Bisexual, Transgender and Intersex people. Changes should actively protect the human and civil rights of older adults to ensure they live their later lives in dignity and without the destructive impact of ageism. When those who have not reached the 'third' or 'forth' age advocate and support the needs of older adults they are creating the basis of long-term support for their older selves.

Any interventions that are introduced in the care of older citizens should ensure that familiar, social connections can be sustained and new social networks are fostered, that can assist older adults to maintain and develop a sense of autonomy, purpose, interest and meaning around their activities. (O'Rourke et al., 2018). We need to capture and value the inherent wisdom in older people by fostering intergenerational engagement and exchange. Exemplars of intergenerational programs, some detailed in public media programs such are the integration of care for pre-school children and aged care residents, and older adults as guides and mentors to youth, appear to hold considerable promise as a means of achieving these goals (Parisi et al., 2009). Employers have a role to play in showing leadership by addressing the marginalisation of older people in the workplace and publicly recognising the value older people bring because of their accumulated wisdom of experience and stability. Importantly, older people themselves must become engaged with their own emancipation from ageist stereotypes. In doing so they must challenge their own strongly held stereotypes and assumptions about what older people can and cannot do. This is not only important for one's own health and wellbeing, but also has the power to influence how younger people feel about ageing and older people.

12 Conclusion

The ageing of populations world-wide does not need to be regarded as a calamity. Regarded wisely, the potential contributions of this growing segment of all populations has abundant 'wisdom of experience' to offer that can assist their communities to live with uncertainty and ambiguity through turbulent times. Globally, all governments and communities have access to extensive information, guidance and resources from the UN and the WHO that can be translated and transformed to meet local needs particularly those that must address sites of poverty and inequality that some older people currently experience. Accessing, interpreting these resources and devising wise plans for their implementation at the local level must include older citizens themselves. Their collective and unique life histories are important in shaping their futures and the unique futures of those that will follow.

References

Abdi, S., Spann, A., Borilovic, J., de Witte, L., & Hawley, M. (2019). Understanding the care and support needs of older people: A scoping review and categorisation using the WHO International Classification of Functioning, Disability and Health Framework (ICF). *BMC Geriatrics, 19*(1), 1–15.

Ardelt, M. (1997). Wisdom and life satisfaction in old age. *The Journals of Gerontology Series B: Psychological Sciences and Social Sciences, 52*(1), P15–P27.

Ardelt, M. (2008). Self-development through selflessness: The paradoxical process of growing wiser. In H. A. Wayment & J. J. Bauer (Eds.), *Decade of behavior: Transcending self-interest: Psychological explorations of the quiet ego* (pp. 221–233). American Psychological Association.

Ardelt, M. (2011a). The measurement of wisdom: A commentary on Taylor, Bates, and Webster's comparison of the SAWS and 3D-WS. *Experimental Aging Research, 37*(2), 241–255.

Ardelt, M. (2011b). Wisdom, age, and well-being. In W. K. Schaie & S. L. Willis (Eds.), *Handbook of the psychology of aging* (7th ed., pp. 279–291). Elsevier Science & Technology.

Australian Association of Social Work. (2013). *Ageing in Australia: Position paper.* https://www.aasw.asn.au/document/item/4356

Baltes, P. B., & Smith, J. (1990). Toward a psychology of wisdom and its ontogenesis. In R. J. Sternberg (Ed.), *Wisdom: Its nature, origins and development* (pp. 87–120). Cambridge University Press.

Benoit-Dubé, L., Jean, E. K., Aguilar, M. A., Zuniga, A.-M., Bier, N., Couture, M., Lussier, M., Lajoie, X., & Belchior, P. (2020). What facilitates the acceptance of technology to promote social participation in later life? A systematic review. *Disability and Rehabilitation: Assistive Technology*, 1–11.

Bruggencate, T. T., Luijkx, K. G., & Sturm, J. (2018). Social needs of older people: A systematic literature review. *Ageing and Society, 38*(9), 1745–1770.

Brugman, G. M. (2006). Twenty: Wisdom and aging. In J. E. Birren, K. W. Schaie, R. P. Abeles, M. Gatz, & T. A. Salthouse (Eds.), *Handbook of the psychology of aging* (6th ed., pp. 445–476). Academic Press.

Butler, R. N. (1980). Ageism: A foreword. *Journal of Social Issues, 36*(2), 8–11.

Charles, S. T., & Carstensen, L. L. (2010). Social and emotional aging. *Annual Review of Psychology, 61*(1), 383–409.

Charlton, J. I. (1998). *Nothing about us without us: Disability oppression and empowerment.* University of California Press.

De Vaus, D. A., Stanton, D. I., & Gray, M. (2003). *Measuring the value of unpaid household, caring and voluntary work of older Australians.* Australian Institute of Family Studies.

Dionigi, R. A. (2015). Stereotypes of aging: Their effects on the health of older adults. *Journal of Geriatrics, 9.* https://doi.org/10.1155/2015/954027

Fung, H. H. (2013). Aging in culture. *The Gerontologist, 53*(3), 369–377.

Gide, A., & Frechtman, B. (2012). *Oscar Wilde: Reminiscences.* Philosophical Library/Open Road.

Gong, C., & Kendig, H. (2016). Ageing and social change in Australia. In H. Kendig, P. McDonald, & J. Piggott (Eds.), *Population ageing and Australia's future* (pp. 19–45). Australian University Press.

Gratton, L., & Scott, A. (2016, November 14). Our assumptions about old and young workers are wrong. *Harvard Business Review.* https://hbr.org/2016/11/our-assumptions-about-old-and-young-workers-are-wrong

Healy, J. (2004). *The benefits of an ageing population.* Australia Institute.

Human Mortality Database. (2015). *Berkeley and Rostock: University of California and Max Planck Institute for Demographic Research.* https://www.mortality.org/

Jalland, P. (2015). *Old age in Australia: A history.* Melbourne University Press.

Jeste, D. V., Ardelt, M., Blazer, D., Kraemer, H. C., Vaillant, G., & Meeks, T. W. (2010). Expert consensus on characteristics of wisdom: A Delphi method study. *The Gerontologist, 50*(5), 668–680.

Latulippe, K., Hamel, C., & Giroux, D. (2020). Co-design to support the development of inclusive eHealth tools for caregivers of functionally dependent older persons: Social justice design. *Journal of Medical Internet Research, 22*(11), e18399–e18399.

Mannheim, K. (1952). The problem of generations. In P. Kecskemeti (Ed.), *Essays on the sociology of knowledge* (pp. 276–320). Routledge & Kegan Paul.

Minichiello, V., & Coulson, I. (2005). *Contemporary issues in gerontology: Promoting positive ageing*. Allen & Unwin.

Novak, M. (2012). *Issues in aging* (3rd ed.). Pearson.

O'Loughlin, K., & Kendig, H. (2017). Attitudes to ageing. In K. O'Loughlin, C. Browning, & H. Kendig (Eds.), *Ageing in Australia* (pp. 29–45). Springer.

Orem, D. (1991). *Nursing: Concepts of practice*. Mosby.

O'Rourke, H. M., Collins, L., & Sidani, S. (2018). Interventions to address social connectedness and loneliness for older adults: A scoping review. *BMC Geriatrics, 18*(1), 1–13.

Parisi, J. M., Rebok, G. W., Carlson, M. C., Fried, L. P., Seeman, T. E., Tan, E. J., Tanner, E. K., & Piferi, R. L. (2009). Can the wisdom of aging be activated and make a difference societally? *Educational Gerontology, 35*(10), 867–879.

Podger, A. (2016). Conclusions: An historic triumph that presents big challenges for public policy. In H. Kendig, P. McDonald, & J. Piggott (Eds.), *Population ageing and Australia's future* (pp. 303–312). ANU Press for the Academy of Social Sciences in Australia.

Rasi, P., Lindberg, J., & Airola, E. (2021). Older service users' experiences of learning to use eHealth applications in sparsely populated healthcare settings in Northern Sweden and Finland. *Educational Gerontology, 47*(1), 25–35.

Ranzijn, R., Harford, J., & Andrews, G. (2002). Ageing and the economy: Costs and benefits. *Australasian Journal on Ageing, 21*(3), 145–151.

Riley, M. W. (1978). Aging, social change, and the power of ideas. *Daedalus, 107*(4), 39–52.

Robine, J.-M., & Michel, J.-P. (2004). Looking forward to a general theory on population aging. *The Journals of Gerontology: Series A, 59*(6), M590–M597.

Skropeta, C. M., Colvin, A., & Sladen, S. (2014). An evaluative study of the benefits of participating in intergenerational playgroups in aged care for older people. *BMC Geriatrics, 14*(1), 109.

Sundberg, L., Agahi, N., Fritzell, J., & Fors, S. (2018). Why is the gender gap in life expectancy decreasing? The impact of age- and cause-specific mortality in Sweden 1997–2014. *International Journal of Public Health, 63*(6), 673–681.

The Benevolent Society. (2017). *The drivers of ageism: Foundational research to inform a national advocacy campaign for tackling ageism and its impacts in Australia.*

https://d3n8a8pro7vhmx.cloudfront.net/benevolent/pages/393/attachments/original/1538977350/Ageism_Full_Report_Final.pdf?1538977350=

Tronto, J. C. (1993). *Moral boundaries: A political argument for an ethic of care.* Routledge.

Turnbull, S., Cabral, C., Hay, A., & Lucas, P. J. (2020). Health equity in the effectiveness of web-based health interventions for the self-care of people with chronic health conditions: Systematic review. *Journal of Medical Internet Research, 22*(6), e17849–e17849.

United Nations Department of Economic and Social Affairs. (2019). *World population ageing 2019: Highlights.* https://www.un.org/en/development/desa/population/publications/pdf/ageing/WorldPopulationAgeing2019-Highlights.pdf

Vaillant, G. E. (2002). *Aging well: Surprising guideposts to a happier life from the landmark Harvard study of adult development.* Little Brown.

Vos, W. H., van Boekel, L. C., Janssen, M. M., Leenders, R. T. A. J., & Luijkx, K. G. (2020). Exploring the impact of social network change: Experiences of older adults ageing in place. *Health & Social Care in the Community, 28*(1), 116–126.

Walsh, R. (2015). What is wisdom? Cross-cultural and cross-disciplinary syntheses. *Review of General Psychology, 19*(3), 278–293.

Wrath, L. (2016). The WHO global network of age-friendly cities and communities: Origins, developments and challenges. In T. Moulaert & S. Garon (Eds.), *Age-friendly cities and communities in international comparison* (pp. 37–46). Springer International Publishing.

World Health Organization (WHO). (2002). *Active ageing: A policy framework.* https://apps.who.int/iris/bitstream/handle/10665/67215/WHO_NMH_NPH_02.8.pdf;jsessionid=608573E506FBE2F0E6D9996E8771FB2B?sequence=1

World Health Organization (WHO). (2015). *World report on ageing and health.* Author.

Xiao, L. D., Willis, E., Harrington, A., Gillham, D., De Bellis, A., Morey, W., & Jeffers, L. (2017). Resident and family member perceptions of cultural diversity in aged care homes. *Nursing & Health Sciences, 19*(1), 59–65.

CHAPTER 20

Young People Shaping Wise Futures

Skye Tasker and Philippa Collin

Abstract

Young people play a vital role in shaping wiser futures. This chapter critically reflects on ways of conceptualising youth leadership to unsettle assumptions about 'youth' and 'leadership' that are entrenched in scholarly policy and popular debates. By analysing the diverse ways young people create change by subverting the 'normal ways of doing things' we propose a notion of 'youthful acts of leadership' and illustrate these with three case studies from the Australian context. We argue that greater attention to how 'youthful acts of leadership' matter as a positive force for change is essential to shaping wiser futures.

Keywords

youth leadership – citizenship – resistance – participation – recognition

1 Introduction

Engaging with young people's contribution to shaping wise futures, as a practice requires us to challenge past assumptions of 'youth' and 'leadership'. It is a practice, which requires wisdom from new and diverse perspectives in order to understand complex problems and achieve social change. In this chapter we argue that in order to learn from and be guided by young people, we must expand our conception of youth leadership from individual acts by the most visible and exceptional young people (who we most certainly admire and can also learn from), to encompass every day and collective practices of resistance and change. Moreover, we propose that, to reimagine our world, we need to work with and be guided by all those who will be there to witness the future. Leadership, therefore, is not merely a set of skills, capabilities or practices, but a politic. We posit that politics of leadership must, necessarily, challenge dominant ideas, power structures and routine ways of thinking and doing that order society.

 | DOI: 10.1163/9789004505544_024

To do so, throughout this chapter we draw on Isin's (2008) notion of 'acts of citizenship' to examine how young people, and the 'scenes' they 'bring into being', challenge the status quo. We explore three examples of how young people are doing this: for climate justice, justice for women and victims of sexual violence, and for Indigenous Australians. Through these examples, we develop a contextual understanding of current and recognised youth leaders and propose new ways of exploring and conceptualising youth leadership. By analysing how some young people subvert the 'normal ways of doing things', we propose a notion of 'youthful acts of leadership'. We conclude with a discussion of the theoretical, ethical and practical considerations that the examples discussed offer for understanding why 'youthful acts of leadership' matter as a positive force for shaping wiser futures. We suggest that 'acts of leadership' emphasise the politicised relations which constitute how we recognise and respond to those engaged in social change. We argue that acts of leadership are inherently political processes, agonistic and contentious.

In writing this chapter we are conscious that as authors we approach this task with specific investments and from particular vantage points. Our views reflect those of a 'young person-scholar' and an 'adult ally-scholar' whose knowledge is built predominantly on western ways of knowing and influenced by decades of advocacy, child rights and youth movements. Our aim, therefore, is not to have the definitive word on 'youth leadership' but to advance ways to learn from and amplify the role of young people in achieving wiser futures: by attending to the new 'sites' of knowing and knowledge-exchange that come into being when young people challenge the status quo. Additionally, as co-authors, we incorporated an iterative and reflexive approach to learn from and to ethically respond to current and impactful youth led movements, social justice issues of our time and each other. Regular dialogue and critical reflection with our embodied and philosophical experience of current events during the process of writing this chapter reflected hearing and knowledge-sharing inherent in wiser practices. We use these reflections to situate and contextualise the chapter, increase our capacity building and explore the ways we all collectively contribute to and enact social change.

2 A Critical Reflection on Contemporary Notions of Youth Leadership

In January 2021, we witnessed 26-year-old Grace Tame being awarded 'Australian of the Year' and her stirring and awakening speech about the power of being heard. Grace Tame has been a driving force in the #LetHerSpeak campaign and an advocate for victims of sexual assault to have the right to speak openly about their experiences of sexual abuse. From her own experiences of abuse, Grace has passionately fought for and contributed to a movement of women asserting their right to be heard for more than 11 years. Now, her personal and political fight, hard work, persistence against adversity and vehement leadership has been acknowledged on a national scale.

Her fight has not been linear or purely skills based. It has been turbulent and influenced by diverse actors, changing socio-political conditions regarding the treatment of women in society and the inevitable relapses which occur when an individual, their family and community recover from complex trauma. And yet we wonder; is being awarded for her individual achievements in the form of 'Australian of the Year' the political acknowledgement that is required for the cause and change she represents?

As a young woman, Skye has followed Grace's story and has been deeply affected by her work and the growing movement of women who are finding their voice. However, Skye watched Grace's speech with conflict in her heart. From a personal perspective, she wondered how we acknowledge as a country that Grace was not on that podium by herself, but in fact joined by a "chorus of voices that will not be silenced" (Tame, 2021). All voices which have, and continue to rise up, in many nuanced ways, in everyday life, against extreme and intersectional adversity.

From a theoretical perspective Skye pondered the impact of this type of award and acknowledgement for young leaders in our communities. On one hand, Grace's courage, persistence, dedication and continued fight for systemic change since she was a child, has propelled her into the national limelight. Her story is inspirational, and her achievement is exemplary. But on the other hand; what is the toll of asking an individual to bear this burden, representation and responsibility? And what is the effect on those young people who are not heard, acknowledged, or afforded the same social support to fight for their human rights and for justice?

Is it neoliberal 'leadership qualities' that should be acknowledged in the form of an award to celebrate an individual's remarkable achievements? Do such awards appropriate forms of resistance and calls for change by absorbing them back into the institutions responsible for the perpetuation of injustice? Or should all the actors and small acts of leadership involved in creating social change be acknowledged? How can true acknowledgement of the "chorus of voices who will not be silenced" that Grace dedicates her award to in her speech be the subject of recognition?

In relation to young people, further questions arise. What assumptions underpinning concepts of 'youth' and 'leadership' must be challenged to open up the possibilities of youthful knowledge and action to create wiser futures? And what can the example of Grace being awarded "Australian of the Year" in

2021 (seven years after the #metoo movement was created by Tarana Burke and the #LetHerSpeak campaign initiated in 2019) tell us about the politics of youth leadership in this current political climate?

This chapter is dedicated to conceptualising and illuminating youthful acts of leadership for creating a wiser future.

3 Contesting Ideas of 'Youth' and 'Leadership'

While young people are some of the most affected by the short and long-term consequences of social challenges such as poverty, health inequalities and climate change, they are also the most disenfranchised in society. Young people are intensely governed by the state and aggressively targeted by markets, however in most countries they are not accorded full political rights and recognition until they are 18 years old. Even then, young people's relative economic disadvantage means they are sidelined by other political interests. Under the conditions of advanced liberal capitalism, young people – especially young women – are expected to self-manage the intensifying risks of contemporary society (Harris, 2004, 2012). Their failure to successfully complete education, gain employment, contribute positively to the community or maintain good health are often deemed to be the result of poor choices, regardless of structural inequalities (Furlong & Cartmel, 2007).

Contradictory forces similarly constitute youth leadership in social change. Firstly, it is heavily proscribed and managed through top-down adult-led processes and programs that say what leadership should look like (Bessant, 2004; Collin, 2015; Harris, 2012; Vromen, 2003). However, when young people challenge corporate policy or social injustices, they are routinely dismissed and misrecognised as unimportant, ineffectual or misguided (Bessant & Lohmeyer, 2021; Walsh & Black, 2018). Nevertheless, in Australia young people have been heavily involved in – and sometimes at the forefront of – initiatives and movements to address complex problems such as social justice, mental health and climate change (Collin, 2015; Walsh & Black, 2011). These dynamics demonstrate the inherently political nature of 'youth leadership'. We now unpack this politics of youth leadership, beginning with the contested concepts, 'youth' and 'leadership'.

4 The Concept of 'Youth'

The term 'youth' is a social category that is regularly used, yet ambiguously defined and understood. Youth, as a concept, has emerged from different disciplinary, epistemological and theoretical standpoints. Influenced by western psychology and developmental sociology in the early 1900s, youth became understood as a universal, biological stage with a set of pathways and transition points into adulthood (Hall, 1904; Piaget, 1972). During the 1960s, studies of social reproduction and transformation challenged essentialist accounts of youth by pointing to how social structures impacted on young people's experiences and opportunities (Allen, 1968). Critiques of essentialist conceptions of youth highlight how they impose normative behaviours and attitudes associated with successful attainment of adulthood, pathologising 'risk' and proscribing interventions to 'correct' individual or group behaviour (White & Wyn, 2004). In contrast with developmentalist constructions of transitions, a sociological understanding of youth considers the social structures and specific contexts young people negotiate as they experience 'emerging adulthood'. These include the contradictory expectations of individualism and making 'choices' about life while being simultaneously subjected to social forces such as class, gender and culture (Morgan & Idriss, 2012; Threadgold, 2018).

Contemporary sociological studies of youth transitions also show the nonlinearity of emerging adulthood. These studies explore how many of the social factors and experiences of adulthood are unattainable to young people well into their 40s due to social and economic changes beyond their control (Furlong & Cartmel, 2007). Along with problematising the linear and 'naturalistic' idea of a 'normal' trajectory towards adulthood, youth studies challenge the very notion of "youth as liminal" and "adulthood as stable" (Theadgold, 2018, p. 15). However, the idea of transitions 'as development' is powerfully reproduced through social institutions such as education – for instance constructing the 'young person' as a site for training and capacity building – rather than acknowledging existing capabilities or young people as change makers in their own right and time of life. As such, the concept of transitions is most useful, rendering visible the *struggles* of youth to navigate and contest normative social and moral expectations as they move from one fantastical but proscribed 'state' to another: child to adult, present to future, minor to citizen (Third et al., 2019; Threadgold, 2018). Acknowledging youth as a social and political construct also allows us to explore how particular visions of youth have limited the way that youth leadership is fostered and acknowledged in society.

5 The Political Construction of Youth

The experience of youth is not natural, but shaped by individual agency, social structures and macro processes such as globalisation and individualisation

(Harris, 2012), policies and laws of a place (White et al., 2017), media portrayals and in the way stories of young people's actions and activities are ignored or mis-told (Bessant & Lohmeyer, 2021). Young people's role in social change, thus, hinges on the way youth is constructed within existing power structures from the local to the global. For example, since 2015, the United Nations (UN) has recognised and advocated for the role of young people in social change and contributing to global development, such as creating a Special Envoy on Youth, youth campaigning platforms and global youth conferences. However, such models situate the role of young people within processes that replicate existing institutions and power structures, which reproduce entrenched ideologies already inherent in international policy and governance processes (Bersaglio et al., 2015; Fergusson & Yeates, 2013; Kwon, 2018; Sukarieh, 2012; Sukarieh & Tannock, 2008). Studying youth participation in UN initiatives, Kwon (2018) highlights tensions in the way youth and leadership are constructed and how these affect meaningful youth participation and engagement with global development issues in the UN. She argues that the expectation that good young leaders will participate in existing platforms is a form of neoliberal self-governance: young people internalise expectations of particular 'expert' forms of participation:

> [The] ideal global youth citizen-subject today is marked by one's enactment of compulsory participation to instrumentally advance one's life chances against the insecurities of social risks posed on an individual in the retreat of state provisions. (Kwon, 2018, p. 13)

This reflects a pervasive neoliberal ideology, which propagates internalised self-governance and rationalises inequality for the sake of competition and market growth (Brown, 2006). When youth is constructed as "asset", "risk" and "good citizens-in-the-making" (Bersaglio et al., 2015, p. 57), young people are positioned as neoliberal subjects.

Youth as a category is, therefore, leveraged to (paradoxically) both relieve and create a particular set of social and political anxieties (Third et al., 2019; Woodman & Wyn, 2011). When young people are positioned as an 'asset' for achieving a 'good and just' society they soothe political concerns for the future. On the other hand, when they challenge adult-centric ideals of political participation in the form of digital engagement and disruptive activism, they are constructed as a 'risk' to traditional societal expectations and practices (Third et al., 2019). For example, students involved in the #SchoolStrike4Climate express desire to participate in shaping society and addressing complex problems associated with climate change. However, they are also portrayed as disruptive and as anti-social for skipping school and challenging existing processes and institutions of policy making (Collin & Matthews, 2021).

Such tensions show how the capacities and expectations of young people are performed within social and political contexts through policy and popular discourse. Understanding youth as conceptually and politically contested, therefore, opens up possibilities to 'see' the experiences of young people differently in relation to a multitude of social forces, structures, relations and associated concepts, including leadership.

6 The Concept of 'Leadership'

Once attributed to a social position or natural gift one was born with, leadership was thought to be a trait one embodied (MacNeil, 2006). During the mid-twentieth century, the increasing popularity of psychoanalytic and behavioural theories in psychology shifted the focus of leadership from individual agents to *a process* reliant on feedback and social context. According to MacNeil (2006) leadership has come to be understood as:

> … a relational process combining ability (knowledge, skills, and talents) with authority (voice, influence, and decision-making power) to positively influence and impact diverse individuals, organizations, and communities. (p. 29)

Although MacNeil (2006) argues for a relational understanding of leadership, whereby its constitutive parts can be recognised in places where change takes place, leadership is still seen as something that is 'done' principally by individuals. Even in more recent understandings of leadership, which highlight contextual influences on leadership, and the becoming of leaders (Oc, 2018), there is a continued emphasis on individualised notions of leadership. Moreover, the requirement for leadership to manifest as 'talent', 'influence' and 'positive' impact excludes ways of being that are currently not acknowledged – and are actively silenced – due to entrenched social, political and cultural norms, institutions and structures.

Theories of distributed leadership challenge binary notions of leader and follower, to explore how agency manifests among actors to influence social change. Distributed leadership refers to a decentralised notion of leadership which focuses on the relationships and interactions between subjects, rather than the hierarchical, top-down notion of leader as commander, and followers as passive recipients (Chatwani, 2018; Spillane, 2012). Ideas of distributed leadership also bring into view the role of materials and organisational structures that are constitutive of practice (Chatwani, 2018). Associated concepts such as 'counterpublics' (Fraser, 1990) further help recognise alternative spaces and actors through which social change can be differently envisaged (O'Donoghue, 2006). Counterpublics reflect alternative ways of being and acting including everyday acts of resistance that can be viewed by the mainstream as 'anti-social'. For example, climate activist Greta Thunberg's initial school strike on the steps of the Swedish parliament was met with disapproval from many teachers, passers-by, commentators and politicians. Similarly, when Aboriginal students do not attend school, or challenge police authority, their behaviour is frequently characterised as anti-social and a reflection of bad choices by bad individuals.

To achieve more equitable futures, it is precisely the inequalities and injustices that are perpetuated through entrenched norms and values that must be surfaced and challenged. Young people play active roles as agents of change even when that agency is uncomfortable or undermined. How, then, can we recognise and respond to less visible and 'leaderless' forms of organising and action favoured by many young people today? How can we consider or engage with those forms that are deemed 'anti-social' or challenge the status quo? In the next section we explore the constraints of contemporary discourses of youth leadership.

7 Problematising Youth Leadership

Despite the potential for youth leadership to be understood in more radical terms, it is commonly conceptualised within the youth development literature as skills acquisition and individual attainment (Dempster et al., 2011). Problematically this framing of youth leadership limits our understanding of how youth have been at the forefront of leading collective movements on issues from mental health to climate justice (Collin, 2015; Walsh & Black, 2009, 2011). Rather than a force for social change, young people in general, and as leaders, are largely constructed as labour potential (Collin, 2015). Such policy, and popular discourses of youth leadership further fail to challenge the adult-centricity of policy domains and workplaces (Houghton & DiLiello, 2010) and are exacerbated by a lack of youth perspectives and concern for their broader influence (Collin, 2015; MacNeil, 2006).

By contrast, the literature on youth participation, which has been substantially influenced by critical studies of student leadership, reveals a much wider range of concerns (Black et al., 2014). These include the ways young people's participation (and disengagement) actively contests, positively shapes and demands responsiveness from adult-centric institutions and processes (Collin, 2015: Farthing, 2010; Harris, 2012; Pickard & Bessant, 2018). For example, while student leadership often aims to recognise 'voice' and provide for young people's active role in influencing decisions, it does so for students who fit within the confines and power dynamics of the school as an adult-run institution. In response, Mayes et al. (2019) argue for a reconceptualisation of childhood within the school environment, to promote youth participation and 'voice' within schools via interventions such as peer mentoring. Such programs can disrupt the adult/child power imbalances and encourage young people to work together to influence school reform (Mayes et al., 2019). Research, which promotes such initiations in a local setting, can allow young people to connect their experience as a citizen of a school community to their wider membership and rights in society (Black et al., 2014).

However, while youth leadership could be a concept through which to envision alternative futures by drawing on young people's perspectives about what is needed in the present, young people as leaders continue to be discursively constructed as 'futurity' (Third et al., 2019). They are evermore 'monetised' within leadership programs and services (de St Croix et al., 2020) further emphasising the economic potential of youth, rather than existing influence and decision-making capability. We argue that restricting youth leadership to operate within discourses that define youth as (future economic) subjects and citizens, inhibits opportunities to truly understand how acts of youth leadership are already creating social change. Instead, we argue for a much more radical approach that transcends existing theories of youth leadership by paying attention to the ways young people can and do shape wiser futures. We propose that by attending to instances where young people are calling for change by subverting the 'normal' way of doing things, we can inform more fruitful and innovative thinking about the role of leadership. To do this, we turn to sociologist Engin Isin whose theories of 'acts of citizenship' help us reimagine how alternative forms of leadership manifest in everyday life.

8 From Young Leaders to 'Youthful Acts of Leadership'

To understand how youth leadership might co-constitute wiser futures, we argue for the need to recognise and respond to young people's leadership practices that break with established (adult) discourses of both youth and leadership. This involves focusing on how young people push back on the expectations that are set for them and in ways that unsettle dominant forms of knowledge and initiate processes of social change. In his work on citizenship, Isin (2008) argues that research has struggled to move beyond accepted notions of citizenship as either legal status or the 'habitus' – or 'enduring dispositions' – that maintains cultural expectations of a political community (Bourdieu, 1994). As such, scholarship has failed to really explain how transformations in political communities occur – whereby people make 'rights claims' by breaking with the expected routines of behaviour (Isin, 2008). We argue that the same can be said for youth leadership, which to date has focused on increasing the status of young people within adult discourses and institutions without sufficiently challenging the legitimacy of the norms and values on which they are based.

Isin (2008) proposes the concept of 'acts of citizenship', which are related to, but distinct from actors and actions:

> … an enactment inevitably creates a scene where there are selves and others defined in relation to each other. (p. 18)

Isin (2008) argues that in contrast with citizenship, which depends on citizens complying with expected routines of behaviour, "acts of citizenship" are the "rupture in the given" (pp. 24–25). Moreover, he proposes that acts are different from actions and actors, instead describing an 'act' as "as an expression of the need to be heard" (p. 24).

This desire to be heard through breaking the 'habitus' of youth and leadership is one way we can distinguish 'youthful acts of leadership'. For example, the School Strike 4 Climate instigated by Greta Thunberg has been replicated around the world by millions of school students all expressing this desire to be heard. Youth leadership on climate action, therefore, cannot be reduced to one or several people in the climate movement as it is a collective expression and act, evolving over time and space. While Isin (2008) suggests that acts are iterative and multiple and have moments where they start and end, he also emphasises that acts have an "internal continuity and accrete over time" (p. 23). Building on Isin we add that while citizenship is about making claims about otherness, for leadership to have substantive value in materialising better futures, it must be rethought as making claims about – and therefore generating – new forms of solidarity.

In the next section we consider three case studies of the way young people enact resistance to entwined systems of oppression that play out in the routines of everyday life. From this we propose rebuilding a concept of 'youthful acts of leadership' that can support the practice of wise futures.

9 Resistance and Leadership – Learning from 'Youthful Acts of Citizenship'

In this section we present three case studies that have been selected because each example illuminates where young people engage in everyday – and sometimes collective – actions that challenge or expose inequity and injustice. These case studies also demonstrate 'youthful acts of leadership' that unlock potential to facilitate social change and wiser futures. These acts are sometimes simple, or they can be more complex. In essence, they are acts, which expand our understanding by disrupting assumptions about what 'youth' and 'leadership' are and their role in creating social change. They also expose the political nature of youth leadership for a wiser future. Each example demonstrates young people's expression of the need to be heard on what is wrong in the world, as well as what kinds of change are required to achieve more equitable and just futures.

9.1 *Case Study 1: Breaking the Silence – The Need to Be Heard as a Rights Claim*

> We do transform as individuals, and we do transform as a community. When I first reported I was shamed and ridiculed by some, but now my truth is helping to reconnect us. (Tame, 2021)

Grace's story was introduced at the start of this chapter to raise key questions and to propose new ways of embracing youth leadership in the future. When Grace was 15 years of age in 2010, she became victim to grooming and repeated sexual abuse by a man called Nicolaas Bester, who was her maths teacher at the elite St Michael's Collegiate Girls' school in Hobart. A year later, Grace reported this abuse to the school and Nicolaas was charged, spending two and a half years in jail. Shortly after his release from jail, Nicholaas was interviewed and shared his version of events with multiple media outlets. When Grace went to share her side, she discovered that it was against the law: out-dated gagging laws in the Australian state of Tasmania, denied victims of convicted offenders the right to be named in the media (Australian Broadcasting Corporation, 2019). Any media outlet who named a victim could be liable for significant fines and therefore they are required to keep victims anonymous, blurred out and, in effect, invisible to the public eye.

Invisibility is a form of silencing and Grace's experience depicts one of many where young people and women are silenced from sharing their thoughts, opinions and stories. As she explains:

> Communication breeds understanding, and understanding is the foundation of progress. Lived experience informs structural and social change. When we share, we heal. (Tame, 2021)

Grace's story contests understandings of youth and leadership in many ways. Initially, her fight to share her version of events from a childhood experience challenged the notion that young people should not have a voice and that they need to be protected by remaining silent and compliant. Her story, instead, revealed the importance of young people feeling able to disclose violence against them. As a young person and women speaking out about what is a deeply affecting and challenging issue in our society, Grace expands and pushes back against maintaining the 'status quo' of being feminine, quiet and respectable. Using her intellect and vulnerability, Grace has drawn on her personal experience to question, educate and challenge how power is distributed to adults over children, which can exacerbate violence that is perpetuated by this abuse of power. She advocates not only for her voice and experience to be heard, but those of every person who has first-hand experience that can lead to social change. She advocates for first-hand experiences to be the key when educating people and institutions about the insidious nature of grooming and issues in society that are uncomfortable and unknown.

Leadership ideals that render invisible young people's experiences, opinions and values, limit our solutions to complex societal problems. As Grace explains:

> Just as the impacts of evil are borne by all of us, so too are solutions borne of all of us. (Tame, 2021)

Exploring youth leadership through this perspective, it becomes apparent that not only do diverse voices and experiences need to be heard and acknowledged, but also that we are *all* responsible for social change. Everyone has a part to play in creating wiser futures. So why should this responsibility be seen as the burden of any one individual? And how do political acknowledgements such as 'Australian of the Year' perpetuate these ideals?

Australian of the Year awards honour "our most exceptional Australians".[1] Since the award ceremony's inception in 1960, this event is one of the largest, most recognised political acknowledgements in the country. This ceremony is designed to spotlight individuals who are exemplary in their efforts to contribute to society and facilitate social change. While all are worthy and deserving, it is only in the speeches of some recipients that the collective efforts that have supported their personal journeys are acknowledged and provoke interest in the social movements which have propelled their causes.

Grace acknowledges the multiple actors who were involved in her story. The ones that made her achievements possible and supported her to not only recover from trauma, but to draw on her experiences to facilitate social change. She pays respect to those that have come before her and others in society who have different identities and intersectional experiences: the people who represent the "many voices, yet to be heard" (Tame, 2021). She also acknowledges the other survivors who are and have been vital to fighting for change. The #LetHerSpeak campaign which was initiated in 2019 by Nina Furnell and the #metoo movement initiated in 2006 fundamentally disrupted organisations and institutions that covered up abuse and exposed predators who have benefitted from living in a patriarchal society. We can learn from these acknowledgements that leadership is not an individual pursuit but, rather, a collective endeavour. The need to recognise all voices in our society and the relational components of leadership can aid our imagination of youth leadership for shaping wiser futures.

9.2 *Case Study 2: The Intergenerational and Relational Threads of Youth Leadership*

> … what I want is a normal life of just being me. And what I mean by me is, I want to be an Aborigine. (Dujuan Hoosan, as quoted in Newell, 2019)

We have come to know Dujuan and his story through the 2019 documentary *In My Blood It Runs*. This documentary follows the everyday life of Dujuan Hoosan, a 10-year-old Arrente boy growing up in Alice Springs to unpack some of complex issues regarding the mistreatment of Indigenous peoples in Australia. A grassroots project, this documentary explores the everyday conflicts experienced by young people growing up Aboriginal in a Western colonised society and education system. Dujuan's everyday life includes the ever-present threat of being taken away from his family by the government. The documentary shows Dujuan's journey through primary school and his confusion and inner conflict about what he was learning in comparison to the knowledge and teachings of his family and community. It depicts Dujuan resisting the oppression of his people and misrecognition of their knowledge, whilst managing the constant threat of incarceration for children as young as 10-years-old from his community. His direct experience reflects a national issue of an overrepresentation of Indigenous people in Australia's gaols, as well as entrenched systemic racism and oppression in the education system and how this affects young peoples' health and education trajectories. In 2019, when the Australian government resisted change, Dujuan pursued his advocacy for lowering the age of criminalisation in Australia and spoke at the UN in Geneva to make heard the of his people. To this day he continues to be the representative for this entrenched issue in Australia.

Youthful acts of leadership can challenge the way young people have paradoxically been seen as 'at risk' and simultaneously 'a risk' to society. Dujuan often ran away from home to reclaim his freedom and feel the land under his feet. His mother Megan says, "He thinks he can go anywhere, he has got his own mind" (Newell, 2019). But she also explains that when young Indigenous kids are out after dark with no adult supervision (in overly policed communities such as Mparntwe otherwise known as Alice Springs), they are often confronted and escorted home or to the station in a paddy wagon. Here, Dujuan's acts of freedom place him at risk of being harmed and constructed as a risk to the community. By contrast, Dujuan sees himself as a defender of Aboriginal rights:

> The first one's that had the magic was the first people that had the land. History runs into all the Aboriginals, it travels all the way through to my blood pipes, all the way to the brain. And when I'm a man, I'm going to fight for rights for black people. When I see a crowd walking past, I am going to lift up my son and say 'Leave black kids alone!'. And I'll try to speak to the Prime Minister. I'm going to say 'Stop killing Aboriginal people!' (Dujuan Hoosan, as quoted in Newell, 2019)

Creative documentation and Dujuan's own words reveal his everyday youthful acts of leadership. This type of documentation provokes our imagination of the everyday acts of leadership, which are not always recognised. The documentary highlights Dujuan's everyday acts of resistance, just by being who he is, which are often invisible to our public eye and oppressed in our political systems. It also showcases the collective act of elevating young people's voices and everyday experiences, including Dujuan's mother, grandmother, teachers at school and Maya the producer of 'In my blood it runs'. All are actors integral to supporting and resisting social inequality and helping facilitate youthful acts of leadership in everyday settings, institutions and daily life.

Intergenerational forms of injustice for Indigenous people involve all people from the community, young and old, to have the right and need to be involved in healing and fighting for systemic change. Dujuan's story is one of the many experiences of intergenerational trauma for Indigenous children and adults who have been enslaved and incarcerated since colonisation. His acts of leadership exist in relation to his people, to his country and to the opposing forces of colonisation that seek to oppress him and his people. In this sense, acts of leadership transcend Dujuan as an individual young 'leader' fighting against all odds and occur through intergenerational acts of resistance that are inclusive of adults, children and ancestors alike:

> The healing power gives me a vision of everything. When I die my powers will decide to find a new person. Maybe take it on to my son, maybe my daughter. It's always here. (Dujuan Hoosan, as quoted in Newell, 2019)

Dujuan's story exposes unity and division, in a community, our nation and the world. The issue of Indigenous slavery, oppression and incarceration is not recent or bound to a single place or time. We have seen in Australia efforts to increase the minimum age of incarceration from 10 to 14 in policy, advocated for across the community and with guidance from the UN. This 'scene' has been sustained by solidarity between policy makers and advocacy groups who have put this agenda on the table. Catalysed by Dujuan's youthful acts of leadership, Maya Newell's ability to capture and communicate these disruptions and Dujuan's follow through to speak at the UN about his experience of growing up in Alice Springs have contributed to international effort for justice.

9.3 *Case Study 3: The Accumulation of Collective Expressions of Resistance*

On 15 March 2019, approximately 1.4 million young people and their allies gathered in towns and cities around the world to protest for Climate Change to be declared an international emergency. Instead of going to school, young people sacrificed a day of education, rebelling against normative practices of school adherence, to claim their right to a future that is safe and sustainable. The initial strike was made by school student Greta Thunberg who, since August 2018, has been sitting in front of the Swedish parliament with her 'Skolstrejk för klimatet' sign. This act, in combination with Greta's passionate demeanour and ability to communicate directly and succinctly, inspired many youthful acts of leadership regarding the need for Climate Action and propelled Greta into the limelight, speaking at the 2018 United Nations Climate Change Conference and getting into twitter debates with then-American president Donald Trump. Twitter was not just used for Greta to challenge the opinions of a lead political figure and adult authority, but was a platform for many young people to have the opportunity to voice their concerns to a global audience (Boulianne et al., 2020).

Inspired by Greta, in 2018, school students from Castlemaine, Victoria, organised with peers to demand that parliamentarians take urgent action on climate change. Organised by word of mouth, a group of classmates undertook eight weekly school strikes in the Castlemaine region, journeying every week to the offices of different members of parliament in their region. These initial strikes attracted between 20 and 50 students and drew the attention and support of the youth-led Australian Youth Climate Coalition (AYCC). Together with AYCC the Castlemaine students created a webpage for their movement, developed a campaign strategy, were trained in organising and, importantly, generated a social media presence to allow a decentralised model that would support students anywhere in Australia to organise and coordinate their own school strikes for climate action.

An online community grew, and students across Australia began to coordinate and organise in their own regions. On 30 November 2018, an estimated 15,000 students temporarily left school to attend rallies in 30 locations around Australia making rights claims to be heard on matters of climate justice. By 20 September 2019, School Strike 4 Climate Australia (SS4C) organisers reported 130 climate actions were held around Australia, from Adelaide to Tennant Creek to Launceston, and estimated attendance had grown to 350,000 people.[2] Even under the global pandemic of 2020, students created new breaks in the everyday expectations of protest. On 25 September 2020, students engaged in a mass distributed protest of 600 different events around Australia.[3] As of January 2021, Australian students are among an estimated 14 million strikers in over 7,900 cities in 213 countries who continue to protest for climate justice as part of Fridays for Future (FFF).[4]

The cumulative effects of all those (young) people building on Greta's initial parliamentary steps protest, Fridays for Future school protests all over the world and well renowned scientists and academics pledging allegiance to declaring Climate Change a global emergency, have inspired and been leveraged into other youthful acts of leadership. For example, in 2020 a group of Australian young people and allies made a seminal class action against Whitehaven's Vickery coal mine. The injunction was made on behalf of young people everywhere – and claimed that approving an extension of the coal mine will harm generations to come by contributing to Climate Change.

10 Conclusion

In this chapter we have questioned how the politics of youth and leadership inhibits recognition and responsiveness to instances of youth leadership in everyday life. We argue that the politicisation of youth and youth leadership undermines the potential for these concepts to be re-imagined and therefore utilised when progressing our understanding of youth leadership for wiser futures. Instead, we suggest that working with the idea of 'youthful acts of citizenship' helps render visible the multiple, accumulating actors, networks and sites of action that emerge when we expand our view. In our own act of leadership, we have contested the persistent framing of youth leadership as futurity and economic and young people as actors who can only be valued for their potential to advance neoliberal adult institutions and ways of thinking. Instead, we propose new attention be paid to the ways young people are disrupting assumptions underpinning these institutions and are crucial for creating new possibilities for wiser future practice.

The second part of this chapter focused on case studies that expand our understanding of what constitutes 'youthful acts of leadership'. We did this by illuminating acts that expose entrenched systemic injustice by challenging 'the normal way of doing things' and, in turn, transcend limiting ideals of the 'youth leader' archetype. This allowed us to unpack and explore how acts create commotion and upheaval and highlight the different and multiple actors over space and time who are implicated in and sustain the scene. By re-imaging youth leadership, we have shown through the case studies of Grace Tame, Dujuan Hoosan and the SS4C how intergenerational solidarities and collective action is generated and sustained, prompting further resistance and action against injustice. They show us how recognition of acts can aid our endeavour at creating wiser future practices.

We all need to reassess the expectations we have of individual actors in leading collective social change. Creating a wiser future is a responsibility for us all. It does not and should not rest upon the shoulders of a lone individual, but on *all* our shoulders. Moreover, we highlight how leadership – like social change – is relational, not exercised by autonomous individuals. Thus, we propose a re-framing of youth leadership to focus on acts and scenes, rather than individual youth leaders, allowing us to be responsive and receptive to the acts that disrupt the status quo and facilitate social change.

We propose that by diverting responsibility from the individuals who represent ideal and/or exceptional youth leaders[5] and redirecting attention onto the acts where the status quo is disrupted we can become more receptive to these scenarios and new acts of leadership into the future. Highlighting the multiple actors involved in social change also resists neoliberal individualist notions of leadership, which we passionately defy. We argue that it is our collective responsibility to recognise and acknowledge the role young people already play in this endeavour and take greater action in promoting an environment which can better support participation from more diverse perspectives in society.

To contribute to wiser futures, we must create new practices, tools and perspectives to challenge injustice. We start this endeavour by proposing new ways to see and listen to young people's acts of leadership, which may have been neglected or oppressed to-date. We believe that to reimagine our world, we need to be represented and led by all those who will be there to witness the future. Therefore, we question why some acts and actors may not have been acknowledged. By facilitating this debate, we expose and call forth the politics of youth leadership. We argue that this is necessary as it is young people's lived experiences, fresh perspectives and youthful acts of leadership, which can illuminate wiser futures.

Notes

1 https://www.australianoftheyear.org.au/
2 https://www.schoolstrike4climate.com
3 https://www.schoolstrike4climate.com
4 https://fridaysforfuture.org/what-we-do/strike-statistics/
5 Whilst also acknowledging their strength and resilience.

References

Allen, S. (1968). Some theoretical problems in the study of youth. *The Sociological Review, 16*(3), 319–331.

Australian Broadcasting Corporation. (2019, August 13). *Gagged by a law, Grace Tame can finally tell her story: 7.30 Report* [Video]. YouTube. https://www.youtube.com/watch?v=E7TsDaQfaC4

Bersaglio, B., Enns, C., & Kepe, T. (2015). Youth under construction: The United Nations' representations of youth in the global conversation on the post-2015 development agenda. *Canadian Journal of Development Studies/Revue canadienne d'études du développement, 36*(1), 57–71.

Bessant, J. (2004). Mixed messages: Youth participation and democratic practice. *Australian Journal of Political Science, 39*(2), 387–404.

Bessant, J., & Lohmeyer, B. A. (2021). Politics of recognition when students protest. In J. Bessant, A. Mejia Mesinas, & S. Pickard (Eds.), *When students protest (Vol. 1): Secondary school students* (pp. 37 to 54). Rowman & Littlefield.

Black, R., Walsh, L., Magee, J., Hutchins, L., Berman, N., & Groundwater-Smith, S. (2014). *Student leadership: A review of effective practice*. Australian Research Alliance for Children and Youth.

Boulianne, S., Lalancette, M., & Ilkiw, D. (2020). 'School Strike 4 Climate': Social media and the international youth protest on climate change. *Media and Communication, 8*(2), 208–218.

Bourdieu, P. (1994). *Practical reason: On the theory of action*. Stanford University Press.

Brown, W. (2006). American nightmare: Neoliberalism, neoconservatism, and de-democratization. *Political Theory, 34*(6), 690–714.

Chatwani, N. (Ed.). (2018). *Distributed leadership*. Palgrave Macmillan.

Collin, P. (2015). *Young citizens and political participation in a digital society: Addressing the democratic disconnect*. Palgrave Macmillan.

Collin, P., & Matthews, I. (2021). School Strike for Climate: Australian students renegotiating citizenship. In J. Bessant, A. Mejia Mesinas, & S. Pickard (Eds.), *When students protest (Vol. 1): Secondary school students* (pp. 13–24). Rowman and Littlefield.

Dempster, N., Stevens, E., & Keeffe, M. (2011). Student and youth leadership: A focused literature review. *Leading and Managing, 17*(2), 1–20.

de St Croix, T., McGimpsey, I., & Owens, J. (2020). Feeding young people to the social investment machine: The financialisation of public services. *Critical Social Policy, 40*(3), 450–470.

Farthing, R. (2010). The politics of youthful antipolitics: Representing the 'issue' of youth participation in politics. *Journal of Youth Studies, 13*(2), 181–195.

Fergusson, R., & Yeates, N. (2013). Business, as usual: The policy priorities of the World Bank's discourses on youth unemployment, and the global financial crisis. *Journal of International and Comparative Social Policy, 29*(1), 64–78.

Fraser, N. (1990). Rethinking the public sphere: A contribution to the critique of actually existing democracy. *Social Text, 25/26*, 56–80.

Furlong, A., & Cartmel, F. (2007). *Youth and social change: New perspectives* (2nd ed.). McGraw Hill.

Hall, G. S. (1904). *Adolescence: Its psychology and its relations to physiology, anthropology, sociology, sex, crime, religion, and education* (Vol. I & II). D. Appleton & Co.

Harris, A. (2004). *Future girl: Young women in the twenty-first century*. Routledge.

Harris, A. (2012). Citizenship stories. In N. Lesko & S. Talburt (Eds.), *Keywords in youth studies: Tracing affects, movements, knowledges* (pp. 143–153). Routledge.

Houghton, J. D., & DiLiello, T. C. (2010). Leadership development: The key to unlocking individual creativity in organizations. *Leadership & Organization Development Journal, 31*(3), 230–245.

Isin, E. F. (2008). Theorizing acts of citizenship. In E. F. Isin & G. M. Nielsen (Eds.), *Acts of citizenship* (pp. 15–43). Palgrave Macmillan.

Kwon, S. A. (2018). The politics of global youth participation. *Journal of Youth Studies, 22*(7), 926–940.

MacNeil, C. A. (2006). Bridging generations: Applying 'adult' leadership theories to youth leadership development. *New Directions for Youth Development, 2006*(109), 27–43.

Mayes, E., Finneran, R., & Black, R. (2019). The challenges of student voice in primary schools: Students 'having a voice' and 'speaking for' others. *The Australian Journal of Education, 63*(2), 157–172.

Morgan, G., & Idriss, S. (2012). 'Corsages on their parents' jackets': Employment and aspiration among Arabic-speaking youth in Western Sydney. *Journal of Youth Studies, 15*(7), 929–943.

Newell, M. (Director). (2019). *In my blood it runs* [Documentary]. Closer Productions. https://inmyblooditruns.com/screenings/

Oc, B. (2018). Contextual leadership: A systematic review of how contextual factors shape leadership and its outcomes. *The Leadership Quarterly, 29*(1), 218–235.

O'Donoghue, J. L. (2006). 'Taking their own power': Urban youth, community-based youth organizations, and public efficacy. In S. Ginwright, P. Noguera, & J. Cammorota (Eds.), *Beyond resistance! Youth activism and community change: New democratic possibilities for practice and policy for America's youth* (pp. 229–246). Routledge.

Piaget J. (1972). Intellectual evolution from adolescence to adulthood. *Human Development, 15*(1), 1–12.

Pickard, S., & Bessant, J. (Eds.). (2018). *Young people re-generating politics in times of crises.* Palgrave Macmillan.

Spillane, J. P. (2012). *Distributed leadership* (Vol. 4). John Wiley & Sons.

Sukarieh, M. (2012). From terrorists to revolutionaries: The emergence of 'youth' in the Arab world and the discourse of globalization. *Interface, 4*(2), 424–437.

Sukarieh, M., & Tannock, S. 2008. In the best interests of youth or neoliberalism? The World Bank and the New Global Youth Empowerment Project. *Journal of Youth Studies, 11*(3), 301–312.

Tame, G. (2021, January 26), 'Hear me now': Australian of the Year Grace Tame's speech in full. *ABC News.* https://www.abc.net.au/news/2021-01-26/grace-tame-australian-of-the-year-speech-in-full/13091710

Third, A., Collin, P., Walsh, L., & Black, R. (2019). *Young people in digital society: Control shift.* Palgrave Macmillan.

Threadgold, S. (2018). *Youth, class and everyday struggles.* Routledge.

Vromen, A. (2003). 'People try to put us down': Participatory citizenship of 'Generation X'. *Australian Journal of Political Science, 38*(1), 78–99.

Walsh, L., & Black, R. (2009). *Students in the lead: Increasing participation by young people in a distributed leadership framework.* Centre for Strategic Education.

Walsh, L., & Black, R. (Eds.). (2011). *In their own hands: Can young people change Australia?* ACER Press.

Walsh, L., & Black, R. (2018). Off the radar democracy: Young people's alternative acts of citizenship in Australia. In S. Pickard & J. Bessant (Eds.), *Young people re-generating politics in times of crises* (pp. 217–232). Palgrave Macmillan.

White, R., & Wyn, J. (2004). *Youth and society: Exploring the social dynamics of youth.* Oxford University Press.

White, R., Wyn, J., & Robards, B. (2017). *Youth and society* (4th ed.). Oxford University Press.

Woodman, D., & Wyn, J. (2011). Youth research in a changing world. In S. Beadle, R. Holdsworth, & J. Wyn (Eds.), *For we are young and ...? Young people in a time of uncertainty* (pp. 5–28). Melbourne University Press.

CHAPTER 21

The Essential Roles of Ethics, Humanity and Social Justice in Any Future Worth Living

Andrew Dutney

Abstract

As the COVID-19 pandemic shattered assumptions about what is "normal", minds have turned to the future and what a "new normal" could and should look like. This is an inherently ethical exercise. The succession of case studies in human diversity delivered by the pandemic has challenged the universalising tendencies of traditional ethics and ethical authorities, accelerating the shift towards ethical naturalism. It disrupted the field of bioethics in particular, where deontological and principle-ist alternatives have continued to be favoured. The pandemic forced a more naturalistic approach to moral decision-making in clinical settings. At the same time, however, it drew attention to the wider socio-economic and environmental context and its relevance to the clinical situation. In this way the pandemic led to a recovery of the broader understanding of "bioethics" as intended when the term was coined. In this way the pandemic has delivered a creative moment in which diverse coalitions of scholars, practitioners and stakeholders have begun to engage in a new, multi-faceted science of bioethics, which identifies "Survival as a Goal for Wisdom".

Keywords

ethics – bioethics – naturalism – COVID-19 pandemic

•••

The COVID-19 pandemic has tested not only political economies across the world, but also cultural and social norms and assumptions. Behaviour that was considered necessary, inevitable, or even self-evidently good prior to the pandemic became risky. Greeting people by shaking hands, hugging or kissing, gathering in large family groups to celebrate weddings, birthdays or funerals, international travel, gathering with colleagues for business meetings or conferences, and so forth. The pandemic has sharpened questions about the relation

 | DOI: 10.1163/9789004505544_025

between the human species and other species and the environment. It has thrown a spotlight on inequalities between developed and developing countries, between successful and disadvantaged members within a given society, and between different generations in the same family or community. And it has certainly turned minds to the future. Not only have individuals been forced to reconsider their personal expectations and plans. Almost all fields of human enterprise have had to improvise and innovate. Now they are each in their own way working out what they might look like next year, or in five or ten years' time.

As the world moves into its future there will be a period of reconsidering and re-establishing the cultural and social norms and assumptions that have been so disrupted. Ethics, as a discipline of imaginative reasoning, has a crucial role to play as communities, organisations, and legislators consciously negotiate the new practices and behaviours that, in due course, will be taken for granted. At the same time, ethics too is specific to its cultural context. Having been disrupted by the pandemic ethics itself will also be subject to the same process of renegotiation.

In this essay I will consider the way ethics has engaged with the experience of the pandemic, with particular reference to bioethics. I will discuss how it has been affected as a discipline, and its ongoing role in the global community.

1 Ethics and the Pandemic

The COVID-19 pandemic has engaged people in a succession of case studies on the profound diversity in human cultures and political economies. The media has responded to the understandable interest in the different ways communities, governments and health systems have experienced and responded to the pandemic. People have been curious about what makes a particular response possible or necessary in one context when it would not be in another. It began with lessons on what "wet markets" are and why they are a normal feature of some large modern cities like Wuhan. It included explanations of the differences in the way, for example, the United States and New Zealand negotiate a balance between the rights of the individual and the public good in relation to measures such as social isolation and wearing facemasks (Fischer, 2012). Watching the way different democracies managed to conduct elections during a pandemic was a lesson in diversity – from established democracies like France or the United States, to newer ones like South Korea or Burundi (Maizland, 2020). It was a moment to see through the lie that "COVID-19 does not discriminate". Its impact in poorer, less developed countries was confronting.

So too the vulnerability of socially and economically disadvantaged communities within richer, developed countries became clear (Patel et al., 2020). *National Geographic*, one of the world's most widely read magazines, devoted its November 2020 issue to the way the pandemic was changing lives globally. It included stories of its impact in Indonesian villages and cities, on what lockdown means for refugees in Jordan, on how it had forced 100 million people into extreme poverty, on the impetus it could give to addressing climate change, and on what the pandemic has meant to American 18–25 year olds. All of this was accompanied by dozens of high quality, graphic photographs to carry the narrative. Since the pandemic began, people have been fascinated by each other. People have been especially focussed on differences in the way the pandemic has been experienced and responded to. It has amounted to a mass-education in human diversity – economic, cultural and political.

In relation to the moral imagination, this awakening to human diversity has had the effect of adding to challenges to the universalising tendencies of traditional ethics and ethical authorities. In the face of globalising capitalism, traditional systems of moral duty have been in decline for many decades. This has strengthened the "naturalistic" movement in ethics, displacing deontological approaches and even principle-ist alternatives, which identify particular moral duties, or at least general moral principles, that apply universally regardless of context. Instead utilitarian and consequentialist accounts of morality are increasingly favoured for the way they accommodate human diversity more convincingly. As Margaret Urban Walker (2008) describes naturalism in ethics, it rejects the claim that morality comes into the world from "somewhere else" – from a supernatural or non-natural realm. Sound moral judgement does not require types of reasoning beyond what we already count on as reliable ways of knowing about the world. So ethical naturalism is "self-reflexive, socially inquisitive, politically critical, and inclusive" (Walker, 2008, p. 5). It is "empirically nourished, but also acutely aware that ethical theory is the practice of particular people in particular times, places, cultures, and professional environments" (ibid., p. 5). Naturalistic approaches to ethics give weight not only to reason, but also to affect, empirical evidence, practice and persons in their context. All of these aspects of moral judgement have been amplified by the pandemic, accelerating the shift towards ethical naturalism. And in the context of this volume, I note that practice wisdom belongs on the naturalistic spectrum.

There have been a handful of scholarly works in ethics that investigate the experience of the pandemic dealing, for example, with geopolitical issues in ethics such as migration, refugees and the management of borders (Aitchison, 2021) or corporate issues like the ethics of crisis management (Branicki, 2020). But, unsurprisingly, the weight of scholarly work has been in the field of bioethics. There have been hundreds, if not thousands of scholarly articles published on different aspects of the experience and management of the pandemic from this perspective since 2020 – especially from the subfields of medical, clinical, nursing and public health ethics. Themes explored have included the sharing of scarce medical resources (Sabatello et al., 2020), whether and how to continue to conduct clinical research trials during the pandemic (Meagher et al., 2020), moral distress in health care workers in unprepared or overwhelmed health systems (Robert et al., 2020), the moral challenge of shifting from patient centred ethics to public health ethics (Angelos, 2020), and whether in the face of a global pandemic medical ethics' "four pillars" – autonomy, beneficence, non-maleficence and justice – could bear the weight of the decisions that had to be made in clinical practice (Arora & Arora, 2020). However, none of these themes have been discussed with the cool confidence of the professional bioethicist. Rather, authors consistently acknowledge that the pandemic has disrupted the way we usually go about making moral judgements.

For example, in Intensive Care Units the need to triage on public health criteria has clashed with the more established practice of person-centred decision-making. Similarly, providing what has long been regarded as quality end-of-life support for patients and their families has also been compromised by the requirement to separate seriously ill patients from all but their medical carers. Healthcare workers, patients and relatives have had to accept "less than perfect solutions" and the moral distress that involved (Robert et al., 2020). Acknowledging that particular moral judgements are just the best that we can manage under the circumstances has its own destabilizing effect on traditional approaches to bioethics. A case in point is the confusing public statements by Catholic bishops on the morality of receiving vaccines developed using cell lines from aborted foetuses (Dyer, 2021), and the tortured logic of the Congregation for the Doctrine of the Faith (2020) in its Note on the matter.

While the disruption of decision-making at the "bedside" properly received attention from ethicists, so did the wider social context and its relevance to the immediate clinical situation. In the United States, for example, this included, "the social determinates of illness and health, the structural racism that magnifies the burden of disease for people of colour, and the effects of dismantling the infrastructure for public health" (Churchill et al., 2020, p. 54). Or again, in South Africa it was an opportunity to see that "the most powerful health-promoting forces are social" (Benatar, 2020, p. 1). Solomon Benatar, Emeritus Professor of Medicine at the University of Cape Town, observed that improved living conditions bring improved health outcomes even without medical intervention. And even in wealthy countries more than half of the factors compromising health are societal. He noted "This proportion is much greater in Africa, disadvantaged by a legacy of previous exploitation that continues through internal and external processes" (ibid., p. 1). He argued that through the experience of the COVID-19 pandemic it had become clear that "striving ethically for health" requires "a paradigm shift from a competitive anthropocentric focus towards a cooperative ecological perspective on all aspects of life and health" (ibid., p. 2).

As bioethics focussed less on the clinical phenomena of the pandemic and more on the wider context within which moral judgements are being made there has been a recovery of the broader understanding of "bioethics" that the oncologist Van Rensselaer Potter intended when he first coined the term (Potter 1970, 1971). Potter, like Benatar more than a generation later, recognised that threats to human health were misunderstood if viewed exclusively through a medical lens. Pollution, environmental degradation, population growth, and the excessive consumption and waste of the earth's resources all had to be taken into account. "Bioethics", as he framed it, addressed an ecological crisis that was at the same time a crisis in western civilization that was affecting (infecting) the whole world. In the Preface to his book, *Bioethics: Bridge to the Future*, Potter (1971) wrote:

> What we must now face up to is the fact that human ethics cannot be separated from a realistic understanding of ecology in the broadest sense. Ethical values cannot be separated from biological facts. We are in great need of a Land Ethic, a Wildlife Ethic, a Population Ethic, a Consumption Ethic, an Urban Ethic, an International Ethic, a Geriatric Ethic, and so on. All of these problems call for action based on values and biological facts. All of these involve Bioethics, and the survival of the total ecosystem is the test of the value system. (pp. VII–VIII)

"Bioethics" was Potter's term for a new multi-faceted science directed towards "Survival as a Goal for Wisdom" (Potter, 1971). Half a century later, the field known as bioethics is recovering that awareness of the broader context of moral judgement. The bioethical agenda still includes, health, medicine and the human lifecycle, but it also includes the environment, biodiversity, biotechnology, social justice, governance, international solidarity and humanity. It is an agenda being re-shaped in the context of climate change, an extinction emergency and, indeed, the COVID-19 pandemic.

2 The Creative Moment

One of the effects of the experience of the pandemic has been to relativise people's assumptions and plans for the future, immediate and also long-term.

We suddenly found ourselves having to do things we had never anticipated, and also prevented from doing things we'd always assumed would be possible or even required. This has been highly stressful for individuals, communities and political economies and there are widespread reports of an increase in rates of mental illness. However, in those moments when it becomes possible once again to do something "normal", like meeting friends in a café or seeing your children off to school or attending a cinema, people display deep appreciation for the activity. Whereas they had previously taken it for granted, now they savour it mindfully. People have been known to weep with wonder and appreciation for something that had once been entirely mundane. Both the stress and the mindfulness are manifestations of an acute awareness of life's "contingency".

Of course there is nothing new about the sudden consciousness of the contingent nature of life – that things are like this but could just as easily be completely different. Philosophers have names for it. Paul Tillich called it "metaphysical shock". Joseph Sittler called it "primitive astonishment". Friedrich Schleiermacher called it "the immediate feeling of absolute dependence". And it led the Hebrew philosopher of the book of Ecclesiastes to the conclusion, "Vanity of vanities, all is vanity". This state of consciousness is usually experienced by individuals, or perhaps family groups, who have been subject to a significant, unexpected change in their circumstances while the rest of the world goes on as usual, but without them. A sudden reversal of fortune, a challenging diagnosis, and accident, or bereavement can throw a spotlight on all the things you have been taking for granted. A feature of the pandemic, however, has been that this "metaphysical shock" is being experienced by whole societies, indeed the whole world, at once. As people move through the acute phases of the pandemic, when it is all just about survival and the immediate existential trauma of losing so much that was familiar and trusted, there is a creative moment delivered by the sudden consciousness of contingency. Will things ever go back to the way they were? Can they? Do things have to go back to the way they were? In fact, could we help things to be different, "better" in the future? And that is an inherently ethical question. What would count as "better"?

At the conclusion of a searing critique of the Indian government's response to the pandemic, the author Arundhati Roy observed that, "Historically, pandemics have forced humans to break with the past and imagine their world anew" (p. 12). In that respect, she said, the pandemic is "a portal".

> We can choose to walk through it, dragging the carcasses of our prejudice and hatred, our avarice, and data banks and dead ideas, our dead rivers

> and smoky skies behind us. Or we can walk through lightly, with little luggage, ready to imagine another world. And ready to fight for it. (Roy, 2020, p. 12)

The Australian sociologist and ethicist, Hugh Mackay (2021), takes a similar view, asking,

> Is it too much to hope that the lessons learned under the pressure of restrictions might be applied more generically? Might we finally stamp out racism, sexism and ageism? (p. 14)

Questions like this resonate with the broader understanding of bioethics that has begun to be recovered during the pandemic. To address them, diverse coalitions of scholars, practitioners and stakeholders have formed in a variety of settings around the world. While few of the people involved would describe themselves as "ethicists", what they are doing together is nonetheless the "bioethics" that Potter imagined half a century ago.

One example is an Australian project published under the title *Upturn: A Better Normal after COVID-19*. More than thirty contributors offered their proposals for a new and better "normal" in fields as diverse as healthcare, industrial relations, the environment, education, housing, and the arts (Plibersek, 2020). In her Introduction to the collection, the editor offered a high level survey of some of the themes that emerged in the project. These included some specific goals for Australia's future including full employment with decent pay and conditions, environmentally sustainable economic growth, becoming "a country that makes things, powered by cleaner, cheaper renewable energy", having "infrastructure that makes our cities and towns more efficient and more liveable", and a shared commitment to address poverty, racism, violence, and climate change (Plibersek, 2020, pp. 3–4). She also identified the simple aspiration that had crystallised under the restrictions and deprivations of the pandemic:

> Australians have had time to think about what matters to them: a secure job and a roof over their heads, but also connection with family, friends and community. (ibid., p. 5)

This summary statement echoes Freud's apocryphal aphorism, "Love and work are the cornerstones of our humanness" (Erikson, 1963, pp. 264–265). Being able to love and to work is the definition of a healthy human being and, at the same time, love and work are the foundation of human health and happiness. But, of course, there is any number of different ways that this aspiration could be met. Indeed, part of the point of the *Upturn* project was to identify ways to fulfil that aspiration that are "better" than the ones that had been snatched away during the pandemic. So the editor also named some of the principles guiding progress towards such goals. These included core values such as inclusiveness, fairness and environmental responsibility. They also included the principles of practice by which we get things done: "We need to bring a spirit of open-minded thoughtfulness and co-operative problem solving" to all the issues associated with our survival and health, both within Australia and internationally.

It is just a beginning, but the experience and response to the COVID-19 pandemic may finally deliver a bioethics that understands human health holistically – involving justice, inclusion, dignity and ecological sustainability. It is a bioethics that knows that, understood in this holistic way; survival is the goal of wisdom.

References

Aitchison, G. (2021). Beyond lockdown? The ethics of global movement in a new era. *Ethics & Global Politics, 14*(1), 36–49.

Angelos, P. (2020). Surgeons, ethics, and COVID-19: Early lessons learned. *Journal of the American College of Surgeons, 230*(6), 1119–1120.

Arora, A., & Arora, A. (2020). Ethics in the age of COVID-19. *Internal and Emergency Medicine, 15*, 889–890.

Benatar, S. (2020). More eyes on COVID-19: Perspectives from ethics: The most powerful health-promoting forces in COVID-19 are social. *South African Journal of Science, 116*(7/8), 1–2.

Branicki, L. J. (2020). COVID-19, ethics of care and feminist crisis management. *Gender Work & Organization, 27*(5), 872–883.

Churchill, L. R., King, M. M. P., & Henderson, G. E. (2020). The future of bioethics: It shouldn't take a pandemic. *Hastings Centre Report, 50*(3), 54–56.

Congregation for the Doctrine of the Faith. (2020). *Note on the morality of using some anti-Covid-19 vaccines.* https://www.vatican.va/roman_curia/congregations/cfaith/documents/rc_con_cfaith_doc_20201221_nota-vaccini-anticovid_en.html

Dyer, O. (2021). Covid-19: US Catholics split after bishops' conference recommends against Johnson and Johnson vaccine. *British Medical Journal.* https://doi.org/10.1136/bmj.n666

Erikson, E. (1963). *Childhood and society* (2nd ed.). Norton.

Fischer, D. H. (2012). *Fairness and freedom: A history of two open societies, New Zealand and the United States.* Oxford University Press.

Mackay, H. (2021). *The kindness revolution: How we can rebuild trust, restore hope and live with generosity and optimism.* Allen & Unwin.

Maizland, L. (2020, September 17). *How countries are holding elections during the COVID-19 pandemic.* Council on Foreign Relations. https://www.cfr.org/backgrounder/how-countries-are-holding-elections-during-covid-19-pandemic

Meagher, K. M., Cummins, N. W., Bharucha, A. E., Badley, A. D., Chlan, L. L., & Wright, R. S. (2020). COVID-19 ethics and research. *Mayo Clinic Proceedings, 95*(6), 1119–1123.

Patel, J. A., Neilsen, F. B. H., Badiani, A. A., Assi, S., Unadkat, V. A., Patel, B., Ravindrane, R., & Wardle, H. (2020). Poverty, inequality and COVID-19: The forgotten vulnerable. *Public Health, 183*, 110–111.

Plibersek, T. (Ed.). (2020). *Upturn: A better normal after COVID-19.* Newsouth.

Potter, V. R. (1970). Bioethics: The science of survival. *Perspectives in Biology and Medicine, 14*(3), 18–23.

Potter, V. R. (1971). *Bioethics: Bridge to the future.* Prentice-Hall.

Robert, R., Kentish-Barnes, N., Boyer, A., Laurent, A., Azoulay, E., & Reignier, J. (2020). Ethical dilemmas due to the COVID-19 pandemic. *Annals of Intensive Care, 10*(84). https://doi.org/10.1186/s13613-020-00702-7

Roy, A. (2020, April 4). The pandemic is a portal. *The Financial Times.* https://www.ft.com/content/10d8f5e8-74eb-11ea-95fe-fcd274e920ca

Sabatello, M., Burke, T. B., McDonald, K. E., & Appelbaum, P. S. (2020). Disability, ethics, and health care in the COVID-19 pandemic. *American Journal of Public Health, 110*, 1523–1527.

Walker, M. U. (2008). Introduction: Groningen naturalism in bioethics. In M. V. Hilde Lindemann & M. U. Walker (Eds.), *Naturalized bioethics: Toward responsible knowing and practice* (pp. 1–20). Cambridge University Press.

www.ingramcontent.com/pod-product-compliance
Lightning Source LLC
LaVergne TN
LVHW020631300926
849161LV00004B/668